Groovin' High

Groovin' High

‖ The Life of Dizzy Gillespie ‖

Alyn Shipton

NEW YORK   OXFORD
OXFORD UNIVERSITY PRESS
1999

Oxford University Press

Oxford   New York

Athens   Auckland   Bangkok   Bogotá   Buenos Aires   Calcutta
Cape Town   Chennai   Dar es Salaam   Delhi   Florence   Hong Kong   Istanbul
Karachi   Kuala Lumpur   Madrid   Melbourne   Mexico City   Mumbai
Nairobi   Paris   São Paulo   Singapore   Taipei   Tokyo   Toronto   Warsaw

and associated companies in

Berlin   Ibadan

Published by Oxford University Press, Inc.
198 Madison Avenue, New York, New York 10016

Oxford is a registered trademark of Oxford University Press

Library of Congress Cataloging-in-Publication Data
Shipton, Alyn.
Groovin' high : the life of Dizzy Gillespie / by Alyn Shipton.
p.   cm.
Includes bibliographical references and index.
ISBN 0-19-509132-9
1. Gillespie, Dizzy, 1917–1993.   2. Jazz musicians—United States—
Biography.   I. Title.
ML419.G54S55   1999   788.9'2165'092—dc21   [B]   98-27684

9 8 7 6 5 4 3 2 1

Printed in the United States of America
on acid-free paper

Contents

Preface

Jazz is a music full of thrilling sounds. It can also span the full breadth of human emotion from exhilaration to profound sadness, from love to alienation, from celebration to commiseration. All the greatest jazz musicians have had the ability to touch their listeners in one or more of these areas, but, for me, Dizzy Gillespie's music has managed to inhabit all of them, while simultaneously conveying more of the sheer joy and excitement of jazz than that of any other musician. There are countless such moments in his recorded output, from his sure touch on his very first recorded solo in 1937, Teddy Hill's "King Porter Stomp," to the brief cameos with his United Nation Orchestra half a century later, where his horn elbows its distinctive way between his protégés and friends to make his last great statements.

In researching this book, I have tried to listen to as much as possible of his recorded legacy, which is never less than impressive, and, even in those periods when his career flagged a little, full of moments of surprise and delight, part of an extraordinarily prolific output at the highest level. I have talked to many of his friends and musical associates from all periods of his life and feel I have come to know many aspects of this complex and brilliant man.

"Why should another book on Dizzy be needed?" I was often asked, during the time this was being written. After all, his own autobiography, which is full of brief contributions from those who knew him, has often been hailed as a landmark in oral history, and there are numerous other biographies such as those by Raymond Horricks, Tony Gentry, and Barry McRae, or the lavish photo-books by Lee Tanner and Dany Gignoux. In other languages there are yet more books, by Jürgen Wölfer, Laurent Clarke, and Franck Verdun.

The answer is that to some extent all these books (which mostly appeared during Dizzy's lifetime) took their cues from him as to the shape and pattern of his life. For example, if Dizzy said that he had heard Roy Eldridge on the radio in Cheraw as a boy, who was to deny it? Yet when I found out that this must have been impossible, that Roy had not broadcast during the years Dizzy was still in South Carolina, I began to realize that, without in any way detracting from Dizzy's immense achievement, there was more to be discovered about the influences on him and the path that led him to be a key member of the generation that revolutionized jazz in the 1940s.

Dizzy was always modest about his own contribution to bebop. Partly in deference to the memory of Charlie Parker, he always stressed Parker's input at the expense of his own. I have attempted to show how Dizzy's contribution was in many ways more important. By being the one who organized the principal ideas of the beboppers into an intellectual framework, Dizzy was the key figure who allowed the music to progress beyond a small and restricted circle of after-hours enthusiasts. This was a major element in his life, and virtually everyone to whom I spoke stressed Dizzy's exceptional generosity with his time in explaining and exploring musical ideas. Modern jazz might have happened without Dizzy, but it would not have had so clearly articulated a set of harmonic and rhythmic precepts, nor so dramatic a set of recorded examples of these being put into practice.

Dizzy's other achievements are many and hard to quantify, but I have been struck by how he was the main pioneer of the transfer of bebop to the big band environment and how he stayed with the idea against financial and commercial odds. Something of the large band environment in which he grew up remained with him throughout his life, and his final years were marked out by the successful triumphs of yet another generation of large ensembles.

For over half a century, his life and work were supported by his long and stable marriage to Lorraine Gillespie, and the world owes her a great debt for astutely managing much of his career. I have not attempted to gloss over other sides of Dizzy's character, but this is always in the knowledge that Dizzy (as he told Nat Hentoff) "was willing to do what I did for her—walk the straight line."

The other main attribute that has arisen in anecdote after anecdote and interview after interview is that Dizzy was a genuinely funny man. I hope that this also comes across in the text, although spontaneous wit never transfers easily to print. Some biographers fall in or out of love with their subject as they progress—I am more convinced than ever that I have been privileged to examine the life of one of the great human beings of the twentieth century.

No book such as this can be undertaken without the aid of others, and I should like to thank everyone who has helped me along the way. In particular I would like to single out John Chilton, who over the years that I have been his editor at various publishers has shown me by example what it means to be a jazz researcher and has consistently been a source of ideas, encouragement, and assistance. Equally, for the last ten years I have enjoyed working with Derek Drescher at BBC Radio 3, who first encouraged me to investigate Dizzy's life for a memorial series of documentaries in 1993, which was the genesis for this book and the source for many of the interviews in it. Derek also produced my subsequent series on Cab Calloway and helped in obtaining permission to use material from further BBC interviews, a national treasure of oral history.

In my earlier book on Fats Waller I was indebted to Franz Hoffman in Berlin for his diligent research in the U.S. black press. I am again grateful to him for assisting me with material from *Jazz Advertised* and *Jazz Reviewed*, his two ongoing research projects, and for his specific investigations into Dizzy's career. Howard Rye has been a good friend and publishing colleague on a number of books, and I am grateful to him for commenting on drafts of several chapters. Chris Sheridan has also kindly shared research information with me for his forthcoming Greenwood Press bio-discographies of Milt Jackson and Thelonious Monk. He and Howard Rye, together with my father, Donald Shipton, did an enormous amount of work in establishing a full recording chronology of Dizzy, which helped to sort out many aspects of his career but has had to be excluded (on grounds of sheer size) from the final book. I should also like to thank Sheldon Meyer, my editor at Oxford University Press and my role model as a jazz publisher, for all his insightful suggestions on the draft manuscript.

Thanks are due to the following musicians for their assistance: Benny Bailey, Danny Barker, Ray Brown, Dave Brubeck, Ray Bryant, Jeanie Bryson, Ian Carr, Al Casey, Doc Cheatham, Buck Clayton, Alan Cohen, Hank Crawford, Bob Cunningham, John Dankworth, Dr. Art Davis, Bill Dillard, Bill Doggett, Harry "Sweets" Edison, Jon Faddis, Benny Golson, Benny Green, Mike Hennessey, Milt Hinton, Illinois Jacquet, Ahmad Jamal, Jonah Jones, Mundell Lowe, Jimmy McGriff, James Moody, Danilo Perez, Roy Porter, Norman Powe, George Russell, Arturo Sandoval, Lalo Schifrin, Scott Stroman, Grady Tate, Billy Taylor, Cedar Walton, Joe Wilder, Jackie Williams, Jimmy Woode, and Leo Wright.

I should also like to acknowledge help from Dick Bank, Bruce Bastin, Dave Bennett, Geneviève Broutechoux (Média 7), Connie Bryson, Felix Carey (BBC), Terry Carter (BBC Pebble Mill), Ron Clough, James Lincoln Collier, Stanley Dance, Grainne Devine (BMG), Nancy Miller Elliott, Suzanne Flandreau (Center for Black Music Research, Columbia College, Chicago), Jim Gallagher (School of Communication Newspaper Archive, Boston University), Brian Gibbon (Start Audio and Video), Jackie Gill (BMG), Maxine Gordon, Jan Hart (BBC), Oliver Jones (BBC World Service), Zane Knauss, Lisa Knorr (Telarc and Atlantic

Records), Charles "Whale" Lake, Gene Lees, Geraldine Marshall (BBC), Jeremy Mitchell (Open University), Karen Mix (Cab Calloway Archive, Mugar Memorial Library, Boston University), Alun Morgan, Robert Andrew Parker, Peter Pullman (Verve, New York), Bruce Boyd Raeburn (William Ransom Hogan Jazz Archive, Howard-Tilton Memorial Library, Tulane University), Henri Renaud, Ron's Jazz Services (Oxford and Bournemouth), Tony Russell, Grover Sales, Margaret Sarkissian, Keith Shadwick, Becky Stevenson (Verve Records), Steve Voce, Sharon L. Toon (Publications and Records Division, Selective Service System, Arlington, Virginia), and Tony Williams (Spotlite Records).

The book would not have been possible without the initial encouragement of Peter Clayton, Charles Fox, and Max Jones, whose interviews for radio and magazines underlie much of my understanding of jazz. The late Roy Plomley's insightful interview with Dizzy was also of great assistance.

The illustrations are from the collections of Jeanie Bryson, Frank Driggs, David Redfern, and Howard Rye. Additional credits are given in the captions.

Finally I should like to thank my family—Siobhan, Christopher, Lizzy, and Angharad—for all their support while this was being written.

Oxford, England   ALYN SHIPTON
August 1998

Groovin' High

1

The Boy from Cheraw

he sight of John Birks "Dizzy" Gillespie, the bell of his upswept trumpet pointing skyward, his cheeks distended into hamster-like pouches, and his ubiquitous beret, goatee, horn-rimmed spectacles, and pinstripe suit, became the archetypal image of a jazz musician. Even when he forsook these trappings in favor of African robes and headgear, or crisp tweed jackets and casual sweaters, Dizzy's presence was synonymous with style and his playing synonymous with jazz. From his first visit to France with Teddy Hill as a gauche nineteen-year-old to overseas tours with his own band in the 1950s, Dizzy became an indefatigable musical ambassador, a passion that never left him right up until the days of his United Nation Orchestra in the late 1980s. When Dizzy died in January 1993, the world lost the man who had taken over Louis Armstrong's role as the father figure of the music; it also lost one of the major innovators in what became known as the modern jazz or "bebop" revolution of the 1940s.

Perhaps because of Dizzy's longevity compared to bebop's other principal character, Charlie Parker, who burned out at the age of thirty-four in 1955, and perhaps also because of his cheerful demeanor and obvious talents as a showman and entertainer, his contribution to jazz's major revolutionary movement has been consistently underrated. Yet in many ways he was a far more wide-ranging, original, and innovative musician than Parker, possessed of a similarly miraculous instrumental talent, but with a ruthless determination to achieve and, for much of his life, a clear sense of direction. At a stage when Parker had retreated to relative obscurity in the Midwest, Dizzy pioneered small group bebop on New York's 52nd Street and then went on to pursue his dream of transferring the style to a big band format. With Chano Pozo (who was dramatically murdered at the height of his career), Dizzy developed Afro-Cuban jazz, and later, with pianist and composer Lalo Schifrin, he produced major works for the concert hall and took a hand in the bossa-nova craze. From a background of grinding poverty he developed a reputation for financial astuteness, yet poured a fortune into keeping his big band going. He was also a respected teacher and inspiration for many younger players, and passed on many of his technical and musical ideas to a new generation that included such disciples as Jon Faddis and Arturo Sandoval.

Beneath the professionalism, his craft as a bandleader honed by long years in the swing bands of leaders like Cab Calloway, Lucky Millinder, and Earl Hines, Dizzy remained an enigma. Outwardly, his lifestyle was in sharp contrast to the self-destructive lives of other beboppers like Fats Navarro, Bud Powell, and Charlie Parker. He enjoyed a stable marriage for over half a century and seemed always to be on the best of terms with his fellow musicians, who appeared universally to adore him. Yet, dig a little deeper and this turns out to be only part of the picture. Dizzy had a penchant for womanizing, he kindled unprecedented animosity among a number of his colleagues, and he had a mean streak that could surface without warning and was by no means restricted to the copious practical jokes for which he became well known during his days with Cab Calloway.

A man of formidable intelligence, who was a keen chess player and a master of the complex arts of composition and arranging, Dizzy often found it impossible to resist the challenge of putting himself one up on an opponent, even after he had outwardly espoused the benign principles of Baha'i; yet others found him so generous with his time and ideas that it became impossible to repay his kindness.

Drummer Kenny Clarke, for example, had no doubts: "Dizzy is different; he's a saint . . . and he was an extraordinary musician, too, just on the verge of genius, in some ways more than a genius. He gave a lot more of himself than any musician I know of—much more than Bird [Charlie Parker], because Bird was like a prophet who brings a message, leaves that message and then disappears."[1]

Yet this describes the same man who broke off from a long, serious interview on his career to tell English critic Charles Fox: "I'm staying at the Mayfair Hotel, and there's a guy down there, one of the hall porters, that plays backgammon. From about five years ago, he's been promising me to teach me how to play this game, you see. Now I've learned it by myself, and he doesn't know that I know it. So what I'm going to do, I'm going to go down and make him get out the backgammon set, saying, 'Maybe you'll teach me now?'

"He's going to think this is the first time, because I'm going to say 'How do you set it up?' I'm not going to know how to set up the board or anything, and he's going to have to explain to me: 'Now when you throw this, *boom*, you have to move here,' and 'This doesn't look too hot, maybe this would be better?'

"And then I'm going to *kill* him, so he says, 'Boy, and I thought *I* was a good player!' "[2]

Few people would go so far out of their way to play a practical joke, and there are plenty of other instances. Dizzy was most fond of recalling his duo session with Oscar Peterson, for Pablo in 1974, when he arrived well ahead of the agreed time for the recording and had completed his warm-up before Peterson arrived. From years of Jazz at the Philharmonic tours together, Peterson knew that Dizzy needed a number or two to get going, so he relaxed when he saw Dizzy stretched out and apparently asleep behind the studio door. He could barely keep up when Dizzy sprang into the opening number, "Caravan." Having related this, Dizzy would then go into paroxysms of laughter at the discomfiture he had caused.[3]

These complexities of Dizzy's character never stood in the way of his achievement in becoming the elder statesman of jazz. As fellow trumpeter Joe Newman observed, "If there's anyone to follow Louis in the public's mind and eye, it will be Dizzy Gillespie, in spite of his clowning."[4] The public loved him almost from the moment he began to lead his own bands in the 1940s, and at its height the bebop craze rivaled Beatlemania. Hordes of fans would turn up at Dizzy's concerts in lookalike berets and horn-rimmed glasses. His generous extrovert character contributed to the lives of many fellow musicians, including Dave Brubeck, who recalled: "When my kids were still quite young they were with me at the [1960] Newport Jazz Festival. I was on stage when the riot began. It was Dizzy who rounded up my children who were out front and herded them to safety backstage. He kept them with him until my wife and I could escort them safely out of the festival grounds. A number of years later, when my sons Darius, Chris, and Dan were performing with me at the Grande Parade du Jazz in Nice, Dizzy decided to take them on a sightseeing tour of the Riviera. According to my sons' description, it was like Mr. Toad's Wild Ride at Disney World, but in spite of being scared to death, [they] had the wildest most joyful time of their lives."[5] Yet other musicians, including many disposed to adore him, fell foul of the perverse side of his nature, such as English bassist Dave Green, who showed Dizzy a rare 78-rpm recording in the band room at Ronnie Scott's, only to look on aghast as Dizzy smashed the disc.[6]

This was bizarre behavior indeed, but part of a pattern that led more than one commentator to the conclusion that Dizzy was "crazy as a fox," outwardly zany (and clearly not always in total control) but simultaneously a shrewd operator who meticulously filed away in his mind any shred of fact or information that might come in handy some day.

So what were the elements that went to make up this complex man: one of the most gifted trumpeters in musical history, one of jazz's great

original thinkers, and, in later life, the guardian of the whole jazz tradition?

Dizzy's contradictory character, his instrumental prowess, and his
will to succeed all have their origins in his childhood in the small South
Carolina town of Cheraw, where he was born John Birks Gillespie on
October 21, 1917. It was then, as it is now, a sleepy backwater on the
Pee Dee River, referred to in tourist literature as "alive with the grace of
the Old South on its shaded streets." The town was laid out in 1768,
and its Episcopal church of St. David was the last pre-Revolutionary
church built in the Carolinas during the reign of George III. John Birks
was the youngest of nine Gillespie children (of whom there were seven
survivors), and the family lived at 335 Huger Street, a north-south thor-
oughfare that runs down toward Market Street with its town green and
Cheraw's fine collection of pre–Civil War buildings.

The "Old South" and its antebellum grace were always the last
things on Gillespie's mind when he was interviewed about his childhood—a period, incidentally, that predates his nickname "Dizzy." He
was known until he reached Philadelphia in 1935 as John Birks, or some
phonetic variation of that name.

"I was scared," he recalled. "Scared of my father. He was super
austere, and never showed emotion. He'd give me a whipping every Sunday morning, me and my brothers, for what we had done bad during the
week. Some weeks we didn't do anything, but we still got a whipping,
so I began to spend the week doing something to get the whipping for.
I guess people thought I was pretty bad, something of a gangster. I'd be
throwing rocks, chewing gum and sticking it in girls' hair, and fighting
every day.

"The only time my father spoke up for me was when I got into
trouble on my first day at school for whistling in the class. I could already
read, count, and do my alphabet backwards, so when I got to school I
just whistled. The teacher, Mrs. Miller, beat me and my father got furious. I didn't know the rules of school, but I knew there was going to
be trouble. But when he went to see the teacher that was the only time
he ever spoke up for me."[7]

John Birks's father, James Gillespie, was a member of a family well
established in the Cheraw area. Many cousins still live in the region, as
do members of John Birks's mother, Lottie's, family, the Powes. Seventeen years separated John Birks and his eldest brother, Edward Leroy
(known as Sonny), and they never got to know one another because
Sonny left home early and died by 1935. The next brother, James Penfold
Jr., ran away from home when John Birks was three or four years old,
although they later shared a room in New York City, where "J. P.," as

he was known, did various casual jobs and eventually became a cabdriver. John's three sisters—Mattie, Hattie, and Eugenia—lived at home for most of his childhood, but he was closest in age and temperament to his youngest brother, Wesley, who had been born in March 1915. Because of John's quick intelligence, he soon caught up the two school years that separated him from Wesley, and (after the initial embarrassment and knock to Wesley's pride) they went through grade school together.

James Gillespie Sr. seems to have been just as contradictory a character as his son John was later to become. He was a bricklayer or "brickmason" by trade, working hard all week; then on Saturdays he transformed into a musician, playing piano with the local band, whose instruments were stored at the Gillespie house. Yet this respected local builder and musician was also the harsh and sadistic father who regularly beat his children. He was so cruel to J. P. when the boy worked with him on a building site that the family's second son ran away. It is tempting to attribute John Birks's own mean streak to his father's behavior and personality (not to mention his uncles, who had reputations as hotheads), but there is also evidence from the adult Dizzy himself that part of his drive as a musician came from a desire to prove his worth to his father, even though James died in 1927.

"I don't remember exactly what my father played. But he had all the instruments, piano, drums, the only bass violin in town—they weren't playing it in jazz at that time, they were still using tubas—and he had a mandolin and clarinet. My mother said he played them all. It's a drag he didn't live to see me become a musician. He died when I was ten, and I hadn't really begun to show an interest in music then. I always enjoyed music though, and when I was two and a half I used to fool around on the piano, playing 'Coon Shine Lady.' I always did have a fascination for the piano through my whole life."[8]

In countless interviews, variations on these views emerge. The adult Dizzy always admitted that he ran scared of his father, yet balanced this with a grudging admiration for the man who had been the only other musician in the family and a sorrow that they never got to share this experience. James forced all the other children to take piano lessons, but none of them stuck to music after their childhood.

The only contemporary on whom John Birks didn't vent his own pugnacious character as he grew up was his brother Wesley. "I used to fight anybody, big, small, white or colored. I was just a devil, a strong devil. I could whip all the guys my brother's size, but I never could whip him. I guess he knew my secrets."[9] In his brother, John Birks found someone who could depend on him emotionally. He helped Wesley overcome violent nightmares—often on the subject of the "wood man," a spectacularly ugly old white man who sold wood and was an object of terror for all the neighborhood children. On one such occasion, Wesley's nocturnal thrashing about in terror was sufficiently severe that he knocked over a pitcher of water and cut his hand so badly that he was unable to go to his regular weekend job at "Son" Harrington's Shoe Shop and Ice Cream Parlor. John Birks took his brother's place, shining shoes and serving portions of ice cream.

As it turned out, John Birks's initial education came from Son's wife, Mrs. Amanda Harrington. The Harringtons and their son James (known as "Brother") lived virtually next door at 329 Huger Street. Between their houses were two vacant lots, and as a small child John would run through them to his neighbors' home, where Amanda, a retired schoolteacher, taught him to read and write before he arrived at kindergarten.

Outside his instrument-filled home, the earliest other musical influence on John Birks was the church. The Harringtons were one of only two black families in Cheraw to be Catholics, and their religion was remote to the Gillespies, who were Methodists. Although one of the Methodist elders had a son, John Burch (whose name was often confused with John Birks's), who played snare drum, the real influence came from the Sanctified Church further up Huger Street, where the sounds of gospel music swelled out during the weekly meetings. As the adult Dizzy was often to say (and to prove in his playing), the rural blues had no impact on him because he never came into contact with it, but the rhythmical handclapping and singing of the Sanctified Church left a lasting impression.

Little or nothing is known about the music played by James Gillespie's band. In later life, Dizzy recalled the instruments rather than the music they played, and his only other childhood memory of music was his maternal grandfather "putting on a show" in the yard near their house. So it seems that it was at the Robert Smalls School in Cheraw where music really took hold of him. By the time it did, his father had died suddenly from an asthma attack in 1927. The year before his death, he had paid to send his two youngest sons and their mother to Philadelphia and New York, where there were various members of the extended family. Not least because of the multitudinous varieties of ice cream available up North, John Birks knew that this was where he wanted to end up in later life, but after his father's death the family was left in such abject poverty that the prospect seemed unlikely.

Lottie Gillespie (who had devoted her life to bringing up the family's many children) began taking in washing and earning a living of a kind, but her entire savings vanished when the head of the local bank absconded with most of the town's money at the start of the Depression, leaving the family destitute. At the same time, without the stern beatings from his father, and facing a penniless future, John Birks became wilder and more uncontrollable, picking fights and carrying out pointless feats of derring-do.

He had passed through kindergarten, first, and second grades rapidly and without major incident, except for his penchant for getting into scrapes and fights. But once he had been left fatherless, it was his third grade teacher, Miss Alice Wilson, who took him in hand, acting as a mentor for him, eventually gaining the boy's confidence and encouraging to take an interest in his academic work. "I was a good English student," he recalled, "for the simple reason that that was the easiest subject to me. I very seldom made a grammatical mistake, like putting a future tense where a past is supposed to be, and those kind of things. I learned very thoroughly there in school."[10]

Gillespie never failed to pay tribute to Alice Wilson in later life, praising her as "the young woman who started me off; the cause of my being in music . . . who took an ornery cuss who's not worth a dime from the start."[11]

The event that precipitated John Birks into a musical career was the arrival at the school around early 1929 of a collection of musical instruments donated by the state. These were farmed out to pupils who expressed an interest, and the eleven-year-old John Birks was allocated a trombone. "Everyone wanted an instrument, but the bigger ones got the chance to get what they wanted. I was too small to reach fifth position on the trombone, but I was so eager I'd even have taken a harmonica. I taught myself scales by using my ear." Before long, Alice Wilson had formed a little band to play for the morning "march in" to the schoolroom and also for a show at least once a year that featured her pupils singing, playing, and dancing. She played the piano herself. "She couldn't read music," Gillespie remembered, "but she was a very gifted composer with a good ear. She'd hear songs on the radio and pick them out. We had a little minstrel show at school . . . and she taught us all the tunes, made arrangements of them, entirely by ear, telling each of us: 'Here's the note you play!' "[12]

Without the stern presence of his father at home, John Birks practiced his trombone long and loudly. That Christmas, James "Brother" Harrington, the boy next door, was given a trumpet. It was an object of interest for him, but one of utter fascination for his younger neighbor, John Birks: "I saw it on the Christmas tree—a long shiny silver-plate trumpet. I saw that horn and went crazy.

" 'Go ahead and try it!' said James.

"He let me practice on it, and I'd keep on running next door to play. If either of us made too much noise, then we'd just run across to the other person's house and carry on. I became pretty fair at the trumpet."[13]

Within a short time, it became obvious to Miss Wilson that John Birks would have to be given a school trumpet to play, and he became a regular member of her little group with trumpet, trombone, snare and bass drums, and herself at the piano. The adult Dizzy often paid tribute to the band's bass drummer, Wes Buchanan, who subsequently led the band when it was booked to play engagements away from school. "I never have heard anyone since play the bass drum in a jazz orchestra like this guy. He'd sit and play it with one knee up against the head. Whenever he wanted a different sound, he'd move his knee forward or back, just like some guys do today with their elbow."[14]

Even in 1930, when he started to play in the school band, John Birks never received any formal training on the trumpet. Given the for-midable heights to which he took trumpet technique in the 1940s, play-ing faster, higher, and more accurately than any brass player before him, in any sphere of music, the fact that his formative years were entirely without any kind of training makes this achievement utterly remarkable. Yet every available source confirms that this was the case: because his schoolteacher, Alice Wilson, was musically illiterate and there were no experienced brass players around to pass on hints about technique to the young boy, everything he learned about the instrument he either taught himself or discovered in trial-and-error sessions with Brother Harring-ton. He soon learned Miss Wilson's limitations when Sonny Matthews, the pianist son of a neighbor, invited him to jam and John Birks discov-ered he could only play in the key of B flat, the one key in which his teacher played the piano. Another self-taught musician might have been daunted by this discovery, but for John Birks it held no terrors: "I said, 'Boy, I'm going to learn how to play in those other keys.' "[15]

He taught himself harmony, working out scales and chords at the piano and applying what he learned to the trumpet. He also started to play alongside his cousin, Norman Powe, a trombonist, and the two boys used each other as practice partners, trying every new scale or harmony together. Powe had had a few lessons from another relative and pain-stakingly taught his cousin to read music, initially in the bass clef used by the trombone. John Birks worked out for himself how to decipher the treble clef and then tried to pass on some of his knowledge to his fellow young musicians, including pianist Bernis or Bernie Tillman, whom the boys cajoled into playing at a dance for a neighboring white school, and who then joined the group regularly for local dances and parties within a few miles' radius of Cheraw. "We played for house rent parties and things like that in Cheraw, and we played for high school dances," remembered Gillespie.[16]

Whether or not he was booked to perform, John Birks made efforts to get to as many of these events as possible, and, if he was not required to play trumpet, he would show off elaborate dance steps in the hope of earning some small change. The bass drummer Wes Buchanan doubled as a dancer with the band, and it was common for the touring bands that occasionally visited the area to bring with them novelty dancers to prance about in front of the musicians. John Birks learned at an early age how to move in front of a group, as well as the principles of showmanship. He subsequently never had difficulty in dancing to even his most revolutionary musical experiments, and his own bandleading always owed something to his early passion for dancing. His relaxed movements around the stage mirrored those of fellow bandleaders such as Tiny Bradshaw or, later, Illinois Jacquet, who both began their careers as dancers.

There were not many other prospects for earning money for a young man about to leave junior high school during the Depression. With nothing else on the horizon, when John Birks left school in 1933 he followed most of his contemporaries into the obvious sources of local employment—the cotton fields and the job creation projects run on a massive scale throughout the impoverished South by the WPA (Works Progress Administration) that had been set up to build roads and public buildings. "I did work on the WPA," he recalled, "but I didn't pick cotton too well."[17]

Many of his fellow black workers in the fields and on the roads had no prospects of looking any further for their eventual employment. The adult Dizzy was to recall that few of them, including some of his own brothers, were literate, and what little opportunity there was for manual labor was the only work going. It was not much better for those who could read and write well. Although there were high schools in the area for white students, there were almost none for black pupils. One of the very few was about thirty miles or so away in North Carolina, at Laurinburg, and it was here that a lucky chance gave John Birks an educational opportunity.

The Laurinburg Institute was a coeducational boarding and day college, catering to black students from ninth grade upward. It had about two hundred on the roll and had been founded in 1904 by Frank McDuffy, who still owned and ran the school in the 1930s. It was established on the principle of a trade school, similar to the pioneering Tuskegee College in Alabama, where pianist Teddy Wilson's parents were teachers. Wilson observed that that school's intake included "adults up to the age of twenty . . . still on the elementary level, because of conditions under which Negroes were living in the southern states of the U.S. in those days."[18]

Laurinburg drew some of its staff from Tuskegee, and both schools offered generous scholarships to exceedingly poor students who showed promise, as well as the opportunity to earn money toward the cost of fees or living expenses by working on the school farm. The wife of the school's founder, Mrs. E. M. McDuffy, was interviewed in 1975 at the age of ninety-four and said: "I had very high hopes of my students. I wanted them to be best at mixing with people, at living with people, and not be ashamed of being black. At that time, they didn't know anything about those things. They would come to me and sit round in big groups and listen to me. . . . I told them the story of Booker T. Washington, of Tuskegee and Hampton, Virginia, and schools like that, and how people gave their lives for higher education, their hands as well as their heads. People who can do things can be somebody."[19]

The McDuffys' own son (Frank Jr., who much later took over the running of the school) had been one of the school's most promising musicians, a trombonist. He and his cousin, Isaac Johnson, a trumpeter, had left in June 1933, creating two vacancies for brass players in the school band, and one of John Birks's neighbors, Catherine McKay, recommended him and his cousin Norman Powe to Mr. McDuffy as possible replacements. The cousins were accepted, and, in view of their impoverished backgrounds, both were taken in during September 1933 on a scholarship basis, without fees, although John Birks did some work on the school farm.

Besides continuing some of the academic work John Birks had begun at school in Cheraw, the trade school element of Laurinburg meant that he had to study a vocational course. Because he had done manual work in the fields round Cheraw and now worked on the Laurinburg farm, the choice was more or less made for him: "Agriculture was an easy subject, and I didn't have to spend too much time studying agriculture. . . . I made good grades and I didn't have to study, because I knew all about those things. You see, I worked on the farm. I plowed, I know how to plow. I know how to protect the soil from generation to generation, and what to plant. Like you make a winter cover crop, they call it, like clover, and in the spring you plow that under, and it ferments and it causes good fertilizer. If anybody wants to find out about the art of farming, see me, because I'm a master farmer! . . . I was very close to the soil—I used to sleep out on the soil a lot! I loved being out, but boy, there was some hard work down there in North Carolina, you know, picking cotton ain't no easy job."[20]

Reading between the lines of this and and other accounts of his time at Laurinburg, John Birks was still desperately poor. Although his tuition fees and board were taken care of, he recalls borrowing clothes from other students and joining the football team (in which he showed some considerable determination and ability) because the footballers received better food. (During the 1933–34 season, he abandoned football on the advice of the school's band coach, Shorty Hall, who pointed out that no would-be trumpeter should ever risk his teeth on the football field.) The farm was the easiest and most obvious source of sufficient extra income to pay for clothes and shoes, and he spent the entire summer of 1934, between semesters, working there. The other ready source of income, however, was music.

Nominally, John Birks was on a music scholarship, and the Institute's music teacher (who arrived some time after John Birks) was a proficient cornet player. For the first time in his life, it seemed that another brass player might be available to coach Gillespie, but Shorty Hall's time was spent helping young players who had far less knowledge than John Birks and so, ironically, he found himself once more responsible for his own musical education. "I was mostly interested in music, and then there was nobody to teach me, so I had to practice all the time by myself. This other guy, Norman Powe, and I practiced incessantly. Man, we would wake up people early in the morning, midnight, and they made us shut up, but we practiced!"[21]

At least part of this practice was on John Birks's original instrument, the piano. Norman Powe remembers him playing with the school band and beginning a party trick that he was to continue for much of his life—jumping across from the trumpet section to play on the piano. Besides the school band, John Birks and Norman Powe continued to play whenever they could with their old colleagues from Cheraw, and complicated transport arrangements were made with relatives or friends who could provide cars. The summers from the Laurinburg years involved plenty of musical dances, picnics, and parties, and John Birks got something of a reputation for disappearing into the fields with girls. On one memorable occasion he lost his mouthpiece when the arrival of an established boyfriend scared him away from a particular young lady with whom he was in a clinch. A showman and dancer, he was popular with girls, one of whom apparently even planned briefly to lure him to the altar.

It is hard to assess exactly what musical influences affected John Birks while he was at Laurinburg. For reasons that will become clear in subsequent chapters, he did not fall under the influence of Roy Eldridge at this stage, as he was often to claim in print. Gillespie himself said, "I wasn't hip to King Oliver and I knew very little about Louis

Armstrong."[22] Yet these comments were made at a time when Gillespie wanted to be regarded as the heir to Roy Eldridge rather than the less fashionable figure of Armstrong. From comments made by other musicians about his playing when he arrived in Philadelphia in 1935, it seems that, in common with almost every other aspiring jazz trumpeter, John Birks had fallen under Armstrong's sway.

In the story of recorded jazz, Armstrong's revolutionary recordings with Joe "King" Oliver and then with his own Hot Five and Hot Seven from the mid-1920s, cut in Chicago at the start of a brief flowering of what became known as "classic jazz" on record, proved immensely influential. In his hometown of New Orleans, Armstrong's every disc was sought out and copied by his admirers—men like trumpeter Lee Collins who followed him into King Oliver's band. All over the United States, musicians interested in jazz, which was still a relatively new music, began to interpret the pop songs of the day in the idiom of their favorite recording or broadcasting artists.

By the early 1930s, when John Birks went to Laurinburg, jazz in Chicago and New York had moved on a few steps. Bigger ensembles than Oliver or Armstrong's pioneering small groups were commonplace, generally made up of around ten players, and the rigid two-beat style of the 1920s was being replaced by the smooth four-beats-to-the-measure rhythms of prototype swing bands. Tubas were replaced by double basses, banjos by guitars, and rolling snare drums by lighter cymbals.

Outside the main urban centers of the North, however, these changes took place slowly and sporadically, and we can be reasonably sure from John Birks's own account of hearing tubas rather than double basses and from discs made in the region at the time that in the Carolinas the prevailing orthodoxy in popular dance bands was the late 1920s style of big band jazz, as played in Chicago by bands like Tiny Parham, Erskine Tate, or Earl Hines; in New York by Duke Ellington, Luis Russell, and Fletcher Henderson; or in Detroit by McKinney's Cotton Pickers. By 1929, though, there was unquestionably one major figure who would have been a predominant influence on any would-be trumpeter almost anywhere in North America: Louis Armstrong.

Armstrong's playing and singing were widely available on disc, and he had broadcast regularly over several networks starting with relays from New York's Connie's Inn in 1929. Louis's gravelly vocals were widely imitated (according to guitarist Danny Barker, they were the envy of many a trumpeter) and so was his bravura trumpet style, with its effortless high notes and beautifully balanced phrasing.

Not only was this influence felt via records or the radio, but also through oral transmission from players who themselves had heard Armstrong and been influenced by him. This is likely to have been the main route of stylistic influence on the young John Birks, since Norman Powe confirmed to the author that the boys did not have access to a phonograph and that nowhere in their rural backwater would it have been possible to buy records.[23]

In Cheraw, before they arrived at Laurinburg, there was also limited access to broadcasts. "We didn't have a radio set," recalled Gillespie, "in fact some of the time we didn't even have electricity because we were cut off. But once we had a penny for the meter we could get the lights on again . . . but our neighbors [the Harringtons] had a huge radio set, and we used to go and listen at their house."[24]

Bands that visited Cheraw and Laurinburg included various touring groups playing jazz. Most were relatively local, but a small number were national figures, including the band led by Louis Armstrong's own mentor, King Oliver.

Despite Gillespie's protestations to the contrary, it seems unlikely that the presence of such a major figure in a Carolina backwater would not have made some impact on an aspiring young musician, even though by the early 1930s this New Orleans veteran was in decline, his heyday of the late 1920s long past. Oliver apparently invited the teenage John Birks and his cousin Norman Powe to join him before his band set off again on its weary way through the small towns and villages of the South. John Birks did not accept, but clearly remembered the great trumpeter and his oddly protruding eye. This is not least because Powe did take up the veteran trumpeter's offer—his two or three months of itinerant employment at the age of seventeen constituted his first "professional" job, although, as he told the author, Oliver was no longer much of a professional: the band was seldom on time in its dilapidated bus, and the pay was meager—just a couple of dollars a night if they were lucky. Their agent, O. R. Wall, never seemed able to get them any decently paying jobs.[25]

Powe left Laurinburg some months before Dizzy, so this event either took place around July 5, 1934, when eight of Oliver's sidemen quit at once after reaching Charlotte during a poorly paid tour of the Carolinas, or in the band's subsequent visits to the region in October 1934 or May 1935. Judging by the reports from Oliver's other musicians, it had not been a rewarding business touring the South in the depths of the Depression for some months before Powe joined them.[26] However, Oliver's presence in the area gives us a clue as to some possible direct influences on John Birks. Oliver's own playing was past its prime, and, although he could still play well on a good day, Powe remembers him taking few solos and having endless trouble with his teeth. Consequently, on the band's 1934 visits, the main solos were taken by two other trumpeters, Deek Phillips and "Red" Elkins. Elkins is remembered by his colleagues for mastering Henry "Red" Allen's style, and Allen's influence on Gillespie is discussed in Chapter 4. Phillips, by contrast, modeled his playing on Armstrong's, even adopting a shallow mouthpiece to try and emulate Louis's range. Because he was with the Oliver band on most of its visits to the Carolinas during John Birks's formative years, he would certainly have conveyed something of the Armstrong style. For the 1935 tour, Phillips's place had been taken by Hosea Sapp, a player whose main recorded work dates from his 1940s rhythm and blues sessions; but solos on pieces like Roy Milton's "Milton's Boogie" suggest a strong Armstrong influence in his phrasing and high notes, while his muted work on "R.M. Blues" from the same period shows a strong hint of Oliver's own playing.[27]

Most of the other groups to pass through Cheraw and Laurinburg were "territory" bands. Generally this term is applied to groups based in the South, Southwest, or Midwest who spent much of their time on the road. Only a small number of these ventured as far as the Carolinas, on long straggling itineraries from Kansas City or Texas, but most of the bands that came to Cheraw or Laurinburg were East Coast groups. The Carolinas had a handful of local bands who mainly worked in the Southeast, although the history of music in the area is still so underresearched that it is hard to be sure about how any of these—like Doc Pettiford's, Billy Stewart's, Kelly's Jazz Hounds (all from Fayetteville), and the Capitol City Aces (from Raleigh)—might have sounded. Gillespie claims to have sat in with the orchestra led in Charlotte by pianist Bill Davis, but unfortunately Davis's career is undocumented, so it is not possible to conjecture about his trumpeters.

The other principal band in the region that Gillespie recalled hearing has at least something of its sound preserved on disc. Also based in Charlotte, about ninety miles from Laurinburg, it was initially led by violinist Dave Taylor and then by pianist Jimmie Gunn. Norman Powe joined Gunn in 1937 and remembered that the band never strayed far from Charlotte and the surrounding area "because Jimmie was a schoolteacher. He always had to get home after the job so he could be at school the next morning. He was very popular in the area, and he had a very good band. We only traveled any distance during the summer vacation when he didn't have to be back for school. The band mainly worked in the Athaneum Ballroom in Charlotte, in a few clubs in the city and in the surrounding area. Some of the guys had extra jobs, like Jimmie himself, but we worked enough that you could make a good living just from music."[28]

The trumpeter who solos on the band's first two records, cut in 1931 as Taylor's Dixie Orchestra, is generally accepted to be Joe Jordan. His colleague in the trumpet section was Lester Mitchell, who, like many members of the band, was attending the Johnson C. Smith University in Charlotte, the city where Victor's engineers recorded them. The tunes are standards—"Everybody Loves My Baby" and "Wabash Blues"—but despite a slightly ragged feel, there is a genuine jazz sense present, and alto soloist Skeets Tolbert (who later made a name for himself in New York) is outstanding. Overall, despite players hailing from a wide variey of regional backgrounds who had come together in and around Smith University, this band captures something of the style of the St. Louis territory bands, most notably the Missourians. Jordan's trumpet is closest to the King Oliver–derived on-the-beat phrasing and tight, slightly cliché syncopations of trumpeters Lammar Wright and R. Q. Dickerson, who led that band. Even more notably, the Missourians' flamboyant tuba player, Jimmy Smith, was ably echoed in Taylor's North Carolina band by Harry Prather, whose agile playing anchors the rhythm section and produces a lively and melodic solo, based on the tune, in "Wabash Blues."

One of the band's saxophonists, Leslie Johnakins, remembered: "We broadcast regularly over the CBS Dixie Network Program, which originated in Charlotte, for about three or four years and this gave the band a good following."[29] He dates this from September 1930, so it is probable that John Birks heard this band frequently, both in person and on the air. During the years 1931 to 1936, when what had become Jimmie Gunn's Orchestra was again recorded by Victor for the Bluebird label, the band expanded and its personnel changed. By 1936, the trumpets were Dave Pugh, Herman Franklin, and Charles Daniels, although it is known that another player called Billy Douglas was also briefly in the section.

Daniels was the band's main arranger and later taught the basis of arranging to Norman Powe when the two roomed together in the late 1930s. Pugh had been a pupil at Laurinburg, where his mother still taught when John Birks and Norman Powe were students there, and he was a well-known and influential player in the region. Even in the late 1930s, when Norman Powe himself was in Gunn's band, they continued to broadcast. "There was a lot of prejudice going on in the South at that time, so it was a big deal for a black band like ours to broadcast, but we were well known as one of the first black bands to play over the local radio networks, even though when I played with Gunn our broadcasts were down to one or two a year."[30]

In his recorded vocals, Dave Pugh is immediately redolent of Armstrong, his gravelly voice accurately emulating Armstrong's tenor range from the period on "To My Levee Home" and "Star Dust." During the five years since the band's earlier recordings, Prather had moved to double bass, and Alton (or "Guy") Harrington had swapped his banjo for a guitar. Jimmie Gunn himself, though an accomplished pianist, had decided to front the band and hired a fluent, capable player called William Shavers to take his place. Even in North Carolina, the changes in fashion that had gone on in New York had permeated the local jazz scene, and the arrangements and rhythm section sound offer a good approximation of Armstrong's current backing band, the Luis Russell Orchestra.

The surprise is how little Armstrong influence is actually present in the playing rather than the vocals. Several of the tracks have a muted trumpet that plays melodic introductions in the style of Doc Cheatham's work with McKinney's Cotton Pickers or Cab Calloway's band. Only "I've Found a New Baby" shows a genuine Armstrong influence in the phrasing of the trumpet solo and the timing of the final high notes that stand out against the rest of the band. For the most part, whichever of Gunn's trumpeters was the key soloist, the inspiration is earlier territory band styles, rather than overwhelmingly Armstrong. Perhaps this is the kind of playing Gillespie meant when he described his playing shortly after leaving Laurinburg with the phrase, "I was still playing Southern." After all, during the years leading up to their 1936 record date, these were the local trumpeters a would-be player like John Birks would have heard most often, and their swing-inspired playing in a large band context may explain Gillespie's lifelong affinity for big band jazz. Curiously, one of Gunn's recordings, "The Operator Special," has another quite distinct characteristic. Its unison ensemble introduction has a strong Caribbean flavor in both the melody and the subtle underlying lilt in the rhythm. Maybe this suggests a starting point for Gillespie's lifelong interest in unusual rhythms and in particular what came to be known as Afro-Cuban jazz.[31]

We do know for certain that, before leaving the Carolinas, John Birks heard one other large ensemble that played a ragged and exciting brand of jazz: the Jenkins Orphanage Band from Charleston, South Carolina. Known initially as a "piccaninny band," this group of young musicians toured all over the United States and in Europe, raising money to keep the black orphanage in Charleston in funds. Numerous reviews talk of this band's exciting, highly rhythmic style, including *Melody Maker*, describing a contingent from Jenkins who appeared in London in 1929: "The trumpet and trombone were shooting off some hot stuff, which, though crude, had a positively irresistible rhythm." Duke Ellington's future trumpeter Cat Anderson toured the Carolinas with this band

in the early 1930s (usually playing trombone) and then revisited the area
again in a territory band known as the Carolina Cotton Pickers. He is
just one of the many distinguished Jenkins musicians that John Birks is
likely to have heard during his formative years as a trumpeter.[32]

At Laurinburg, in addition to trying to make sure they caught up
with touring jazz groups, Norman Powe recalled that much of his and
John Birks's study was of classical music, but they also listened to broadcasts by Duke Ellington and Cab Calloway on the radio. "These were
the two events we did not miss, when Cab's band or the Ellington band
were on the air, they broadcast from the Cotton Club something like
twice a week, and we would always hear them."[33] The main soloists in
Cab's band during the Laurinburg years were Edwin Swayze and Lammar Wright, both of them playing in the style favored by Jimmie Gunn's
band. Ellington's main soloist was Cootie Williams.

The other main legacy of Laurinburg on John Birks was its brand
of moral and ethical education. There is evidence (including his own
account) that he was no less hot-tempered at Laurinburg than he had
been during his tearaway phase in Cheraw immediately following his
father's death. On one occasion he pulled a knife on another pupil in
rehearsal, but managed to talk his way out of trouble. He also tells of
accepting punishment when necessary from Principal McDuffy, and
seems to demonstrate that the McDuffy ideals had rubbed off on him:
"With all the deprivation and as hard as we had it down South, he
managed to uplift us and instill in us a sense of dignity."[34]

For some years to come, John Birks would still be a wild character,
prone to draw his knife in the heat of anger, but Laurinburg had im-
planted some measure of pride in him, and some measure of his own
worth. "I got so tired of the little G'lespie boy," recalled Mrs. McDuffy,
when she was interviewed alongside Gillespie, "but I had patience with
you, or you wouldn't be where you are today!"[35] Even if, as later chapters
show, he was not as defiant of the U.S. draft as he suggested in his
autobiography, by the end of the 1930s he held one clearly established
view as a consequence of his upbringing in the South: "The enemy, by
that period, was not the Germans, it was above all the white Americans
who kicked us in the butt every day, physically and morally."[36]

By the start of 1935, the time drew closer when John Birks would
have to leave the South. Early that year, to try and escape the economic
burdens of surviving in Cheraw, his mother packed up and moved to
Philadelphia. "They wanted me to stay down there and finish," recalled
Gillespie,[37] but his work went to pieces. Before the school year was out,
he had flunked physics, which meant he could not obtain his high school

diploma without staying another year. He was unprepared to do this and he eventually dropped out of school, with the aim of joining his family up North.

Much later, as the leader of his own big band, he interrupted a tour of the South to collect his diploma from the Laurinburg Institute. By then he was a famous son of the community and nobody was going to worry about grades in physics. "I was on the road with Ella Fitzgerald, and we stopped in Laurinburg. We played a free concert in the daytime, with Ella, and in the middle of the concert Mr. McDuffy walked out on stage and said, 'Here's something you left!'

"It was my high school diploma dated 1934 and my football letter. So I'm not a high school dropout any more."[38]

2

Philadelphia and the First Bands

The period Gillespie spent in Philadelphia is the most obscure in his early career. From the time he left Laurinburg in the early summer of 1935 until his arrival in New York in 1937, we really know very little about this crucial formative stage in John Birks's musical development, during which he matured from a high school dropout, self-taught as a trumpeter, to the accomplished musician who joined Teddy Hill's Orchestra within a few weeks of arriving in New York.

Gillespie arrived in Philadelphia around the end of May 1935, having returned for a day or two from Laurinburg to Cheraw and then hitching a lift northward with a friend. He joined his mother and other members of his extended family in a smallish apartment at 637 Pine Street, in the black heartland of South Philadelphia, at its junction with Seventh Street. Bill, the husband of John Birks's oldest sister Mattie, bought him a trumpet at a pawn shop and within a few days of his arrival he had a job with a trio, paying $8 per week.

John Birks had found it hard to attend to his work at Laurinburg almost from the moment his mother moved north and was no longer a few miles away, so when he eventually rejoined his family, he was reluctant to leave home again for long, even when quite large sums of money were involved.[1] Consequently, the Philadelphia years became a period of consolidation, during which John Birks remained close to his family before finally launching himself on New York and a full-fledged musical career. It was also a time in which he grew from boy to man, and his autobiography rather bashfully describes his early sexual experiences, including his first encounter with a white woman. "I don't think I even enjoyed it because I was too scared," he recalled. "I'd never been with a white girl before."[2] Yet before long "Peggy" collected him from the gig again and again, and soon he was involved in a relationship—albeit not yet a serious one. It was not to be the last such romance; even throughout his long and stable marriage, the adult Dizzy continued to be fascinated by miscegenation. In the late 1930s, before he was married, he pursued white whores in London and Paris, the more relaxed racial climate in Europe perhaps encouraging him to shed some of his ingrained southern inhibitions. In the odd pockets of liberal attitudes and behavior that he then encountered in the United States, such as at Camp Unity, he continued to experiment. Later accounts of his tours in Europe suggest that he never quite abandoned this interest and he formed one serious liaison with a white partner on the American side of the Atlantic later in his life.[3]

For such a significant center of American musical development, Philadelphia lacks a comprehensive account of its fertile and varied history of vernacular music. When John Birks lived there, it was a vibrant city, the home of dozens of musicians who were or became first-order jazz players. In midtown, the Earle Theatre on 11th and Market Streets presented visiting jazz orchestras and its Friday morning shows combined films, comedians, and vaudeville acts with out-of-town jazz presentations. Big name black bands played more regularly at the Pearl Theatre, on Ridge, near 23rd Street, and similar groups—including those of Teddy Hill, Tiny Bradshaw, Lucky Millinder, and Cab Calloway—played the Lincoln Theater at Broad Street and Lombard Street. Later these visitors appeared at the Nixon Grand Theatre in North Philadelphia.

The main black neighborhood centered on South Street, between 15th and 16th Streets, with an atmosphere similar to the Harlem of the time. Photographer Irv Kline captured its spirit in pictures taken while John Birks lived and worked there. Within a block or two, in an area crammed with restaurants, bars, food and clothing stores, barbershops, and billiard parlors, Kline found blind guitarists singing the blues on street corners, a female brass quartet playing hymn tunes, and skyward speakers on the sidewalk outside the record shops playing the latest "race" records. He recalled stopping by the jam sessions at Teddy Burke's music store, or in the basement of the Douglas Hotel, where local players like John Birks would mingle with stars from whichever visiting big band was in town.[4]

The Green Gate Inn on 12th and Bainbridge Streets, where Gillespie had his first job, was rowdy, and before long John Birks (who was already getting known by other musicians for the eccentric habit of carrying his newly acquired trumpet around in a paper bag) had migrated to another job at a South Street joint that paid a little more. He also took steps to join the recently reestablished black local of the AFM, the musicians' union.

There had been a flourishing black local (number 591) in Philadelphia before the Depression, but it had fallen victim to financial hardship and closed. A new local, number 274, was established at the start of 1935, and its first secretary was trombonist Frankie Fairfax.[5]

"Fax" was a well-connected and influential figure on the Philadelphia music scene. He does not appear to have made any records, but his band became a nursery for a number of musicians who played with some of the most influential Swing Era leaders. He was remembered by his pianist, Bill Doggett, as hailing from West Virginia and coming north with a college band led by another West Virginian, Chappie Willett.[6] In the late 1920s, the itinerant trombonist Clyde Bernhardt had bumped into Fairfax in the South, recalling him as the "college man" who played tuba and trumpet in McClane's Society Orchestra in Huntingdon, West Virginia,[7] and it is probable that this band became the nucleus for Willett's. By 1934, Fairfax had settled on trombone as his instrument; by this time he was already based in Philadelphia, from where he traveled widely in Willett's band. The black press carried pictures of the group (including Fairfax) on a tour to Detroit that year.[8]

According to Doggett, Fax made all Willett's sidemen charter members of the new local and, soon after, took over leadership of the band himself. It swiftly became one of the city's three main black big bands, holding down a Saturday-night residency at the Strand Ballroom. Fax was a canny bandleader and organizer, whose ambition was to front the city's finest orchestra, and in his quest for suitable musicians, Doggett remembered that he recruited some of the best players from his main rival, Jimmy Gorham.

Willett is an even more shadowy figure than Fairfax, but it is known that he gave up leading to write, subsequently providing arrangements for many leaders, including the up-and-coming Lucius "Lucky" Millinder, a bandleader who had been hired by the powerful Irving Mills Agency to front its Blue Rhythm Band in New York.[9] Fairfax, assisted by his former boss Willett, was to develop close ties with Millinder and some years later set up a complete band for him, as he was also to do for other leaders. It was, it seems, quite common in Philadelphia for bands to be "borrowed" for road tours by established leaders, and Andy Kirk, for example, recalled "lending" his band to Blanche Calloway in 1931 for a gig at the Pearl Theater and a recording at nearby Camden, New Jersey. This practice squares with Irv Kline's description of his hometown as "corrupt and contented" before World War Two. It seems that Fax fitted well into such an ambience.

Fairfax had a reputation for consistently finding work for his bands, but he also got taken to task from time to time for swindling his men out of part of their earnings. In 1935, Bill Doggett led a walkout over money and took the musicians off to Atlantic City for a season, leaving

Fairfax temporarily without a band, although the two men were later reunited. Nevertheless, Fairfax remained a union official until more or less the time that the black and white locals were combined, many years later, as Local 77. Obviously his "contented corruption" was not acceptable to everyone, and in later years trumpeter Charlie Shavers could be roused to anger by mere mention of the name Fairfax: "If he walked in here right now, you wouldn't be able to stop me going for him!" he told musician and author John Chilton.[10]

Before his spectacular departure from Fairfax's band, Bill Doggett had provided most of the group's music. He had arrived at a simplified method of jotting down notes that made his scores hard to read for the uninitiated, and when Gillespie first tried out for the band he found it impossible to decipher Doggett's attenuated script and failed his audition. Gillespie suggests in his autobiography that this caused some friction between himself and Doggett, although clearly it did not last.

Rejected by Fairfax in the late summer of 1935, John Birks continued to play in the many clubs in South Philadelphia and to visit any household where he might learn more about music. He and Doggett became frequent visitors to one another's homes, and Doggett confirmed that John Birks had developed sufficient powers of execution on trumpet by 1935 to play whatever ideas entered his head, backed by a sound knowledge of harmony, based on his piano playing. The two men would swap instruments to investigate more about harmonies and chords, and detailed, lengthy discussions went on in the area's after-hours restaurants.[11] Doggett was never a serious trumpeter, although, like a lot of musicians, he loved fooling about on other instruments. He gave up messing on trumpet a few months after he met Gillespie, but he was sure that it had been beneficial for both players to swap. He got the chance to understand some of John Birks's burgeoning harmonic ideas by listening to him working them out on piano, and John Birks considered it worth the trip to North Philadelphia to Doggett's house (or persuading Doggett to make the journey southward) to find out more about the structure of big band charts and how to voice chords for sections. During this period he started to learn firsthand many of the arranging skills he was to employ later.[12]

Another haunt was the home of the McGriff family. Organist Jimmy McGriff was the son of a local Philadelphia stride pianist, a man who played "dance piano," and who became one of John Birks's closest friends. Jimmy himself was born during the time John Birks was living in the city, but as a small child he remembers Gillespie keeping up his regular visits to the house whenever he was in town, and that his father would later go along to hear him whenever he returned to Philadelphia, leaving his young son in the car outside where he could listen to the music.[13] McGriff is sure that his father was "at school" with John Birks during those years, "studying music," and this equates with comments from Gillespie's later colleague Bill Dillard, who thought John Birks had been "at school" in Jersey or Pennsylvania before his arrival in New York.[14] There is scant evidence that Gillespie had any kind of formal education during the Philadelphia years, and plenty to suggest that from late 1935 there would have been little or no time for any further schooling because Frankie Fairfax offered him a job in his new orchestra, a band recruited to replace the one spirited away by Bill Doggett.

It was the Fairfax band that, within a few days of his arrival in it, conferred Gillespie's nickname on him. Trumpeter Palmer Davis noticed the empty trumpet chair at a rehearsal when John Birks was fooling around on piano and called over to the drummer, Norman Dibble, "Where's Dizzy?" The name stuck, and became better known than the trumpeter's own from then on, although a few other Philadelphia colleagues, such as Charlie Shavers, also called him the "Cheraw Flash" for the remainder of the 1930s.

Dizzy was a member of Fairfax's group from the end of 1935 until the spring of 1937. There were few other founding members of this new band who achieved anything other than local fame, save for Dizzy's fellow trumpeter Jimmy Hamilton, who had worked with Fairfax on and off

The Frankie Fairfax Orchestra, Philadelphia, 1935. Fairfax (center) with music; Dizzy Gillespie kneeling on the right. (Frank Driggs collection)

from 1934 on trumpet, but who made the transition to clarinetist during Dizzy's time in the orchestra. Hamilton's career is a remarkable parallel of Dizzy's. He was born the same year as Gillespie into a rural South Carolina community where his father played in a local band, and in due course moved with his family to Philadelphia. After the Fairfax days, he remained in contact with Dizzy, briefly working with him some years later in Benny Carter's band before going on to become the principal clarinet with Duke Ellington, in place of Barney Bigard. Fairfax's bassist, Oscar Smith, remembered earnest conversations about music between Hamilton and Dizzy in his father's pool hall, at 1306 Brown Street.

Around Christmas 1935 and New Year's 1936, in a characteristic move, Fairfax hired his entire band, with the exception of himself, to the New York bandleader, Tiny Bradshaw, for a tour to the South. In his autobiography, Dizzy lists a partial personnel for the musicians who traveled with Bradshaw, who was a drummer, pianist, and singer, and recalls that they played in Charlotte, North Carolina. This event was etched in Dizzy's memory because he saved the life of Palmer Davis, who was being asphyxiated by fumes from a gas fire in his hotel room when Dizzy discovered him in the nick of time.

Charlotte was the final destination on the tour, which began with a week apiece at the Royal in Baltimore and the Howard in Washington. The band was nearly stranded at their third engagement in Richmond, Virginia, although it is as a consequence of this unfortunate gig that we have a full list of the personnel on the tour because they deposited their union cards there with Local 38. There was a quaint protectionist custom then in place in the United States under which a band from "out of town" was required to deposit its details with the local branch of the AFM. The idea was to protect local jobs and incomes by preventing the importation of contract labor at reduced rates. In the case of jazz musicians traveling round the country, a 10% levy was payable by the employer to the local branch of the AFM for any band hired from outside the area.

Bradshaw's personnel included trumpeters John Gillespie, Pete Brown, and P. J. (Palmer) Davis; trombonist Bert Claggett (listed as Cliggett); saxophonists Tascell (or Tasso) Richardson and Shorty Cawthorn (listed as James "Squashy" Hawthorne); guitarist Sam Saddler (or Sadler); bassist Oscar Smith; and drummers Norman Dibble (or Dibbles) and Rossier "Shadow" Wilson (listed as Williams, and whose presence doubling Dibble's is hard to explain). There were also two other members for whom instruments are not identified: Harry Carter and James Alexander.[15] After a week in the Richmond Theatre, their next job (at a restaurant and club) fell through and the band survived on tinned sardines until the job in Charlotte was confirmed. Even there they spent several days eating turkey in every possible recipe after no tickets were sold for a Christmas dance at which they were to appear.[16]

Back in Philadelphia, and reunited with Fairfax in early 1936, the band underwent a shake-up in personnel. John Brown and Harold Reid came in on saxophones alongside Richardson and Hawthorn, and at Reid's suggestion Jimmy Hamilton and Pete Brown were replaced on trumpets by Charlie Shavers and Carl "Bama" Warwick.[17] These two trumpeters had more or less grown up together in New York after Warwick had moved north from his native Brookside, Alabama, to New Jersey in 1930.

Shavers's father had a barbershop close to the Savoy in Harlem, and in the shadow of the famous ballroom the two young men absorbed the jazz atmosphere of New York together. Despite markedly contrasting physical characteristics—Shavers was short, tubby, and dark-skinned; Warwick was tall and sufficiently light-skinned to "pass" as white—they referred to each other as brothers. "Of course, he isn't really my brother," Shavers told British journalist Sinclair Traill, "but he was brought up in our house and went to school with me and lived with us for so long, I always think of him as my real brother. . . . My brother was a real good trumpet player and I'm not kidding. They hired me in those days because my brother was such a good first trumpet."[18]

With the arrival of these two talented trumpeters, his exact contemporaries, and with a blend of skills and experience that perfectly complemented his own, Dizzy blossomed. Here was the chance he had never had before to try out new ideas, discuss technique, experiment and then put the ideas to the test for real every night on the bandstand.

Dizzy recalls in his autobiography that, when Shavers and Warwick arrived, he was "still playing Southern. I'd learned a couple of Roy Eldridge's licks and would play them and whatever else I could pick up from playing the piano." He had clearly used his time at Laurinburg to develop his technique as a trumpeter, but, despite Dizzy's own recollections, we can be certain that he had not fallen under the spell of Roy Eldridge during his time there. Instead, we know, from bassist Oscar Smith, that "his trumpet solos were imitations of Louis Armstrong."[19]

So what led Dizzy to alter his playing? And could it actually have been Charlie Shavers, who was the first musician to exert a dominant influence on Dizzy's mature style and moved his playing in the direction of that of Roy Eldridge?

The recorded evidence of Dizzy's first discs, made soon after his arrival in New York in May 1937, certainly show that by then he had made a remarkably complete assimilation of Roy Eldridge's approach to the trumpet. Clearly, during his two short years in Philadelphia, Dizzy somehow absorbed many of Eldridge's ideas, but what is truly remarkable is that he can only have had very limited direct exposure to Eldridge's own playing. Yet he not only seems to have taken on the older man's style, but by 1939 had used it as the springboard for his own. (For a comparative discussion of Eldridge and Dizzy's styles, see the account of Dizzy's first records in Chapter 4.)

Roy Eldridge, who was born in 1911 in Pittsburgh, is generally seen as the stylistic link between Dizzy and the father of jazz trumpet, Louis Armstrong. Eldridge, nicknamed "Little Jazz," was in many ways the prototypical swing trumpeter, able to inject energy and pace into only a few bars of solo space in a big band recording, yet also capable of sustaining almost limitless invention in after-hours jam sessions. He and Chu Berry, the tenor sax player with Teddy Hill (and later a colleague of Gillespie's in Cab Calloway's band), were famous for "going on the rampage" in Harlem, as guitarist Danny Barker put it, and sitting in at club after club, where their endlessly competitive sparring would raise the temperature and the standard of playing of those around them.[20]

Eldridge was working in various parts of the East and Midwest during the years that Dizzy was growing up, and played with Cecil Scott, Elmer Snowden, and Charlie Johnson in New York during the early 1930s before a brief stay in early 1933 with Teddy Hill. He went off in 1933 on a road tour of Fats Waller's *Hot Chocolates* revue; led a band in Pittsburgh with his saxophonist brother, Joe, the same year; and then joined McKinney's band in Baltimore. He did not rejoin Teddy Hill until early 1935.

Almost every published account of Dizzy's life repeats the assertion from his autobiography that he heard Roy Eldridge and Chu Berry broadcasting with Teddy Hill's band from the Savoy in New York while he was still living in Cheraw. He tells the story of sitting in with Bill Davis, while aged fifteen, at the Elks Hall in Cheraw, successfully navigating a couple of choruses of "China Boy" in the key of F, before rushing to his neighbor Mrs. Amanda Harrington's house to hear Eldridge, Berry, and trombonist Dicky Wells over her radio in a live network relay from the Savoy.[21]

In his later years, there was no doubt in Dizzy's mind that he first heard Eldridge with the Hill band on the radio "from down South," since he related the same story on numerous occasions.[22] Yet the only possible time that Dizzy could have heard Eldridge on the air from Cheraw was during the short time between leaving Laurinburg and deciding to travel north to join his family in Philadelphia. Although Eldridge had been briefly with the Teddy Hill band in 1933, the band was not broadcasting at that time, nor had Chu Berry joined.

Hill's first broadcast was during the week of June 22, 1935, four months after the band had cut its first records and in all probability around the time those discs were actually released since there tended to be about a three-month lead time from recording to release.[23] So before the broadcasts began, only those who had heard Eldridge in person would be fully aware of his revolutionary style.

Hill was quickly hailed as "the newest sensation in the realm of orchestra leaders over NBC" by the *New York Age*,[24] and the *Amsterdam News* confirmed: "Teddy now goes out on the red network of WJZ three times a week: Thursdays 5–5:30, Fridays 4:30–4:45, Saturdays 4:45–5:15." It went on to say, "Teddy Hill and his band hit the metropolitan critics right between the eyes the very first time on their national hookup."[25]

This suggests that a convenient piece of romance crept into Dizzy's memory. Although there is no doubt that he did develop a deep stylistic debt to Eldridge, he could not have heard Hill's band over a national network in 1933, and, even when it was possible to hear it in 1935, the broadcasts took place in the afternoon or early evening, not late at night. The story made a fitting climax to his account of his Cheraw years, but the reality is that he almost certainly heard Teddy Hill's broadcasts from the northern urban sprawl of Philadelphia.

The most telling clue to what actually happened is Dizzy's recollection that, when he met trumpeter Charlie Shavers at the start of 1936, "he knew all of Roy's solos. Everything." Once Shavers had settled in Philadelphia, he and Dizzy played side by side in the Frankie Fairfax band for some months and Dizzy confessed, "I . . . learned all of Roy's solos from Charlie."[26]

Usually when players talk in this way, they are referring to recorded solos. Ray Brown, for example, recalled that only a year or two later, as kids in Pittsburgh, he and his musical friends would learn all Lester Young's solos from records as soon as they were released. To be let into a friend's house you'd have to whistle the latest solo through the door.[27] Danny Barker made similar claims for New Orleans trumpeters in the 1920s, recalling how Lee Collins would learn all Louis Armstrong's solos from the famous Hot Five and Hot Seven records as they appeared.[28] The implication from Dizzy is that he and Shavers mastered the solos that Roy Eldridge had recorded, although there were so few of these that Shavers must have brought into the equation his personal experience of hearing Eldridge frequently over a lengthy period in New York.

Teddy Hill's session of February 26, 1935, was actually Eldridge's first record date (there is no proof he is on Clarence Williams's session of July 1930), and the four sides produced are his only recordings with Hill's Orchestra. Later that year came discs with Putney Dandridge, Teddy Wilson, Billie Holiday, and the Delta Four, while in early 1936 there were influential discs with Gene Krupa and Eldridge's new boss, Fletcher Henderson, that began to show what Eldridge could do. Yet there were still far fewer examples of Eldridge's playing available than, say, Louis Armstrong's. Eldridge's regular radio broadcasts under his own name from the Three Deuces in Chicago did not begin until relatively late in Dizzy's period in Philadelphia.

It is also possible that, around the time of the Hill band's afternoon radio shows in 1935, Dizzy first heard Eldridge in person on one of a handful of live dates with Hill (and in the subsequent after-hours jam sessions) in Philadelphia because it was at one such gathering that Hill first recalled seeing Dizzy.[29] The Hill band played a few one-nighters at the Pearl in 1935 in which Eldridge appeared. He was back the following year at the Nixon Grand when he returned with Fletcher Henderson.

Yet, even for a musician as talented and assiduous as Dizzy, it would be hard to assimilate an overall style from hearing a few solo moments in afternoon broadcasts, a handful of records, and fleeting appearances on live dates where the band played second place to singers and dancers.

What this suggests above all is that Dizzy's main exposure to Eldridge was secondhand, both explaining a joke about this in his autobiography and pointing to Shavers (whom Oscar Smith said had already used his own remarkable facility to extend elements of Eldridge's style by 1936) as a much more important musical influence on Dizzy than tends to be acknowledged. When hearing Shavers and Eldridge together on their Jazz at the Philharmonic recordings from the 1950s, their stylistic affinities are obvious. Dizzy's protracted contact with Shavers would have offered him the perfect opportunity to discover ways of tackling solos in almost all musical contexts with a consistency of approach indebted to Eldridge but aurally transmitted by Shavers. It equipped Dizzy with an understanding of Eldridge's style that would have been virtually impossible to acquire from records and broadcasts alone.

The Frankie Fairfax band remained at the Strand most Saturdays in 1936, and from time to time traveled out into the Pennsylvania countryside, up into the mountains, or into the state's mining and industrial belt. Bill Doggett recalled that the band was often booked on a regular circuit that took in Lancaster, Throop, Scranton, and Hazelton, among other places. Doggett thought that any band was likely to exhaust the playing opportunities of the area in a relatively short while and was glad of the opportunity to play for new listeners during his runaway season in Atlantic City.[30]

Doggett's departure allowed Fax to take his new band of completely different musicians playing new arrangements (some of them by Shavers) back round the circuit that had been growing tired of his old band. For much of the first half of 1936 this was the pattern of Dizzy's life, before Tiny Bradshaw reappeared and lured Shavers and Warwick away for good with the offer of more money, travel, and fame. Bradshaw wanted Dizzy to go along as well, but this time Gillespie refused, preferring to stay close to his mother and family. Dizzy remained with Fairfax, alongside trumpeter Palmer Davis.

Dizzy was content to stay with Fairfax until a few months into 1937 when he got a phone call from Shavers and Warwick, who had moved on from Bradshaw to the Mills Blue Rhythm Orchestra headed by Lucky Millinder and were passing through Philadelphia. This was a name band, only a rung or two below Cab Calloway's or Ellington's, and handled by the same high-profile agency, and the two trumpeters were keen for their former partner to join them. They persuaded Millinder to agree, and he hired Dizzy, paying him to come to New York plus a few weeks' salary, even though he had not heard Dizzy play.

Lucius "Lucky" Millinder was considered by many of those who played for him to be a great band director, even though he made no pretense of being a musician himself. Drummer Art Blakey, who later played with Millinder, summed him up: "Lucky couldn't read a note if it jumped up out the floor and slapped him on the head, but you've never seen talent like his. All you had to do in his band with an arrangement was sit there and follow him. You can't make a mistake, because he knows everything that's happening. An amazing man, he didn't know one note from another but he had ears as big as an elephant's. He was a hell of a band director, but I don't know where he learned."[31]

Doggett, who also was to work with Millinder, agreed. "He was one of those leaders who just fronted a band with a baton. But his style of directing was unique at that time. He used to jump up high in the air, and I remember one of his tricks was to jump up onto the lid of the grand piano while I was playing, and leap off again onto the floor without missing a beat of the baton."[32]

The only problem for Dizzy was that, at the time Shavers and Warwick coerced Lucky into letting their friend join the band, the chair he was to fill was actually occupied by one of the giants of Swing Era trumpet, Harry "Sweets" Edison. Sweets not only had no intention of leaving, but was clearly unaware of the arrangements made by his colleagues. He was also playing as well as at any time in his career, making Lucky more and more reluctant to fire him. Danny Barker (who played guitar in the band) recalled them "cutting" the Count Basie Orchestra in a battle of music a few months later, and Sweets agreed: "I would say 'yes' we beat Count Basie, and I think that group with myself, Billy Kyle on piano, and Charlie Shavers, who was playing very interesting stuff on trumpet, was just about Lucky's best ever band."[33]

Lured by the offer of joining a New York "name" band, Dizzy gave his notice to Fairfax, packed his bags, and set off to stay with his older brother J. P. in Harlem. But the job never opened up for him, and he was soon in New York without work and none of the reputation he had acquired in Philadelphia.

Ironically, it is just as well Dizzy did not join Millinder. Lucky had recently bought out the rights to the band name from the Mills Agency: "I own my band," he told the *Baltimore Afro-American* in a 1937 interview,[34] and it was not long before he was running himself into serious debt. A few weeks into 1938 he laid his band off in New York, and to try and recoup some of his losses did a deal with Frankie Fairfax's friend Hayes Pugh in Philadelphia and a new agent, Tommy Wharton, to front Bill Doggett's band on a tour of the South. Doggett was promised that they'd return to New York and the band would be billed as "under the musical direction of Bill Doggett." This never happened, and Lucky sank further toward finally being declared bankrupt in 1939.

Shavers and Kyle left within a few months of each other before the 1938 layoff to join John Kirby. The other musicians who had waited loyally for him until they found out he'd betrayed them to front Doggett's band offered him no comfort. Barker, whose memoirs are bitter on the subject of Millinder's betrayal, joined Benny Carter, and Edison joined Count Basie to become a mainstay of Basie's band for well over a decade. In due course, Bill Doggett helped Lucky rebuild his band and career, and in the early 1940s they were to recruit Dizzy, but in the meantime a new opportunity was on the horizon for Gillespie.

3

Teddy Hill and Edgar Hayes

Once he had arrived in New York, in the late spring of 1937, Dizzy never entertained the thought of returning to Philadelphia and his family. Despite having to share a single room with his brother and arranging matters so that he slept during the day while his brother was at work and went out all night so J. P. could get some rest, Dizzy had discovered the most vibrant and active jazz scene in the world. Simultaneously, with few of the inhibitions of his early sexual encounters from Philadelphia remaining, he made full use of his brother's daytime absences to bring back to their 142nd Street room many of the attractive young women he encountered in the city's throbbing nightlife. Dizzy's innate skills as a dancer made him a sought after dancing partner at venues like the 400 Club, where his energetic style was based on the Lindy Hop.[1]

In his autobiography, Dizzy lists the after hours joints where he was one of a coterie of sitters-in, despite the attempts of the American Federation of Musicians to discourage jam sessions. The union disliked club owners who paid a trio and, by encouraging guests, ended up appearing to present a full band, but Dizzy and his fellow trumpeters Charlie Shavers and Bama Warwick took every chance to flex their musical muscles, and ran rings round the union officials who checked up on clubs like George's, the Yeah Man, the Victoria, the 101 Ranch, and Clark Monroe's Uptown House.

Shavers, despite a heavy working schedule with Lucky Millinder's band, continued to act as a mentor for Dizzy and introduced him to other musicians, including drummer Kenny Clarke and trumpeters Benny Harris and Bobby Moore. Harris and Clarke were later to play an important role in pioneering modern jazz, but Dizzy himself paid tribute on several occasions to Moore, a former member of Count Basie's Orchestra, who eventually ended up in a mental hospital but who still promised in 1937 to be one of jazz's most innovative soloists.

"Little Bobby was the best of our crowd," recalled Gillespie in 1977. "He's in a state hospital now, since 1937, and they offered me his old job with Basie. But I wouldn't take Bobby's job as we were such close friends and used to jam together all the time. It was a team, Charlie Shavers, little Bobby, Benny Harris, Bama and me. We used to go in all the clubs down in the Village or in Harlem and after the union delegate had left, we'd check them out and jam."[2]

Buck Clayton, who worked alongside Moore in Basie's band, recalled that, before his mental problems, Moore had had some dentistry done on his two front teeth, which, together with the poor state of the rest of his mouth, left him virtually unable to play. Before this, remembered Clayton, "He was a wonderful little trumpet player, about sixteen years old and trying to play like Roy Eldridge."[3] Clayton, who arrived in New York with Basie at the very start of 1937, thought Moore was a little too young and inexperienced to shine in some of the company that jammed at Monroe's club. Yet it is obvious from his remarks that Roy Eldridge's approach to playing trumpet was the common bond that bound Dizzy, Moore, and their circle of friends together.

As the weeks went by, Dizzy began to spend more and more time at the Savoy Ballroom, the "home of happy feet" in Harlem at 596 Lenox Avenue. Before long he became sufficiently well known at the club, run throughout its existence by Charlie Buchanan, that he could get in without paying. Dizzy talked his way into playing a few numbers with many of the famous bands that played there, such as the Savoy Sultans and Chick Webb's Orchestra, in which he was one of the few guests ever encouraged to sit in. "Chick took a liking to me when I was very young," Gillespie told British critic Charles Fox. "I'd never seen anyone sit in with Chick's band before, but every time I'd go to the Savoy I'd have my horn (you know, I had that everywhere) and Chick would motion me to come to the bandstand."[4] Dizzy would take Taft Jordan's place and sit alongside Cuban trumpeter and saxophonist Mario Bauza (who was later to introduce Dizzy to the concept of Afro-Cuban music and be a colleague in the Cab Calloway Orchestra). Another of Webb's sidemen at the time was alto saxophonist Louis Jordan, who was already being featured as a vocalist. Dizzy would have had firsthand exposure to Jordan's slick showmanship and this may have had a bearing on his own subsequent stage persona.

The Savoy was one of the most popular dance halls in Harlem. "It had two stages that could hold twelve-piece bands," remembered trumpeter Bill Dillard, who played there with Luis Russell and Teddy Hill. "They always had two orchestras. So you'd play your set, then you'd be off and the other band would play. They had ten dancing girls, dime-a-dance girls, because at that time all over many of the largest cities in the states they had these dime-a-dance places, where you'd get ten tickets to dance for a dollar and the fellow who bought the tickets would go on the dance floor with one of the girls until the music stopped and the girl would take one of the tickets. The dances varied from jitterbugs to slow numbers, but it was a dime ticket for every dance.

"We also had many people coming there from Europe, and along the perimeter of the dance-floor they had tables that would seat four people, that were out there for people who just came to listen to the music and watch the lindy-hopping and drink up the happy atmosphere that the dancers projected."[5]

Dillard spent many months at the Savoy in various bands, but his observations confirm that the venue had a reputation that was more than just local. The dance hall catered both to listeners and dancers, and with a change of at least one of the resident bands every week, it had a throughput of many of New York's most accomplished jazz players. The majority of bands were black, but from time to time the great white swing orchestras like Benny Goodman's appeared there in "battles of music" with one or other of the regular resident orchestras.

As Dizzy related the story many times, it was a casual meeting with bandleader Teddy Hill at the Savoy that secured his first professional job after arriving in New York. Hill asked Dizzy if he knew where he could find a trumpeter to replace Frankie Newton, who was unwilling to travel to Europe with Hill for a lengthy tour (since, according to fellow trumpeter Bill Dillard, Newton had been rehearsing his own five-piece group for an engagement in Greenwich Village). Dizzy immediately agreed and was signed up there and then. But as is so often the case, there was more to it than that.

Hill recalls (in Dizzy's autobiography) that Gillespie was one of a number of trumpeters who called him when the news got out that Newton was to be replaced for the trip to Europe. Hill remembers Dizzy auditioning (still wearing his coat and gloves, which would seem a bit far-fetched for the mild climate of May 1937, when the events took pace), and that he moved Shad Collins from second trumpet to third and gave Dizzy the second chair and the lion's share of the solos. Frankie Newton, and Dizzy's idol Roy Eldridge before him, had played third trumpet, the least demanding in the section, to conserve his strength for solos. Gillespie's reading skill got him the second chair plus the solos, and provoked a coolness between him and Collins that was to last for many years.

Even this is not the full story. Normally, like many other bandleaders, Hill would have asked the opinion of his sidemen before even auditioning a new trumpeter. Both saxophonist Howard Johnson and guitarist John "Smitty" Smith claim that they lobbied for Hill to hire

Gillespie, loyalty that was later repaid when both of them worked in Dizzy's own bands. "I had got Dizzy his job in Teddy Hill's band," recalled Smith in 1980, "so in return he hired me for his big band."[6]

Teddy Hill himself was well liked by his fellow musicians and had worked his way up through the bands of George Howe and Luis Russell before leading his own orchestra from 1932 onward. Born in Birmingham, Alabama, in 1909, he had had lessons from John Tuggle "Fess" Whatley, a leading black teacher and bandleader in Birmingham, whose career as an instructor at the Industrial High School and as leader of his "Jazz Demons" lasted from 1917 until 1962. After learning trumpet in Whatley's Industrial High band, Hill subsequently specialized on tenor saxophone from 1924, although he doubled on the other reeds, and he became a regular member of New York pit bands for shows and revues as well as a sideman in some of the late 1920s bands where Chicagoan and New York influences merged.

Although he was a competent section player, Hill's solo playing was undistinguished, and, as time went by, he largely forsook his saxophone for the conductor's baton. His band started out at the Ubangi Club, where he had an eight-month residency in 1932–33, and later he worked at the Roseland Ballroom before landing a regular job at the Savoy. His 1935 broadcasts gave him a wide following, and he adopted the name "NBC Orchestra" for his band to reinforce this, keeping the title after their airshots came to an end. Even in distant Birmingham, Hill's reputation was enhanced, as "Fess" Whatley "set Teddy up before the students as a model young man who has achieved the kind of success other Industrial High graduates should go after." School principal A. H. Parker came to Radio City in New York to make a presentation to Teddy of his alma mater's appreciation, and other press releases of the time stressed Teddy's "family" image—"having a wife and daughter living in Harlem."[7]

Teddy's fatherly instincts were called on to obtain a passport and other travel papers for Dizzy at short notice, and, since any paperwork surviving from Cheraw was deficient, Hill made the trip to Philadelphia to get the necessary documents signed by Dizzy's mother. Dizzy was still only nineteen and perfectly happy to spend time at Hill's house playing childish games with Teddy's infant daughter. In later years he hotly denied rumors that Teddy used him as a babysitter and that this was the main reason he was hired.

So what kind of band was Hill's, and where did it stand in the league table of 1930s swing orchestras? Many critics align themselves with Gunther Schuller, who, basing his judgment entirely on recorded evidence, classifies the group as "one of the poorest bands to come out of Harlem," responsible for a "ramshackle collection of recordings."[8] But in view of the band's reputation among musicians, and the considerable influence exerted by its principal soloists of 1935 and 1936, Chu Berry and Roy Eldridge, Schuller's judgment would seem to be a little harsh. The band's overall recorded output does have a high proportion of Dillard's mannered vocals, and it swings more in the late 1920s style of Luis Russell than some of the better mid-1930s groups, but it never sounds less than a professional, competent dance orchestra.

Long-term members of the group like John Smith and Howard Johnson thought highly of it. "I wanted some glamour," recalled Smith, who stayed from 1932 to 1939. "The Savoy was a wonderful place and we used to be there about six months at a time and then go on tour . . . to the Apollo Theatre in New York, the Lincoln in Philadelphia, the Royal Theatre in Baltimore and the Howard Theatre in Washington."[9] Working at this level and consistently being rebooked on the main East Coast circuit does not suggest a band that was all that lacking in musicality. Johnson is more forthright: "Teddy's was a very good band, but somehow we never seemed to get much of a reputation."[10]

At least part of the responsibility for such success as the band did enjoy was due to Hill himself. "The fellows in the band considered Teddy a good business man, because he kept us working," said Johnson. "He was a good looking fellow, and he used to get up there and wave a long stick. . . . He had played tenor saxophone with Luis Russell . . . then he got an alto and played it in this band." Hill's business acumen and his management skills were to have an important role in Dizzy's later career and the development of bebop, but in May 1937, Hill came up with what Dizzy most needed at the time—the firm offer of a job.

The band was to sail for Paris at the end of May—a story about them that appeared in the *Pittsburgh Courier* on June 5 is datelined "Mid-Atlantic 2 June"—and they did not arrive back in New York until late September. The French backers of the tour timed it to coincide with the Exposition Universelle of 1937, hoping that there would be a large potential audience visiting Paris for the exhibition. It is unclear how much, if at all, Dizzy worked with the band before they left. Certainly he was to have difficulty holding onto his job once he returned from Europe (because he belonged to the Philadelphia, not the New York, branch of the musicians' union), so it is highly likely that, if he played publicly with Hill at all before the band quit New York, it would have been for just a handful of evenings. But Dizzy did go into the studios with Hill on May 17, ten days or so before they sailed, and they cut a series of six sides that are discussed in the next chapter.

Because Dizzy had joined the band at relatively short notice and

Teddy Hill's Orchestra, Randall's Island, New York, May 1938. (Left to right) Dicky Wells, Earl Hardy (trombones), Dizzy (partially obscured by Shad Collins, leaning forward), Bill Beason, Sam Allen. (Photo: Dunc Butler; Frank Driggs collection)

had only previously sat in sporadically with Hill at the Savoy up until the time of the record session, no one in the band had any real idea of his overall capabilities. "It was all fine," recalled Bill Dillard, "until we got on the boat and started rehearsing our charts. It took over a week to sail from New York to Paris in those days, so every day we rehearsed, and we found out that Diz had never really played in a proper big band section before."[11]

Given the large book of arrangements that the Hill band had amassed, and the discipline they had built up over years of broadcasting and recording between 1935 and 1937, Dizzy's experience with Frankie Fairfax was not adequate for him to play with the control that Hill's men took for granted. "My job as first trumpet player," recalled Dillard, "was to keep the brass section playing together, phrasing together, attacking together and so forth. Diz just hadn't done anything like that properly, so I helped him in every way I could to phrase and attack with the section."

In his autobiography, Dizzy defends his abilities and suggests that he could read anything that was put in front of him (which tallies with Bill Doggett's impressions from Philadelphia) and that "Bill [Dillard] helped me change the things that I did that weren't professional." Dizzy also singles out Shad Collins and trombonist Dicky Wells as members of a clique in the band who were against him. When asked about this, Bill Dillard said that not only did the older, more established men in the band resent Dizzy being hired when he was clearly deficient in his section playing, but that "when he took solos he was obviously different from the way we swung and played with a certain kind of a lilting rhythm. He played a different story in his solo playing. Sometimes he'd play very high and fast, and he'd produce a row of notes that were dissonant or did not blend with what he had hoped to do. He would stop playing and start laughing." This happy-go-lucky demeanor along with Dizzy's obviously different ideas seem to have been the basis for the rift that grew wider as the band's trip to Europe progressed.

Some of those who met the Hill sidemen during that visit, like expatriate Canadian trumpeter Alfie Noakes, a veteran of Ambrose's Orchestra, observed the open dislike of some of the band members for Dizzy. He related his observations to John Chilton, telling him "the situation was exacerbated because Dizzy had a money-lending scheme in operation. The older guys borrowed from him and had to pay him back with swingeing interest."[12] Chilton himself confirmed how some members of the band felt: "The dislike was real enough and long-lasting. I remember the abhorrence in Dicky Wells's voice when he talked about Dizzy. Russell Procope [one of the reed players] confirmed the band's attitude." The principal event that seems to have sealed the distance between Dizzy and many of his fellow bandsmen was a recording session organized in Paris for the visiting Americans by Hugues Panassié, from which Dizzy was very obviously excluded.

The Hill band arrived in Paris early in June. Their rehearsals aboard ship (most probably the *Lafayette*, but recalled by one or two band members as the *Ile de France*) had been treated as free entertainment by the passengers. Not only had the band itself been rehearsing to acquaint its new members—Gillespie, saxophonist Bob Carroll, and trombonist Wilbur de Paris—with the arrangements, but it was to be featured as part of the Cotton Club Revue, and so rehearsed the accompaniments to a selection of tap dancers, singers, and novelty acts in a program of largely new material by Benny Davis and Fred Coots. Chief among the dancers was Bill Bailey (singer Pearl Bailey's brother) who was later to be a colleague of Dizzy's in the Cab Calloway entourage. There was a second novelty band on the bill called the "Tramp Band" that featured kazoos and a washboard in its lineup.[13]

The Cotton Club Revue ran for six weeks at the Moulin Rouge,[14] before the whole company transferred to London on July 23, three days before they opened for a further five weeks at the London Palladium. In his autobiography, Dizzy makes the point that most of the principal Cotton Club dancers (like Bill Robinson) were not in Paris with the Revue. Yet despite the absence of star dancers, the revue was a great success. "The show was very varied," recalled discographer and author Maurice Cullaz. "There were prestigious dancers, and it was the first time anyone in Paris had seen the Lindy Hop."[15] Cullaz went almost every night, sometimes taking along the former Teddy Hill trumpeter Bill Coleman (who had settled in Paris) and their wives. Another visitor was Hugues Panassié, editor of *Jazz Hot* and president of the Hot Club of France. He wrote, "Besides Duke Ellington's Orchestra, this is the best band which ever came to France. . . . Their style generally resembled that of Fletcher Henderson with touches of Chick Webb."[16]

At the time, Panassié and his fellow critic Charles Delauney had just set up their new record label, Swing. Its object, besides recording the Hot Club's "house band" (the string quintet with Stephane Grappelli and Django Reinhardt), was to record U. S. visitors to Paris, and Panassié no doubt enlisted the advice of Bill Coleman in deciding which of Coleman's former colleagues in the orchestra to record.

Coleman did not already know the playing of the young Gillespie, who had arrived in New York after Coleman left for Europe, and had little opportunity to hear Dizzy with the show since "there were not many solos. The band accompanied the actors and only played an overture number before the first and second parts of the show."[17] So, similarly unaware of Gillespie's talent and anxious to record some of the better known names in the orchestra, Panassié assembled a band with trumpeters Shad Collins and Bill Dillard alongside Coleman, plus bassist Richard Fullbright and drummer Bill Beason, to record with Django Reinhardt on guitar. The nominal leader was trombonist Dicky Wells, one of the men whom Dizzy felt to be part of the clique in Hill's Orchestra who disliked him, and they went, as Dillard recalls, to "a big studio at the end of the Champs Elysées" and cut several sides on July 7. They returned on July 12, with pianist Sam Allen and saxophonist Howard Johnson, for a second session, where Reinhardt's place was taken by his Hot Club colleague Roger Chaput.

That he should be excluded from the recording activities of the band clearly rankled Dizzy, and, even though Panassié's review in *Jazz Hot* was very favorable concerning him, he was still complaining about the record dates when interviewed in France as late as 1989.[18] Instead, he sought solace in sightseeing, in his growing interest in photography, but above all in the whorehouses, accompanied by guitarist John Smith, whose presence in the recording studio was rendered unnecessary by Reinhardt and Chaput.[19] The availability of white prostitutes (whom Dizzy would occasionally hire in pairs) continued the interest begun in Philadelphia in his association with "Peggy." Things were not much different in London, and musician and raconteur Benny Green recalled that, during a return to Britain in the 1970s, Dizzy followed up a visit to the offices of *Punch* magazine (where he outraged convention by eating the formal lunch without using a plate) by strolling with Green toward Tottenham Court Road. The ostensible purpose of the stroll was to look at the plethora of camera shops in the area, but Dizzy confessed his real motive was to see the site of a prostitute's room where, after conducting his business, he had accidentally (and painfully) washed his private parts in Lysol in a dimly lit bathroom during his 1937 visit with the Hill band.[20]

On both sides of the English Channel, audiences had relatively few opportunities to hear the Hill band playing in its own right. Dizzy's own recollections back up those of Bill Coleman, although Dizzy also remembers the band playing for dancing at the Moulin Rouge after the formal revue had ended. "The band was set up on the floor," he recalled. "We had to play for dancing, and the trumpets and saxophones were right at the back [behind the rhythm section] . . . but it really sounded good. We participated in the whole show, and it was after all the different acts were over that we played a few numbers for dancing. The show was very similar to what went on at the Cotton Club, with singers and dancers, and we had Roland Smith [*sic*] with us, who became very well known for his interpretation of 'Old Man River'. There was a large restaurant, lots of tables, and the stage projected a long way into the room."[21]

Dizzy remembers being "dragged" off to nightclubs afterwards, and that Paris really "sent" him, because the city never slept. The band members were staying close to the Moulin Rouge and found a friendly after-hours bar near the club where they could relax at the end of the gig if they were not going out on the town. We do not know for certain which clubs Dizzy went to, or whether he jammed with local musicians, as he was to do at the Nest Club in London a few weeks later, but we do know something of what he sounded like.

"He was already playing in a way that differentiated him from Roy Eldridge," recalled Maurice Cullaz. "He had a very varied and powerful style . . . all the [local] trumpeters came and asked Dizzy to show them his trumpet and his embouchure, because he was easily playing through two octaves above middle C, and everyone was fascinated by the apparent ease with which he played."[22]

His embouchure was all the more remarkable because of his characteristic and totally individual method of pushing his jaw forward and playing with his cheeks puffed out. This contradicted every aspect of good practice in the standard textbooks of the day and fueled the amazement of the Parisian musicians, who were flabbergasted by the results that could be achieved with such an unorthodox technique. "He always played that way," remembered Bill Dillard. "I think he taught himself to play, and without an instructor he didn't realize that that wasn't the typical way of playing. But by the time he found that out, there was no point in changing it. He started that because he wasn't aware how to play without his cheeks puffed out."[23]

The circumstances under which the band appeared in London were such that audiences had even less opportunity to hear Dizzy than in Paris. During the 1930s, a spirit of growing protectionism had led the Musicians' Union and the Ministry of Labour to clamp down on the issuing of work permits to visiting American bands. Individual musicians like Fats Waller, Coleman Hawkins, and Benny Carter were granted permission to work, but, after 1935, the likelihood of entire U.S. orchestras like those of Duke Ellington and Cab Calloway (who had appeared in 1933 and 1934, respectively) visiting Britain became increasingly remote.

Only four months before Teddy Hill's band appeared at the London Palladium, the Jimmie Lunceford Orchestra, which arrived in Britain en route to the United States after a tour of the Continent, was refused permission to appear. Its members had to content themselves with some after-hours sessions at the Nest Club in London's Kingly Street.

Hill's band was granted a permit only because it provided the accompaniments for a revue, and the Ministry stipulated that the band had to appear on stage behind the dancers and avoid movement except insofar as it was necessary to operate their instruments. The *Melody Maker* correspondent clearly felt that the band was denied the opportunity to shine, being "obviously handicapped" by its position, although it is worth noting that in the 1920s several shows imported from the United States featured the band on stage with the singers and dancers as a matter of course. *Melody Maker* also reported a "weakness in the saxophone section—thin, ragged and out of tune" during some of the stock arrangements that went with the dance routines. "When it goes to town it is something like a real Harlem band," ran the piece, which nevertheless praised the show itself extravagantly: "The dizzy speed of the dancing, the garish colors of the settings and costumes, the restless music and whirling movement of the whole production appeared to leave the public in a daze as they walked out."

Having been extended to a five-week run, the Cotton Club Revue finally closed in London on August 28; some of the company returned home, while the majority continued to Dublin, where they played for a week as Harlem on Parade at the Royal Theatre. The company re-crossed the Irish Sea for a final week as the Cotton Club of New York at the Palace Theatre in Manchester, before finally setting sail for home on September 14. Mancunian audiences alone had the opportunity of regularly hearing members of the band outside the setting of the stage show because the city's Ritz ballroom presented a number of afternoon dances at which they sat in with Rowland Hyatt's Orchestra, the resident group. One member of Hyatt's band had poor vision, and to help him read the arrangements, he had had the bell of his trumpet altered to point upward so he could peer more closely at the music. It is possible that this inspired Dizzy's own upswept horn, and that the idea lay dormant for the best part of fifteen years before he had such a horn made.[24]

Members of the Teddy Hill Orchestra and the cast of Harlem on Parade at the Theatre Royal, Dublin, August 31, 1937, celebrating the victory of Joe Louis over boxing champion Bobby Farr. Dizzy waving his hat on the left. (Howard Rye, by permission of the Dublin *Evening Herald* and the British Library)

When Dizzy got back to New York, the proud possessor of a British tweed overcoat and several hundred dollars better off after three months in Europe at $70 per week, it was to find that he was prevented by the AFM from continuing to play with Hill. He had left his original "transfer" from Philadelphia with the New York Local, but his journey to Europe invalidated it, and he was obliged to deposit his card all over again and avoid taking any regular engagement for three months. He was allowed to play one-off engagements, but any band hiring him on a regular basis would be charged a 10% levy by the union. Consequently, Dizzy did very little work for the last few months of 1937, except for a few jobs in the outer suburbs with a West Indian musical saw player, Cass Carr, and spot jobs (and a couple of illicit tours out of town) with the big band led by pianist and arranger Edgar Hayes. His money quickly evaporated, and he had a rough few months compared to the relative luxury of his life in Europe.

Once Dizzy got permission to work in New York again, in January 1938, he spent the next eighteen months in a variety of bands. For the most part, he worked with Teddy Hill's band, or with Hayes. Dizzy also worked at the Apollo Theatre with the Savoy Sultans when they enlarged their group for gigs away from their "home" at the Savoy, and he worked at the Savoy itself with flautist Albert Socarras.

This period was one in which Dizzy's musical life benefited from a variety of influences; it also was one in which he underwent a radical change in his personal life.

Scarcely recovered from his carousing in Paris, Dizzy returned to New York nightlife, and, before his funds ran out, carried on his previous routine with his brother in their small room at 216 West 139th Street. On a trip upstate to Camp Unity, a holiday center run on leftwing lines at Allaben Acres, Wingdale, where Dizzy went with Cass Carr, he observed: "Almost everybody up there was mixed. White-black relationships were very close among the communists . . . a lot of white girls were there, oh yes."[25]

But all this was to change when Dizzy met a dancer called Gussie Lorraine Willis, known generally as Lorraine. He first saw her during a brief visit to Washington with Edgar Hayes in late 1937 (a trip he should not really have made under the conditions of his union card). Lorraine, who had been brought up in South Carolina and whose first marriage ended in the premature death of her husband, was not starstruck by the glamour of Dizzy's job as a musician, and she tended to go home rather than look for nightlife after her evening's work was done. Her very unattainability attracted Dizzy, and he courted her assiduously by letter once they were back in New York. He became increasingly penniless as the days ticked by before he was allowed to work regularly, but she was back in her regular job at the Apollo. A fellow dancer, Alice Lyons, was go-between. For a long time, their meetings were restricted to the few minutes between shows at the Apollo or between sets at wherever Dizzy was playing.

In due course, Lorraine, a powerful and strong character despite her delicate appearance, was to become Dizzy's regular partner and eventually his wife. She helped him financially while he waited for his transfer to be accepted, and she was to provide a firm home base for him as well as good business sense during the years ahead. Dizzy's brother moved out of their room on 139th Street some time before Dizzy's transfer came through and Lorraine eased the financial burden by giving Dizzy the portion of her salary she had previously sent home to her mother. Before long they set up home together, although they did not marry for some years.

Nicknamed "Striver's Row," 139th Street was, even in 1937, a desirable address. It consisted mainly of elegant brownstones, many wholly occupied by members of Harlem's professional classes. Nevertheless, some of the houses were let out as rooms, and the street was consequently a mecca for musicians, including Fletcher Henderson, Chick Webb (who shared his house with Taft Jordan and Bob Carroll), guitarist Al Casey, trumpeters Paul and Freddie Webster, and reed player Garvin Bushell. Based in J. P.'s former room, Dizzy and Lorraine became a regular part of that musical neighborhood.[26]

With his personal life stabilized, Dizzy used the period following his return from Europe to accelerate the development of his own musical identity in earnest. He was still thought of as a trumpeter in the Eldridge mold, but, as we know from his playing in Paris, his own personality was emerging and he brought a number of new factors into the equation.

Teddy Hill's band parted company with a number of its older musicians on the return to New York and during Dizzy's forced period of absence. When he returned to the group, the new trumpet section included Al Killian and Joe Guy, both forward-looking musicians whose ideas were far closer to Dizzy's than Dillard's and Collins's had been. Had Hill's working pattern been as it was before the tour of Europe, Dizzy might well have worked only with Hill once his AFM transfer came through. However, Hill's was no longer the full-time resident band at the Savoy and so it worked less regularly. The reputation it had built up in Europe was of no use in obtaining work back in the United States. It continued to appear at the Savoy occasionally, interspersed with a number of other bands, including Chick Webb's, invariably opposite the Savoy Sultans, who remained there week in, week out. The Moe Gale

Agency booked Hill's band alongside Edgar Hayes's Orchestra on a tour of the South, playing "Battles of the Bands" during some of the weeks they were not at the Savoy.

Because his band could not work continually, most of Hill's musicians obtained other jobs and Dizzy frequently found himself alongside his old jam-session friends Bama Warwick and Benny Harris in Edgar Hayes's lineup. Dizzy said that it was on a trip to Detroit, which he made with Hayes while waiting for his transfer in late 1937, that he first worked regularly with drummer Kenny Clarke. Clarke's rhythmic innovations will be discussed more fully in relation to his recordings with Dizzy's big band, but Clarke was already playing in a style markedly different from other drummers, using the traditional snare and bass drum combination to accent beats other than the conventional first and third note of each bar. Hayes was out of the country (without Dizzy) on tour to Sweden from February to May 1938,[27] and Clarke went with him. After Hayes's return, Clarke and Gillespie were to work frequently together during late 1938 and early 1939, laying much of the foundation for their later friendship during the early development of bebop. It is highly probable that Dizzy misdated the beginning of his association with Clarke, since trombonist Clyde Bernhardt, who was a long-term member of Hayes's band, did not concur with Dizzy's dating and recalled Dizzy's first gigs alongside Clarke within Edgar Hayes's lineup being in the following summer.

Bernhardt's memory (aided by diaries and notes) was such that he was probably correct to recall Clarke's bringing Dizzy to a rehearsal just before the band opened at the Apollo on July 15, 1938. Bernhardt remembers the band's third trumpeter, Cyril Newman, being unable to cut a couple of new arrangements satisfactorily. Dizzy, by contrast, played Hayes's "Bugle Call Rag" at sight, and after a second run-through had memorized the whole complex part. He got the job for the Apollo run and remained with the band on and off for some months.[28]

"Edgar let us play a little of the new music that we were beginning to work out at that time," said Dizzy. "Later, when I rejoined Teddy Hill at the Savoy, I brought Kenny with me."[29] (Hill was not impressed with Clarke's unorthodox drumming, nicknaming it a "klook-a-mop" style, a name that was for a short period used to describe what became known as bebop, and stuck permanently as Clarke's nickname.)

Hayes, who made his name with a recording of Hoagy Carmichael's "Star Dust," seems to have been a man much given to rehearsal, with a genuine curiosity about the forward-looking developments in jazz. He produced new arrangements for Dizzy that featured him as a soloist, providing settings that were particularly suited to his style, in place of Teddy Hill's aging charts in which Dizzy played parts conceived for Roy

Eldridge or Frankie Newton. Hayes's other sidemen included saxophonist Rudy Powell, who set Dizzy thinking about new harmonic ideas.
Dizzy credits Powell with alerting him to the possibilities of the "flatted
fifth," one of the most obvious harmonic devices in bebop.[30] When Hayes
reduced his group to a quintet, Powell and Gillespie stayed on as the
front line.

Clyde Bernhardt's colorful recollections (which, unusual for an oral
history, aptly capture the larger-than-life character of the man himself
with its curious mixture of humorous charm and pedantry) give us a good
insight into Dizzy's personality in the late 1930s. He was already disguising his shrewd mind and formidable musical talent behind a smoke-
screen of clowning. "One time during a number he slid off his seat and
sat on the floor, blowing and turning his horn all kinds of funny ways,"
remembered Bernhardt, who also describes Dizzy jumping up from his
seat while playing, elbowing Hayes aside from the piano stool, and comping some extra harmony with his left hand while continuing the trumpet
part perfectly. This was a trick Dizzy used often, and trumpeter Benny
Bailey remembers seeing Dizzy perform similar antics in Billy Eckstine's
band some six years later. Audiences loved the horseplay and clowning—
musicians who thought about it realized the extraordinary talent of someone who could lark about so effortlessly yet remain musically competent
on two instruments at once.

A particularly insightful reminiscence involves Hayes's bassist John
Drummond, who had become tired of hearing Dizzy's relentless practice
echoing through the courtyard of a Detroit hotel. Drummond pretended
to be an angry old lady, complaining about the noise, and phoned Dizzy's
room. "Yes, ma'am!" Dizzy meekly agreed, to her requests that he stop
practicing forthwith and for the rest of his stay. Dizzy found it hard to
understand the band's mirth when he told them how he'd told her to go
to hell. "Man, I laid that bitch's ass out." Strangely, he did not find it
necessary to practice in his room for the rest of the stay, but used the
distant basement instead. This is a particularly graphic example of
Dizzy's tendency to economize with the truth when it was less than
favorable to him, and makes it advisable to treat many of the more colorful stories in his memoirs with caution.

Although his colleagues in Hayes's band helped to develop Dizzy's
harmonic and technical skills, his rhythmic imagination was extended
through his association with Albert Socarras. Socarras was only an occasional visitor to the Savoy during this period, although he worked
regularly at the Cotton Club, which had moved downtown to Broadway
and 48th Street. His group had a regular big band lineup, but he featured
himself on flute rather than saxophone, and employed a three-piece

string section that, together with his Cuban arrangements, gave the band a very individual sound.[31]

Socarras tended to feature a strong jazz player on tenor and on trumpet to take improvised solos over the band's Latin beat. His saxophone players included Prince Robinson and Cecil Scott, both well-respected soloists, and he found that Gillespie's openness to Latin rhythms made him ideal on trumpet. Socarras left New York for an ill-fated visit to Europe in 1939 that was brought to an abrupt end by the gathering war clouds, but Dizzy certainly got to know and play with him during 1938 and was to rejoin him a few years later.

Socarras was much in demand as a sideman when not leading his own band, and he spent some of the period after Dizzy's return from Europe in the big band of trumpeter Erskine Hawkins. Although Dizzy never cited Hawkins, (whose powerful high note playing brought him the nickname "20th-Century Gabriel") as an influence, he was much impressed by Hawkins's other principal trumpeter Dud Bascomb. He later told Dan Morgenstern about his admiration for Bascomb's harmonic ideas, and, during one of his late 1930s visits to Washington, also congratulated Hawkins's arranger Sammy Lowe on a chart for "All the Things You Are," written for Bascomb.[32]

In many accounts and interviews concerning the middle part of 1939, Dizzy related the story of Teddy Hill's breaking up his orchestra, apparently because the Savoy Ballroom would not pay him the proper union scale for playing at the 1939 World's Fair in New York, where a stand had been erected to recreate the main features of the dance hall. Moe Gale, head of the Gale Booking Agency and the main shareholder in the Savoy, was always seen by Dizzy as the main culprit.

"We had a show with the Lindy Hoppers and Teddy's Band and we were doing between eight and twelve shows a day on and off," Dizzy recalled. "We figured this was a class 'A' engagement, but the union thought it should be third-class, because they were in cahoots with the booking agency. The guy who owned the Savoy, he was a brother-in-law of the secretary of the union, so we had a meeting at the union to thrash this out. They got mad at Teddy Hill, the Gales who owned the Savoy, and they never gave Teddy a job no more, and that was Teddy's main job in the Savoy."[33]

It appears from the press of the time that not only had Teddy stopped being the main resident band at the ballroom at the time he left for Europe, but that the carrot of a high-profile engagement at the World's Fair was offered to several of the other bands that played the Savoy off and on. It was therefore not a foregone conclusion (as Dizzy suggests) that the Hill band would secure the job for the duration of the fair. The successful bands who eventually took over the afternoon and evening stints there were led by bassist Lee Norman and the eccentric clarinetist and comedian Fess Williams. "Lee had a very good and friendly connection with Charlie Buchanan, the man who used to run the Savoy," recalled Norman's lead trumpeter Harvey Davis.[34] (Buchanan was the minority shareholder in the dance hall, and managed it for Gale.)

"Lee 'had an inside' on getting the job there," said Davis. But for months the press had been circulating rumors that the job would go to Hill or to Edgar Hayes.[35] The truth seems to be that by taking a stance against Gale, Hill lost any chance he might have had in holding on to the World's Fair job, especially having already forfeited the main band slot at the dance hall by going to Europe. By a twist of fate, the Savoy Sultans were to lose it too—Gale and Buchanan hired Lee Norman's band to come into the Savoy itself after the World's Fair ended. One reason that Hill's actions would have irked Gale so greatly is that, only four years earlier, he was using Hill to advertise his fair treatment of the bands he employed. "Teddy Hill, current at the Savoy and whose band is under the management of Gale Inc., related his obtaining union wages whenever he works at the Savoy and told of their fair and equitable treatment of him and his orchestra," ran a piece in the *New York Age* in August 1935.[36]

So, Dizzy's firm and frequently repeated conviction that Hill's band broke up for good with the demise of the World's Fair job is hardly accurate, since he was actually playing with Hill at the Apollo when he eventually secured the job with Cab Calloway that made his name.

Dizzy was with Edgar Hayes for the first part of August in 1939 before joining Teddy Hill at the Apollo for seven days on Friday, August 11. Hayes did not pay Dizzy at the time for his few evenings with the quintet, and, when Dizzy went for his money, already secure in the knowledge he was to join Cab Calloway, Hayes suggested he would not need it now he had such a well-paying job. Dizzy's schoolboy temper flashed and he flailed at Hayes, snatching his spectacles and cutting his hand in the process. When he began work with Cab, his hand was still wounded, and he started his tenure with Calloway as he was to leave it— in a hot-tempered fight.

4

The First Records

The recording career of the Teddy Hill band lasted just over two years, from February 1935 until May 1937. Within that brief span, Hill had the distinction of presiding over the recording debuts of both Roy Eldridge and Dizzy Gillespie, on the band's first and last sessions, respectively. There is a marked improvement in the sound of the orchestra over that two-year period, with crisper ensemble playing, a more driving rhythm section, and some more aggressive and confident solos, even though the first sides do include the vitality and interest of Chu Berry and Roy Eldridge. Their four issued sides from 1935 give us only a tantalizing glimpse of how the band must have sounded in its thrice-weekly broadcasts a few months later. Yet, to understand something of the influence that Roy Eldridge had over Dizzy from broadcasts and recordings, it is necessary to look further than the half-handful of discs he made in Hill's band. The following year, when Eldridge and Berry had switched their allegiance to the Fletcher Henderson Orchestra, they cut twenty sides—the largest body of recordings of Eldridge in a big band context that would have been available for Dizzy to study during his last few months in Philadelphia.

But why was Eldridge such an important influence? And why did trumpeters like Shavers and Gillespie attempt to emulate him? To some extent, it was because Eldridge was the first of the generation ten years younger than Louis Armstrong to make a significant impact on the role of the solo trumpet in jazz. His technique involved a different, more oblique, way of attacking notes from Armstrong's. Of the pioneer 1920s trumpeters, perhaps only Jabbo Smith (in a brief recording career followed by years of obscurity) showed that there were ways other than Armstrong's of approaching solos, through combining elements of surprise with fleet negotiation of the trumpet's entire range. Eldridge denied any direct influence from Smith, preferring to cite Hot Lips Page and Rex Stewart as instrumental in shaping his ideas. Perhaps more important was an influence who did not even play a brass instrument. In his mid-teens Eldridge began learning Coleman Hawkins's recorded solos note for note, and to sight-read his brother Joe's saxophone exercises. At least part of Eldridge's revolutionary speed came from his efforts to assimilate saxophone phrasing into his trumpet technique. Nevertheless, Eldridge's playing, however it was inspired, developed the direction first taken on trumpet by Jabbo Smith, and Roy's recorded solos, such as the one on Fletcher Henderson's "Jangled Nerves," demonstrate why his playing caused such a sensation among other trumpeters.

The solo follows Chu Berry's and extends over two choruses. Instead of working up gradually through the registers to a stately last-note climax, as Armstrong might have done, Eldridge's bustling first chorus on the twelve-bar blues sequence leads to an array of dazzling high notes, placed just as he moves into the next chorus, far earlier in his solo than was generally the convention. He forces the listener's attention by providing high drama as early as possible and then keeping up a barrage of equally dramatic devices. This and his timing, which finely balanced a combination of pushing urgency and the ability to relax and play behind the beat, rather than Louis's majestic on-the-beat phrasing, epitomized what was new and exciting about Eldridge.

But that is only part of the story. Among musicians, the buzz of excitement was fueled by Eldridge's unremittingly combative personality. Whereas, as Gunther Schuller has pointed out, there was an inexorable certainty about Armstrong's playing, a sense of the "rightness" of his notes as if he was merely uncovering preordained phrases of great majesty and beauty, Eldridge's playing is full of the scent of battle, the instinct of the chase. "You couldn't see nobody for Roy," recalled Dizzy.[1] "He was standing up there all by himself. He was the most incredible trumpet player I've ever seen. He wanted to play better than anybody—just to wipe out everybody else. I was never that kind of trumpet player, you know, trying to play against somebody. I play what I know and that's it. But Roy just wouldn't be satisfied until he'd blown, and if his performance didn't come up to his expectations, well, he'd be very unhappy. Roy has really got the competitive spirit."

At this distance in time, it is sometimes hard to appreciate the rapid pace at which developments in jazz were taking place in the 1930s. Eldridge's career was only a couple of years or so ahead of Dizzy's own, and it is a sign of his enormous influence that the effects of his innovations spread so rapidly through the jazz community between his first recordings in 1935 and Dizzy's session for Hill just over two years later. Yet, just as Dizzy himself had initially been indebted to Louis Armstrong, Eldridge's own style could be seen to owe something to what had gone before, and it was not completely formed in the mid-1930s.

In his early recordings with Hill and Henderson, Eldridge's playing falls into three distinct categories. The first is consciously derivative and owes its firm on-the-beat phrasing and understated melodic approach to the direct influence of Louis Armstrong, exemplified in a track like Henderson's "Shoe Shine Boy" from August 1936, where Eldridge sings in a style that also echoes Armstrong's work with his big band of the same period. The timbre of Eldridge's solo here is unusual, using a mute-and-microphone technique that gives a slightly muffled, buzzing effect, which he also uses in the second category, pieces like "Mary Had a Little Lamb" from Henderson's previous session in May. This track, with its subtle paraphrase of the nursery melody moving further away from the original in each eight-bar segment, is looser than Eldridge's ballad playing, but like much of his muted work is relatively introspective, stressing flattened passing notes, and not the all-out free blowing that we find in the third group of recordings. These are pieces like "Jangled Nerves" and "Riffin,' " in which Eldridge's powerful open horn is well back from the microphone as he displays all the firepower of his jam-session style. It is in this third group that Eldridge's influence on other horn players was most effective.

Careful listening to this latter group of pieces shows that Eldridge was not necessarily building solos that had the architectural integrity of Armstrong, or even of Chu Berry, but were constructed from a mass of little formulaic patterns that tripped easily off the valves. Leaps between registers, the repeated high notes that open his second chorus of "Jangled Nerves," or the four-notes-up-four-notes-down trademark that wraps up his first sixteen bars of "Riffin,' " (and, by coincidence, opens his solo on Gene Krupa's "Swing Is Here" from the same year) were all ideas that could be copied and absorbed by a technically proficient student.

Dizzy's contribution to his own first recording session includes four solos, and it is a fascinating exercise to see that in the midst of his own emerging style, each draws on elements of the three broad categories to be found in Eldridge's work. The most celebrated is his lengthy contribution to "King Porter Stomp," but, before examining this, it is informative to look in detail at his other three solos—on "Yours and Mine," "I'm Happy, Darling," and "Blue Rhythm Fantasy."

"Yours and Mine" has a half-chorus of clear and forthright trumpet, punching out the melody firmly on the beat, very much in the Armstrong-based manner of Eldridge's "Shoe Shine Boy." Only a telltale downward moving flurry at the end of the passage hints at Dizzy's naturally more fluid approach, but that, coupled with the consistency of the attack here with the high-note playing on "King Porter," confirms that he rather than Shad Collins takes this solo. Dizzy, like Eldridge, was not keen to acknowledge in press statements or interviews the Armstrong influence on his playing, although in the 1950s Dizzy recorded the affectionate and outrageous parody of Armstrong called "Pops' Confessin'," which demonstrates how thoroughly he had assimilated Armstrong's mannerisms. Armstrong, in the fast-moving world of the young, hip jazz musician of the mid-1930s, was already felt to be an anachronism, and, although no jazz trumpeter could avoid a debt to him, many chose to look forward rather than backward when discussing questions of style. "Yours and Mine" offers one of the few glimpses of Dizzy's original "down South" playing that predated the impact of Charlie Shavers and Roy Eldridge on his thinking, but which is also, in its way, influenced by Eldridge.

By contrast, "I'm Happy, Darling" offers only the briefest of trumpet vignettes in what is otherwise largely a vehicle for the singing of Bill Dillard. (Dillard was still singing, dancing, and playing throughout the 1980s, when "One Mo' Time" and its sequel "Further Mo'" gave him the opportunity to delight New York and London audiences with his solo features. He was harshly treated by critics for his vocal work with Hill, and, despite his historical connections with so many important swing orchestras, virtually ignored by jazz researchers—although, in common with his near contemporaries Doc Cheatham and Johnny Letman, he retained the "gentle lilt" of his prewar style and remained untouched by the bebop revolution.) Dizzy's trumpet contribution to "I'm Happy, Darling" captures the buzzy muted sound of Eldridge's playing on "Mary Had a Little Lamb," and its pickup phrase, which climbs to a flattened third, shows an intuitive understanding by Dizzy of the way Eldridge used eight measure windows in a big band chart to stamp his personality on a performance. "[Dizzy] was very very shrewd in the way that he came in on solos," recalled Edgar Hayes. "He'd always have his horn ready to fill in on something—to the extent of filling in on what you call 'breaks.'"[2]

Dizzy himself was more concerned about mastering the technicalities of recording. In just the same way that he devoted hours to practice, both on piano and trumpet, so that he genuinely understood the structure of what he was playing, he felt he had to master the art of playing on record. "I had never made a record before. They kept telling me to point toward the microphone," he remembered. "I didn't have the technique of recording, but I finally got it together."[3]

In any event, Dizzy seems to have mastered not only the art of playing on record but of capturing that element of Eldridge's sound that was uniquely possible by playing into a microphone. The "buzzy" quality of the muted horn would not otherwise carry over a big band.

Several listeners who heard Dizzy often in the flesh were to observe that he made intelligent use of the microphone throughout his career, from the date of those first recordings onward. "If you heard him without a microphone he had a noticeably thin tone," wrote John Chilton.[4] "It was as though the microphone 'loved' him in the same way the camera 'loves' some film stars. Whenever he blew into a microphone, either in a club or a studio, his tone usually sounded handsomely full."

The third of the sides Dizzy cut with Teddy Hill is unusual in that "Blue Rhythm Fantasy" is the only piece the Hill band recorded twice, having originally recorded it exactly a year earlier with Frankie Newton on trumpet. Newton's solo is not one of his best, but it compares in style to the discs he made under his own name for Hugues Panassié in New York in 1939. There is no sign of Newton's playing leaving any mark at all on Dizzy's solo in the same piece.

Dizzy's 1937 version of "Blue Rhythm Fantasy" is at a slightly brisker tempo, and there is more confidence all round, despite the messy collision early on between Howard Johnson's alto sax and Russell Procope's clarinet that seems to be a weakness of the arrangement, rather than on the part of any individual player. Procope's solo opens with a corny quote, but builds in confidence before Dizzy takes up the chase.

Dizzy's opening phrase is a middle register repeated figure that leads into one of Eldridge's trademark four-notes-up-four-notes-down figures before the whole solo disintegrates in a sequence of flurrying fragments. Quite possibly this is an example of Dizzy's trying to overreach himself, but it brings to mind the towering influence of another mid-1930s trumpeter whose work is almost never mentioned in connection with Dizzy: Henry "Red" Allen.

Second only to Armstrong in the pantheon of New Orleans trumpeters, Allen created a highly individual blurry style, phrases tumbling after one another from the bell of his horn, just as his vocals always took on a frantic, urgent quality in which it seemed there might never be room for the whole lyric to appear. His work would have been as well known to Dizzy as Armstrong's (in whose band Allen had played) because Allen had made dozens of records. His varied career included a first-rate series of small band sides cut from 1929 onward to rival Armstrong's popular discs. Allen had also been featured with Lucky Millinder and the Mills Blue Rhythm Orchestra. (Millinder had cut a version of "Blue Rhythm Fantasy" earlier in 1937, with his new trumpet team of Shavers, Warwick, and Edison, but there is no evidence that this influenced Dizzy's playing on Hill's remake of the tune.)

Gunther Schuller has written of Allen's tacit influence on Eldridge and astutely pointed out the areas where Eldridge's playing appears to have absorbed Allen's creative approach to form and harmonic experiments (including Eldridge's own first disc for Teddy Hill, "Here Comes Cookie").[5] For someone as steeped in music as Dizzy, and as fanatically interested (as his colleagues in the Fairfax and Hill bands remember him to have been) in every aspect of jazz trumpet, it would be hard for him not to have absorbed something of the Henry Allen influence, even if he did so by the indirect route of "filtering" Allen's ideas through Eldridge's playing.

Henry Allen had been Eldridge's predecessor as the main trumpet soloist in the Fletcher Henderson orchestra, and, although his influence was less fashionable than that of Eldridge and Berry when they joined Henderson in 1936, Allen had done much in his recordings with the band to extend the role of the big band soloist, particularly in the context of Henderson's own arrangements.

One of the best known of all Henderson's arrangements was "King Porter Stomp," a thorough reworking of Jelly Roll Morton's old piano rag into a romping vehicle for a large swing band. It was most famously recorded by Benny Goodman in July 1935, one of the series of Henderson charts that launched Goodman's phenomenal popular success. Compared to the recordings of the piece by several of the black swing orchestras of the period and despite a poised contribution by trumpeter Bunny Berigan, Goodman's version sounds ponderous. Nevertheless, Goodman's disc adheres to the form of the piece that Henderson conceived, with an opening trumpet solo, and then, after a modulation ushered in through a four-measure bridge by the saxophone section, a series of solo and riff choruses on Morton's closing chord sequence (a sequence of repeated two-measure patterns returning for the most part to the home key of D flat major) in which the trumpet takes a second solo chorus.

Teddy Hill's disc, made two years after Goodman's and with Dizzy taking the Allen/Berigan role, still adheres broadly to the Henderson arrangement, although it is closest in spirit to the late 1930s version cut for broadcasting by Chick Webb's band.[6] There are signs that Hill's was a "head" arrangement for the band—in other words, a piece so well known that no written "chart" existed and the band based the piece on its collective knowledge of the popular Henderson and Goodman records. Russell Procope, Dicky Wells, and Bob Carroll all take solos in the space used by Goodman for his own clarinet feature, and the Hill band adds a snappy little trumpet lick to the familiar riffs of the final choruses. Dizzy's horn stands out during those measures as he leads the section across the beat, in a continuation of his solo playing that dominates the first and central portions of the performance.

Dizzy's opening choruses, with some precisely placed high notes, punched out with real power, strings together a series of Eldridge's familiar motifs in a convincing solo that is, in the opinion of many critics, one of the most effective assimilations of Eldridge's approach by any

other player. In much of Dizzy's future playing, and especially his choruses with Cab Calloway's Orchestra, this was the style he was to develop
and make his own. But his second solo, later in the disc, is more interesting, and owes as much to Allen as it does to Eldridge. It is not a direct
quote of Allen's solo on his August 1933 recording of Henderson's original arrangement,[7] but it uses many of Allen's characteristic devices, from
the urgent repeated opening figure to the augmented seventh that Gillespie hangs onto for almost a bar.

In later years, there are few overt signs of Henry Allen's influence
remaining in Dizzy's work, but plenty to suggest that Dizzy kept an ear
cocked toward the ongoing development of Roy Eldridge's style. Dizzy
himself acknowledged his debt to Eldridge on his first discs, but also
that he was prepared to try anything and put whatever came into his
head into his playing.[8] These discs are a long way from the triumphs of
the following decade, but they were made early enough to document
Dizzy's playing before his own characteristics had fully emerged and
show a range of influences a little wider than generally supposed.

5

Cab Calloway and the Dawn of Bebop

"Cab didn't know anything about music, he was a performer and a singer," recalled Gillespie in a radio interview. "He knew very little about what was going on, but he did have a good band. He relied on other people to tell him how good a guy was . . . and these guys were at the top of their profession. It was the best job in New York City at that time, and here I was just twenty-two years old, with a job like that."[1]

Perhaps because of the acrimonious manner in which Dizzy left Calloway's band just over two years after he joined, he seldom had much of a good word to say about Cab himself in many of the written and recorded interviews that survive. Yet those two years he spent with Calloway from 1939 put Dizzy on the map as a trumpet soloist, as a member of one of the most commercially successful bands in the United States. Constant exposure to Cab's polished stage act, showmanship, and exemplary discipline had more of an effect on Dizzy than he cared to acknowledge, and more than any other pioneer of bebop, Gillespie upheld these show-business big band traditions in his own work. The dark glasses, goatee, beret, and upswept horn became trademarks as familiar for Dizzy as Calloway's own costume was for him: that famous white zoot suit, "the color of old piano keys" as British critic Peter Clayton described it. Dizzy's mumbling scat-singing and "Oop-pop-a-da" lyrics have similar parallels to Calloway's "Hi-de-ho" and hipster's language.

Cab Calloway, born on Christmas Day 1907, had been at the top of his profession for the best part of a decade when Gillespie joined his band in the summer of 1939. Calloway's childhood was spent in Baltimore, where his paternal grandfather ran a pool hall, and even Cab described the old man as a prototype of Sportin' Life, the roguish anti-hero of Gershwin's *Porgy and Bess*, allegedly modeled on Cab himself. The larger-than-life world of the pool hall, with its shadowy characters, made the young Cab far more streetwise than might normally be the case for the son of a well-to-do middle-class black lawyer. But Cabell Calloway Sr. had a nervous breakdown, was institutionalized, and died while Cab was still a boy, and Cab was brought up by his mother and stepfather "Papa Jack." The memory of his father's values competed with his widowed mother's struggles to bring up her young family.

Cab soon modeled his own behavior on his grandfather, hustling on the streets when he should have been in school, and at one point being sent away to a boarding institution where his mother hoped his character would be reformed. Instead, he chose the stage as an alternative form of rebellion, and followed his sister Blanche into show business, abandoning a promising start as a basketball player and forsaking college to travel to Chicago with the revue Plantation Days.

Before long, Cab was fronting a territory band, the Alabamians, led by Marion Hardy. He came with them to New York, and, after winning a vote as most popular leader (despite the Alabamians themselves being beaten) at the Savoy Ballroom, he assumed the leadership of the victorious band, the Missourians.

The Missourians were swiftly renamed Cab Calloway's Orchestra, booked by Irving Mills (who also managed Duke Ellington) and enjoying the protection of the Mob. Through broadcasts from the Cotton Club and a string of successful records built around the Harlem drug culture of "Minnie the Moocher" and "Smoky Joe," Calloway became a national star. He was popular and wealthy enough to travel in style, avoiding many (though not all) of the privations of black bands on the road by using his own private Pullman cars, one of which contained Cab's Lincoln, which he would drive off the train as they arrived at the venue for each touring engagement.

Cab may not have been as musically adept a leader as, say, Lucky Millinder, but he knew from his hard-won route to fame how to get to the top and stay there, and he brought his streetwise toughness to leading the band. The band's earning power was a direct consequence of Calloway's own popularity. His was the top-earning black band in the United States at the time, grossing $7,000 a week. The runners up, in a league table published by the Baltimore Afro-American, were, in descending order of revenue: Louis Armstrong, Fats Waller, Chick Webb, Duke Ellington, and Jimmie Lunceford.[2]

Cab had devised an act that communicated an irrepressible bonhomie to the public, but concealed a firm and ruthless control over his band members. British arranger Alan Cohen worked with Cab in the 1980s and recalled that he used the dance movements of his stage act to direct the band, and that the huge grin vanished from his face as he turned to face his musicians, scowling disapproval at anyone remotely out of line, before reappearing as he turned once more to the audience.[3]

In the late 1930s, Cab's band was undergoing a major overhaul.

Since taking over the Missourians, he had weeded out the older style players, the unreliable, or the less musically adept, making slow but progressive changes. "From 1931, he'd fired one Missourian of the original band at a time," said Danny Barker, his guitarist. "He fired them because he had a hard time getting them to listen to that baton. So to get his revenge, just like Lucky Millinder, he fired one at a time. It was a process to break up a clique, and make sure no one joins the clique."[4]

Now the process was accelerating. The pace picked up in 1937, when Chu Berry replaced Ben Webster as the band's tenor soloist. Chu was musically restless, and, unlike Webster, who sat in with local musicians wherever the band went and kept up a stream of freelance playing engagements and record dates alongside his work with Calloway, Berry decided to make changes inside the band. As guitarist Morris White and drummer Leroy Maxey left, and Danny Barker and Cozy Cole joined, Berry worked on Cab to let the band record more instrumentals and encouraged a new enthusiasm for rehearsal.

To a great extent this stemmed from the rhythm section, where Cole's modern drum style, Barker's fat guitar chords, and Milt Hinton's mobile basslines were already achieving much of the departure from precedent that was to crystallize into bebop. Hinton's playing was almost as flexible as Jimmy Blanton's with Ellington, and he allowed the Calloway section to move a long way from the heavy two-beat of the mid-1930s with Al Morgan and Leroy Maxey.

"Cab wasn't interested in rehearsing the band," recalled Hinton. "He was an artist. We were good players, we loved each other, and it was our chance to try and cook a rhythm section together. We organized that band ourselves. The trombones would get together and have a trombone rehearsal, the trumpets the same. We did the dynamics of the orchestra ourselves, because this was our chance to try to do something together. I remember the trumpets discussing whether to use hand vibrato or lip vibrato on a particular arrangement. We took it very seriously."[5]

Dizzy's arrival into the Calloway band at this point was fortunate for the young trumpeter. Berry had succeeded in persuading Cab to let the band make instrumental records with no vocals from the leader, and there were growing allocations of solo space on Cab's own records. Outside the band, and unaware of the changes going on, potential recruits were concerned that they might not get the chance to solo, and when Doc Cheatham decided to leave the trumpet section in the early summer of 1939 because of ill health, Cab's first choice as replacement, Jonah Jones, turned him down.

In most accounts of Gillespie's arrival in the band, the story is told that the Cuban trumpeter Mario Bauza, who became something of a mentor to Dizzy, lent Gillespie his uniform and had Dizzy play in his place at the Cotton Club. Bauza claims he pretended to be sick and sent Dizzy as a last-minute replacement for three days, returning himself to play alongside Dizzy on the fourth. "Cab say to me: 'How you like that new fella?' And I say, 'He ain't bad.' Two days later Cab say, 'Do you want that guy in the band?' I say, 'We need this guy. Once you really hear what this guy has to offer, you progress the band.' "[6]

But this is not how Cheatham remembered it, nor does it tally with Cab's own contribution to Dizzy's autobiography. The exact date of Cheatham's departure is not known. He left some time in the late spring or early summer, exhausted with the band's life on the road and doing several theatre shows a day in New York before a nighttime stint at the Cotton Club downtown. By August, when Dizzy joined, Doc was in Europe on an ill-fated trip to France that coincided with the outbreak of war.

The one thing that is certain is that when Doc left, Cab's first priority would be to find a lead player, rather than a soloist, although he might have persuaded Lammar Wright to resume the lead duties he had given up in 1932 when Cheatham joined. For many years, Wright, whose high-register technique was so formidable he could double his parts an octave higher, had played second trumpet and soloist, sharing the solo duties with the third trumpeter, originally Edwin Swayzee and later Irving "Mouse" Randolph. Doc had specialized in lead playing, plus the occasional ballad, and, on an earlier leave of absence in 1937, his job had been taken over in its entirety by Shad Collins.

The man Cab wanted to hire was Jonah Jones, who in 1939 was sharing the front-line duties with violinist Stuff Smith in Stuff's spirited small group, from which Cab had already poached Cozy Cole. Cab's reasoning was that Jonah could combine playing lead with his exciting Armstrong-influenced solos. But Jonah was of two minds about the offer because he enjoyed the endless solo space he had in Stuff's group, despite Stuff's perilously fast-lane lifestyle.

"I figured Cab's band wasn't the place for solos, because his show was so big. He had eleven boy singers and tap dancers, Bill Bailey, Pearl's brother, the Miller Brothers and Lois, it was wonderful! What a show. But there were no chances for trumpet solos, whereas with Stuff I had all the solos I wanted. I'd be there blowing, and Stuff would be playing riffs on his violin, muttering into my ear 'One more, Jonah! One more!'

"I nearly went to Cab then, though, because of all the drinking with Stuff. I was drinking 100% proof and smoking marijuana because Stuff wanted you high every night. One time, before Cozy went to Cab, me and Cozy decided to stop drinking. We got to work and Stuff kicked off 'Stomping at the Savoy.' Then we went into 'Mood Indigo.' Stuff turned round: 'Something's wrong! Cozy? You high? Jonah? You high?' We told him we were taking it easy. Stuff said, 'If everyone's not high by the time we come back off the break, there'll be a $10 fine for anyone who isn't high.' And he brandished the little flask he kept in his pocket for emergencies. We went out the back and got loaded just to avoid that $10 fine, and Stuff was happy."[7]

This was in sharp contrast to Jonah's recollections of Cab doing the rounds of dressing rooms threatening to fire anyone caught smoking marijuana, and, when Jones eventually did join Cab in 1941, it was with the knowledge that Cab's disciplinarian style would straighten him out.

Undeterred by the initial rebuff, Cab kept calling Jonah (and according to Jones continued to do so until he eventually came into the band two years later). So it is not, as many people supposed, a mistake on Cab's part that he stated in Dizzy's autobiography that it was Jones who recommended Dizzy.[8] Almost certainly, Jonah thought of Gillespie, Teddy Hill's trumpeter and energetic sitter-in, as being both an exciting soloist and available, so he recommended him to Calloway.

Cheatham agreed. "When I left the Cotton Club downtown in 1939, Dizzy was there at the rehearsal. But ... they were undecided about Dizzy, what he was doing. So they decided to get another guy and they chose Mario Bauza. He made the job, did a good job on lead. Dizzy wasn't interested in that anyway. So Dizzy and Mario joined the band at the same time."[9]

In effect, the iron-lipped Bauza, already seasoned as lead trumpeter with Chick Webb, although equally proficient as a saxophonist, took Cheatham's place and Dizzy replaced Randolph, leaving Wright to continue as a section rather than lead player, a job he did not resume until Bauza himself left (and then only for a few months until Shad Collins rejoined). Mario came into the band a little earlier than Dizzy, since he is present on the band's July 17 record date in New York, and Dizzy does not appear until the following month's session on August 30, having finished his gig with Teddy Hill at the Apollo during the week's shows starting on August 11. The most likely chain of events is that Dizzy auditioned for Cheatham's job, failed to get it, but secured the solo chair on the strength of his audition shortly after Mario Bauza was installed as lead, when Randolph decided to quit.

Whatever the exact sequence, it seems highly unlikely that Bauza would have risked his new job in such a high-profile band by sending Dizzy along in his place within days of landing the position, and it seems equally unlikely that Dizzy would have wished to record that he failed an audition in his autobiography. What is certain, however, is that in Cab's mind Dizzy was always his second choice, and he would continue to try to recruit Jonah Jones during Dizzy's entire stay with the band.

Once Dizzy had actually arrived in the band, he found that, despite the gradual replacement of the older players, he was very much younger than the rest of the band. Up until then, the "baby" of the band had been bassist Milt Hinton, and, although he was born in 1910, three years later than Cab, Milt always felt somewhat isolated by his age. "The rest of the band were my seniors by five to ten years, and although that seems nothing today, at that time it made a lot of difference."[10]

The young Gillespie and Hinton quickly formed an alliance driven as much by their relative youth as by any musical affinity they might have had. "When Dizzy came into the band, he was broke. He didn't have any money. And the mouthpiece he had was so brassed it was going to eat right through his lip. I remember giving him $5 to go down to have that mouthpiece plated. God knows he's paid me back ten thousand times for that, through our friendship. As he went on and got more famous, he always kept that family relationship going. He and Lorraine had no children, but my wife Mona and Lorraine became friends, and Dizzy and Lorraine were so delighted when my daughter Charlotte was born, Lorraine went down to the store and bought lots of clothes for Charlotte. She didn't have any idea about children's clothes or the sizes, so she just bought up everything she could see!" Dizzy's friendship with Milt extended to a mutual interest in photography and the associated gadgetry. For years after he left Calloway, whenever Dizzy found a piece of photographic equipment he thought would interest his old friend, he packed it up and sent it off to the Hinton household.[11]

The perception of Dizzy within the band was mixed. Doc Cheatham's description of the musical reaction as "undecided" is about right. In Dizzy's own mind, by the time he joined he had developed a clear stylistic identity: "The development had jelled. Where my style is concerned, I'm almost playing the same way now [1979] that I played then."[12] The recorded evidence supports this. As will become clear in the discussion of the discs Dizzy made between 1939 and 1941 in the next chapter, most aspects of his mature style are discernible in these recordings and it is therefore highly dubious that Dizzy's main development as a soloist happened after his meeting with Charlie Parker in 1940.

The conventional view of bebop history is that Parker, and his fellow members of the Jay McShann Orchestra, influenced a whole generation. As Ross Russell put it, discussing McShann's 1940 transcription recordings featuring Parker and trumpeter Buddy Anderson: "Anderson's work foreshadows developments to follow in the bebop period and the playing of Fats Navarro and Dizzy Gillespie."[13] The evidence of Gillespie's recordings may show that Dizzy's syntax was not fully developed, but by 1939–40 his bop vocabulary was largely in place, and when he cut his 1939 records he had not heard Charlie Parker or felt his influence.

The indecision felt by Calloway's sidemen was a mixture of suspicion at the unfamiliar turn that Gillespie's solos were taking and the recognition that some of his ideas lay beyond his (already formidable) technical capabilities. Coupled with Dizzy's complex personality, his shrewd mind, and innate business acumen concealed behind a facade of clowning, it is not surprising that the band found it hard to know what to make of him.

"When he came in the band he wasn't the best trumpet player we had . . . but he had these beautiful ideas and a great mind" (Hinton).[14]

"He wasn't Dizzy at all—just young, vigorous and restless. Some in the band resented the liberties he took. He acted restless, because the arrangements seemed trivial to him, as he had played at the Savoy Ballroom and heard the music of many great black arrangers . . . you had to listen because his new sounds kept you off-balance until he came back in on time" (Barker).[15]

"The premier thing about him was that he was a good musician. . . . His improvisation of jazz was just what he was thinking all that time, and he put it into his playing. And all those intricate changes that he would make on his horn . . . nobody had ever heard anything like this before" (Calloway).[16]

"From time to time, during a performance, Dizzy would just take off in double time. Man, it was wild. . . . Cab was very meticulous about music and he'd get as mad as hell. 'What the hell you tryin' to do with my band?' Cab would holler at Dizzy. Dizzy would just smile and all Cab could say was 'Just play it the way it's written' " (Bennie Payne).[17]

All in all, Danny Barker's writer's eye probably sums up Dizzy in 1939 most effectively: young, vigorous, restless. And when this is put together with Payne's accounts of Dizzy coercing the trumpet section to "cut loose" from the arrangements (following the example of altoist Hilton Jefferson, whose additions to the scores were so perfect Calloway complained when his replacement Rudy Powell left them out); Dizzy's antics at miming football passes behind Cab's most romantic vocals; and Dizzy's growing penchant for practical jokes like spitballs and igniting sheets of cellophane on sleeping musicians in the band bus or train, it is clear why Cab described Dizzy in his autobiography as "a pain in the neck" and why he continued to phone Jonah Jones to persuade him to join the band.

Nevertheless, from August 1939 until September 1941, Dizzy was

Part of Cab Calloway's Orchestra, late 1939. (Left to right) Keg Johnson (trombone), Chu Berry (tenor), Claude Jones (trombone), Andy Brown (alto), Dizzy, Chauncey Haughton (alto), Mario Bauzá (partially obscured). (Frank Driggs collection)

a trumpet soloist in Cab's orchestra, and to start with he took the lion's share of the solos. During the latter part of 1940 the number of solos he was allowed declined, as Cab featured other members of the band, and, after Jonah Jones eventually joined the trumpet section alongside Dizzy in March 1941, the solo space available to Gillespie became severely limited. This pattern is generally thought to mirror Dizzy's growing affinities with bebop and Calloway's dislike for the style. At the same time, it is argued, Dizzy's disenchantment with the relatively straightforward arrangements the band played made him musically disaffected with Cab, however fast the musical company in the band might be. Dizzy also hints that he was unfairly excluded from the "band-within-a-band," the Cab Jivers, which were a popular part of Cab's stage act.

A number of factors combine to suggest that this is not the whole story. It is undeniably true that Cab did not care for bebop, yet he did not object to many bop-inflected solos from Dizzy on his records and broadcasts from 1939 and 1940. Cab also encouraged Dizzy to record his novel arrangement "Pickin' the Cabbage" (as well as his arrangement of "Paradiddle" for Cozy Cole), and so it is clear that he did not obstruct Dizzy's progress to begin with. Dizzy, as we know, felt his style did not change greatly during the Calloway years, and he was challenged by the demands of soloing on some of the band's more forward-looking arrangements like Don Redman's "Cupid's Nightmare." Dizzy was also an enthusiastic coach for Milt Hinton and Danny Barker (who were in the Cab Jivers), suggesting newer and more interesting chord substitutions and harmonies that they might use in their accompaniments and solos.

Equally, although Dizzy may not have been challenged by the content of many of the band's arrangements, there was no shortage of new material to play. With broadcasts and recording sessions, tours, and several shows a day to perform, Cab's orchestra ate up new charts at a great rate. (Doc Cheatham recalled the queue of hopeful arrangers who would wait to see Cab during the band's regular residencies at the Cotton Club, trying to sell him arrangements, and that people like Harold Arlen would be among those from whom Cab regularly acquired material.)[18]

Almost certainly the thing that wore down the relationship was Dizzy's attitude to Cab's disciplinarian style. Dizzy constantly tested Cab's authority, and the relentless pranks and horseplay on stage began to outweigh Dizzy's very real musical contribution to the band. While tolerating Dizzy, it must have irked Cab to see glowing press reports about the man he really wanted in the band, Jonah Jones.[19] When Jonah finally arrived, Cab showered privileges on him that must have hurt Dizzy deeply.

"He had Buster Harding, whom I'd known in Buffalo, write a chart for me, called 'Jonah Joins the Cab,'" recalled Jonah. "I never thought that would happen. Cab would sing 'Here comes Jonah, blowing on his trumpet' and I'd walk round in front of the band, and I'd do a chorus in F, one in F sharp, one in G and so on 'til I ended up in C. I was the first one in the band ever to do that, to go out in front on my own and solo, and have Cab announce my name. After I'd been doing it for about six months, he let Hilton Jefferson do the same, on a nice number for him, 'Sophisticated Lady.' Of course after that all the guys in the band were clamoring 'Let me come down . . . feature me!'"[20]

Of course, Jonah was allowed to join the Cab Jivers as well. Cab, by featuring Jones in this way, created a tension between the personalities in his band that could not last, but it is also possible that this is the reason Gillespie, scarred by the experience, adopted the role of stern disciplinarian himself once he became a bandleader in his own right.

The music played by Cab's band when Dizzy joined was conventional big band fare. Tenorist Walter "Foots" Thomas, a veteran of the Mis-

sourians, was the staff arranger as well as the senior member of the saxophone section, but in their record dates around the time of Dizzy's
arrival the band also played charts by Edgar Battle, Earl Bostic, Benny
Carter, Andy Gibson, Buster Harding, Don Redman, and Chappie Willett.[21] These were the cream of arrangers at the time, but they were not,
with the exception of Redman, venturing far from the conventional
thirty-two-bar popular song structure in the majority of their work, nor
were they challenging existing notions of jazz harmony or rhythm. Even
Mario Bauza's arrival in the band had barely jogged them out of routine,
and only "Chili Con Conga" from the record date of October 17, 1939,
suggests that his Afro-Cuban influences were at work.

It was this orthodoxy Dizzy set out to challenge in his musical
contribution to the orchestra. His own arrangement of "Pickin' the Cabbage" is discussed in the next chapter, but it indicates that his ideas as
an arranger were moving away from popular songs in the "I Got Rhythm"
model and starting to explore similar territory to Redman's chromatic
landscape in "Cupid's Nightmare."[22] We have already seen how his fellow
musicians reacted to his work as an instrumentalist in their attempts to
describe his unfamiliar approach to constructing a solo.

Dizzy found his most sympathetic following in the rhythm section
(as might be expected because they had to follow his trumpet solos as he
was playing them), and, almost from the moment of his arrival in the
band, he began to involve his friend Milt Hinton and guitarist Danny
Barker in his attempts to explain the chord extensions and diminutions
that underpinned his harmonic thinking.

Hinton has told the story many times about his initiation into modern harmonic thinking from Dizzy: "In the intermissions at the Cotton
Club (we did two shows every night, one at eight o'clock and another at
eleven thirty) and after the eight o'clock show, the guys would go out
drinking and hanging around, but Dizzy and I would sit around and start
talking about changes. Dizzy had been uptown, playing with Teddy Hill,
and he was picking up on all the new changes and substitution chords.
We were now beginning to use an A minor chord instead of a C chord,
emphasizing the A in there which is the sixth. Dizzy was enlightening
me about all these different changes, the different combinations of
sounds they made and I just loved that. So, as it was the summer time,
we'd go up on the roof of the Cotton Club, up a little stairway from
backstage, a winding fire stairway, and I would take my bass, and we
would practice what he was telling me about. He'd show me these new
changes. We'd get off at three o'clock, and we'd go to Minton's, which
was up in Harlem, to play there. He'd say there's a lot of kids there

playing, and they're going to get in our way, so let's move all these changes all around and they won't know what the heck we're doing."[23]

Danny Barker remembered these experiments going on in empty rooms in the theatres where the band was on tour. "After a while I would give an excuse, because the more we would jam and discuss music in depth I began to find myself sitting there listening and holding my guitar in my lap." Yet Danny also accommodated Dizzy's solos in the chords he played with the band: "I would figure on playing chords that would be strange to some people, but would be correct with his extensions, chord-wise." He also noted alterations in drummer Cozy Cole's playing behind Dizzy's solos: "When Diz would be blowing his things to come, he was machine-gunned with Cozy's military diddles . . . he was doing the flamadiddles, explosions and rimshots that Klook-a-mop (Kenny Clarke) was doing: bop—bebop! In a different theory."[24]

Like Hinton, Barker recalled Dizzy and Milt going uptown to sit in at Minton's, although he doesn't confirm that this was after playing at the Cotton Club.

Based on Barker and Hinton's testimonies, and the reputation of Minton's as the birthplace of bebop, most historians date Dizzy's after-hours experiments to 1940, the year Teddy Hill took over as manager and started the Monday night bebop jam sessions there. Yet it is more likely that Dizzy's forays into the after-hours sessions that partly spawned bebop began in 1939. An investigation of the date sheets for Calloway's band shows that they were in New York relatively little in the summer of 1940 and during that period Calloway did not work at the Cotton Club. It is, however, entirely likely that Dizzy and Hinton had gone uptown after their Cotton Club shows in 1939 to sit in at another after-hours venue, Clark Monroe's Uptown House, which had been open for a couple of years and was already attracting musicians interested in the new music. It was there, not at Minton's, where Dizzy was recorded creating a fledgling bebop solo on a piece called "Kerouac," in May 1941. So, those summertime rooftop practices at the Cotton Club recalled by Hinton were almost certainly while the band was there in September 1939.[25]

Eighteen months later, Dizzy was still working out new changes with Hinton when Jonah Jones joined the band. "He used to take Milton Hinton downstairs to tell him what notes to run . . . it got so he could play what was later called bebop," Jones said. "Cab didn't like it. Dizzy'd do something different in his solos, and Cab'd say 'I don't want that.' Then Dizzy'd do it again, and Cab would say, 'Give that chorus to Jonah!'

"I didn't have any idea what Diz was doing, so he started taking me downstairs too. I put some of his ideas in one of my solos, and Cab yelled at me, 'You too? Play like that and I'm going to fire you!' So I went back to my old way of playing."[26]

The implication of all this is that Dizzy was continually experimenting throughout his time with Cab, and that in the same way as Hinton had at one time joined Ben Webster on his forays to sit in with local musicians wherever the band went, Milt now did the same with Gillespie. Dizzy was clearly absorbing influences from many places, initially from Monroe's, later from Minton's, and eventually from many of the new locales he visited on Calloway's taxing itinerary of cross-country travel. Barker, for example, recalls eavesdropping on a rehearsal of the Harlan Leonard band directed by Tadd Dameron while the band was in Kansas City. "This arrangement seemed difficult to them . . . [Dameron] did not say anything, but the wrinkle on his brow spoke: 'What's wrong? Can't they hear?' "[27]

"Hearing" the new harmonies of bebop was what Dizzy was trying to instill in his Calloway colleagues, and he was successful with Hinton and to a lesser extent with Barker and Cole. The only other member of the band Dizzy singled out for praise was the remarkably talented altoist Hilton Jefferson.

The incident with Dameron suggests that in quite separate locations all over the United States, musicians were experimenting with new sounds. There is, however, a generally held view that the principal catalyst was Charlie Parker.

Parker, like Harlan Leonard's band based in Kansas City, had joined the newly formed Jay McShann Orchestra there in 1939. Dizzy always maintained that he met Parker in 1940, and that they were introduced by McShann's trumpeter, Buddy Anderson, following which he jammed for several hours with Parker, for the most part playing piano himself. This story is corroborated by Anderson.

But when did it take place? How early was Dizzy exposed to Parker's genius? There are some scholars who suggest the meeting could have occurred as early as 1939, but this is unlikely. Calloway's band was only in Kansas City for less than twenty-four hours after Dizzy joined them that year, when they played a Thanksgiving concert at the Municipal Auditorium on November 30. There was no opportunity for Dizzy to spend any time with Parker because the band would have set off overnight in its Pullman car to travel to their next gig at Omaha, Nebraska, the following day. Nor could they have met prior to Cab's appearance on the thirtieth, since on the twenty-ninth they had been in Wichita, and before that in Joplin, Missouri. All these centers, although relatively close in U.S. terms, were interconnected by rail, and there is little reason to suppose that Calloway's established traveling practice of moving overnight after each gig would have been altered for that one night in Kansas City.

The following year, however, the band returned to Kansas City on June 23, for at least one night at Fairyland Park, an amusement area that ran evening entertainment throughout the summer season every year and had been home to Andy Kirk's band in the mid-1930s. After playing there, Cab's band left Kansas City in time to make a record date in Chicago on June 27, 1940. Not only were McShann's Orchestra (including Parker) resident at Fairyland Park that same summer, but Harlan Leonard was back in Kansas City after his New York debut at the Golden Gate in February.

This dating is further backed up by Buddy Anderson, who brought about the meeting. "We were the house band and Cab played it as a one-nighter . . . I went out to dig Cab and dug Dizzy. He knocked us out."[28] Anderson is credited by Ross Russell among others for being a bebop innovator on the trumpet, and indeed Dizzy recognized that Anderson shared many of his own interests in extending the scope of the trumpet solo in jazz, but Anderson clearly felt that Dizzy was way ahead by the time they met. Bebop was, he said, "already going. Dizzy and them had something out East already going by then."[29]

This was Calloway's only visit to Kansas that year, so it seems a safe assumption that the Parker/Gillespie meeting actually took place on June 24, 1940, and during that same visit it is also possible that Dizzy met Dameron, the twenty-three-year-old arranger of the Harlan Leonard band.

The historic meeting came about after Anderson and McShann's other trumpeter, Orville Minor, took Diz to a Kansas City jam session at the Kentucky Barbecue, once the Calloway band had finished at Fairyland Park. Dizzy played, impressing many of the local musicians who gathered there with his original style. Chu Berry also played. Parker failed to show that night, and Anderson met Diz at noon the following day outside the Kentucky and introduced him to Parker, from where they made their way to AFM Local 627 and clustered round the piano on the first floor. (In his memoirs, and in other interviews, such as in Art Taylor's *Notes and Tones*, Dizzy says this went on at the Booker T. Washington Hotel, but Anderson offered such a detailed recollection in several different interviews over many years that it seems appropriate to trust his memory, including, "There was a piano there and dog shit too. The president of the local kept his hunting dogs up there.")[30]

In Anderson's view, at that time Dizzy generally showed little interest in the innovations of other musicians, even Charlie Christian, whom they knew in common, and Dizzy exhibited little keenness about Parker until the moment he heard him play. As Dizzy himself said, he'd worked regularly with Chu Berry every night for nearly a year and had recorded with Ben Webster and Coleman Hawkins as well as jammed with Lester Young, so he wasn't likely to get excited about just any saxophonist. When Parker did play, it was exceptional: "The things Yard [Parker] was doing, the ideas that were flowing . . . I couldn't believe it. He'd be playing one song and he'd throw in another, but it was perfect."[31]

Although Parker, born in 1920, had grown up in and around Kansas City, he had failed to make much of a name for himself until 1940. An abortive trip to New York in 1939 did not lead to musical employment and, although he worked for a time in the kitchens of a club where Art Tatum played, most of his music-making took place in after-hours jam sessions. Nevertheless, by late 1939 or early 1940, he had drawn together the original ideas behind his playing, put them into a theoretical framework that made sense by playing melodic improvisations based around the extensions into ninths and thirteenths above conventional root chords, and had worked long and hard at his instrumental technique. This musical originality and facility, coupled with a flawed and addictive personality that sought drugs and booze, with an appetite for knowledge (many who knew him recall he would hold informed and intelligent conversations on almost any subject), and with a radiant charm and ready wit, when not too overcome by narcotics, made him a mesmerizing individual. Most of those who knew him agree (with a consensus absent from comparable appraisals of Gillespie) that Parker had the aura of genius about him.

Pianist Jay McShann hired Parker both before and after the visit to New York, after first hearing him in 1938 from outside Barlett Duke's club in Kansas. McShann thought he knew every player in town, but this one sounded different. Parker said he'd just been on a long tour of the Ozarks with the territory band led by George Lee and had got some "woodshedding" done. Many accounts say that the youthful Parker had not got his playing together until about this time and that he was erratic and undisciplined, but McShann remembers a change in Parker after the New York trip in 1939. He tells the story in several versions of Parker woodshedding (or assiduously practicing) the band book in a very short time in order to outplay the regular first altoist John Jackson. McShann recalls: "After we got the band together, he used to rehearse the reed section, and he was pretty strict with those guys, you know."[32] Parker's theoretical knowledge may not at that stage have rivaled Gillespie's (which was reckoned, even by the high standards of Calloway's band, to be extraordinary), but Anderson thought Bird's [Parker's] knowledge was "highly advanced theoretically, too."[33] Orville Minor concurs, believing that musically Parker was "a leader, and he set all the riffs." The band's most forward-looking head arrangements were generally agreed to be Parker's work.[34]

When Dizzy was asked to define the difference in their contributions to the early development of bebop at the time they met, he said: "My contribution was mostly rhythm and harmonic. I figured out all the chord changes to all the things and, you know, the substitute chords. . . . And the contribution of Charlie Parker was mostly in . . . the phrasing."[35] The head versus heart distinction carried over into their lives as well. "I was blessed that I got married early and had a good wife. That sort of kept me straight," Dizzy said in 1976. "Probably I would have been like Charlie Parker, you know, involved in drugs or alcohol or something like that if I hadn't had this stability."[36] Dizzy had finally married Lorraine in Boston on May 9, just a few weeks before he and Parker met.

Apart from the odd chance encounter on the road, it was several months before Parker and Gillespie met again, in the after-hours clubs of New York some time after Dizzy had left Calloway and after McShann had come to New York in February 1942. Parker had not made any records by the time he and Gillespie met and was not to do so until 1941, when his solo on "Swingmatism" with McShann's Orchestra, the first of a series of forward-looking charts to be recorded by the band, shows a soloist with just as much flair and originality as Gillespie brought to his work with Calloway. Transcription discs exist of Parker's playing from late November and early December 1940, but these did not receive wide circulation, and, for the year after they met, it continued to be Gillespie, through his exposure with Calloway's band, who was the more widely heard of the main bebop innovators.

The year 1940 was also when Dizzy registered for the draft. Like all United States males between twenty-one and thirty-five years old, he would have been required to register during October. Dizzy says that he thought being on the road with Cab might hinder those who sent out the papers in finding him. He claims he was tracked down in Pittsburgh, but in fact his draft registration card shows that he presented himself to his local board at Lenox Avenue in Harlem, four days before the October 20 deadline.

In his autobiography, Dizzy gives an account of his attendance at the selection board in New York. Although such boards were manned by local volunteers (including volunteer medical staff), rather than government bureaucrats, and they varied in the degree to which they would accept the various excuses offered by musicians (folklore about what to say and how to behave was rife in the big bands), it is highly unlikely that Dizzy behaved in quite the manner he suggests in his book. There he says that when asked his views about fighting he replied: "The white man's foot has been in my ass hole buried up to his knee in my ass hole . . . so if you put me out there with a gun in my hand and tell me to shoot the enemy, I'm liable to create a case of 'mistaken identity' about who I might shoot."

This incident almost certainly never took place. If something similar did happen, then it did not occur during 1940. Call-up was by lottery, but prior to that men were classified for service on medical grounds. This was done in the first instance by questionnaire, and Dizzy's was not returned until February 1941. The following May, he was notified that he had been classified 1-A (fit for general duty). Even then, his name did not come up in the lottery and his first appearance before a selection board was not until 1943, when he was rejected and reclassified 4-F (unfit for physical, mental, or moral reasons) on September 11. No record of his interview survives, as all such paperwork relating to men conscripted before 1980 has now been destroyed.

The whole episode, as related in Dizzy's autobiography, is redolent of Clyde Bernhardt's recollections of Dizzy's attitude to John Drummond's practical joke in the Edgar Hayes band: Diz was as meek as a lamb at the time, but told the world afterward how he'd blustered it out. Nevertheless, it is true that he avoided the draft and was to continue to do so on the subsequent occasions when he went before a board, being repeatedly placed in Classification 4 in 1944 and 1946.

Although Dizzy elaborated on the truth regarding his draft, there is no doubt about how he came to leave the Calloway band in September 1941. By mid-1941, Jonah Jones, who had joined by the beginning of March that year, was increasingly taking all the trumpet solos. Cab's popularity was as strong as ever and the band continued its regular criss-crossing of the United States. Prior to Jones's arrival they'd been out on the West Coast for a season at Topsy's Roost in Hollywood, where no doubt Gillespie met for the first time many of the local musicians he was to meet again five years later when he brought his own bebop group to Billy Berg's. He may not (as Buddy Anderson suggests) have been over-keen on going out to hear new talents, but he was as indefatigable as Ben Webster had been about sitting in and showing off his own playing with local groups, and there is little doubt that this activity increased as his "official" solo duties with Cab diminished. Illinois Jacquet, for instance, recalls in Dizzy's autobiography how he met Dizzy while Cab was in Chicago, and how they jammed together before making for Jacquet's hotel room, where Dizzy continued to play his muted horn.

Occasionally there were excitements, such as a night in Omaha, Nebraska, when Dizzy and Jonah Jones forgot their rivalry and went out after work together to hear Jay McShann's Orchestra. "We went by to hear the band," recalled Jonah. "We sat at a table near the bandstand, and I was listening to the trumpeter [Anderson]. Then Dizzy hunched me: 'Listen to that sax player!' he said. My attention went back to the trumpet, but when the saxophonist played again, he hunched me again. It was Charlie Parker, and Diz wanted me to hear him running all those chords."[37]

Deprived of the ability to solo in Cab's band, the traveling to Virginia, Ohio, New England, and Chicago, among other places, must have become irksome for Dizzy. There is evidence that this led him to develop his penchant for onstage comedy and horseplay while still working away behind the scenes at his musical development. One of the last press notices to mention his work in the band points out that Dizzy provided "the comic relief, both on and off the bandstand."[38] Milt Hinton remembers that during the band's usual summer in New York the Cotton Club rooftop practices continued, and that, although he did not play in the Cab Jivers himself, Dizzy was working with Hinton on how to develop as a bass soloist. Substitute chords and melody lines with "flatted fifths" were among the ideas Dizzy encouraged Milt to try in his bowed bass solos with the small group.[39]

The Cab Jivers had a regular feature whenever the band played a theatre, and on Sunday September 21, 1941, the band played three shows at the State Theater in Hartford, Connecticut, before returning to New York for a four-day gig at the Brooklyn Strand Theatre.

"For my solo," remembers Hinton, "Dizzy was teaching me some new chords on 'Girl of My Dreams.' He taught the solo to me arco style, like a Slam Stewart solo, and for the end, he ended it on a flatted fifth. Now, I couldn't hear a flatted fifth in those days, and most of the times I would try to make it, I would miss it.

"If I made it correctly, I'd look back at Dizzy, and he'd make a circle with his thumb and finger to mean 'OK! That's good.' And if I missed it, he would put his fingers up to his nose and say 'You stink!' Now this one time in Hartford, I missed the heck out of it, and I turned round and Dizzy made the 'You stink!' sign, and waved his hand at me to say, like, 'Get away from here!'

"At the same time, sitting next to him was Jonah Jones, with a big wad of paper in his hand. Jonah thumped the wad of wet paper up into the air beneath his music stand, and it landed in the spotlight on the stage right beside me. Cab was standing in the wings with a couple of ladies, and he saw the paper land in the spotlight. He looked across and saw Dizzy waving his hand, and he was sure Dizzy did it."

After the show, Cab accused Dizzy of throwing the spitball. Unusually, he was innocent, despite his track record for playing about, and he protested to "Fess" Calloway: "Fess, I didn't do it!" Calloway then accused Dizzy of lying, and made to slap him, whereupon Dizzy drew a knife. Hinton was putting his bass back on the bandstand and saw what was about to happen. "I tell you, Cab would have been long gone, if I hadn't been there. Dizzy was larger than I, but I just interfered with the blow as he was striking Cab with the knife. Cab grabbed Dizzy's wrist and the two of them began to scuffle, and it took two big pachyderms, Chu Berry and Bennie Payne, to pull them apart.

"When Cab got to his dressing room, he found his beautiful white suit had red all the way down the pants. When I interfered with the knife I'd stopped it going in his body, but it had gone in his leg. He came back up and told the fellows, 'This kid cut me!', and he told Dizzy to get his horn and get out."[40]

Dizzy left at once. Although he and Lorraine were waiting at the Theresa Hotel in Harlem when the band bus finally got back to New York after the evening shows, Cab was in no mood to accept an apology, and Dizzy left the band. For years Cab did not know the truth about the incident, but many years later Dizzy was reconciled with him in a public concert where Dizzy characteristically made light of the incident by singing, "Who threw the spitball?"

Jonah Jones still remains diplomatically silent on the subject, although he makes no secret of the fact that Cab openly preferred him to Dizzy. *Down Beat* reported Dizzy's departure and noted: "Gillespie found a knife and started to carve the Calloway posterior.... Cab Calloway still has a sore end ... Cabell took ten stitches from a doctor."[41]

Dizzy returned to his freelance career, moving from band to band over the following few months, and was seldom forthcoming on his Calloway days. Nevertheless, according to Calloway, Dizzy and Tadd Dameron brought some music down to the Strand Theatre in New York a year or two after Dizzy left Cab, in order to hear the guys "go up to the rehearsal hall and play this arrangement."[42] Although Cab's band did not ever feature the chart, it was to become part of Dizzy's own big band repertoire. This suggests that, whatever hard feelings there may have been between Dizzy and Calloway, Dizzy still recognized the musicianship of the band and its exceptional ability to run down a complex chart at sight.

Dizzy himself was gracious enough to acknowledge one thing that his two years with Cab brought to him: "Discipline! That's the word—with no deviations from it. . . . Working in his band taught me to do what I was supposed to do." It is the greatest irony that Dizzy's departure was brought about when Jonah Jones, a poacher turned gamekeeper if ever there was one after he left the wildness of Stuff Smith for the orthodoxy of Cab, was the one who let the discipline slip. Milt Hinton sees the knife incident as a turning point, after which Dizzy became a mature musician, ready to become a leader himself.

6

The Calloway
Recordings

I figured that there was something deeper, there was more to me;
and there was more to evolve from the instrument, the trumpet,
than what Roy had created," wrote Dizzy about his 1939 recordings.[1]

After a two-year gap since his last discs with Teddy Hill,
Dizzy came back to the studios with Cab Calloway for the first of a series
of regular sessions on August 30, 1939. This date marks the start of a
prolific recording career that never again flagged, apart from the ban on
commercial recording imposed by the AFM in 1943. Almost all the
subsequent stages of Dizzy's work are firmly charted on disc.

In his early days with Calloway, Dizzy shared the bulk of the solo
honors with Eldridge's former partner Chu Berry, taking anything from
eight to sixteen bars on a large number of the band's 1939–40 discs.
Since, during this period, he also contributed to one major freelance
session and, a little later, was informally recorded at Monroe's Uptown
House, we can form an idea of where Dizzy had got to in his development as a soloist. His limited solo opportunities with Cab make it possible only to glimpse the degree to which his style had gelled, but he had
clearly come further than the derogatory assessment of his playing by his
eventual Earl Hines big band colleague Scoops Carry, who said: "Dizzy
popularized the flatted fifth. But Tatum was doing that. I'd say it was
Tatum from the start."[2]

Art Tatum's use of unusual intervals was essentially decorative: the
underlying harmonic context of Tatum's work never deviated from standard swing chording. Dizzy's playing, as we know from his own account
and from Milt Hinton's description of their rehearsals together, was essentially concerned with reharmonizing passages within the twelve, sixteen, and thirty-two bar structures of popular songs to alter or enhance
their underlying chording. Furthermore, in his playing, substitute chords
were exactly that—harmonies that did not eliminate the effect of the
original underlying chords of a tune, but enhanced them. Often it is
possible to hear Dizzy imposing altered chords over the Calloway band

as the rhythm section chugs happily away at the original sequence.³ His efforts as an arranger, as well as the structure of his solos, give us an idea of the way his mind was working harmonically, bringing his investigations at the piano into both his playing and writing.

In this he was helped by Calloway's attitude toward records and by the ongoing revolution in the band brought about by Chu Berry. "We didn't have much solo work to play in Cab's band, because it was all featuring him," recalled Milt Hinton.⁴ "But Chu Berry made a great turnabout in that band. 'You've got all these great musicians in the band,' Chu told Cab, 'You should really let the guys play sometimes.'

"Cab wasn't a star who was made by records, and didn't really like to make recordings—radio was what made him and every night you could hear him coast-to-coast hi-de-ho-ing. He didn't *need* records to make him famous, and wherever we went with the band, people flocked to hear him, like they would a rock star today, because of his fame from broadcasting. Chu knew this, and he carried on: 'Next time we make a record, why don't you sing on one side and feature the guys on the other side.'

"So when we did get to the studio, Cab said, 'OK, why don't you guys do something for the other side!' And that's how we began to get features like my 'Ebony Silhouette' or 'Pluckin' the Bass,' or Cozy Cole's 'Paradiddle.' It's Dizzy that takes the trumpet solo on 'Pluckin' the Bass,' and that was the first time he was really featured on record."

Fortunately for Dizzy, Calloway's band cut "Pluckin' the Bass" (a feature written for Hinton by Roy Eldridge and his brother Joe, and later recorded in an inferior version by the Eldridge brothers) on Dizzy's very first session. His arrival on record with the band was announced by the flattened interval that crops up within a bar or two of the start of his brief solo on the first tune they cut, "For the Last Time" (even if the rest of that solo is conservative in style, rather like the Armstrong-influenced "Yours and Mine" Dizzy made for Teddy Hill). Calloway confirmed Dizzy's presence by shouting "Take it, Dizzy!" in the flurry of short solos in the otherwise forgettable novelty number "Twee-Twee-Tweet," which was cut next.

If the originally issued take of "Pluckin' the Bass" were the only version of the piece that existed, we might be forgiven for thinking that Dizzy was inhibited by the surroundings of Calloway's band and adopting a consciously more conservative style than on "King Porter Stomp" from two years before, despite being given a whole chorus to stretch his wings. His solo on this first cut only gives a couple of glimpses of a more exciting way of playing, with some high notes in the second eight bars, and an urgent, repeated phrase after the middle eight or "channel."

Fortunately, a second take was made, with Hinton sounding more confident, better dynamics from the orchestra, a splendid solo from Chu Berry (whose work on the issued take is also excellent), and a completely different and inspired solo from Dizzy. Sounding far less inhibited, presumably because a perfectly acceptable take was in the bag already, Dizzy is much more confident and adventurous. He blisters into his higher register within a couple of bars, produces in the second and final eights the first recorded example of one of his later trademarks—a phrase in which a note is repeated several times with minor variations in pitch and timbre by using substitute fingerings—adds one of the Eldridge four-up-four-down figures, and manages to free himself completely from the melody during the middle eight, rather than being fettered by it as he was on take one.

The fluency of Dizzy's ideas, the rapid execution of the trumpet figures, and the excitement he generates, not only build a perfect platform for Berry's solo with supporting rimshots from drummer Cozy Cole but show Dizzy beginning to find his own voice. Like Eldridge, he uses stock phrases to construct elements of his solo, but there is a compositional quality to his playing that is absent in much of Eldridge's work (and on Dizzy's own first attempt at the solo). This solo offers the first glimpse on record of a new maturity in Dizzy's work, supporting his view that many of the elements of bebop were already present in his style by 1939. Because the second take of "Pluckin' the Bass" was not issued at the time, it has tended to be overlooked in much of the literature.

In the sessions he subsequently played with Calloway, Dizzy preserved for posterity the nascent forms of many of the trumpet figures he was to incorporate into bebop, but few of those records were to have the same critical impact as his solo playing on his first freelance date, cut for Lionel Hampton, just twelve days after "Pluckin' the Bass."

From the moment he came East, after joining Benny Goodman's Quartet in California in August 1936, vibraphonist and drummer Lionel Hampton was an indefatigable organizer of freelance record dates. Some were quite haphazard affairs—Milt Hinton recalls an unidentified customer in a bar giving Hampton $300 to turn up for a record date the following day.[5] Yet many of Hampton's sessions, made up with friends and colleagues from all the leading big bands of the day, have an electric mixture of spontaneity and formal planning. Some are out-and-out jam sessions, including "Wizzin' the Wizz" from April 1939, where Hampton and Chu Berry work with just a rhythm section and feature Hampton's extraordinary two-fingered piano playing. Others, like a Chicago date in October 1938 that produced "Down Home Jump" and "Rock Hill Special," are more organized affairs, with a band largely drawn from

Earl Hines's orchestra falling naturally into disciplined section playing and giving a richness to the "head" arrangements that sounds composed.

The common element in all Hampton's sessions was his supreme confidence in his own ability to produce dazzling improvisations on the vibes or dramatic drum solos at will, which would guarantee popular and saleable discs. Raised in Chicago, and a veteran of newsboys' bands there, Hampton had moved to California in the mid-1920s to work with band-leader Les Hite. When that job fell through, he scuffled for work, ending up in Paul Howard's Quality Serenaders, a band that he used as a launch-ing pad to a successful career in the West, eventually becoming a resident attraction at Frank Sebastian's New Cotton Club in Culver City, where he was billed as "The World's Fastest Drummer." Before long he had recorded on vibes with Louis Armstrong, started his own short-lived big band, and become a byword for after-hours jam sessions. "Discovered" by Benny Goodman at a club called the Paradise, he became an inter-national star in Goodman's small group and toured the United States alongside the full Goodman orchestra.[6]

Perhaps because of his own addiction to freelance recording, Good-man never resented Hampton's frequent excursions to the studios under his own name, and, enjoying the fame his career with Goodman brought him, Hampton made the most of his opportunities.[7] The band he put together on September 11, 1939, was, however, an extraordinary lineup even by his standards. From Cab Calloway's band he borrowed drummer Cozy Cole, bassist Milt Hinton, Chu Berry, and Dizzy Gillespie. He added the virtuoso guitarist Charlie Christian, pianist Clyde Hart, plus three of the most famous saxophonists in jazz: Coleman Hawkins, Benny Carter, and Ben Webster. Using Carter's arranging skill to provide out-line routines for the four sides they cut, the results were among the most celebrated of Hampton's prolific output.

"Roy wasn't in town, probably Charlie Shavers wasn't in town, so then I got the job," recalled Gillespie.[8] "Milt and Cozy were on the date, so they told Hamp: 'Hey, we got a little trumpet player in Cab's band that you might be able to use.'

"And I went on the record date, and looked up and I saw Ben Webster, Chu Berry, Benny Carter, Coleman Hawkins—*the* saxo-phones. And then there was Charlie Christian and Clyde Hart. I was used to Cozy and Milt, but when I saw these other guys I was *ner-vous*, because I didn't know them too well. That was a real state of nervousness, that record."

To Hinton it was a common occurrence to be in such stellar com-pany. "To you now it may seem an extraordinary thing," he told the author,[9] "but to us it was just a nice get-together. We were all young guys who'd meet down on 52nd Street, or jam during an intermission just for a half-hour or so. We were all in town together with our various bands, we all knew one another, and when Lionel got a date, he'd say, 'You guys, come down there.' It was the same with Teddy Wilson, whom I knew from Chicago like I knew Lionel. When he got dates with Billie Holiday I'd get to be the bass player."

Webster and Hawkins were featured, respectively, on "Early Session Hop" and "One Sweet Letter from You," leaving little space for Gillespie to make his presence felt. His cup-muted lead, however, ushers in both takes of "When Lights Are Low," a Benny Carter original, with some neat scoring for the saxophones behind the trumpet. This piece is worth noting, because until the Uptown House jam-session recordings of a year or two later, it offers the first chance to hear Gillespie playing in a small-group ensemble. The context is undeniably swing, but the overall "feel" of the horns, shadowing the trumpet lead in unison or close harmony, is comparable to a bebop group, especially in the little rushed upward phrase in the eleventh bar, where there are hints of the rapid unison articulation of a head arrangement that would become commonplace in Gillespie's groups within the next five years.

By 1939, this kind of arrangement, in which a riff-based or unison "head" led into a sequence of solos, was the *lingua franca* of small swing groups. Fats Waller's little band used the technique in numbers like "Yacht Club Swing," the Goodman sextet put it to good use in many arrangements, but the preeminent practitioners of the style were bassist John Kirby's small group. Kirby, with a front line of Charlie Shavers, Russell Procope, and Buster Bailey, perfected a kind of chamber jazz, in which Shavers's tightly muted lead would be shadowed through intricate lines by Procope and Bailey. Given the close friendship between Shavers and Gillespie, it has always seemed likely that the tight ensemble playing and overall approach to small-group playing developed by Kirby played a role in Dizzy's thinking during the formative stages of bebop. Dizzy's playing on "When Lights Are Low" is evidence of his assimilation of the style, despite acquiring almost all his playing experience in big bands.

The track that has drawn the most critical attention, however, and by whose title the session has always been known, is "Hot Mallets." Gillespie's opening cup-muted solo has rightly been identified as a harbinger of bebop, although only the descending figure that follows the opening quote from Irving Berlin's "Cheek to Cheek" and the subsequent "same-note-repeated-using-different-fingering" pattern leading into an Eldridge four-up-four-down flare, familiar from "Pluckin' the Bass" could genuinely be said to have carried over into Gillespie's subsequent vocabulary. Instead, it is the timbre of his muted solo that so stands out, prefiguring his later athletic efforts with the mute in the 1945 sextets with Charlie Parker. Perhaps buoyed by the previous success of his second attempt at a full chorus solo on "Pluckin' the Bass" Gillespie delivers a completely confident, rounded solo here, with a clear shape and none of the fumbles that decimated his playing on Hill's "Blue Rhythm Fantasy" or that are even noticeable on his few bars of "I Ain't Gettin' Nowhere Fast," the final track from the August 30 Calloway session.

Ever since the "Hot Mallets" session, Lionel Hampton himself was at pains to point out its significance. "The first time bebop was played on trumpet," he told Charles Fox, "was when Dizzy played on 'Hot Mallets.'"[10] Hampton related in his autobiography that he had heard Dizzy a few days before at the Apollo (no doubt during his last week with Teddy Hill) and thought that he was playing in a different style from anything that had been heard before. He resolved to use Dizzy on record as soon as possible.[11]

Unfortunately, Dizzy did not follow up this one date with any comparable freelance sessions during the remainder of his time with Cab, so we only have hearsay, like Hampton's recollections, to assess the impact of his small-group playing beyond what survives on record. (His muted work behind singer Alice O'Connell, on a session made when organist Glenn Hardman recruited Dizzy and Cozy Cole from the next door studio where they were working with Cab, consists entirely of understated obbligatos behind the vocals.)

Cab himself had an ambivalent attitude to his musicians moonlighting on other leaders' sessions. At first, a few years earlier, when Ben Webster and Milt Hinton started the trend, Cab was furious. "I don't want my musicians making everyone else sound good!" he raged.[12] But after Webster threatened to quit, Cab uneasily accepted the situation, and by the time Chu Berry joined he had sensibly revised his views: "I'm glad to know I've got musicians everyone else wants," he purred at Hinton. Nevertheless, the relentless work schedule that Cab imposed on his band acted as a disincentive to undertake too much extra playing, and Dizzy preferred, as we know, to linger backstage with Hinton talking chords, or informally to sit in after hours in Harlem, or at local clubs wherever the band went on tour.

Dizzy had no solo appearances on Cab's October record session, five weeks after "Hot Mallets," although two aspects are worth noting. First, in the band's initial attempt at a Latin arrangement, "Chili Con Conga," Mario Bauza's incisive lead helps the brass phrase crisply across the rumbling rhythm section. Dizzy always acknowledged his debt to Bauza for introducing him to the polyrhythmic texture of Latin music and developing his knowledge of it from his earlier connection with Albert Socarras. "I became enthralled with it, when I met Bauza," recalled Dizzy. "You could say I'm just freakish for that, for Latin music, because it's multirhythmic. That's what I like. Some musicians, say the rhythm section, think that for all of them to come in right together, and *boom!*, they think that is the epitome of it, they look at one another and grin, and you know what they did. But the idea of multirhythm is more subtle and it takes care of all the beats in the bar, you know, all the in-between beats."[13]

Compared to a genuine Latin band's work, "Chili Con Conga" is a rather stodgy attempt, but in some respects it is remarkable that Calloway recorded it at all. In Dizzy's development, however, it is not only relevant for Bauza's disciplined lead (an enthusiasm Bauza shared with his predecessor Doc Cheatham, who went on to work alongside him with Machito) but because Dizzy's first arrangement for the band "Pickin' the Cabbage" further explores some of the polyrhythmic ideas in Latin music.

The second track from October 17 worth noting is "Vuelva," another gently Latin piece, in which the arrangement features the clarinet harmonized over the rest of the reed section—an idea that may also have been in Dizzy's mind when he paired clarinet and trumpet on "Pickin' the Cabbage."

Dizzy makes brief appearances on all four sides from the band's next date in November. Introducing himself as "Diz the Wiz" (along with "Chu the Fool" and other band members), he takes a few bars on "A Bee Gezindt," and an authoritative half-chorus on "Give, Baby, Give." There is a trumpet introduction to "Sincere Love" and a conventional solo on "Do It Again." But it is the next session from March 1940 that marks the high point of Dizzy's recording career with Calloway.

Made during one of the band's visits to Chicago, "Pickin' the Cabbage" was Dizzy's first arrangement to be recorded. It consists of a minor theme over a repeated ostinato bass pattern, in which Hinton's bass doubles with Andrew Brown's baritone. Various commentators have drawn attention to the unusual chordal structure of the opening with its eleventh and thirteenth chords, but even Gunther Schuller's notation of this[14] avoids the problem of capturing on paper the off-center accents of the ostinato, with Brown's baritone honks anticipating and emphasizing the fourth beat of every bar, for the most part paralleled by Cole's rimshots. The rhythmic effect is to destabilize the normal four-four swing structure (which is only allowed to gain hold in the middle eight).[15] By running the theme for Jerry Blake's clarinet and Dizzy's muted trumpet over the top, with its stress on a slightly anticipated first beat of every bar, the piece creates a sense of contrary motion and an underlying hint of Latin rhythm. Dizzy's own solo, which works best in the minor sections of the piece, is confident enough for him to get out of trouble in the middle eight, but less impressive than the vision revealed by the whole arrangement. It may be, in Gunther Schuller's pun, a "minor effort," but it is genuinely unusual within the oeuvre of the Calloway band, and an exploration of the rhythmic texture possible from section writing (rather than depending on piano, bass, drums, and guitar to create the entire rhythmic impetus).

A second aspect of Dizzy's arranging skills is revealed on the same session with his feature for drummer Cozy Cole, "Paradiddle." Dizzy became increasingly fascinated with percussion throughout his career, and Kenny Clarke believed that Dizzy educated many drummers in the elements of bebop drumming that he (Clarke) had pioneered as a side effect of this fascination.[16] By working closely with Cole (even though Cozy was never to develop stylistically beyond his work in Calloway's band), Dizzy had the chance to create an arrangement for one of the most effective and popular of all swing drummers and to understand how to write in such a way as to show off the drums to best advantage. The fact that none of Cole's other features worked so well is tribute to Dizzy's innate sympathy for percussion, even if unkind critics felt that the piece simply allowed Cole to carry on his relentless dressing-room assaults on the practice pad. (When the author met Cole in 1976, he was still as assiduous in his practice routines as he was said to have been in the 1930s.)

"Paradiddle" obviously depends for much of its length on Cole's playing solo, but the interest in the arrangement comes from the full band chorus at the start as well as the voicings of the orchestral punctuations between the drums in the second chorus. The third and fourth choruses are for drums (with a central passage for cymbals) before the orchestra returns briefly to ride out the disc. None of the orchestral voicings would disgrace Tadd Dameron, Gil Fuller, or any of the other arrangers who were to work with Gillespie from 1946 onward. Dizzy's eventual persistence in running a bebop big band probably had its foundations here. It was a chance to write challenging music for one of the best swing orchestras of the age, which was prepared to rise to that challenge as an antidote to its regular job of accompanying Cab. The gusto with which the trombones tear into their passages at the end of the middle eight suggests real enthusiasm for the chart from Dizzy's fellow band members, and it is sad that this record date represents the only recorded examples of his work as arranger for the band.

For another year, Dizzy was to continue to be featured on records with Calloway before the arrival of Jonah Jones marked virtually his last appearance as a soloist. Instead of investigating every brief solo glimpse of Dizzy in more than fifty further tracks the band cut before he left, a clear sense of his development can be gathered by focusing on a relatively small number of extended solos, and on one "live" recording by the band, that shows them unrestrained by the necessities of studio work and 78-rpm playing times.

Two of Dizzy's commercially recorded solos ("Calling All Bars" and "Topsy Turvy") date from May 15, Dizzy's last session before he met Charlie Parker, and the remainder of the material follows their June 1940 meeting. It would be too much to expect the meeting with Parker to have had a radical and immediate impact on Dizzy and, if one accepts his statement from his autobiography (even though he contradicted it in one or two other passages) that his style was effectively formed anyway when they met, then to look for a magical transformation would be misleading. (Dizzy was not above describing it as a magical transformation, as he did in relating the effect of meeting Parker to Gene Lees: "I was playing like Roy Eldridge at the time. In about a month's time I was playing like Charlie Parker."[17] Even in his dialogue with Lees he immediately contradicted himself by saying why he did not play like Parker: "I'm not a copyist of somebody else's music.") It would not be until Parker and Gillespie worked side by side in Earl Hines's band a couple of years later that the real effects of cross-fertilization would take effect in subtle modification of Dizzy's phrasing and the extension of his speed and range. Perhaps the most balanced critical assessment of their mutual effect on one another and on other players at the time they met is in Thomas Owens's masterly survey *Bebop*: "Some players copied Parker directly, others copied players who copied Parker, and a few, such as Gillespie, copied the swing-era players that Parker copied."[18]

"Calling All Bars" is a long circuitous solo, and it is hard not to dismiss it as Gunther Schuller does as "circular and repetitious."[19] But "Topsy Turvy" shows a side of Dizzy's playing that was not to reemerge until later, with his famous recording of "I Can't Get Started"—the ability to construct a logical, powerful, and measured solo on a ballad sequence, in this case over a thirty-two bar sequence in B flat minor. He begins by working on the D flat of the vocal line, but extends his solo outward, to produce a paraphrase figure that is repeated in two different registers in the second eight bars. This motif is reintroduced for the opening of the channel and ultimately inverted in a series of descending diminished figures in the last eight. This is playing of a level only rarely achieved by Eldridge. Dizzy is revealing a solo, much as Armstrong did, where there is an inevitability about the rightness of the notes and phrases, but this time using his own vocabulary.

The band played the same arrangement at its residency at the Meadowbrook Inn in New Jersey on July 27 when its performance was recorded. Dizzy attempts to replicate his solo from the May studio session, but, despite shouts of encouragement from Calloway, almost loses his way in the channel and, after a couple of fumbles, fails to wrap up the last eight bars so effectively. This does suggest, however, that Dizzy was following the example of every major trumpeter since Armstrong and working out effective solo patterns that he could recreate night after night on particular tunes. It is clear from its vocabulary that this solo is his, and not the work of the song's arranger Edgar Battle.

The Meadowbrook Inn recording also shows Dizzy in fine form on the up tempo "Limehouse Blues" and on "King Porter Stomp" (offering a chance to compare his playing with the 1937 Hill disc). On "Limehouse," he turns in a splendid solo that shows his growing mastery of the "downhill run," long tumbling figures that descend rapidly from a few introductory high notes. The last four of his sixteen bars show him negotiating a pattern that would become a staple of his bebop playing.

A more harmonically challenging moment occurs in Dizzy's two brief solos on Don Redman's "Cupid's Nightmare" from the same session. This piece was a highly unusual composition for the period, exploring chromatic harmonies and whole tone scales,[20] and Dizzy (offered twice the space he occupies on the band's commercial disc of the tune, cut a month later) adds his own incandescent glow to Redman's sinister landscape.

In the rest of his Calloway output, two of Dizzy's solos stand out. The first is on the band's flagwaving "Bye Bye Blues." Following Chu Berry at blistering tempo, it displays Dizzy's growing mastery of intricate phrases at high speed. Harmonically, it barely strays from the underlying sequence, but it does show (particularly in the octave leaps at the end) the formidable technique that Dizzy had developed, which was to underpin his bebop playing. It also stands out for the control with which Dizzy manipulates the pace of his phrasing, alternating slower figures with the rapid patterns that were to be his trademark.

The final track that deserves mention here is "Boo-Wah Boo-Wah." In his second eight, Dizzy introduces a sequence of triplets that was to develop into one of his most characteristic solo motifs and is identified by Thomas Owens[21] as dating in its complete form from around 1943. Owens notates the passage as it ultimately appears in "Woody 'n' You," but in this precursor, over a B flat chord sequence, Dizzy pitches it lower and plays it slower than he was ultimately to do.

No individual solo from the Calloway years could be described as a full-fledged bebop solo. But in terms of Dizzy's harmonic language, his technical skill, and arsenal of solo motifs or phrases, he had put clear

water between himself and Eldridge and consolidated a sufficiently individual style for it to grow alongside rather than as a consequence of
Charlie Parker's innovations. The context of Dizzy's solos on record with
Cab is often seasoned with elements of Cab's showmanship, and hearing
Cab's shouts of encouragement and banter on the Meadowbrook disc is
a distant pre-echo of Gillespie's own stage persona in his later live big
band discs. By the parting of the ways at Hartford, Connecticut, a useful
apprenticeship had been served out.

7

Horn for Hire

Mr. Minton, who was the first black delegate of Local 802, wanted to head this club, and he put Teddy Hill in charge," recalled Dizzy in 1976. "He had Monk and Kenny Clarke (I think Kenny was the leader) and Kermit Scott and Joe Guy. Joe had worked in Teddy's band before. Then Charlie Christian used to come down every night and all of us used to congregate in Minton's and then after hours at the Uptown House. Those two places were the spawning grounds of our music."[1]

The legendary status afforded to Minton's (which was in the basement of the Cecil Hotel at 210 West 118th Street), based on such oral reminiscences as Dizzy's, has made the club into one of the sacred cows of jazz history. It is celebrated as the place where bebop was forged in the heat of the after-hours jam session, and where the great and the good clamored to sit in. Those with no knowledge of the rhythmic and harmonic changes afoot in bebop were systematically excluded as the musicians on the bandstand played ever more esoteric chord changes and improvised melodic lines built of increasingly complex chordal extensions at greater and greater speed.

Accounts of Minton's Playhouse appear so widely in the written and oral history of jazz that the underlying substance of its role as a "spawning ground" is undeniably true. But in Dizzy's own case, as we already know from Chapter 5, it is more likely that he visited Monroe's Uptown House after his earliest experiments with Milt Hinton, and we can assume that Minton's played its most important role for him during whatever short spells Dizzy was in New York from Teddy Hill's arrival there as manager in 1940 until around the time he left Calloway in September 1941. In terms of Dizzy's own development, rather than the development of the style as a whole, it did not regain similar importance until after Charlie Parker's arrival in New York with Jay McShann during February 1942, and, from Dizzy's accounts to several interviewers, he and Parker did not actually jam together there all that often. Their real cooperation began the following year when both men joined Earl Hines.

There are several reasons why Minton's is such a focal point in oral history. First, as we know from Dizzy's previous statement, Minton had been a prominent member of Local 802 and its first black delegate. He had also had a role in managing the Rhythm Club during its declining years, an establishment that was beloved by the whole generation of 1930s New York jazz musicians. The conjunction of as politically and socially important a figure as Minton and ex-bandleader Teddy Hill as his manager was a potent one, and Hill's connections throughout the "show-people" world of the Savoy and the Apollo brought in a wide cross-section of musicians and entertainers as part of the club's late-night clientele. The club became famous for its food, and it also encouraged listening: "In Minton's there was complete quiet: very little talking, no glasses clinking, no kinds of noises," wrote Danny Barker of his visits there with Dizzy and Milt Hinton.[2]

Barker's description is a brilliant romantic evocation of all that was new and exciting about the club, and his account dwells on the dramatic interplay between Clarke and Thelonious Monk. "Monk started. Klook fell in, dropped in, dived in, sneaked in; by hook or by crook, he was in. . . . You would look, hear the off-, off-, off-beat explosion, and think 'fireworks,' and then the color patterns formed in the high sky of your mind."

The romance of a club where experimental sounds could be heard without hindrance, and the club's relative longevity (it opened in 1938, but was not a popular venue for after-hours musicians until Teddy Hill's arrival as manager in 1940 to the 1950s),[3] combined with its popularity among Harlem entertainers who congregated for the Monday night open-house suppers and jam sessions promoted by Hill, are all factors that have tended to inflate its importance. In much of the literature it forms such a convenient landmark in the story of the emergence of modern jazz that other parts of the story can easily be overlooked. Clark Monroe's Uptown House on 134th Street was founded earlier, by at least 1937, tended to stay open later, and, until it moved downtown to 52nd Street in 1943, was no less important than Minton's. Equally, from accounts that survive, plenty of jam-session space at Minton's appears to have been taken up by Swing Era giants like Roy Eldridge, Ben Webster, and Art Tatum, who were certainly not forging a new style, while numerous members of Minton's house band, like bassist Nick Fenton and trumpeter Joe Guy, faded quickly into obscurity. (Kenny Clarke himself left within a year.)

Both these venues, separately or together, were a relatively small part of a movement in jazz that was gathering momentum in many regions of the United States, but above all in the buses and backstage dressing rooms of the great big bands. In New York, but also in cities like Chicago, Philadelphia, and Pittsburgh, after-hours clubs were places to come and display ideas that, certainly in the case of Dizzy, had already been worked out on the roof of the Cotton Club and in convenient rehearsal spaces wherever the Calloway band had found itself. From shortly after he left Calloway in September 1941, an equally important focus was Dizzy's own apartment at 2040 Seventh Avenue, where he and Lorraine settled after their marriage and where musicians dropped by at all times to work out ideas with Dizzy on his battered piano.[4]

Judging by what recorded evidence survives, however, and backed up by accounts such as Barker's, there was one aspect of the after-hours clubs that was essential. It was there that the fundamental changes to the rhythm section were able to gel. However much Dizzy and his big band colleagues were able to explore new chord changes in the course of their regular work, there was no opportunity to pull everything together in front of a rhythm team that was complementing their melodic and harmonic exploration with rhythmic innovation. With no requirement to satisfy dancers, Monroe's and Minton's were platforms for this process to take place, even if the initial results were slow to appear.

The paradox at the heart of the bebop movement is that it began as small band music from ideas propounded by those who, for the most part, garnered their experience in large bands. That this should coincide with a period when the American Federation of Musicians fell into dispute with the main record companies and effectively put an end to recording from late 1942 until over a year later has also made it hard to chart the precise evolution of the new jazz, with recorded evidence giving the misleading impression of a sudden leap forward by 1944.

To understand what was happening, and the respective roles of Dizzy and the after-hours clubs in the process, it is helpful to analyze the elements that combined to become bebop.

Musically, the development took place in all three critical areas: melody, harmony, and rhythm. Based on more complex underlying harmonies, improvisers created melody lines that were asymmetrical, avoiding both the standard metrical conventions of swing, such as the formal division into four- or eight-bar phrases and the conventional forms of harmonic resolution. At the same time, rhythm sections began to break up the firm four-to-the-bar pulse of swing and, by carrying forward momentum on the double bass and ride cymbal, to use harmonic instruments such as the piano or guitar to introduce prodding, occasional chords instead of evenly spaced beats, and to use the snare and bass drums for accents that were no longer placed regularly on the "on" (first and third) or "off" (second and fourth) beats of each measure. Besides contributing to and delineating many of the harmonic developments in bebop, Dizzy himself pioneered both Latin rhythms as part of this mix and the idea of the double bass playing motifs or "patterns" rather than the "walking" lines of the Swing Era.[5]

Lorraine and Dizzy Gillespie in Harlem, 1940. (Photo: Danny Barker)

Socially, a major consequence of the "new" jazz was that it was no longer dance music, which had very much been a function of swing. The loyalty of the dancing public, from the early 1940s, increasingly migrated to the emergent forms of urban blues and rhythm and blues, thereby almost guaranteeing that much modern jazz would need to find different consumers if it were to achieve comparable levels of popularity to swing. Promoters continued to book the emerging modern jazz artists on the traditional circuits, but, as Dizzy was later to find with his "Hep-sations of 1945" tour, this was not an automatic route to success.

So far, we have been able to chart Dizzy's own development as a soloist and to observe some of the characteristics in his playing that were to become the foundations of his bebop style. By late 1941, when Dizzy left Calloway, many of the general developments that were to coalesce into the mature form of bebop were under way, but their combination was to be ragged and uneven. The after-hours clubs enjoy such prominence in musicians' memories because they were focal points for that combination of elements, even if in reality much of the endless time spent jamming did not actually enhance the development of bop very far. The clubs were a meeting ground for like-minded individuals drawn from several different bands (in which their new ideas were likely to be an individual or minority interest) where it was possible for ideas to cross-fertilize.

From a handful of private recordings made by an enthusiast called

Jerry Newman at Monroe's Uptown House around May 1941, when Dizzy was still in the Calloway band and enjoying a few days in New York between visits to Boston and Chicago, we have an opportunity to glimpse the process of integration beginning to happen, just as Dean Benedetti's subsequent eavesdropping captured an equivalent stage in Charlie Parker's development.

The recordings that survive by Dizzy are two versions of "Star Dust" and a long medium-tempo piece based on "Exactly Like You" that Newman titled "Kerouac" after the beat novelist who was a regular at Monroe's. Dizzy has solos at the beginning and end of "Kerouac," which is accompanied, like one of the cuts of "Star Dust," by a trio that almost certainly included Kenny Kersey on piano, Nick Fenton on bass, and Kenny Clarke on drums. The second "Star Dust" is from a different session, and only Don Byas on tenor is known for certain to have been there, along with an anonymous trio and a welter of horns that blow soft chords over the last few notes.

The most noticeable thing about these discs is the degree to which Dizzy's thinking appears to be more advanced than that of those around him. On "Kerouac," for instance, Clarke's forceful brushwork is straight four-to-the-bar rhythm playing, with not even the same rhythmic variety that is found in his Edgar Hayes recordings. What "klook-a-mop-ing" there is uses a well-known cliché of Sid Catlett's that involves the rapid repetition of a punctuation, creating a two-note figure slightly ahead of the fourth beat of a bar to propel the band forward into the next measure. (Clarke was a firm friend of Catlett's, who coached him for a short-lived stint in Louis Armstrong's big band a month or so after these discs were cut.)

Kersey's piano work has nimble single-line right-hand solos, along with prodding comping chords, but it is not markedly more advanced than, say, a swing musician like Billy Kyle's playing of the same period. By contrast, Dizzy's playing resembles a series of architectural drawings. He experiments with the structure of chorus after chorus, imposing a clear design on each, from upward moving diminished chords to many of the descending figures he had worked out in his Calloway solos. There is a high incidence of flattened fifths and one or two other such harmonic devices, and in the last group of choruses Dizzy experiments with groups of high notes. (An analysis by Jonathan Finkelman of part of his second solo on "Kerouac" draws attention to a pattern that later reemerged in Dizzy's big band version of "One Bass Hit.")[6] The rhythm section follows him through his explorations, but at this stage they were still unequal partners, giving credence to Dizzy's view that what was going on was an "evolution" rather than a new development altogether.[7]

The rhythm section is even more in the background on the two takes of "Star Dust," of which the second (with Byas) involves a long open-horn ballad solo by Dizzy of great beauty and poise. He would have known the piece well from his work in Edgar Hayes's small group, which featured the tune as its theme, but here he invokes many of the melodic twists and turns that would become features of his later ballad vehicles like "I Can't Get Started." His pickup after Byas's solo is masterly and shows a degree of maturity as a soloist that is hard to equate with the stories of his wild and unruly temperament. A more prosaic solo on the other "Star Dust" is interesting only because Dizzy uses the cup mute in a way that shows a development in his technique from the "Hot Mallets" session; it clearly indicates the muted timbre he was to employ in his own bebop quintets.

Clarke's playing is more extroverted on some of his other after-hours sessions captured by Newman (notably those with Charlie Christian),[8] but at this distance it is hard to see from the recorded evidence of his playing what all the fuss was about. Several witnesses, including Dizzy, recall Clarke's drumming as notably innovative in his work with Teddy Hill during 1939, and trombonist Henri Woode is said to have taken great exception to Clarke's playing with Hill, inspiring Hill's "klook-a-mop" description. Virtually no examples of such playing can be heard on Clarke's recordings from 1940 and 1941. On "One O'clock Jump" with Sidney Bechet, from February 1940, there are occasional hints of uneven accents in Clarke's otherwise forceful, but conventional swing drumming and the same is true of his one session with Count Basie's band in May 1941, at almost exactly the time of the Uptown House discs. The exceptional aspect of his work with Basie is the way his dynamics and accents fit the arrangement in "Down, Down, Down." Basie was not to have such a musically adept drummer again until Gus Johnson joined him some years later. In Billie Holiday's session for Eddie Heywood in March 1941 there are some clearly recorded examples of Clarke's small band work, but only the deft brushwork on an uptempo "Romance in the Dark" suggests anything other than a meek swing drummer.

Clarke once said that the origins of his style owed something to fast and furious tempi, and that in pieces like Hill's "Harlem Twister" he used to rest his bass drum foot from playing every beat and play accents instead.[9] Possibly musicians used to a four-square bass drum rhythm felt lost without it, but certainly Clarke does not "break up the rhythm" very noticeably on the majority of his 1940–41 discs. It seems that Clarke's main innovations happened during the years after he led the backing quartet at Minton's.

Dizzy himself backed up Clarke's ergonomic theory of why the drum style changed when he suggested that Clarke's economy of style in the after-hours sessions was due to his self-preservation instincts: "It's pretty hard on the drummer in a rhythm section when one guy plays eight choruses, another guy plays twelve, and by the time they get around to you the rhythm section is pretty tired from pushing."[10] Continuing this line of argument, Dizzy suggested to Charles Fox that he and Monk devised more complex harmonic and rhythmic arrangements not so much to "scare away the no-talent guys" as to keep jam sessions within a reasonable length without so many endless solos that the rhythm team ended up exhausted and uninspired.

For much of the period when Minton's was in its heyday, Dizzy was no more than an occasional visitor. "I never worked there. I never got paid for working there," he said. "On Monday nights all the performers from the Apollo Theatre would come up and do a number. Other than that, those other nights we'd go and jam. Teddy would let us come in without money, and then he'd feed us, because they had a good kitchen."[11] But for a major part of the year after he left Calloway, Dizzy was working so late that his regular job coincided with after-hours clubs. At Kelly's Stable, the sets were at 11:30 and 3 A.M., not finishing until 4:30 A.M., and Dizzy spent several months there or at the Famous Door, where the hours were only marginally earlier. It is likely that he and Kenny Clarke did much of their formative thinking about bebop well away from Minton's because from almost the moment Dizzy left Calloway he worked with Clarke every night for two long spells, first in Ella Fitzgerald's orchestra and then in Benny Carter's group. (Clearly, although the exact chronology of his movements has never been completely sorted out, during the last quarter of 1941 Clarke was no longer the house drummer at Minton's.)

Dizzy joined Ella Fitzgerald, replacing Taft Jordan, in early October 1941, and remained until no later than November 5. Ella finished a week at the Apollo just two days before the spitball incident and the band went north to Boston for around three weeks. Ella's straw boss Teddy McRae recalls Dizzy subbing in the band for "about four weeks" and accounts vary as to whether the Boston residency they played was the Cocoanut Grove or Levaggi's.[12] This no doubt took place between Ella's two New York recording sessions on October 6 and 28, respectively. Both involve a small group (with Clarke playing a quiet supporting role on drums), but are interesting in that the musical directorship of Ella's band passed from Teddy McRae to Eddie Barefield during the Boston gig. Whereas McRae is the soloist on the October 6 date, his place is taken by Barefield on October 28.[13]

To Dizzy (who played no part in the recordings and was simply a sideman in the Boston residency) the musical chairs of the leaders and the poor management of Ella's band, in which musical and financial issues were settled over her head between her musical director and the Moe Gale Agency, were more reasons to dislike the way that Gale and the Savoy had treated his old boss Teddy Hill and did nothing to improve his view of them.[14] The main legacy of his brief stay in Ella's band was that Dizzy used his three weeks or so of working with Clarke to sort out an arrangement based on a John Kirby riff for what later became his own composition "Salt Peanuts."[15]

Back in New York, Dizzy was recommended by guitarist John Collins as a suitable replacement for Little Benny Harris to play trumpet in Benny Carter's small group. Carter had recently come off the road after a lengthy big band tour of the Cotton Belt, the West, and Southwest, with singer Maxine Sullivan, and on October 23 his sextet settled into Henry "Red" Allen's former residency at Kelly's Stable at 137 West 52nd Street, opposite Art Tatum and with Nat King Cole's trio, Billy Daniels, and the singer Miss Rhapsody in support.[16]

Benny Carter, who was born in New York in 1907, became one of the most naturally gifted musicians in jazz history. He was widely respected by the early 1940s as a saxophonist and trumpeter, with dazzling proficiency on both reed and brass instruments. His main influence as an arranger was first apparent in his work for Fletcher Henderson and for McKinney's Cotton Pickers, where he continued the pioneering work of Don Redman, and he became internationally famous after a mid-1930s posting as staff arranger to the BBC in London. Surprisingly for such a talented figure, he had a more checkered career as a leader. His career record shows band after band that he set up, provided charts for, and then allowed to fall into a rapid decline. "He would be a sensation," recalled Danny Barker, who played in his band in the late 1930s, "and for some reason I don't know he'd fizzle out. Been doing it for years, fizzling. Got discouraged because he couldn't keep on. Guess he didn't want to go on them one-nighters. But he had quite a name. And that opened doors for him in record companies. Everybody knew him, because he arranged for everybody."[17]

The sense of disappointment that some of his sidemen felt when Carter's bands "fizzled out" was tempered by the fact that Carter enjoyed universal respect among almost all musicians. "They figured if you could play Carter's scores you could play anything," said Barker, and Dizzy notes in numerous sources that Carter was generally the best trumpeter in his own bands, against some stiff competition. The small group that Carter brought into New York in the fall of 1941 was important for two reasons: it was not dependent on endless one-nighters, like Carter's larger groups that preceded and followed it, so it created an opportunity for stable, long-term development; and it was a high-profile enough group to gain critical attention for its music alone, and not, as Calloway's group had, for the quality of its accompanying revue and the leader's stage antics.

In his autobiography, Dizzy suggests that it was at this point that he first worked at Kelly's Stable with Coleman Hawkins, leaving abruptly after a week because of his low salary. But this dating must be inaccurate (and is contradicted by Dizzy himself elsewhere) because Coleman Hawkins was in Chicago for the entire period after Dizzy left Cab. It was not until the fall of 1943 that Dizzy spent a brief spell at the club with Hawkins.[18]

As it turned out, Dizzy's debut with Carter, on November 5, 1941, did not take place at the sawdust-covered, rough-hewn Kelly's Stable, but in the auspicious surroundings of the Museum of Modern Art at 11 West 53rd Street. The Museum presented twice monthly "Coffee Concerts" at 9 P.M. on Wednesdays, each season including a wide variety of music from folk and ethnic artists to classical and jazz players, and Carter was booked to open the new series for the fall of 1941. "Gillespie made his official bow with Carter" there, according to *Down Beat*, in a program that reunited Carter and Maxine Sullivan and also featured harpsichordist Sylvia Marlowe playing her Schubertian arrangement "Who Is Sylvia?" and her "Harpsichord Blues and Boogie Woogie."[19]

The program was built around standards, including "I Got Rhythm" and a number that would later be identified with Dizzy: Vernon Duke's "I Can't Get Started." But the band did play a couple of Carter originals, "Back Bay Boogie" and "Fireside Chat." Because Kelly's Stable did not start its first show until 11:30, no doubt the band went the block or so downtown to play their regular gig after the concert. Carter's group featured Al Gibson on clarinet and tenor, Charlie Drayton on bass, and Sonny White on piano. John Collins, from his own account, was with them on guitar at the outset, but did not stay into 1942. Kenny Clarke had joined on drums, and he and Dizzy worked alongside each other in the group for much of the period until late February 1942, first at Kelly's Stable, and after the New Year at the Famous Door, where Jimmy Hamilton replaced Gibson on clarinet and tenor.

Playing in a sextet regularly for the first time, and benefiting from his proximity to Carter and Clarke, this experience was far more influential on Dizzy's own development than sitting in at Minton's. The tight routine of such a regular working band (even though a *Billboard* reviewer urged Benny to exert more discipline) would have encouraged Dizzy to compress his ideas into "sound bites," brief one- or two-chorus solos, rather than extending his thoughts over several jam-session choruses.

The band played new compositions by several of its members; with un-usual sequences, new arrangements to work on, and the challenge of using solo space as effectively as an old hand like Carter, Dizzy's ground-ing in small-group playing was every bit as significant as his time in Calloway's topflight big band. Few published accounts of Dizzy's life dwell on this period, but it was clearly important to Dizzy, who said of Carter: "Playing with him was my best experience next to playing with Charlie Parker."[20]

So why was it so important, and why be skeptical about Minton's? What can we ascertain about Dizzy's development to support this view-point? Primarily, Carter's band offered Dizzy the boost in confidence and increased solo space that he had systematically been denied with Calloway. Furthermore, the solo opportunities in a sextet were far greater than those for even the most heavily featured trumpet soloist in a big band, and the regularity of a nightly gig in New York for the best part of four months was the first such long-term residency of Dizzy's career. From eyewitness accounts, reviews, and one important piece of recorded evidence, we can be confident that Carter gave Dizzy the opportunity to mature as a soloist, and that however much trial and error or experiment clouded people's perceptions at the time, the soloist who emerged into the limelight in recordings for Les Hite and Lucky Millinder during 1942 was several stages further on in developing his own improvisational style than the player who left Calloway the previous September.

"When Dizzy was in my band at the Famous Door," said Carter, "I was asked to get rid of him because he was playing augmented ninths, etc. They thought he was hitting bad notes."[21] Fortunately, Carter had the musical awareness to understand and appreciate what Dizzy was do-ing. "I could see that Dizzy, when he was with me for several months, was groping for something. And he knew his music . . . I stood up for him."[22] Carter felt that Dizzy's unorthodox humor and overall personality were not as wild and out of control as the stories of his departure from Calloway suggested and went on record to praise Dizzy's musical and business acumen at that period.

Those who saw the band were impressed, both by Carter's instru-mental and arranging skills and Dizzy's playing. Tenorist Frank Socolow was a frequent visitor, and recalled: "[Dizzy] was already into the new thing. . . . The way he played his changes; the way his whole conception was set apart from what was happening."[23] Other musicians went often, including trumpeter and arranger Neal Hefti, who had first encountered Dizzy in Omaha, during a Calloway tour. "When I went to New York in 1941, Dizzy was one of the first people I found. . . . I think the first time I saw him he was working with a little group led by Benny Carter."[24]

Hefti was smitten by Dizzy's work, and claimed Dizzy as the inspiration behind his famous trumpet chorus on Woody Herman's "Caldonia," which was adopted by the entire trumpet section of the band.[25] His infatuation with Gillespie can be traced back to his regular opportunities to hear Dizzy at Kelly's Stable.

This was the first time in his career that Dizzy was being sought out by other musicians as an interesting player and potential influence. It was also the first time he was given sufficient solo space for his live performances to be written about by critics.

His "trumpeting is top notch," wrote Barry Ulanov, in a piece for *Metronome* that dwelt at some length on a comparison between Carter's band and John Kirby's sextet. "Commercially, Benny Carter's small crew might be the first to rival Kirby's in that outfit's almost one-band field. Its performances are not as slick as the latter's yet, nor are its books alive with the saleable novelties that mean so much for the Kirbys. But the material is all here."[26] This assertion, apparently also made by Leonard Feather,[27] confirms the point made in Chapter 6 (concerning "When Lights Are Low"), that Kirby's group was influential in the early development of bop by offering a convincing small band model that could easily be adopted by musicians trained in large orchestras. It also reemphasizes the importance of Charlie Shavers (Kirby's trumpeter) on Dizzy's own stylistic development because Shavers's muted playing with Kirby owed little to Roy Eldridge and was very much an independent line of thinking.

Contrary to Dizzy's recollection that during his stay with the band Benny Carter did not play trumpet until Dizzy coerced him to do so for just one night, late in their run,[28] Ulanov's review clearly shows that Carter was playing trumpet alongside Dizzy, saying: "He's fooling around with half-valve effects now." Ulanov draws attention to the clear structure of Carter's solos on trumpet, and there can be little doubt that this aspect of Carter's musicality rubbed off on Dizzy, whose own solos were already indicating a grasp of structure and form.

For the period between Carter's residency at Kelly's Stable and his move to the Famous Door, Dizzy accepted a job on the road with the large white swing band led by Charlie Barnet. Frankie Newton's band was due to open at Kelly's Stable on December 18, and it seems that Dizzy left Carter before the end of their Kelly's Stable residency, since Harvey Davis remembers replacing Dizzy there and *Down Beat* noted: "John (Dizzy) Gillespie was slated to join Charlie Barnet's orchestra as featured hot trumpeter about December 15 . . . Barnet plans to use the colored ace, who formerly was with Teddy Hill and Cab Calloway and who is now with Benny Carter, only for about three weeks on a tour."[29]

Dizzy's main observation about this experience was the uniform approach of the white musicians to their charts. He felt the black bands he had worked with each asserted an individual approach to their arrangements, but Barnet's men played identically to the way they would have done had they been in a comparable white band like Benny Goodman's or Artie Shaw's.[30] Dizzy stored the experience away and within a few months was producing charts himself that he could sell to white swing band leaders.

The Barnet tour, however, was little more than a useful stopgap to cover the Christmas layoff, and Dizzy, recommending to Barnet that Joe Guy replace him, returned to Carter's band.

The Famous Door residency offers more eyewitness accounts of Dizzy's work. The best known is probably from Leonard Feather, from his 1949 book *Inside Bebop*. The pen portrait he draws of Dizzy is so convincing that it has permeated jazz literature, and his account of Dizzy's unruly behavior with Teddy Hill, "dancing during someone else's turn in a stage show; or putting on his trumpet derby and facing the backdrop instead of the audience," appears in many descriptions of Gillespie by other writers, ascribed to other periods and other places. Not one of the reviews of the Hill band that appeared at the time of Hill's European tour mentions Dizzy's behavior,[31] and, as we know from Maurice Cullaz and even the reluctant Hugues Panassié, the French marveled at his trumpeting technique, not his horseplay. In his book, Feather suggests that Dizzy's habit of starting to read a new arrangement from an interlude or the last chorus rather than the top was abnormal, overlooking the point that most competent sight readers generally study only those parts of an arrangement that may impede the rapidity of their sightreading. With considerable literary skill, Feather makes this entirely normal aspect of Dizzy's behavior appear unusual. Yet his account of Dizzy in Carter's group at the Famous Door is as penetrating as the Hill band description is potentially misleading.

In February 1942, Feather had a vested interest in Gillespie because he was producing a record session for Decca with altoist Pete Brown on which he was to use Dizzy. Feather's skill at writing glowing advance press pieces about artists he was to record, including his own compositions on the session, and then reviewing his own productions as if he were an impartial critic, was almost an art form in itself. Some of his anonymous pieces for the black press give away their origins—only a white Englishman is likely to have used the Gilbert and Sullivan analogy in a critique of Hugues Panassié's recording activity and dub him "the Pooh Bah of swing."[32]

Feather had supplied Benny Carter's group with an arrangement of "Lady Be Good," and, when he went to the Famous Door to hear the band play it, he was somewhat disconcerted: "Dizzy's style [was] alternately fascinating and nerve wracking, this being the effect he had on many listeners at the time, myself included. In fact when I had to assemble a small band for a Pete Brown/Helen Humes date for Decca, and was stuck for a trumpet, I was reluctant to use Diz, since this was a blues session and I could hardly see him as a bluesman."[33] This is a little disingenuous, since although Humes (and Nora Lee King) sang blues lyrics, the arrangements featured a front line modeled on John Kirby's, with Dizzy and Jimmy Hamilton recreating their roles in Carter's group and Pete Brown taking the alto parts and virtually all the solos. Indeed, we know from trumpeter Harvey Davis that Brown's own band—residing at the Onyx club at about this time with Davis on trumpet and "Pazuza" Simon on tenor, while Brown was featured on both trumpet and alto—had some remarkable similarities to Carter's group.

On Brown's discs for Feather, the tight front-line riffs on "Mound Bayou," "Unlucky Woman," and "Gonna Buy Me a Telephone" give us a tantalizing glimpse of how Carter's band might have sounded, espe-

Session at Decca, February 9, 1942. Pete Brown, Dizzy, Charlie Drayton, Sammy Price, Ray Nathan, Helen Humes, Leonard Feather, Jimmy Hamilton. (Frank Driggs collection)

cially as Sammy Price, Decca's house pianist, keeps his habitual boogie-woogie well in check on these tracks. (When he abandons his natural boogie style, Price's best jazz small-group playing from the period is not greatly different from that of Sonny White, Carter's pianist, on the evidence of both men's discs with Sidney Bechet.) The outstanding moment, however, comes in the most blues-like of the four-track session. After some rousing piano boogie from Price to introduce "Cannon Ball," the front-line horns play obbligatos in turn behind Nora Lee King's robust vocals. On her second chorus, Dizzy produces an elegant cup-muted solo to back her up that is well shaped and mature, with some of his characteristic downward runs early on and some repeated high notes toward the close. This is the best glimpse we have of his small band style during his period in Carter's group, and it suggests a small band soloist with poise and control. Plenty of the elements in his solo playing here would be retained in Dizzy's own bebop bands of a couple of years later.

It is possible that even more can be discovered about Dizzy's work during the Benny Carter period because the band appeared in a short movie or "soundie" intended for a kind of film jukebox that was in vogue in the early 1940s. *Case of the Blues* featured Maxine Sullivan and Carter's Sextet from the Famous Door, but while it is listed in various filmographies, a recent project to locate known copies of all soundies failed to establish whether any print survives. Dizzy claims that he first began to finalize the composition that became "Night in Tunisia" (originally known as "Interlude") during a break in rehearsals for this film.[34]

For him, Dizzy's months with Carter had another benefit. He was able to hear Art Tatum and Nat King Cole night after night when they shared the billing at Kelly's Stable. Tatum's rapidity of thought and adventurous solos were inspirational to someone with Dizzy's fascination for the piano. "I learned a lot about harmony from Benny Carter, Art Tatum, and Clyde Hart," he recalled.[35] Yet it was a vocal ballad from Nat Cole's repertoire that he adapted for his own use. Cole sang "How High the Moon" at a medium tempo, but Dizzy realized the potential of its underlying chord sequence for rapid improvisations and hijacked it to become one of the anthems of the bebop jam session as a high-speed instrumental number.[36]

As Dizzy's residency with Carter at the Famous Door drew to a close in February 1942, he looked around for other work. Carter himself formed a new big band to back Billie Holiday on a theatre tour, starting at the Apollo on April 10. Only Al Gibson, John Collins, and Charlie Drayton remained from the small group, with Jimmy Hamilton joining Eddie Heywood, and Kenny Clarke going to Henry "Red" Allen's band. Dizzy sat in at Harry Lim's Sunday afternoon jam sessions at the Village

Vanguard while he cast about for a job. At that stage, what was to become a world famous jazz club had not settled on a single style of music to present, and the Vanguard's regular evening sessions hosted calypso singers, or bluesmen like Leadbelly, who was featured there in what the *New Yorker* called its "smoke filled cellar . . . something like an air-raid shelter."[37]

During the next month or so, Dizzy recalled working with Claude Hopkins and "Fess" Williams. If, as Dizzy claimed, he also worked with Fletcher Henderson for a few days at the Apollo during this stage, then it would have been immediately after he finished with Carter. Henderson, who had recently returned to fronting an orchestra after a period of concentrating on arranging, brought "his own youthful band" into the Apollo for the week of February 20, after a tour of East Coast "theaters and armories."[38]

It was at about this time, during a gap between regular playing engagements, that Dizzy himself tried his hand at arranging for a living, selling his charts to Jimmy Dorsey and Woody Herman. The Herman orchestra arrived in town halfway through March 1942 and took over Benny Goodman's residency at the New Yorker Hotel on 8th Avenue at 34th Street, where they stayed until May 8. Woody Herman recalled Dizzy subbing on theatre dates with the band around this time and told many interviewers that he advised the young man to give up trying to play his unusual style on trumpet and stick to arranging. "I'm glad he ignored me!" Woody told Gene Lees, but so impressed was Woody by Dizzy's arranging that he agreed to pay Dizzy a hundred dollars a chart. The offer, which represented a real vote of confidence, remained a fond memory in Dizzy's mind, and he frequently drew attention to this gesture on Woody's part. In later life, Dizzy did not generally add the second part of the story, which, according to trumpeter Cappy Lewis, is that Woody's financier and lawyer, Mike Vallon, did not get round actually to paying Dizzy until the trumpeter arrived in his office and began to pick his fingernails with a particularly vicious-looking knife.[39]

At least three arrangements changed hands. In July the band made a disc of Dizzy's "Down Under," but for the time being his charts on "Swing Shift" and "Woody 'n' You" went unrecorded. His chart of "Grand Central Getaway," written for Jimmy Dorsey at around the same time, was recorded by Dorsey's big band as a V-Disc a couple of years later.

After a month or so of freelancing, Dizzy found a regular gig with West Coast bandleader Les Hite, who was nearing the end of a lengthy tour of the eastern states. He was almost certainly introduced to the band by Hite's arranger, Walter "Gil" Fuller, who later played a major role in Dizzy's own big bands. Dizzy joined Hite on March 31, immediately after a four-night booking in Brooklyn.

"When Les Hite went into a period of intensive rehearsal after concluding his booking at the Brooklyn Strand Theatre last week, he had a new man in each section," reported the *New York Amsterdam News*. "Most important of the changes was the acquisition of John 'Dizzy' Gillespie, quixotic young man with a horn recently heard with Benny Carter and Charlie Barnet. He replaced Stumpy Whitlock, who went back to his home in Omaha."[40] The other new arrivals were pianist Gerald Wiggins and trombonist Leon Comegys, who replaced the Woodman brothers Coney and Britt, who had been drafted. America's entry into World War Two at the end of 1941 had accelerated the rate at which musicians were compelled to leave the big swing orchestras, and the moves reported in the press of the time involve a mass of substitutions and switchings from band to band to compensate for draft losses.

Dizzy's relatively short stay with Hite (he left when Hite returned to the West on May 19) is mainly remembered because of Dizzy's dislike of drummer Oscar Bradley. A disciple of Cozy Cole, Bradley went into a series of loud ratamacues during one of Dizzy's solos, and Dizzy promptly sat down in protest and stopped playing. (Dizzy always claimed that this was at the Apollo, but this is unlikely, since Hite's band played the Apollo for the week of March 20, two weeks before Dizzy joined them.) Hite was wary of Dizzy, knowing his hot-tempered reputation and that he carried such a wicked-looking knife, so nothing came of the incident, but no doubt Hite was glad when the time came for Dizzy to leave the band. Their association is, however, preserved on disc, since Dizzy solos on "Jersey Bounce," cut around the second week of May 1942 originally for the Elite label, but released as the first discs to be issued by a new label called Hit (which was later to feature Bud Powell's inaugural recordings with Cootie Williams).[41]

The disc was an immediate success (pre-release orders topped 40,000). The soloists in turn are Wiggins, in a sub-Teddy Wilson style, tenorist Quedellis Martin, and guitarist Frank Pasley, before Dizzy enters. His solo is a dramatic piece of work, most noticeable for the way in which his relaxed, laid-back entry is followed by a flurry of descending high notes. This is no longer the voice of a Roy Eldridge disciple, however many stages removed, but quite clearly identifiable as the Dizzy Gillespie of the bebop era. It would seem that his tenure with Carter had allowed him to blossom, and the clever use of a repeated phrase in the center of the solo with its top notes shifted a half-step up the second time through is pure Gillespie.

His next discs were cut at the end of July, in the orchestra of Lucky

Millinder, who had re-formed his big band with the help of Bill Doggett and successfully overcome his financial problems. Quite when Dizzy joined the band is unclear. Millinder seems to have been on the road a lot with his new band, and reports show that in early 1942 he played throughout the South and Midwest, with dates in Nashville, Tampa, San Antonio, Houston, and Indianapolis.[42] During Dizzy's time in Les Hite's band, Lucky was in Chicago, but he made his way back to New York via Detroit, Baltimore, and Washington, D.C., ending up at the Savoy on May 30. It is most likely that Dizzy joined him there and would then have gone into the Apollo with Lucky in mid-June.

The band's discs from July 1942 are standard swing-band fare, with the exception of "Little John Special," which not only includes a version of the "Salt Peanuts" riff that Dizzy and Kenny Clarke had worked out the previous October, but also a fiery solo from Dizzy that confirms that his "Jersey Bounce" feature with Les Hite was not a one-off success and that his style had genuinely matured. This is the best and most consistent playing he recorded before the ban on commercial recording that began in August 1942 (discussed in the next chapter). The fusion of his playing and arranging skills, while operating inside a conventional swing format, is a forerunner of his own large bands of the middle to late 1940s. Dizzy also solos on Millinder's "Mason Flyer," but only the final high note part of his chorus, which is punched out over the whole band, is noteworthy here, showing Dizzy's growing confidence in the upper register and out-doing anything he recorded in his Calloway days.

The Millinder rhythm section swings hard, propelled by the drums of Panama Francis, and on bass is the Minton's bassist Nick Fenton, alongside Bill Doggett on piano. Fenton only spent a short time with Millinder, and Musicians' Union records show that his place was soon taken by George Duvivier. Despite his formative role in bebop, Fenton seems simply to have been in the right place at the right time, and some of his jam-session colleagues (notably pianist Al Tinney, who disliked Fenton's habit of tapping his foot heavily while playing)[43] were dismissive of his efforts. Yet the important aspect to note is that the rhythm section in particular is still playing in a standard swing style, despite the growing bebop influence in the brass phrasing over Dizzy's riff pattern and his own solo.

In several interviews and his autobiography, Dizzy recalls Millinder's curious personality, not only reinforcing Art Blakey's remarks quoted earlier about Millinder's formidable talent as a director but stressing his tendency to fire musicians on a whim. "One time he even fired himself," Dizzy quipped on many occasions. Most histories suggest that Dizzy left fairly soon after the July recording date, but in a couple of

Dizzy's own accounts he recalls that he quit (after a bout of lip trouble) when the band was at the Earle Theatre in Philadelphia. An examination of Lucky's schedule suggests that this must have been quite late in the year because in the band's relatively full itinerary up until mid-September, when they followed up a week at the Apollo with a further week at the Fox in Brooklyn, they do not seem to have spent two weeks in Philadelphia. Dizzy appears to have been with the band toward the end of the year when they toured the Midwest, since his name is listed in the personnel who appeared in Milwaukee with Millinder, and this is likely to have been after they finished in Brooklyn on September 19.

We do know, however, from several sources that Dizzy worked in Philadelphia for approximately two months between his time in Millinder's band and joining the "bebop nursery" of the Earl Hines Orchestra. From an announcement that "Dizzy forms band" in *Metronome*, we can assume that he began this during November 1942.[44]

Millinder, it seems, chose to exercise his penchant for firing musicians on Dizzy, and gave him two-weeks' notice. Since the band was in what amounted to Dizzy's hometown of Philadelphia, Dizzy had no trouble in securing a job for himself locally. To make the point that he had recovered from his lip trouble, he played relentlessly (including through other musicians' solos) for the second week of Millinder's Philadelphia booking. Lucky tried to hire him back for more money, but Dizzy was adamant—he was leaving and he was going to be a bandleader for the first time.

This all sounded very grand, but his gig was at one of Philadelphia's less well-known clubs, the Downbeat, run by Nat (or Nate) Segal. "The Downbeat opened with a bottle of Scotch, a record player and a pinball machine," wrote Irv Kline. "The club nurtured the new music at its very inception [and was] on the first floor of a building on 11th Street, halfway between the Earle Theatre and Chestnut Street. On the ground floor was the Willow Bar, where an old sign still [1991] proclaims: 'The Willow Bar, Where Old Friends Meet New Friends.' "[45] The club was later forced to close, after the U.S. Navy (who placed it off limits to personnel when sailors were caught fraternizing with black hookers) leaned on the city authorities to ensure that it did not continue in business. But in late 1942, the club took on a very similar role in Philadelphia to that of Minton's and Monroe's Uptown House in New York.

Dizzy took his duties as leader seriously, but, since Philadelphia was a short train ride from New York, he made sure he continued to appear in various jam sessions about town. Milt Gabler advertised Dizzy as a frequent participant in his Sunday jam sessions at Jimmy Ryan's,[46] and Dizzy also took a job on many other Sunday afternoons for Monte Kay, who ran similar jam sessions at Kelly's Stable. "Bird started sitting in. Dizzy came to lots of them," wrote Ira Gitler. "He used to come from Philly and pay a $6 fare to make a $10 job."[47] There was an added reason for Dizzy to be a frequent if somewhat underpaid commuter. Because of her work, Lorraine remained in New York and Dizzy spent weeknights at his mother's house in Philadelphia.

In Philadelphia, Dizzy's band included pianist Johnny Acea, his former colleague from Frankie Fairfax's band, Oscar Smith on bass, and a young white drummer called Stan Levey.[48] Smith wrote at some length about this residency, and a few of the points he makes are significant in the history of bebop. First, he remembers the Downbeat as being for a mainly white clientele, and that, despite its unprepossessing site, it featured "big name" jazz musicians. For the most part, these were individuals who were either passing through Philadelphia or had come over from New York for a one-night job and worked with Dizzy's band as an accompanying group. Charlie Shavers, playing his exciting brand of open trumpet (in contrast to his muted work with John Kirby), was one visitor whose chase choruses with Dizzy were an event everyone remembered.[49]

Smith recalls Acea as one of the best pianists he ever worked with, who also doubled on tenor sax. Dizzy would slide onto the piano stool and play chords while Acea took tenor solos. Dizzy was also keen to teach Stan Levey the intricacies of bebop rhythm and occasionally grabbed the drumsticks to show him a complex pattern. When a white guitarist, Teddy Walters, joined the band, Smith remembers the dazzling tempi that the band would strike up to show off the talents of visiting soloists, or of Dizzy himself, and also that "as a four-piece rhythm section, we met Dizzy's concept of harmony." Few testimonies so eloquently bear out Kenny Clarke's contention that Dizzy was a generous teacher and an evangelist for the new ideas that he and Clarke had worked out. It is also noteworthy that, in this early stage of the development of bebop, two members of this pioneering group were white. Dizzy's association with Levey was to continue on his pioneering trip to California in late 1945, and Smith summed up Levey in late 1942 as "a white guy who played well and sort of passed for black."[50]

From accounts of Charlie Parker's career at a similar point, it would seem that, as so often was the case, while Parker scuffled, Dizzy had landed a secure, relatively high-profile job in Philadelphia, with plenty of opportunity both to continue experimenting and working out how small group new jazz might be played with a schooled rhythm section. He also had the chance, both on his regular gig and his frequent visits to New York, to jostle with other talented and stimulating musicians. Parker, by contrast, had left Jay McShann's big band and worked for most of the time for small amounts of money with the house band at Monroe's Uptown House. Eyewitness accounts suggest that he became increasingly unkempt and disheveled as his personal life disintegrated into a round of drink and drugs and he lost the regular income and discipline offered by McShann. Parker appeared at many of the Sunday jam sessions frequented by Dizzy and they blew together on such dates, but their real association was to begin early in 1943 when they joined Earl Hines.

Most accounts have them together in Hines's band by the week of January 15, 1943, when Hines was at the Apollo in New York, shortly after Dizzy was billed as a featured soloist in an afternoon swing concert at the Savoy on January 9. This does not tally with Oscar Smith's memoirs, however, as he recalls the engagement with Gillespie in Philadelphia running on later into 1943. Smith is clear that he joined the group at the Downbeat after he left Warwick State Training School for Boys in New York, where he had been an instructor, at the end of the fall term (probably in December 1942), and remained with Dizzy until not long before he was drafted in March 1943. We know that Dizzy was in the Hines band by February 15, when a private recording of his jamming in Parker's hotel room was made. One of the first photographs of him with the trumpet section, taken on February 27, appears in the *Chicago Defender* of March 6, but it is probable that he was recruited to the band later than most earlier histories suggest and that for the first few weeks of 1943 he continued the work begun with Benny Carter in refining his ideas about small-group jazz.[51]

8

From Earl Hines to 52nd Street

When Earl Hines was asked what he thought about the experiments of Charlie Parker and Dizzy Gillespie in his 1943 band, he said, "No, I didn't like it. It was getting away from the melody a lot. But then we had to stay with what the young people were asking for at that particular time. And I knew these boys were ambitious and I always left a field for any improvement if they wanted to do it. I told them I didn't like these things, but Dizzy made me some arrangements, so did Charlie, and I had about a dozen bebop arrangements in my book."[1]

Earl Hines was one of the most influential figures in the development of jazz piano. He is mainly credited for creating the "trumpet" style in which the right hand doubles a melody line in octaves and adopts linear phrasing comparable to that of a trumpet soloist, rather than using all the harmonic possibilities open to a pianist. Several musicians, including Dizzy, have pointed out that this had a direct bearing on the bebop playing of people like Bud Powell and Al Haig, whose right-hand solo lines emulated those of bebop trumpets or saxophones.

Hines's influence was important to many pianists in the transitional period from swing to bop. Teddy Wilson, for example, praised Hines's touch, especially "the power of the whole hand behind the touch, not just the individual finger . . . he would always come at that keyboard and play each note with complete control and intention, no matter how loud, whereas many players, when they get carried away with emotion . . . stiffen and begin to hit the piano and consequently lose the rhythm."[2] In his autobiography, Wilson describes the technicalities of Hines's technique and demonstrates the lineage that filtered from Hines through his own playing and that of Art Tatum to the early boppers like Bud Powell and Al Haig. Yet this meant nothing to most members of the general public in the early 1940s for whom Hines was simply a successful bandleader who employed a heartthrob vocalist, Billy Eckstine, known as the "Sepia Sinatra." Hines's pioneering piano work from the 1920s onward, when he had matched the dazzling innovations of Louis Armstrong with an equally forward-looking keyboard style, was almost forgotten.[3]

In 1940, Hines did a deal with the Chicago "mob" and bought out the ownership of the band he had led in the city for twelve years, mainly at the Grand Terrace, and went on the road. Hines made no secret of the fact that his career had been significantly advanced by the patronage and protection of Al Capone and other notorious Chicago gangsters, recalling their kindnesses to him and his musicians with a gratitude that tended to overlook their wholesale involvement in corruption and violence. Once out on the road, Hines never again enjoyed the same long-term security and stability of employment that he had during the 1930s, and, from the time he finally broke up his band in 1948 to join Louis Armstrong's All Stars, his career had rather more troughs than peaks.

The early 1940s was the pinnacle of Hines's career as a leader, bringing with it considerable commercial success. On a trip to the West in 1940, their first year of "freedom," Eckstine and Hines recorded a simple blues called "Jelly Jelly," and the band suddenly had a hit on its hands. With further discs like "I Got It Bad and That Ain't Good," and "Stormy Monday Blues" (both from 1942) Hines suddenly found he was more popular than at any stage in his long career, and, after playing to packed houses in New York and Detroit, he received a greeting more familiar to present-day rock stars when he appeared in Philadelphia in November 1942.

"The famed pianist was literally mobbed by admiring jitterbugs. You've never seen anything like it, gang!" screamed the *Chicago Defender*.[4] "The band had played the town to an almost record crowd and on closing day Earl visited the store of a friend and the jam was on . . . so terrific was the jam that Hines lost his hat. His coat was in rags when police finally recovered the exponent of 'Jelly Jelly' blues. Police and old-timers say they haven't seen anything like it since the first visit by Joe Louis to this city of brotherly love. . . . In addition to mauling over Hines, the crowd in the store and outside screamed for Billy Eckstine. They wanted to see the man whose voice has aided in making Earl Hines's band the outfit of the year."

It is not clear whether it was during this visit that Hines, Eckstine, and the band's drummer, Rossier "Shadow" Wilson (Dizzy's former colleague from the Fairfax band in Philadelphia) recruited Dizzy to join the Hines band, apparently telling him that Parker had already agreed to join, and saying the same about Gillespie to Parker. Had Dizzy been aware of Hines's brush with adoring fans, it is probable he would have mentioned it. What he did recall was that "they came through Philadelphia, and cruised me out on the road with Earl Hines. Right after that, maybe two or three weeks later, we needed a tenor player and he got Charlie Parker in the band."[5] In view of the dating discussed in the last chapter, it is more likely that this recruiting mission took place while Hines was in Baltimore in late January 1943. This squares with Dizzy's memory that the band then went out on the road, rather than moving into New York for a few weeks, which is where Hines went after the Philadelphia mobbing of November. If this dating is correct, Charlie Parker would have joined the band as it made its way to Chicago for a short season in Detroit.

What we know beyond all reasonable doubt is that by Valentine's Day 1943, when the band played at the Savoy in Chicago (and living up to the auspicious legend of that date in that city, three people were shot at the ballroom within a single hour during the evening), the two main protagonists of bebop, Dizzy and Parker, were playing regularly together in the ranks of Hines's orchestra. Because of their presence and (as the draft forced further changes in personnel) that of more like-minded players as the months passed, the band is now recognized as having played a vital role in accelerating the development of modern jazz.

Parker did not even own a tenor sax at the time he joined Hines, and in numerous accounts the story is told of how Hines heard him playing alto and bought him a tenor so that he could take the place of Budd Johnson in the band's reed section. The personnel for the band who went on the road with Hines included Dizzy, Maurice "Shorty" McConnell, Gail Brockman, and Jesse Miller on trumpets; Bennie Green, August "Gus" Chappell, and Howard Scott on trombones; Andrew "Goon" Gardner and George Dorman "Scoops" Carry on altos; Thomas Crump and Charlie Parker on tenors; and John "Bearcat" Williams on baritone. The rhythm section, as well as Hines on piano, included Connie Wainwright on guitar, Jesse Simpkins on bass, and Rossier "Shadow" Wilson on drums, with Billy Eckstine as the sole vocalist, although since this list is drawn from AFM records it is probable that singer Madeline Greene was also present since she does not appear to have been a member of that union.[6]

When Dizzy and Parker first joined Hines, there was quite a contrast in the experience each brought. Dizzy, despite the quickfire temper that had gotten him into trouble with Calloway and Hite, was an experienced and widely traveled big band player, with the added benefits of his small-group work with Benny Carter and his own brief foray into leadership. Parker, although he had worked for some time with Jay McShann, was an altogether more erratic proposition. Almost all his experience outside McShann's band consisted of after-hours jamming. Nevertheless, he had already acquired a formidable reputation since

Earl Hines and His Orchestra, Apollo Theatre, 1943. Dizzy at the extreme left and a dark-spectacled Charlie Parker on the extreme right; the female pianist is Sarah Vaughan. (Frank Driggs collection)

arriving in New York, not least on the strength of reviews like Barry Ulanov's *Metronome* coverage of his Savoy residency with McShann: "The jazz set forth by the Parker alto is superb. Parker's tone tends to rubberiness and he has a tendency to play too many notes, but his continual search for wild ideas and the consistency with which he finds them, compensate for weaknesses that should be easily overcome."[7] Although Dizzy did not recall seeing Parker openly using drugs during their time together with Hines,[8] Parker was already the prisoner of a habit that had begun in his teenage years. Many of the anecdotes about his time with Hines focus on his erratic behavior.

Shortly before the band arrived in Chicago, it spent a week at the Paradise Theatre in Detroit. There Parker's habitual missing of occasional shows became apparent, despite Hines's stringent policy of fines. Billy Eckstine recalled Parker's sleeping below the stage during an entire show, having installed himself in the theatre overnight to ensure he would be there on time.[9] He also remembered that, even though Parker's absence from the reeds was immediately obvious to any listener from the way the band played its arrangements, Parker had perfected the art of appearing to play while actually sleeping behind his round-lensed dark glasses on the bandstand. Trumpeter Benny Harris, who joined the band a little later, remembered that the entire band ganged up on Parker when he had missed one show too many, jabbing at his shoulders and making him promise to straighten out—an experience Harris himself endured after experimenting with nembutals.[10]

But if Parker's personal life was chaotic, there was no doubting his musical genius. Hines marveled as Parker memorized arrangement after arrangement, seldom looking at the parts again after the first run-through and indeed often sitting on his "book" and facing a blank music stand as he played each show from memory.[11] This precocious talent was matched by Dizzy's work over the previous few years in trying to formalize his own new ideas into concepts that could be taught and passed on to others. As Parker's instinctive genius met Dizzy's insatiable curiosity to explore the possibilities of the new sounds in jazz, the two men spent many hours together on the road, working out their ideas. This was nothing new to Dizzy, who fell naturally back into the kind of backstage and after-hours rehearsing he had done in Calloway's band.

From very early on in their time in Hines's band, a recording survives made in a hotel room in Chicago the night after the murderous Valentine's Day dance at the Savoy. It was cut by yet another enthusiast with a portable disc recording machine, Bob Redcross. Despite the degradation of the glass and acetate masters, modern transfers of "Sweet Georgia Brown" are of sufficient quality to give a fascinating glimpse of the backroom developments in Dizzy and Parker's playing. Oscar Pettiford is the one-man rhythm section, having carted his bass across a snowy Chicago to Redcross's room at the Savoy Hotel to jam for the microphone.

Although Parker's style is modified through his transfer to tenor sax from his more usual alto, it does allow comparisons to be made between his playing and that of other tenor players. His evenness of tone, with occasional punctuations, is reminiscent of Lester Young, although Young would not have managed the effortless sequence of scalar runs that Parker's first solo is built around, which owes something to the harmonically based style of Chu Berry. Dizzy continues the vein of thought apparent in his Monroe's discs, sharing a few ideas with Parker, but mainly setting out short and distinctive phrases of his own and "worrying" them into a series of subtle variations throughout the length of each chorus before moving on to a new motif in the following chorus. Parker's playing—as one might expect from his respective background—has more to do with long and seamless development of ideas with less "architectural" connection between the phrases within each individual chorus. The same essential distinction remains apparent for much of their recording career together, where even a late recording like the 1953 Massey Hall concert in their mature style shows Dizzy shaping his solos for dramatic effect on a chorus-by-chorus basis, while Parker had a more instinctive and less structured approach.

Redcross's informal recordings are the only evidence of how Dizzy and Parker sounded at the time they were both in Earl Hines's orchestra, since their tenure in what has often been called the bebop "nursery" coincided with a two-year dispute between the major record labels and the American Federation of Musicians. Known as the "Petrillo ban" after AFM president James Petrillo, this effectively prevented any records from being cut between August 1942 and September 1943, when Decca became the first major company to concede to union demands for a royalty to be paid to the AFM for onward distribution to musicians to compensate for the loss of sales brought about by broadcasting. The other major companies settled during 1944, gradually restoring the record industry to normality, but not until after Dizzy and Bird were long gone from Hines's band. Only the testimonies of musicians who heard them, and a handful of reviews, give any clue as to the developments that took place.

"Time and time again when we were playing theatres," remembered Hines, "Dizzy used to go up in Charlie Parker's dressing room and read music out of his exercise book and Charlie Parker sometimes used to go down to Dizzy's and read music out of *his* exercise book. And these are the things that Dizzy and Charlie were playing . . . they had any number of long passages."[12]

This statement by Hines, and others like it, have been taken by many journalists and commentators over the years to mean that the two men simply swapped the books of formal exercises appropriate for their instruments. There might have been some point in this for developing instrumental prowess and mastering figures that were not naturally suited to the valves of the trumpet or the keys of the tenor sax, giving both men the opportunity to incorporate such figures into their respective solos, but Dizzy vehemently denied that this happened.[13] It seems more likely that Hines is referring to the manuscript books in which the two men worked out the core of arrangements that were added to his stock of "charts."

We do not know the details of all the dozen or so arrangements that Parker and Dizzy worked out together, but we do know that these included "Interlude," which was retitled "A Night in Tunisia" during Dizzy's stay with Hines, and also "Salt Peanuts," which had been gently evolving since Dizzy and Kenny Clarke worked it out fourteen months before in Ella Fitzgerald's band. Dizzy also arranged "East of the Sun" for singer Sarah Vaughan,[14] who had joined the band by mid-March 1943 alongside Madeline Greene, whom she eventually replaced.

Such a mythology has grown up around "A Night in Tunisia" that it can be hard to disentangle truth from legend. For example, Norman Weinstein's book on the subject[15] castigates critics like Max Harrison and James Lincoln Collier for being "dogmatically opposed to even considering the possibility of a hitherto unacknowledged link" between the piece and the "imaginative and metaphoric" impact of Africa on jazz, thereby further complicating attempts to take a clear view of how Dizzy wrote and developed the piece. Attractive as the idea is to use the piece as a symbol of "imaginings of Africa," the weight of evidence suggests that the piece existed well before it acquired the "Tunisia" tag, and that it was substantially complete by the time Dizzy left Benny Carter in February 1942 under the title of "Interlude." It did not appear on disc until late 1944, with Boyd Raeburn's big band cutting a full orchestral arrangement titled "Night in Tunisia" for V-Disc on Christmas Day 1944, and Sarah Vaughan recording it as "Interlude," accompanied by Leonard Feather's small group (including Dizzy) just under a week later on New Year's Eve.[16]

Yet we know that twenty months or so before these records were made, Dizzy had introduced an arrangement of the piece into Hines's band. It is probably safe to assume that Art Blakey's account of Dizzy's drafting the composition on a desk improvised from the lid of a garbage can in Houston is fanciful (although Dizzy's ready facility with his arranger's pencil probably led him to sketch out charts on almost any available surface during the Hines band's long road tours). Dizzy told Stanley Dance there was no truth in Blakey's colorful anecdote, and reconfirmed the story from Chapter 7 that it dates from the time of his "soundie" with Maxine Sullivan.[17] Hines himself claimed to have given the piece its "Night in Tunisia" title, as a consequence of the prominence in the contemporary news of the North African campaign of World War Two, and, although Dizzy refutes that story in his autobiography, several independent primary sources confirm Hines's claims.[18]

As originally conceived, "Night in Tunisia" depends for its originality on an extension of Dizzy's ideas from "Pickin' the Cabbage." Just as the earlier tune is built on the platform of an ostinato that undermines the conventional pulse of a big band rhythm section and includes a harmonic tension between major and minor keys, "Night in Tunisia" develops harmonic and rhythmic ideas in parallel. Dizzy built it around an A thirteenth chord resolving to D minor, coupled with the alternation between the Latin ostinato rhythm of the opening section and the straight four-to-the-bar of the bridge section; in his arrangement for Hines it was to be a trombone solo. Trombonist Bennie Green recalled being taught about the underlying bebop harmonies by Dizzy and given the tune to play as his feature with Hines.[19] A year later, when this was almost the only big band chart in the library of Billy Eckstine's band, Eckstine adapted the solo and played it himself on valve trombone, an instrument he took up after aspirations to be a trumpeter throughout his tenure with Hines.[20]

The Earl Hines Orchestra, with Parker and Gillespie, traveled widely throughout the United States for much of 1943, with arduous strings of one-nighters interspersed with full weeks at the usual East Coast theatres. For the most part, the one-night gigs were to entertain the growing number of enlisted servicemen at camps around the country who were awaiting the call to arms that would take them overseas. Between army bases, the band filled in with dances and concerts. Gillespie recalled in several interviews an incident in Pine Bluff, Arkansas (which probably took place during May 1943, in a period for which a full band itinerary is lacking, but during which it is known from AFM deposits that the band toured the South),[21] in which he was attacked and hit on the head with a bottle by a white man who made racist remarks while Dizzy was practicing the piano. Parker, whom Dizzy recalled as being a mine of information, obscure facts, and an impressive vocabulary, sprang to Dizzy's defense: "This guy hit me on the head with a bottle, and what did Charlie Parker say but, 'You took advantage of my friend, you cur!' "[22]

The attacker fell back, and, although Dizzy later related this story as an example of Parker's wit, he remembered: "I didn't appreciate it then, you know. I can realize that afterwards, but blood was all over my uniform." The band uniforms were an important part of Hines's show, and Sarah Vaughan was taken to task when she joined the band for her sloppy approach to hygiene and laundry. Billy Eckstine bought her a suitcase and supervised her wardrobe so that she did not let the side down, and no doubt Dizzy would have been concerned at ruining his jacket. On road tours the band was billeted with black families in many of the southern towns they visited, and laundry was done overnight by the musicians' hosts. With genuine admiration for the way his bandleader ran the operation, Dizzy recalled: "I loved Earl Hines . . . he was a great administrator."

Despite Dizzy's wild image, he was now beginning to show the kind of maturity that would turn his "dizzy" behavior into a marketable persona and conjoin it with a clear sense of a bandleader's values. The old Calloway discipline was ingrained in him, and in Hines he found a leader who combined Cab's stern leadership style with the kind of genuine musical talent that Dizzy, as a pianist, was in awe of.

Knowing Hines's keyboard prowess—and that he was never shy to take a solo—the band used to exploit his solo talents and leave him playing chorus after chorus on his feature numbers, while they delayed their entry. "He could play," remembered Dizzy. "We used to make him play more than one, two or three choruses. We wouldn't come in, and he'd play and play, and he'd be saying, 'Why won't you come in.'" Yet coupled with this gentle teasing was a genuine respect for a leader who was prepared to try new ideas and give Parker and Gillespie a chance to work out their embryonic charts with the full band. "He could put things together on stage with a band," said Dizzy. "With a limited amount of music he could tell them what to play with a 'You do this' and 'Yeah! well done.' We did some things like that, special things and it was very nice."[23]

The opportunities that Hines gave his up-and-coming sidemen were noticed by the musicians who came to hear them as they traveled around the country. In March 1943, the band played a week in Philadelphia. The young Howard McGhee, a trumpeter who greatly admired Dizzy, came to the shows at the Fays Theatre and afterward went back to their hotel with Parker and Gillespie. They blew all night in the kind of session captured on record in Chicago by Bob Redcross, and McGhee was able to learn firsthand from Dizzy and Parker how their ideas were developing.[24] This scene was repeated wherever the band played for the general listening public, enabling interested musicians within striking distance of each gig to go out of their way to hear the group. Even the wayward Parker resumed some of the discipline he had displayed with McShann and complemented the inspiration and genius of his solo playing by corralling the reed section together for rehearsals. Billy Eckstine recalled them gathering in Parker's room in a St. Louis hotel to rehearse until three o'clock in the morning, and, while it is doubtful that nobody knocked on the wall to complain (Eckstine suggesting that the sheer energy of the music forestalled complaints), Parker entered into the spirit of excitement and musical adventure that permeated the band.[25]

On stage, Hines's band was unusual to watch because there were two pianos set up in front of the stage. He sat at one; Sarah Vaughan was at the other. She played chords when Earl got up to direct or talk, and he backed her when she walked to the vocal microphone. It was an arrangement Earl had pioneered in 1920s Chicago, when he and Willie Hamby had shared the piano duties in the band at the Sunset Café where he backed Louis Armstrong. In the 1940s, Sarah's employment on the payroll as a pianist rather than a singer simplified Hines's life, he could treat her as a musician, not a cabaret artiste, and her employment details could be rationalized into the same lists of transfers as the rest of his musicians when the band was on the road. For the same reason, Hines did not discourage Eckstine's efforts at playing brass instruments, and Eckstine traveled as a full-fledged member of the AFM. Sarah was to stay on when, in August 1943, Eckstine along with nine other members of the band quit.

"I had been with Earl going on five years," recalled Eckstine. "He said he was going down South again and I told him: 'Hell, no! I don't want to go down South any more, Earl.' I'd just gotten married so I said: 'I think I'm going to stay around in New York and work down 52nd Street.' So I put my notice in and when I did, nine of the guys put theirs in, too."[26]

The band finished a week at the Royal in Baltimore on August 12 and immediately set off for Winston-Salem, North Carolina, to start a couple of weeks of one-nighters across the South. Even though these would have taken him close to his original hometown, there is no evidence that Dizzy made this trip, and most accounts confirm that he and Parker departed at the same time as Eckstine, leaving Hines to an ill-judged experiment of adding a female string section to his depleted ranks after his return to New York in September.[27]

Initially, the plan was for Eckstine to form his own band, employing many former Hines alumni, but this did not materialize for several months, so Dizzy once more found himself casting about for work. He played briefly with Coleman Hawkins at this point, at Kelly's Stable, and this is the engagement mentioned in Dizzy's autobiography. As Dizzy's own account makes clear, he left before a week was out because Hawk only paid him union scale and not the few dollars more that would indicate a suitable rate for a recognized and well-established soloist.[28]

Within a couple of months, an opportunity presented itself that most jazz musicians in the mid-1940s would have given their eyeteeth for. Duke Ellington's Orchestra came to town to do a month-long season at the Capitol Theatre, in a show that featured Lena Horne, the "World's greatest monopod dancer" Peg-Leg Bates, and the Deep River Boys, a vocal group that had recorded a year or two before with Fats Waller.[29] The show played between screenings of the movie *Phantom of the Opera*. Because Ellington's regular trumpeter Harold "Shorty" Baker did not belong to the New York local of the AFM, he (together with one or two other members of the band) was to be replaced for the engagement by a New York–based substitute. Dizzy took the job and found himself alongside Rex Stewart, Wallace Jones, and Taft Jordan in the trumpet section of the world's most famous jazz orchestra.

"Several men sat in the trumpet section, including for a few quick weeks, Dizzy Gillespie," recalled Rex Stewart,[30] writing about a time of great change in the band in the wake of bassist Jimmy Blanton's death and the departures of mainstays like tenorist Ben Webster and clarinetist Barney Bigard, who was replaced by Dizzy's old Philadelphia colleague Jimmy Hamilton.

But if Stewart remembered the engagement with affection, Dizzy did not, as he felt completely excluded by a band whose lack of com-

Dizzy with Duke Ellington, Capitol Theater, New York City, 1943. (Frank Driggs collection)

munication between one another was legendary. In his autobiography, Dizzy recalled the other members of the trumpet section "silent as high priests in a temple" about the complexities of the arrangements.[31] (Reading Duke's parts depended on a degree of clairvoyance on the part of new members of the band to figure out the alphabetical cues from section to section.) Apart from one evening when one of the other trumpeters was absent and Duke gave Dizzy solo after solo, he was little more than hired help in the Ellington Orchestra and was pleased to leave at the end of the theatre engagement, recalling only Lena Horne's contribution to the stage show as outstanding. He did, however, leave a small number of recordings with Duke for the World Transcription service, which, because it was recording for broadcasting, sidestepped the AFM recording ban.

Unfortunately, Dizzy's presence is virtually undetectable on the eleven different numbers he cut with Duke, some of them running into several takes. The brass section work, however, is exemplary on "Rockin' in Rhythm," and Dizzy's presence can actually be discerned for a fraction of a second on "Blue Skies," when the trumpets engage in some serious competition with one another behind high-note solos from Jordan and Stewart, respectively.

After leaving Ellington, when the Capitol show closed on November 10, a new opportunity opened up for Dizzy as he and bassist Oscar Pettiford got together to lead a quintet. "We turned down $75 a week apiece offered by Kelly's Stable," recalled Pettiford (ironically the same amount that Dizzy says he had held out for with Hawkins). "I had worked at the Onyx Club before, and I was good friends with the owner Mike Westerman, so I asked him if I could be re-engaged. I was welcomed back gladly."[32]

The Onyx was one of the growing number of small clubs that had opened in the basements of the brownstones on 52nd Street. "You went down a few steps and into this long low basement room that held maybe sixty to seventy people, with a small stage at the end," remembered pianist Billy Taylor, "and that's what most of the clubs along the Street were like."[33] Dizzy had worked on the Street before, with Benny Carter at Kelly's Stable, but this opportunity to co-lead a band that he and Pettiford determined would be devoted to the new music was a very significant event, not only in his life and in the history of modern jazz but also for 52nd Street.

The group that opened there was pictured in the *New York Amsterdam News* on December 11, and joining Dizzy and Pettiford were Don Byas on tenor, Max Roach on drums, and Billy Taylor on piano. The newspaper report ignores the fact that the band was co-led, announcing: "The Onyx Club is scoring nightly with the new John (Dizzy) Gillespie Band, led by Gillespie, former trumpet star with Cab Calloway."[34] It appears that for the first few weeks of the engagement, the personnel fluctuated considerably. Bassist and entrepreneur Jimmy Butts listed Thelonious Monk as the pianist and Lester Young as the tenor player, while Taylor made clear that he was taking time off from his regular job with Ben Webster at the Three Deuces to play in the Gillespie/Pettiford group.[35]

"It was never my gig," he told the author. "When they opened, they actually didn't have a piano player, because they wanted to get Bud Powell. So I sat in with Dizzy. As a matter of fact, throughout his long career that's all I ever did with Dizzy, was sit in, because although we worked together quite a bit over the years I was never actually a member of his regular band at any time. I sat in a lot at the Onyx, during that December, and I kept getting back late to play my next set across the Street with Ben Webster, so Ben fired me. I got my job back a little later, but for a while there I was playing quite often at the Onyx, and Monk was doing the same, taking time off from his job with Hawk."[36]

The Onyx Club band, December 1943. (Left to right) Max Roach, drums; Don Byas, tenor; Oscar Pettiford, bass; George Wallington (who had recently taken over from Billy Taylor), piano; Dizzy, trumpet. (Frank Driggs collection)

Dizzy originally hoped to get Charlie Parker and Bud Powell to join this prototype bebop band. Parker, however, had been characteristically inefficient about organizing his union transfer from his home Kansas City branch of the AFM (Local 627). He had never altered his affiliation during his months with Hines (all surviving transfers showing his 627 affiliation, along with baritonist John Williams, amid the predominantly Chicago-based members of Hines's band) so, when he came off the road, along with Eckstine and Dizzy, Parker found he was unable to work in New York, just as Dizzy had been caught out on his return from Europe with Teddy Hill.

Parker returned to Kansas City for a while and apparently never got Dizzy's telegram asking him to join the group at the Onyx. Powell, on the other hand, was a regular member of Cootie Williams's big band, and at nineteen was under Cootie's legal guardianship. Williams refused to allow Powell to quit, and Powell went on to make his first records with Cootie in January 1944. It is fascinating to speculate that, had Powell not remained with Williams, he might never have suffered the appalling head injuries he received during a beating from police in Philadelphia, which began his history of mental decline and set in motion the events that drastically curtailed his musical career.[37]

When Pettiford and Dizzy opened, Don Byas had been appearing opposite them as a soloist with Al Casey's trio and Billie Holiday. (Casey remembers their working at the Onyx and says he was also featured opposite Dizzy at the Downbeat across the Street a few months later. At the Onyx, Casey made way for Pete Brown around the time Dizzy and Pettiford arrived, but returned to back Billie in the New Year after she had been on the road with Teddy McRae.) Casey's trio at the time was pianist Sam Clanton, a gentle Nat Cole-style player mostly forgotten about today, and bassist Al Matthews.[38]

Byas was never an entirely convincing bebopper, but, rather like Coleman Hawkins, he was a sufficiently adaptable tenorist to amend his playing to cope with all the vitality, speed, and harmonic originality of the new jazz, and he rapidly changed bands at the Onyx to work with Dizzy and Pettiford rather than Casey. "He'd worked with just about everybody," recalled Billy Taylor, "Erroll Garner and others up and down the Street. But Don wasn't a big enough name to draw the crowds on his own. In fact, Budd Johnson, who eventually replaced him, was far better known to the general public because he'd been with some high-profile big bands like Earl Hines, which had put him in the public eye more than Don."[39]

During those last weeks of 1943, Dizzy patiently taught Billy Taylor the changes to several of the new compositions the band played. Although he had written down some of the sequences, Dizzy preferred to explain what he was after by demonstrating at the keyboard. Taylor told the author: "Dizzy said, 'I could write out the chords for you, but I want this voicing here, and that voicing there. When I write chord symbols, you have a choice and that doesn't mean you'll play the voicing I'm after.' Of all the people who were taking part in this bebop revolution, Dizzy was the one who really intellectualized it. I'd met him when he was playing the Howard Theatre in Washington, where I grew up, when he came there with Earl Hines. I knew Benny Harris, who was in Earl's trumpet section and who was vital in spreading the word about the changes Diz and Bird were making, and it was Benny who introduced us. And so I already knew Dizzy when I found myself sitting in with his band at the Onyx. In fact, even before Benny introduced us the word was out on Dizzy among musicians. 'Here are some guys to watch in Earl's band: Dizzy and Charlie Parker.' I think Dizzy was so keen to get his new concepts out there that that's why he started writing arrangements. Trying to get the widest group of people to buy in to what he was doing. Once he started teaching me those changes at the Onyx, he became a mentor to me, and I've never forgotten it."[40]

Some cynical observers believe that many of the bop innovations were spontaneously conceived and that the underlying theory was concocted later to justify the unusual sounds. Accounts like Taylor's make clear that this was not the case; right from the outset, Dizzy's profound knowledge of harmony underpinned everything he set out to achieve, with a firmness of resolve and understanding he never lost. Years later, trumpeter Jon Faddis was describing this aspect of Dizzy's work. Hearing Dizzy solo: "You can't really tell what the tune is and you say, 'Well, wait a minute, what's he doing here?' If you say that to Dizzy, he'd go to the piano and say, 'Look! Here's the chord, and here's what I did.' He would pick out this note and you'd say, 'Whoa'—it would just make your mouth drop open."[41]

As 1943 drew to a close, a young white pianist called George Wallington took the piano chair on a permanent basis. Wallington is one of the more obscure characters in the history of bebop. Classically trained, the slender boyish pianist was nicknamed "Lord" Wallington by the other musicians because of his aloof mannerisms. In fact, these concealed a clear focus in his life and work and he consistently sought out musical company where he could learn and extend his ideas, having no qualms about leaving music in due course or turning down an offer to join Gerry Mulligan, an action that led directly to the saxophonist's famous piano-less quartet. Although he had grown up in New York, Wallington (whose real name was Giacinto Figlia) had actually been born in Sicily. After an eighteen-year career in music in which he produced some of modern jazz's most enduring compositions, such as "Godchild" and "Lemon Drop," he went into the family air-conditioning business and only returned to play for a few brief guest appearances and a couple of albums in the mid-1980s, not long before his death (six weeks after Dizzy's) in February 1993.

Musically, Wallington was directly influenced by Bud Powell, and his playing tended to be minimalist in ensembles and a passable equivalent of Powell's style of extended linear right-hand playing when he was allowed a solo. For the teenage pianist, anxious to learn and extend his musical ideas, his partnership with Dizzy was ideal. "Music school was always open on the job," recalled Dizzy,[42] who repeated the coaching he had recently gone through for Taylor with the nineteen-year-old Wallington.

The irascible Pettiford, whose temper was as volatile as Dizzy's and whose fondness for the bottle occasionally led him into violent confrontations, was less accommodating. "White muthafucka, can't play shit!" Pettiford would shout (according to Dizzy[43]) when Wallington missed a chord change. Dizzy had nevertheless made a wise choice of pianist, and we know from Billy Taylor's account that in the band's helter-skelter arrangements and aggressive ensembles the pianist would be dominated by the pounding bass of Pettiford and the swirling drums of the young Max Roach, making Wallington's understated approach ideal for the group.

Roach was Wallington's exact contemporary and had also grown up in and around New York when his parents moved to the north Brooklyn suburb of Bedford-Stuyvesant from the picturesquely named Dismal Swamp on the Virginia/North Carolina border, where he was born. Despite a formal training from a Scot who would hum the drum patterns he wanted the young Roach to play, an abortive attempt at a course in the Manhattan School of Music, and a practical apprenticeship of playing variety shows at the Darktown Follies on Coney Island, Roach's heart was in 52nd Street from his early teens. He would draw on a moustache using his mother's eyeliner and bluff his way into Kelly's Stable and the other clubs, or uptown at the Savoy Ballroom, where he would stand only a few feet away from his idol Chick Webb.

Unlike Kenny Clarke, who was an instinctive big band drummer, Roach's talents were geared toward small-group jazz. "When he met Dizzy and Bird, he changed his style and although he was briefly with Benny Carter's Orchestra, what he was doing didn't sit well in a big band," recalled bassist Ray Brown, who worked with Roach a year or so later. "He was basically a small band drummer."[44] From his teenage years,

Roach had a uniquely identifiable sound, and players like baritone saxophonist Cecil Payne (a boyhood friend) claimed he could identify the drummer from outside any hall he was playing in. Roach's approach was lighter and less dramatic than Clarke's, taking the broken rhythms of Clarke's style as a starting point rather than an end in itself.

In virtually every history of the development of bebop and all the earlier biographies of Dizzy, his band with Johnson, Wallington, Pettiford, and Roach has been the subject of endless speculation. Because it was not known to have recorded, the only evidence of its originality and importance is from eyewitness accounts, or, indeed, from the musicians themselves who played in it. In 1995, however, as part of their work to produce a comprehensive edition of all Gillespie's recordings, the French discographers Alain Tercinet and Philippe Baudoin discovered that Bob Redcross, the man who had recorded Parker and Gillespie together during their stay with Earl Hines, had a single surviving acetate of the Pettiford/Gillespie band on 52nd Street. With the assistance of the collector Jean Portier, they were able to produce a sufficiently clear version of "Night in Tunisia" to be issued. The results unequivocally show that the

The Onyx Club band, early 1944. Roach, Budd Johnson (replacing Byas) on tenor, Pettiford, Wallington, and Dizzy. (Frank Driggs collection)

music being played by the group had developed in virtually every respect into what would now be classified as bebop. Only Dizzy and Roach were playing in ways identical to their well-known bebop recordings of a year or two later, yet the ensemble as a whole is a more unified bebop band than several of the studio groups with which Parker and Gillespie recorded in 1945. Bebop had clearly developed into its full form by late 1943.

Budd Johnson's tenor begins the recording, paraphrasing the "Night in Tunisia" theme, and cascading into a series of Parkeresque runs after a repeated arpeggio figure early in the chorus. Although his style still has firm roots in the rhapsodic tenor ballad approach of Hawkins and Berry, Johnson's choice of notes and intervals is clearly influenced by bebop harmonic thinking, especially in the final eight measures before Dizzy enters for one of his most accomplished solos. All the elements of mature Gillespie are present, from the repeated urgent phrase of the opening to the stately high notes of his middle eight and the rapid downward cascades of the following chorus. But what distinguishes this solo from Dizzy's 1942 work with Millinder is that for the first time the rhythmic setting is right. To prepare the ground, Roach has been breaking up the time with powerful snare and bass drum punctuations from the middle of Johnson's solo and, as Dizzy enters, Roach stirs things up more, echoing Dizzy's phrasing with a flurry of rimshots and snare patterns. The pulse is carried by Pettiford, with stabbing chords from Wallington, whose own solo is a mild disappointment, with some surprisingly archaic stride figures early on. As Johnson and Dizzy bring the opening countermelody back over Wallington's piano, Dizzy slips in a cup mute and the final section has the familiar sound of a Parker/Gillespie quintet, anchored by Dizzy's muted horn. The existence of this vital recorded document confirms the innovations made by the band and that, however great Bird's influence was on the ideas of the group's members, it was not Charlie Parker but Dizzy Gillespie who pioneered bop in the clubs of 52nd Street.

Only a matter of weeks before this documentary disc was cut, Kenny Clarke had introduced Max Roach to Coleman Hawkins, by recommending Max to replace him in the saxophonist's quartet at Kelly's Stable when Clarke was drafted. By the time Roach made his studio recording debut with Hawk's quartet in December 1943, he had left the Stable and was already working each evening in the Gillespie/Pettiford group. Hawkins was sympathetic to the aims of the new band and its musicians, and he must have realized that, as it became established on "the Street," the group was doing something original and innovative. This was not simply confined to the music itself, but to the group's whole approach to its work. What this was is best summed up by the British critic Charles Fox, who perceived "an unspoken policy, a psychological shift on the part of the musicians that performers should create the kind of music they wanted to play. If audiences liked it, so much the better, but this was no longer the first priority."[45]

Hawkins took the opportunity offered by the numerous small record companies that were springing up in the wake of the AFM recording ban to identify himself with this policy and annexed virtually all of Dizzy and Pettiford's band for a couple of recording sessions in February 1944. "He wanted his coat to be pulled with this kind of music, and he wanted to be in first," remembered Budd Johnson.[46]

The group that recorded as "Coleman Hawkins and His Orchestra" consisted of rhythm with a full big band trumpet and saxophone section, but no trombones. The Onyx Club rhythm team of Pettiford and Roach were present, with jam-session supremo Clyde Hart on piano in place of Wallington. Both Don Byas and his replacement at the Onyx, Budd Johnson, were in the saxophone section, along with Leo Parker, Leonard Lowry, and Ray Abrams, while Vic Coulson and Ed Vandever joined Dizzy in the trumpets.

Hart was so comprehensively talented that he was the automatic choice to play piano as the most reliable player to anchor a studio session. Hart's role in the development of modern jazz has often been underestimated. He was the epitome of the transitional player, with a rhythmic sense firmly couched in swing and a natural feeling for conventional swing harmonies, but his ear was so acute and his pianistic ability so great that he easily mastered most of the bebop innovations far more efficiently than almost all his generation of swing players. "Clyde's ability was really respected by Dizzy," Billy Taylor told the author. "I remember being at a jam session in Harlem with a dozen other pianists when Art Tatum was playing. Art pulled off a particularly impressive break, and we asked him how it was done. The only other player in the room who got the hang of it instantly was Clyde Hart, and Dizzy knew and respected this aspect of Clyde's talents."[47]

Despite being titular leader, Hawkins knew that he should not try to make the running in selecting the newer players—or the music to be played—for his "new jazz" session. "Dizzy was the straw boss," recalled Roach.[48] "He did some of the arranging, matter of fact, I guess, most of the arranging on that date. He was the guy who organized and called the musicians and since I was the drummer in his band, of course, he called me in on the date." Johnson and Hart actually provided one of the charts cut on that first session, "Bu-dee-daht," but the most interesting piece from February 16 is Dizzy's "Woody 'n' You" (no doubt slightly amended for the available instrumentation from the arrangement he had produced the previous year for Woody Herman, but not yet recorded by the Herd). In the past, most authorities generally agreed that this was the first genuine bebop recording, although in truth it is only slightly further advanced than Dizzy's efforts with Millinder on "Little John Special," with the exceptions being Dizzy's own solo and the underlying chord progression, and it is not in the same league as Redcross's acetate of the Onyx Club band.

The beginning hints at things to come, and a break from Pettiford suggests a bass pattern that never subsequently recurs as the band struggles for a few bars to regain the opening tempo. In his later recordings of the piece, Dizzy opted for a Latin rhythm, but on this session the band wavers momentarily and then plumps for a four-square pulse. The opening chorus gives Hawkins the melody with some rather slushy sax accompaniment (which survived almost unchanged into Gillespie's later chart for his own big band, retitled "Algo Buena"), with only the trumpets hinting at the bop-inspired phrase of the underlying theme as each eight-bar phrase ends. Hawkins then picks up this bop theme for a powerful solo, with the trumpets following Dizzy through a spontaneous, if ragged, sequence of accompanying punctuations that hint at the absent Latin meter. Then Dizzy's own solo follows—a model of clarity after what has gone before, and with Pettiford and Roach naturally falling into their supporting roles from 52nd Street. Roach punctuates aggressively on snare and bass drum, while his ride cymbal and Pettiford's surging bass keep the rhythm moving forward. In Dizzy's solo the old "Bye Bye Blues" figure reappears in the second part of the middle eight, this time at the pitch in which it was subsequently to appear in much of his recorded work. The closing brass and reed figures are a backdrop for Hawkins, whose final solo is intense and passionate, but during which Roach and Pettiford fall back to supply a conventional swing rhythm.

When the band reconvened a few days later on February 22, they cut a blues, "Disorder at the Border," some of which later resurfaced under the title "Cool Breeze." Pettiford's personality is immediately imposed on the piece, as Hart comps for his solo breaks. With all the horns settling into a riff pattern, Dizzy superimposes a different motif with muted trumpet—a technique he had used successfully in earlier arrangements, but given added drama here by a sudden rimshot punctuation from Roach as Dizzy scurries into his highest register, on open horn.

The Hawkins recordings may not be full-fledged bebop, not least in terms of the leader's own playing, but, taken as a whole, they represent a considerable advance on anything that had gone before. As commercial recordings that appeared at the time, rather than a privately recorded fragment that emerged over half a century later, they were among the most influential discs of the pioneer bebop period.

9
Billy Eckstine

As 1944 began, the Gillespie/Pettiford group was well established at the Onyx Club. With a regular personnel (Budd Johnson on tenor having replaced Byas and George Wallington firmly ensconced on piano), it was able to develop as a unit in much the same way as Benny Carter's sextet had done a couple of years earlier. Before long, apparently due to Dizzy's habit of identifying the next piece for the band by scat-singing a phrase or two from the head arrangement and ending with the syllables "be-bop," the new style of music played by the group acquired a name.

Earl Hines was given to saying that the name had grown up during Dizzy and Parker's tenure in his orchestra: "Their arrangements had any number of long passages in them, and the reporters didn't know what to call that kind of music. At the end of the theme, by the time they got through finishing it, they'd run out of breath. They'd go 'Diddly, diddly, bebop!' And that's why they called it bebop."[1] But although not one review of Hines's famous 1943 orchestra mentioned the word at the time, it started to appear in print following Dizzy's run at the Onyx.

" 'Bebop' is the name of a song written by Dizzy Gillespie," recalled Max Roach in conversation with fellow drummer Art Taylor. "As far as I can remember, critics called the music bebop when they came into the club where we were playing at that particular time on 52nd Street. The music was so unique and unusual, so fresh and original; they asked Dizzy what he called it and perhaps Dizzy misunderstood their question, or maybe he told them the title of the tune . . . we were playing a song called 'Bebop' and they just called all the music bebop."[2] In fact, it seems that the tune in question was "Bu-dee-daht," Budd Johnson's piece that he and Clyde Hart had arranged for the Coleman Hawkins record date. Barry Ulanov, one of the critics who took up the phrase, remembered: "This just as often became 'Bu-re-bop!' Because the emphasis was on the last two notes of the triplet, the tag was best remembered, for humming and other descriptive purposes, as 'rebop.' And because man's taste for the poetic, whether he so identifies it or not, leads him again and again to alliteration, 'rebop' became 'bebop.' "[3]

To make the most of the group's growing body of head arrangements, Budd Johnson persuaded Dizzy to write out lead sheets for most of the tunes so that he and Dizzy could play them in unison or close harmony.[4] Dizzy did so, and this became the moment when a significant body of the new themes he had worked out—first with Kenny Clarke and later with Charlie Parker—were systematically committed to paper. Judging by the recordings of these pieces that surfaced on various record dates during the following year, Dizzy acknowledged his debt to the thematic voicings of the Benny Carter/John Kirby small band tradition in creating the initial core repertoire of bebop.

Although Don Byas had left the band late in 1943 to follow up what proved to be an unsuccessful opportunity to find a place in the Ellington Orchestra (something that did not eventually happen until 1950, when he replaced Charlie Rouse on a European tour), on at least one occasion before he went he had gotten drunk on the bandstand at the Onyx. When this happened, the mean streak in Dizzy's character emerged. He forcibly reminded Don that he could easily best him in any squabble while he was drunk and that Don's playing had fallen apart under the influence of alcohol. For the rest of his stay, Don's playing improved and he kept the drinking under control.[5] The same could not be said of Oscar Pettiford. Dizzy and visiting musicians like trombonist Trummy Young got involved in fights trying to protect Pettiford from the effects of his pugnacious behavior: "Dizzy and I both got beat up trying to help him," remembered Young; even Dizzy's vicious-looking carpet knife failed to keep trouble at bay.[6]

By March, things had come to a head, and Dizzy and Pettiford parted company. Their joint band was still billed at the Onyx at the start of the month (although Dizzy and Al Casey were listed as headliners, with Oscar Pettiford and Billie Holiday as their respective star attractions).[7] By March 25, Dizzy had taken the rest of the band, with Leonard Gaskin replacing Pettiford, to a new residency a few doors away on 52nd Street, not as he recalled in his autobiography (misdating the whole sequence of events by a year) at the Downbeat, but at its forerunner, Chick Goldman's Yacht Club, where he was billed as the "Swingsational Dizzy Gillespie with Budd Johnson." Trummy and Lester Young jointly fronted the other band on the bill, with whom Billy Eckstine was featured vocalist.

Trummy and Eckstine had opened there a week earlier, with pianist and singer Una Mae Carlisle in support, and the Dizzy/Budd Johnson band took her place. "52nd Street, long the home of femme torch singers, gave the male side a chance with the debut of crooner Billy Eckstine, ex-Earl 'Father' Hines vocalist," reported the *New York Age*, and the following week Hines himself, plus Louis Armstrong, were guests of honor at the club's celebrity night to promote Eckstine and the opening of Dizzy's band.[8]

During this period, Eckstine's plans to lead his own big band began to crystallize, and a record date was planned for April 13. Although the band got together in the studio, it was not to become an active unit until June, and in the intervening time Eckstine himself appeared as a solo act opposite Boyd Raeburn at the Apollo, before briefly taking over Pettiford's spot at the Onyx. By May, the new music was no longer being featured every night on the Street. Dizzy left the Yacht Club (which closed around this time, reopening a few weeks later as the Downbeat) and, as he waited to join Eckstine, he briefly took Charlie Shavers's place in John Kirby's sextet at the Aquarium Restaurant, while Pettiford's group (in which Joe Guy had taken Dizzy's role) was finally ousted from the Onyx by ex-Calloway drummer Cozy Cole.

Some accounts suggest (unfairly) that Dizzy was replaced for Kirby's broadcasts by Charlie Shavers, but this is untrue, and the surviving air-shots show Dizzy's apt blending of his new ideas with the Kirby style, further confirming Ulanov and Feather's observation about the close links between the emergent bebop small groups and Kirby's trendsetting orchestra.[9] On a characteristically tight arrangement like Charlie Shavers' "Close Shave," Dizzy stays well within the parameters of Shavers's own approach to this type of chamber jazz, his attack blending perfectly with Buster Bailey's clarinet and George Johnson's alto. The emphasis and pointing of the phrases show how effortlessly Dizzy could cope with this tightly muted ensemble work, and his muted lead and short solos on "Taking a Chance on Love" only hint at his bebop affinities, otherwise remaining well within the swing boundaries laid out by pianist Ram Ramirez and drummer Bill Beason.

A week later, on Dizzy's second session with Kirby to have been recorded off the air, his confidence is up. He contributes a dazzling solo to the closing "Rose Room." Following Bailey's statement of the theme, Dizzy's entrance is nothing short of electrifying, with a series of repeated high notes leading into an elegant countermelody at the very top of his range. In the channel he reuses the "Bye Bye Blues" figure before returning to his opening motif for the final eight bars. This is playing of the same high order as the solo from his quintet with Pettiford, and it would immediately have been tagged as "bebop" were it to have appeared in a commercial recording of the period. Yet it sat happily inside the regular output of Kirby's group, with no uneven boundaries of style. Even Ramirez and Beason adapt to Dizzy's off-center phrasing, although it is his range and choice of notes rather than purely rhythmic elements that mark this solo as unusual, and it holds more interest than his other surviving solos on "Irresistible You" and a wearisomely slow "Perdido."

The imminent formation of the Billy Eckstine big band, however, was to be an event just as important in the history of bebop as the first few months in which the music could be heard every night on 52nd Street or the demonstrable proof of Dizzy's affinities with the style of John Kirby. Despite a short life and constantly fluctuating personnel owing to the war, the Eckstine orchestra acquired a reputation as the first genuine bebop big band, and by Eckstine's stroke of genius in appointing Dizzy as his musical director, Dizzy got his first taste for what was to become the overwhelmingly successful achievement of his career: adapting the modern jazz idiom to the scale of a full-sized big band. No other leader has achieved this as well or as consistently in the history of jazz, yet initially Dizzy and Eckstine's efforts were rewarded by the hostility of critics, notably Leonard Feather.

As noted in Chapter 7, because of his involvement in playing, composing, promoting, and producing, as well as his journalism, Feather was a powerful ally for any musician; consequently, he was an equally formidable adversary. At precisely this time, Feather (closely supported by Ulanov) chose to launch an attack of unprecedented venom on the traditional jazz recordings of Art Hodes, in the *Metronome* column called "The Two Deuces." Apparently offended by some aspect of Hodes's radio show on WNYC (which featured small band jazz and relaunched the careers of veteran musicians like Cow Cow Davenport, who was, ironically, the washroom attendant at the Onyx during Dizzy's residency), Feather described Hodes's Columbia Quintet as "an amateur band entertaining in an air-raid shelter" in the January 1944 issue, beginning a four-month campaign of vitriol. Hodes sued *Metronome* for $100,000 and eventually settled out of court, but, although he technically won his action, the incident proved damaging for Hodes, who lost the opportunity to record with Lester Young when the record company involved pulled out, dismayed by *Metronome*'s reports on Hodes's work.[10]

Clearly, Feather was a dangerous man to tangle with, and initially he was as unimpressed by the early efforts of the beboppers as he was by the simultaneous efforts of New Orleans revivalists Bunk Johnson and George Lewis, whom he described as "hopelessly incapable of producing anything that could be called real music, or real jazz or real anything else except real crap."[11] His writing about Dizzy grew more positive and more affectionate as time passed, but during the Onyx/Eckstine period he was not a supporter of Dizzy's efforts; a reconciliation of sorts was only effected late in 1944, after Dizzy had left Eckstine and Feather included him on a session he produced to feature the singing of Sarah Vaughan. Much that has passed into folklore about the Eckstine band and Dizzy's role in it derives from Feather's *Inside Bebop*, but, just like its coverage of the Teddy Hill days, this is not a reliable source. Taken together with Feather's other writing, it seems that Eckstine had a point when he said: "Leonard Feather, he rapped the shit out of me. Every time we'd come in, 'the band was out of tune,' and the this and the that, and now it's the 'legendary Billy Eckstine band.' "[12]

Feather had shown up frequently at the Onyx, and apparently Pettiford ribbed him about his reluctance to write about Dizzy: "Write something about him. The guy's something else you know." At this point, Feather did not take up the challenge, and Dizzy felt this was because "he wasn't really hip to us and what we were doing musically."[13] Once Eckstine's plans started to coalesce, Feather did write about the band, but generally negatively. One reason for this is the complex relationship between Dizzy, Eckstine, and their agent, Billy Shaw of the William Morris Agency. Clearly there was a tension between Feather and Shaw, and Feather criticized him for his ambivalence over booking Eckstine, and presented the singer as a management "problem." It is Feather who recorded that Shaw had the idea of billing Eckstine as "X-tine," but in a substantial amount of the contemporary editorial copy and advertisements for the band this name form never appears, and the only variation is in the gradual acceptance of "Eckstine" rather than "Eckstein" as the correct way to spell the singer's name.[14] Equally, Feather reported: "The singer had been laying eggs at the Zanzibar, the Yacht and other spots and Shaw was undecided what to do with him." In Feather's account, the formation of the big band was a desperate measure on the part of the promoter to rescue an ailing career. In fact, not only do contemporary accounts suggest that Eckstine was quite successful as a solo artist, but there were two simple reasons why Eckstine formed a big band.[15]

The first was that this had all along been his intention when he left Hines, and, faced with a choice between the prospect of fronting George Hudson's band from St. Louis as if it were his own or picking up the vein of creativity that Dizzy and Parker had unleashed in his last months with Hines, there was no contest. He accepted Budd Johnson and Dizzy's advice to recruit an orchestra built firmly on ex-Hines personnel plus a nucleus of other players who favored the "new jazz."[16]

The second was straightforwardly financial. Immediately following his departure from Hines, Eckstine was a bankable commodity for Billy Shaw as a "single," capitalizing on his hit record of "Jelly Jelly" and his club and cabaret appearances. The introduction of a tax on such venues forced Shaw to rethink, and thus he realized that, despite the risks of setting up and managing a large orchestra, it was potentially more lucrative to put Eckstine back on the theatre circuit, where the tax would not apply. "The 30 percent cabaret tax so ruinous in nightclubs . . . decided him to quit working as a single . . . and form his own band," reported the *New York Age* in a feature on Eckstine by Ted Yates.[17] Shaw gambled that the theatre circuit would pay big money for Hines's former star, and he was right. "The Eckstines are heading for the Regal Theatre in Chicago, where they will be paid $5,500 per week, and a split over $17,000—an unheard of figure for a new band," noted Yates. "It will receive a similar wage at the Apollo in New York." Shaw's management acumen also ensured that the new band was launched with a hit record behind it, a piece of thinking that seems more in tune with the 1970s than the 1940s.

The band's April session had been made for Deluxe, and, like virtually all the discs cut for the label by the group in its short career, the recording quality achieved by this small firm, previously only experienced in producing hillbilly songs, is execrable. Yet the issued disc from this inaugural session, even though it is by a studio band that predates the eventual regular personnel and despite its boxy sound (or, on many re-issues, an appalling artificial echo that was added at the initial transfer to microgroove), is powerfully exciting.

"Good Jelly Blues" (a self-conscious effort to recreate the success of "Jelly Jelly") was backed by "I Stay in the Mood for You," the latter including some dramatic and original arranging by Dizzy in which each section (trumpets, saxes, and trombones) plays modernistic phrases in turn behind Eckstine's vocal, with a soaring final chorus by Gillespie's trumpet over the whole ensemble. The disc seized the imagination of the public and the tiny Deluxe firm found it hard to keep up with demand. "Fortunately for Deluxe [Eckstine] didn't make more," ran one press report. "That company has been unable to keep up with Billy's fans. Able to produce 20,000 waxings a month, the company finds itself with 72,000 requests for 'I Stay in the Mood for You'. . . . Deluxe has all it can do to handle the Eckstine disc."[18]

The chain of events that set up Eckstine's big band—and indeed his relationship with Billy Shaw—owes much to the entrepreneur John Hammond, who had encouraged Shaw to handle the singer, whom he had previously only promoted as part of Earl Hines's entourage. Once Dizzy and Budd Johnson had persuaded Eckstine to set up his own orchestra, Shaw "sent out about forty wires and got back answers from twenty-five of them wanting to know what the dates were."[19] Shaw pulled in deposits from the theatres that were willing to book the package; with this money Eckstine bought the necessary equipment and arrangements to get the band going. Initially they had only a few of Dizzy's scores, but Count Basie generously loaned some of his charts to Eckstine and others were swapped with Boyd Raeburn in return for new arrangements from Dizzy.[20]

The band that gathered in April for the recording date included some of the eventual full-time members of Eckstine's band, notably Shorty McConnell on trumpet, Howard Scott on trombone, Budd Johnson and Thomas Crump on reeds, Connie Wainwright on guitar, and Shadow Wilson on drums. For the eventual band, Eckstine added Gail Brockman on lead trumpet, plus Buddy Anderson from Jay McShann's band. For the trombones he brought in his ex-Hines colleagues Bennie Green and Jerry Valentine (who was a useful arranger and composer as well). The reeds had Charlie Parker and Robert "Junior" Williams on altos, Gene Ammons on tenor, and Leo Parker on baritone. John Malachi, who had been Eckstine's accompanist on the club circuit, joined on piano, and Tommy Potter came in from Trummy Young's little group on bass.[21]

Almost before the band started to work, the draft seized some of its members, and Thomas Crump was replaced by Lucky Thompson, while Shadow Wilson was eventually replaced by Art Blakey, who always maintained that this was simply because Shadow did not want to tour the South. The first date for the band was in Wilmington, Delaware, on June 9. Disaster struck when Dizzy, traveling to the job from New York, went to sleep on the train and woke up several stations further down the line when he arrived at the terminus in Washington, D.C. Shadow Wilson did not make the gig either, and Eckstine was reduced to playing drums himself. "Now I'm really frantic, I don't have Diz there and I don't have any drums," he told Max Jones. "We worked for a week without a drummer. When we got to Tampa, Florida, I picked up a kid called Joe, who played drums." Within a few days, Joe caught a fever and died while the band worked in New Orleans, and Eckstine eventually persuaded Art Blakey to meet the band for their next big engagement in St. Louis at the Plantation.[22]

Despite all these troubles, Eckstine's band began to receive some good reviews, beginning with Johnny Sippel in *Down Beat*, who said: "The handsome 'Sepia Sinatra' is proving a very versatile frontman . . . not far behind the leader is the ever-mugging Dizzy Gillespie." There were constant minor changes of personnel, and by the time the band had "smashed records from opening day on in Detroit, Cleveland, Washington, and other key cities," other players of the new music like Howard McGhee and Dexter Gordon had joined its ranks. "Advance notices proclaim his new band a brilliant one," ran a report in the *Chicago De-*

fender, "chuck full of novel groovie [*sic*] arrangements and a truly grand gang of entertainers." The entertainers included veteran dancers Buck and Bubbles, described as "velvet in motion," and it seems that Dizzy's "mugging" was in the context of the black vaudeville tradition, of which he had had firsthand experience with Calloway, Millinder, and Hite.[23]

One point on which Leonard Feather's writing about the band concurs with other accounts is that Billy Shaw had made clear to Gillespie that, if he handled his duties successfully as musical director of the band, Shaw would help establish Dizzy's own career. "If you do well, this'll be your big chance to straighten out," Feather credits Shaw with having proposed. "After Eckstine is all set and established, I'll go to work on you and build you with your own band."[24] Dizzy did do well, and he also took stock of the stress of keeping a band such as Eckstine's together on the road. The following year he was to launch his own large orchestra, and at that stage he discovered that, between them, he and Shaw still had some lessons to learn. What was not in doubt about Eckstine's band, however, was that despite all the trials and tribulations of fluctuating personnel, mixed reviews, and endless traveling, the band had an enviable *esprit de corps*. Everyone involved in it knew that it was doing something new and exciting.

Art Blakey, for example, regarded it as the most important stage in his early career: "I had the band at the Tic Toc in Boston. Meanwhile Billy had organized his band, and it had Shadow on drums, and they had a certain clique that hung out together: Charlie Parker and Dizzy Gillespie and Freddie Webster and Sarah Vaughan. . . . Shadow left, and in the meantime they had to get somebody to take Shadow's place. So somebody told Billy about me. Billy knew me, but he didn't know about what I was doing, and he sent for me and I came round and joined the band, and that was the turning point of my life.

"I met Sarah Vaughan, big and skinny as a rail, running round there with Dizzy and Charlie Parker. They were running around at rehearsal beating each other with wet towels and acting crazy instead of rehearsing, and I couldn't understand those guys.

"Sarah—they were knocking her down, but she was just as rough as they were and she was cursing around. I said to myself, 'What kind of a band is this? I never heard of a band like this before in my life!' I got mad at one of them cursing, and Billy called me over and said, 'Art, if you're going to be in my band, you've got to be around these guys. You've got to get used to using profanity.' "[25]

Soon, the infectious musical qualities of the band took hold. Art remembered a twenty-four-hours-a-day riot of music-making and a spirit that held the band together even in adverse circumstances: "We were out on the road every night, so we rehearsed every day and played every night. We had to play army camps to keep the bus on the road, to keep buying gasoline for the bus. We were out on the road, and the guys were so crazy. We were riding down in the South and these guys would open up the windows of the bus and they'd be shooting crows. So the FBI came and took the bus.

"I think most of the guys didn't have draft cards. The last time I saw Gene Ammons he was going out the door putting his horn in a pillowcase. When I saw him next he was back in New York. Gone! 'Ain't gonna draft me in no army!'

"The authorities didn't know what to do so finally they got us. They waited until we opened at the Apollo, and then they went down there and sent for all the guys to join the army. They sent for Bird, to come down and join. He went in a telephone booth and went to sleep, and he stayed in there all day and then came out and went back to the gig. They didn't want nothing to do with him. Dizzy went down in a negligee carrying his horn. So soon the whole band was out. They sent me home in a cab with a red card and it said: 'Would be a great risk to the U.S. forces, never to be recalled.'

"Well we had a ball because we weren't interested in nothing else, just wanted to play some music."[26]

Blakey's account, in a rather helter-skelter interview, runs together a number of salient points. The band was given to rehearsing far more than the average. "To get back to the love thing," remembered Eckstine, "We used to get in a town . . . the guys would go on in the hall, set up, jam, or Bird would take the reed section, sit and run through things. . . . When we was working the Riviera [in St. Louis] the people used to move out, we'd rehearse at four o'clock in the morning. Sit right in the room, the reed section would be there blowing all night."[27] He also explained that, with the war on, the shortage of gasoline made it necessary to play army bases. Billy Shaw had concluded that free shows for the troops would ensure that the band was classified as a priority for fuel. But the vehicle itself was eventually commandeered for the war effort, leaving Eckstine to move his musicians by train.

In Blakey's memory this was elided with the effects of the draft itself. But his recollection of Dizzy is not accurate. Dizzy had appeared before the draft board a year earlier in July 1943, when he was with Earl Hines, and it was then that he was classified 4F. He did not appear before a board in 1944.[28]

Blakey was not alone in recalling the spirit and enthusiasm of Eckstine's band. Eckstine himself often wrote and talked of the genuine love and affection for one another between his musicians; so too did many of those musicians themselves, including tenorist Dexter Gordon. He had been in Chicago, playing in Louis Armstrong's big band, when he got a call to join Eckstine. He finally left Louis in Buffalo, and traveled to Washington, D.C., where he arrived just in time for the last night of Eckstine's residency.

"I go backstage and greet all the cats, and Eckstine says, 'You might as well come and do this last show with us,' " he recalled.

"So everyone is saying 'Yeah!,' and I hardly know what's going on. They say, 'Come on, man, you got it!' So we went on stage and did the last show and ended up with a Tadd Dameron arrangement of 'Airmail Special.' It was very rapid and, the next thing I know, 'B' is calling me out to blow. So I went out and played a couple of choruses and started to back off when Bohanna (Art Blakey) did his drum roll and I was right back in there. I guess I must have played seven or eight choruses.

"That was the beginning of the saga. This was [still] the first few months of the Eckstine Bebop Band and it was *très, très* exciting. Sarah Vaughan . . . was a natural singing phenomenon . . . her voice was much lighter then and she was making all these leaps with perfect intonation. This band was so special because we felt we had a mission."[29]

In the following year, mainly because of their collective use of heroin, Gordon and the men who had by then become his reed section colleagues—Sonny Stitt, John Jackson, and Leo Parker—became known as the "unholy four." Eckstine continued to lead the band until 1947, but Dizzy left him in December 1944, when the band came to the Apollo in New York for the Christmas show. Dizzy had gotten what he wanted from Eckstine: the chance to write and arrange for a big band (which he directed and rehearsed), and he had gained the trust of Billy Shaw. The time had come for Dizzy to establish himself as a leader, and he began again where he had left off earlier in the year, on 52nd Street.

Before he left Eckstine, however, he took part in a further recording session with the band, when they returned to New York after a late November engagement in Chicago. Once more, Deluxe did not favor the group with the best possible sound quality on these discs, but the atmosphere of energy and excitement is palpable. There are two takes of Jerry Valentine's arrangement of "Blowing the Blues Away," a vehicle for Gene Ammons and Dexter Gordon to indulge in a tenor "battle." The first take is a muffled and rather ragged affair, but the brass riffing behind Eckstine's vocal is daring and a perfect introduction to the sparring tenorists. The second cut includes both a clearer vocal and a more polished battle from the tenorists, as well as tidier section playing. In both, Dizzy's joyous horn soars over the closing ensembles, demonstrating the skill he was to hone to a fine art in his own bands of dominating even the full-blown power of sixteen other musicians.

"Opus X," the other track of interest from the date, is one of the best early examples of Art Blakey's big band drumming. It is possible to imagine clearly from this how his trademark pressroll would have hauled Dexter Gordon back to the solo spot, as Blakey dictates the dynamics and shading of the entire piece from the drum chair. Apparently he incurred Dizzy's wrath when he first arrived by emulating the shuffle beat and paradiddles of Cozy Cole and Oscar Bradley. There is no trace of that style here, almost six months after he joined the band, with Blakey showing his own snare and bass drum-dominated technique that combines breaking the rhythmic patterns in a similar way to Clarke or Roach with an inevitable sense of forward motion through his use of rimshots, bass drum accents, and the famous pressroll (which here introduces the second eight bars of John Jackson's alto solo in a characteristically forceful manner).

Dizzy and Blakey were not to work regularly together again all that often. Highlights of their subsequent work include Dizzy's early 1950s small groups and the Giants of Jazz tours in the early 1970s, but in "Opus X" Blakey provides a perfect cushion for Dizzy's own eight-bar solo (the last of Dizzy's contributions to Eckstine's band to be recorded), and it is regrettable that their paths did not cross more often in the years that followed.

As 1944 drew to a close, Dizzy contributed to one final recording session, which gives us a glimpse of the girlish Sarah Vaughan as she must have sounded with Eckstine and Hines during her time in common with Dizzy in those bands. This was the session mentioned earlier that was arranged and led by Leonard Feather, which included two of his own compositions, "Signing Off" and "No Smokes Blues." Although "Night in Tunisia" (as "Interlude") was also recorded on the session, with Dizzy himself playing piano before switching to trumpet for a brief eight-bar solo, it suffers overall, like all the other tracks, from the dogged unswerving swing style of the rhythm section. Along with Feather himself at the piano for all but the opening of "Interlude," the team of bassist Jack Lesberg, guitarist Chuck Wayne, and drummer Morey Feld sound anachronistic compared to the modernist drive of the Eckstine band, and Dizzy is the only soloist apart from Sarah who ventures into either the harmonic or rhythmic language of bebop. The contributions of Georgie Auld on tenor and Aaron Sachs on clarinet stay firmly inside the safety of swing phrasing and harmonies. It is tempting to suggest that one of

Feather's reasons for not getting overenthusiastic about bop in his critical writing was his own inability to write or play effectively in the style.

Dizzy himself plays trumpet on this session in the manner he was to adopt subsequently in Jazz at the Philharmonic, where many of the rhythm sections he worked with retained their swing roots. He devised a manner of constructing boppish solos that fitted easily into the swing meter, yet communicated much of the excitement and dash that his playing contained in a more fully bebop context. Just as Charlie Parker was later able to convey much of his own solo style over the lush backing of a string orchestra, Dizzy managed to condense the essence of bop, by using substitute harmonies and daring rhythms coupled with his by now formidable high register, into his choruses in more swing-orientated company. In the 1950s, for much of the time, his own small groups adopted a consciously less boppish approach to rhythm section work and showcased Dizzy's solos and those of his current saxophonist in a manner that is not dissimilar to this session. Yet in 1944, this must have seemed unexciting company for Dizzy, and perhaps this was a session he participated in for political rather than musical reasons, getting himself into Feather's good books and promoting the career of Sarah Vaughan, who was later to record with Dizzy's own small groups. Whatever the case, Feather gave Dizzy only eighteen bars of solo space across four tracks. On "No Smokes Blues," he was once again asked to provide a backing obbligato to the vocal, just as he had on Feather's Pete Brown session almost two years before. Only the bridge on "Interlude" and a thoughtful eighteen bars on "East of the Sun" give any hint of the star soloist who was to captivate 52nd Street in the months that followed.

10

Bird, Big Band, and Berg's

lthough many of the accounts of Dizzy's life suggest that in 1945 he went more or less directly from the Billy Eckstine Orchestra into his quintet with Charlie Parker at the Three Deuces on 52nd Street, the sequence of events that led Dizzy into that quintessential bebop band was a little more complex. Events are further confused by the plethora of recording sessions that were on offer from several small companies attempting to cash in on the inertia of the major houses in the wake of the AFM recording ban. "The ban had created an unprecedented seller's market," wrote Ross Russell, who shortly afterward became the proprietor of Dial Records, typical of the small independent labels that quickly came to an agreement with AFM boss James Petrillo and started recording, while most of the major corporations sought to thrash out more complex arrangements with the musicians' union.[1]

Three of the labels that sprang up in the wake of the AFM ban concerned themselves with the new jazz played by the beboppers. These were Continental, Manor, and Guild, the last of which lived and died between January and December 1945.[2] Dizzy had recorded for Continental with Sarah Vaughan and Leonard Feather on New Year's Eve 1944, and he went on to make further sessions for all three companies as 1945 got under way.

The music produced at these sessions is discussed in the next chapter, but clearly these small labels were exploiting a public hunger for new discs—a situation in which a shortage of worthwhile new performances had been exacerbated by the wartime scarcity of shellac, compounding, for example, the Deluxe company's inability to satisfy popular demand for the Eckstine records noted previously.

Although Parker and Gillespie appeared with one another on record very early in 1945, in Clyde Hart's session with Henry "Rubberlegs" Williams, they were not at that stage, it seems, playing together regularly outside the studio. Five days later, when Oscar Pettiford put together an eighteen-piece band (again with Williams) to record for Manor, Bird was not present, leaving Dizzy to coerce a chaotic collection of musicians (including some of his former 52nd Street associates like Don Byas and Clyde Hart) into some semblance of order, since Pettiford had overlooked the necessity of providing charts for such a big band. When Dizzy led his own sextet on disc, during a later part of the same day's session, Don Byas recreated his former role as Dizzy's reed-playing counterpart.

By mid-January, Dizzy was back in the big band fold, working with the white bandleader Boyd Raeburn, who had been a ready customer for arrangements over the previous year. Dizzy was in the band by January 17 on one of a couple of radio transcription sessions, appearing later on two regular record dates, and for a week at the Apollo Theatre early the following month.[3] Quite how long he stayed is unclear—obviously not the "two and a half years off and on" once quoted by Raeburn himself (although this is a fair estimate of the time of their active association, from the moment they first traded arrangements), but possibly Dizzy stayed longer than the "few one-nighters and a week at the Apollo" he recalled to Leonard Feather.[4]

Raeburn was a curious figure in jazz history. He had been a dance band saxophonist during the 1930s and early 1940s and suddenly acquired an enthusiasm for bebop around 1943, and for four years led a consistently innovative and experimental orchestra, combining a taste for contemporary European concert music with his interest in modern jazz. With the support of a wealthy backer, a West Coast real-estate man with the unlikely name of Stillman Pond, Raeburn was able to convert his enthusiasms into some sort of reality. His most ambitious venture was in 1947, when he rivaled Stan Kenton with a twenty-two piece orchestra, but his 1945 group was equally unusual and included several rising stars, both black and white, including Dizzy, Benny Harris, Oscar Pettiford, Al Cohn, Serge Chaloff, and Shelly Manne.

Many of the arrangements provided for the 1945 band were by George Handy, but several were created by Dizzy as a result of the exchange of scores that followed the Eckstine band's raid on Raeburn's library. "[Raeburn] may have started as a society bandleader in Chicago in the 1930s playing Mickey Mouse junk," said his guitarist, Steve Jordan, "but by 1945 he wanted only the best arrangements and the best players he could find. . . . Many musicians and critics raved about the band, noting that some of our music brought Stravinsky, Bartok, Debussy and Ravel to mind. But though we made it artistically, the band did not succeed commercially." Raeburn appears to have been an enthusiastic and likeable man, who doubled on soprano, alto, and tenor sax, in addition to the bass saxophone that was his trademark. He "played only occasionally with the band," wrote Jordan, "because few of the arrangements included him."[5]

Dizzy's presence in the orchestra added to his reputation as being a "cutting-edge" musician, and his musical personality became identified with the new sounds of Raeburn, just as it had been with the pioneering Eckstine band (in which his place had been taken successfully by Fats Navarro). The same could not be said of all Dizzy's freelance recording activities at this stage, and he made relatively undistinguished contributions to some mainstream discs by Dixieland clarinetist Joe Marsala and blues singer Albinia Jones, as well as some more successful efforts with tenorist Georgie Auld (who was moonlighting from his military service to lead the occasional studio session). About this time, Dizzy began to adopt pseudonyms for some of his discs, since his own efforts as a leader won him an exclusive contract with the Guild label, starting in February 1945.[6]

One reason Guild was keen to snap up Gillespie's services was that in January *Esquire* magazine had voted him "new trumpet star" in its annual jazz awards. The main trumpet category was won by Cootie Williams, with Roy Eldridge claiming "silver" prize. So Dizzy was at last being recognized as an instrumentalist whose gifts put him on a par with his former idols. During February, Dizzy appeared with several of the winners at a Harlem jam session run at the Witoka Club by entrepreneur, bassist, and writer Jimmy Butts, and was billed to appear at Carnegie Hall in April in an official poll-winners' concert, alongside the Lionel Hampton Band.

At the time of the original announcements of the awards, on January 17, *Esquire* had hosted a lengthy radio broadcast to publicize the winners. This duly went out on the "Blue" radio network, but immediately caused controversy because of the omission from those performing of Count Basie and Buck Clayton. "Neither . . . was invited to participate in the concert," reported the *New York Age*, "despite the fact that both were elected to top honors and both were available. . . . It was reported that Leonard Feather, a freelance writer and jazz 'authority' who supervised the concert for *Esquire* magazine, was being sought by Basie's representatives for a full explanation of the concert's snub."[7]

Feather's role as a promoter was plainly still controversial, but, despite his previous antipathy toward bebop, in May 1945 he appeared in the first of a couple of innovative concerts of "Modern Music" at the New York Town Hall, promoted by Monte Kay and Mal Braveman under the rather pompous banner of the "New Jazz Foundation." Feather accompanied Dinah Washington, who was characteristically asked to perform two of his compositions, but the organizers sensibly hired Dizzy's complete quintet with Charlie Parker for the full-blown bebop section of each concert.

This band was by now established at the Three Deuces on 52nd Street. It had opened there during March, and included Al Haig on piano, Max Roach on drums, and Curley Russell on bass. They were the main attraction at the club, playing hourly sets and supported by pianist Erroll Garner plus his trio of drummer Harold "Doc" West and bassist Al Lucas, with guest appearances from the ubiquitous Don Byas. For the Town Hall concert on May 16, because of the chaotic organization of the show and the nonappearance of several headline acts, they found themselves playing the lion's share of the program, including supporting bassist Slam Stewart in his solo features. Despite all this, and the fact that Max Roach had been replaced for the evening by Doc West (albeit familiar with their repertoire from playing opposite them at the Three Deuces), they triumphed.

"Dizzy was in magnificent form. I've never heard him play so well, muff so few notes and reach such inspired heights," wrote Barry Ulanov in the following issue of *Metronome*. "Dizzy's boys played through the first half of the concert unrelieved, and the effect was stunning." Clearly the band had honed its act through the long residency at the Three Deuces, and the legendary skill with which Dizzy and Parker established almost telepathic communication was not lost on the audience. "Dizzy and Charley [*sic*] played their unison passages with fabulous precision, no easy achievement when your lips and fingers are so tangled up in mad running-triplet figures," reported Ulanov, who also noted Bird's penchant for starting his solos with a solo break before the rhythm section was pulled back in his slipstream.

As well as demonstrating that they had arrived at a uniquely compatible method of playing together, Dizzy and Bird (no doubt drawing on the stock of head arrangements sketched out by Dizzy the previous year at the Onyx) had established a core repertoire of their own. The pieces they played at the Town Hall were the same titles they were to record over the next few months, and formed the nucleus of their broadcasts and concerts together well into the start of 1946. They played "Shaw 'Nuff " (named after Billy Shaw), "Night in Tunisia," "Groovin' High," "Be Bop," " 'Round About Midnight," "Salt Peanuts," "Cherokee," "Blue 'n' Boogie," "Dizzy Atmosphere," and "Confirmation."

This was the first formal concert ever played under their own names by Dizzy and Parker together (not counting a Palm Sunday dance and

New York Town Hall, May 1945. Harold "Doc" West, Curley Russell, Charlie
Parker, Dizzy. (Photo: Charles B. Nadeu; Frank Driggs collection)

jam session, at which they appeared at the Lincoln Square Center in late
March for the indefatigable Jimmy Butts). They returned to the Town
Hall for the same promoters on June 22, in what was to be the last New
Jazz Foundation concert presentation for some time. (Concerts later re-
started more modestly as Monte Kay's swing sessions and dances, an-
nounced by "Symphony Sid" Torin.)

Once again Dizzy and Bird acquitted themselves well, but the nonappearance of Coleman Hawkins and Slam Stewart incensed the audience and critics alike; in the aftermath the Foundation gently slid from
the public eye.

Through reviews of the quintet's records in *Down Beat* and accounts
of the group's residency at the Three Deuces, it is obvious that this
Gillespie quintet was the consummation of all that had gone before to
establish bebop into some kind of cohesive and recognizable style. The
mercurial presence of Charlie Parker gave Dizzy's own playing a robust
counterbalance, with greater stylistic empathy than partners like Don
Byas, Budd Johnson, and Dexter Gordon, and the rhythm section was
able to knit together a consistent approach following all the long years

of after-hours experiments. Haig was a more adventurous pianist than Clyde Hart (who died suddenly from tuberculosis during March 1945, only days after recording with Dizzy and Parker), and Russell was a more than adequate ensemble bassist. Roach continued to develop the style that is evident from his Onyx Club and Coleman Hawkins recordings of 1943–44.

Having followed Dizzy's progression to this point, there seems little doubt that his mixture of instrumental brilliance, quest for musical knowledge, and relatively high-profile career came together in this quintet to mark his musical maturity. No critic has captured this phase in Gillespie's career as eloquently or effectively as Whitney Balliett, who wrote: "Few trumpeters have ever been blessed with so much technique. Gillespie never merely started a solo, he erupted into it. A good many bebop solos begin with four- or eight-bar breaks, and Gillespie, taking full advantage of this approach . . . would hurl himself into the break, after a split second pause, with a couple of hundred notes that corkscrewed through several octaves, sometimes in triple time, and were carried, usually in one breath, past the end of the break and well into the solo itself. . . . Gillespie's style at the time gave the impression—with its sharp, slightly acid tone, its cleavered phrase endings, its efflorescence of notes, and its brandishings about in the upper register—of being constantly on the verge of flying apart. However, his playing was held together by his extraordinary rhythmic sense."[8]

Dizzy was the titular leader at the Three Deuces and the band's concert appearances, and his own "ever mugging" stage presence was the persona seized on by the critics in their reviews. Parker's instrumental brilliance was noted, but in the context of his work as a sideman, and there were warning signs that an unrelieved diet of the new music could be indigestible. "Too much of it is repetitious and for that reason dull . . . how great for how long can they be?" ran one review of the June Town Hall Concert.[9]

Yet jazz history appears to have absorbed the myth created by Ross Russell that this achievement of defining small-group bebop was Parker's alone, in which Dizzy and the others played an almost incidental part. Because of Dizzy's increasingly businesslike attitude to the music, which, despite his stage mugging did not involve narcotics or alcohol abuse and not being, to put it mildly, the liability that Parker was, he seems to have been derided by those who identify great music with "the jazz life."

"Dizzy was verbal, witty, extroverted, sunny of disposition—everything Charlie was not. Dizzy was accessible to everyone. You did not elevate such a man to a hierarchy," wrote Russell. "Blowing musicians, who were in the position to know, all agreed that Parker was the fountainhead of the new music. The flow of musical ideas suggested mysterious, primal forces."[10] Dizzy, however, could see that there was more to be done, and his musical restlessness involved further development and exploration, not least drawing on his decade of experience in big bands. Parker's unique talent was all to do with the flow of musical ideas from his saxophone. Put him in an environment where he could improvise and, in his prime, unhindered by illness, drink, or drugs, he could be sublime. But could this be the basis not only of a career, but a whole new chapter in jazz? Dizzy's musical and professional instincts told him otherwise, and even though the chapter he embarked on next was a near disaster, it convinced him of the direction his own career was to take.

Despite the considerable musical success of the quintet, Dizzy still nursed the ambition to lead his own big band and develop the ideas he had nurtured with Eckstine. Billy Shaw had all along anticipated such a stage of Dizzy's career, and so plans were laid to form an eighteen-piece band to go on the road. The quintet left the Three Deuces on Thursday July 5 and Dizzy set out on tour with his big band three days later, as part of a package called "Hep-sations of 1945."

"A big band is different from working with a small band," Dizzy told Charles Fox. "I have an expertise in playing in the cracks, aside from playing solos, playing in between what the band is doing and along with the section. I like that kind of stuff, and then I'm pretty good in front of a big band. I move a lot, and I conduct all right."[11] To help him in his new venture, Dizzy recruited arranger Walter "Gil" Fuller, who had earlier worked with him in the Les Hite band. Initially, Fuller was horrified to discover Dizzy rehearsing his horn section by getting them to sit in alongside him at after-hours joints. He persuaded Dizzy that, to put the band on the road in any sort of shape, proper rehearsals were going to be necessary.

Fuller arranged a loan from Billy Shaw's son Milt, who was jointly promoting the tour, and he hired the Nola studios for some organized rehearsals. He also created the core of the band's library by arranging the Parker–Gillespie Quintet repertoire for eighteen pieces, getting Dizzy to set out the unison lines and harmonic structures, while Fuller repeated the role he had had with Les Hite and rapidly produced playable charts.

The personnel for the touring band initially included Harry Pryor, Kenny Dorham, Elmon Wright, and Ed Lewis alongside Dizzy on trumpets; Al King and Ted Kelly on trombones; Leo Williams and John Walker on altos; Charlie Rouse and Warren Lucky on tenors; and Eddie de Verteuil on baritone. In the rhythm section, Dizzy repaid his old debt of gratitude to Teddy Hill's guitarist John Smith by asking "Smitty" to join his band, together with Howard Anderson on piano, Lloyd Buchanan on bass, and Max Roach on drums.[12] Once the band had actually started its tour (mainly a trawl through the South playing for dances on a circuit booked for Gale by a man named Weinburg), musicians fell by the wayside as the draft, unreceptive audiences, and the South itself took their toll. Consequently, the personnel was somewhat different when the band came into the McKinley Theatre in the Bronx for the week beginning August 31 at the end of the southern leg of the tour. Those who flitted through the ranks are said to have included Benny Harris, Freddie Webster, Miles Davis, and Fats Navarro on trumpets, and baritone saxophonist Leo Parker. There were further changes when the band moved to Chicago toward the end of September.[13]

By all accounts the show that Billy Shaw had booked alongside Dizzy's "Terrific Sizzle Band" was popular. It was built around the famous dance act, the Nicholas Brothers, who, despite the continued popularity of their 1943 film *Stormy Weather*, were trying to revive their stage careers after each had spent time in the armed forces. When the show first went on the road it also included the two overweight comedians Patterson and Jackson (billed as "600 pounds of comedy, singing, and dancing"), Billy's wife June Eckstine on vocals, and the dancer Lovey Lane. Later the "glamorous song stylist" Betty St. Clair, Joe Arena, and the Amazing Lesters were added to the bill. But while the warm reception given to the variety package was one thing, the cool treatment afforded to Dizzy's big band was quite another.

"We didn't fare too well on that tour," recalled Dizzy. "It was a big show that went down South, but they weren't ready for us. They was just ready for the blues down there."[14] In theory, a black big band playing the music of the hour should have been overwhelmingly popular on the tour circuit. "[We went] to Baltimore, to Washington, D.C., through Maryland, Virginia, the Carolinas, Alabama, Texas, playing all black theatres and dance halls," recalled Max Roach. "We stayed in black homes everywhere. Everything we came into contact with was black."[15]

The problem was that the package had been billed as "a great show, plus an evening of dancing to a great new band."[16] In all the dance venues they played, the local black population arrived, dressed to the nines, ready for an evening's dancing. The sound of an eighteen-piece bebop orchestra, sounding off on one of Dizzy's original compositions, left them puzzled and bewildered. A crisis had arrived in the role of jazz as a form of popular music. Up until this point, bands that played for dancing, revue packages, and the touring circuit had been inextricably linked. The "Hepsations of 1945" marks the moment that jazz formally ceased to be the music of black social dance. For some years to come the innate conservatism of agencies, theatres, and dance halls made sure that jazz big bands continued to appear on bills with variety artistes and play for dancing, but the same philosophical movement or "psychological shift" that has already been noted in connection with the boppers on 52nd Street became true of large jazz orchestras. They no longer felt, as part of the bebop revolution, that they needed to play the music audiences wanted to hear.

"Our style of playing, generally, was geared for people just sitting and listening to music," wrote Dizzy later. Yet, with his own natural sense of rhythm and movement, Dizzy himself could never see why it should be hard to dance to his band. "I could dance to it. I could dance my ass off to it. They could've too, if they had tried."[17] In fact, Dizzy was telescoping history. For once, Leonard Feather's account that during this tour Dizzy was nervous and unrelaxed on stage is corroborated by several other sources. With the "Hep-sations" package, his announcements were so poor that the Nicholas Brothers took over the role of comperes, and Dizzy was not his usual self, moving awkwardly and uneasily about the stage. It took another year and another band for him to regain his normal ease of manner in front of a large orchestra, as Feather noted in his account of the following year's tour with Ella Fitzgerald: "Dizzy loosened up, started mugging, spinning around and dancing and became the 'compleat showman.'"[18]

There are several reasons for Dizzy's lack of sparkle on his 1945 tour. First and obviously, he was disappointed that the enthusiasm for a bebop big band that he had felt in New York and was to feel in Chicago at the end of the tour had simply evaporated in the South. Second, he was confronted with all the onerous responsibilities of leadership for the first time, handling the game of musical chairs among his sidemen, the transportation of the band, and other personnel problems like Max Roach's growing drug addiction with the same dedication. (Roach has gone on record as saying that it was Dizzy's devotion to him that caused him to kick the habit during the tour, and there was a general sense among the band that Dizzy was assuming a new maturity as leader.) Third, it is likely that the South itself, with all the memories it conjured up of Dizzy's childhood, poverty, and segregation, had an effect. In the North, Dizzy had used his music as a most effective escape from the hardship and manual labor that had been the lot of his parents and his contemporaries in Cheraw. The rejection of his new music by the black southern population must have been a difficult reaction to handle.

By the end of September, the tour had run its course, and Dizzy shelved his plans to be a big band leader. He returned to small-group work around New York, and, as the Guild records he had made earlier in the year were released, he was booked out on a string of one-nighters with a small group by the William Morris Agency.[19] Because Miles Davis had started playing with Charlie Parker during Dizzy's big band tour, Dizzy did not work regularly again with Parker at this point, although they were united in the studios for the infamous "Koko" session, discussed in the next chapter. Parker was, however, central to a tour to the West Coast that Gillespie planned to make at the end of the year. To join him on this trip to Billy Berg's Club in Hollywood, Dizzy recruited two younger musicians who were rapidly building names for themselves, bassist Ray Brown and vibraphone player Milt Jackson. Both were to be key associates for much of the rest of the decade.

By 1945, the role of the bass in a bebop rhythm section was less clearly defined than that of the piano or drums. Late 1930s innovations by swing players like Milt Hinton and Jimmy Blanton had indicated that there was a flexible solo role for the bass and that supple four-to-the-measure basslines could supplant the walking arpeggios pioneered by men like Pops Foster and Al Morgan and refined in Basie's band by Walter Page. By the mid-1940s, only Oscar Pettiford had pulled these ideas into anything approaching a redefinition of the bass's role, and few other players combined flexible ensemble lines with the solo ability of a horn player as he did. Curley Russell, for example, had been an acceptable ensemble player in Dizzy and Parker's quintet at the Three Deuces, but he was no soloist.

Ray Brown, who had just passed his nineteenth birthday on October 13, 1945, at the point when he met Dizzy for the first time, was the bassist who was to consolidate what had gone before into the definitive role for his instrument in a bebop small group. In Pennsylvania, word was already out on the young bassist from Pittsburgh who would sit in at jam sessions at the black Musicians' Union. Bill Doggett told the author that a year or two earlier he had tried to get the teenage Brown to join Lucky Millinder, but that Brown was still too young and had refused to leave home.[20] By 1945, however, Brown was a seasoned veteran of the southern touring circuit, and had been on the road for some months with the New Orleans bandleader Snookum Russell. One of the attractions of Russell's orchestra was a moment during their show when Brown and tenorist Charles Harman (from Sandusky, Ohio) came to the front of the stand and played a bowed-bass and tenor feature on pieces like "Sometimes I'm Happy," in which they recreated the solos of Slam Stewart and Lester Young from records.

"Then the leader found out that I knew all of Jimmy Blanton's things with Duke Ellington, so he started bringing me out and featuring me and him doing some of Ellington's stuff," recalled Brown. "The next thing I know, they have signs saying 'The Snookum Russell Orchestra, featuring Ray Brown, the World's Greatest Bass Player.' Now this was down South. I mean, I would get hung up by my thumbs if this was New York, but in Mississippi it's OK."[21]

Brown's colleagues were sure of his talent and urged him to try his luck in New York; he was further encouraged when Russell's band tangled with Andy Kirk's in a battle of music, and saxophonist Eddie "Lockjaw" Davis assured him he'd quickly find work in New York. Yet he was reluctant to face the big city on his own and talked four of his fellow musicians with Russell into making the trip with him. To pave the way, he'd sent off a stock of handbills of Russell's band with his "World's Greatest" tag to the managers of several big swing orchestras, using his mother's address in Pittsburgh as a *poste restante*. To his surprise, offers started to arrive at his mother's house, and he decided to leave Russell while the band was in Florida. When the moment came, all four of his colleagues chickened out, and he ended up lugging his bass and suitcase onto the train north to make the two-day journey on his own.[22]

Brown has told the extraordinary story of his arrival in New York many times, but he was gracious enough to do so again for the author.

"I got there and went to my aunt's house uptown. I arrived at eight o'clock in the evening and went up to her apartment, put my stuff in my room, and she gave me something to eat. While I was eating, I was talking to my aunt's son, and I said, 'Where's 52nd Street?'

"He said, 'Oh it's downtown. Just take the subway and it stops two blocks away. After you've eaten, we'll go there.'

"So we got on a train, went downtown, and came round the corner and there were all these clubs, sitting right there, one after another, and the signs outside said 'Art Tatum, Billie Holiday, Coleman Hawkins, Don Byas, Slam Stewart, Stuff Smith.' And I say to myself, 'Wow! This is it!'

"I started looking in these clubs, and when I got to the third club, a place called the Spotlite, it had Coleman Hawkins on. There was a big sign outside that said 'Coleman Hawkins with Thelonious Monk, Al McKibbon and Denzil Best' and below that, there was another smaller sign that said 'Billy Daniels accompanied by Hank Jones.' Now when I first left home, I got a job in Buffalo, playing at a nightclub, and I was staying at the YMCA where I met Hank Jones. We used to play together in the daytime because we were both with different bands in the evening. Later I'd seen him again with Hot Lips Page.

"So I went in there and asked for him. He was sitting in the back room, so I went back with him and sat down. We hadn't seen each other for about three years, and so we started talking. All of a sudden he said: 'Hey! look who's coming in the door!'

"I said, 'Who's that?'

"He said, 'Dizzy Gillespie.'

"Now remember, this is the same night I arrived in New York. I said, 'I wanna meet him.'

"So Hank says, 'Hey! Dizzy! Come over here! I want you to meet a friend of mine, just got in town. A great bass player.'

"I say, 'Hello.'

"Dizzy says, 'You play good?'

"Well, what am I going to say? So I said, 'I can play, you know.'

"He said, 'Do you want a job?'

"Well, I almost had a heart attack. But I said, 'Yeah!'

"He took a card out of his pocket and said, 'Be at my house tomorrow night, seven o'clock.'

"I said, 'Okay!' And the next night I went up to his house and there were four guys there: Dizzy Gillespie, Charlie Parker, Bud Powell, and Max Roach. Not a bad place to be. Scared shitless, but a nice place to be on my second day in New York.

"Well, we rehearsed for a couple of days and then Dizzy said to me, 'Okay! You've got the job.' So I called my mother up and she said, 'Which of those bands did you go with?'

"I said, 'None of them. I took another job, with Dizzy Gillespie.'

"She said, 'Who's that?' "

According to Brown, the quintet worked on 52nd Street for a few weeks before heading for California, but Powell and Roach were not able to make the trip West. Powell's inability to travel, according to Brown, involved narcotics.

Bud Powell had by now left Cootie Williams, and although outwardly recovered from his beating at the hands of Philadelphia police, he was already having mental trouble in addition to his extreme reaction to the use of drink or drugs. Yet his mercurial brilliance at the keyboard has rarely been surpassed, and by all accounts he was at the height of his powers during the mid-1940s, although only a few recordings adequately document his playing from this period. A session recorded with Dexter Gordon in January 1946, only a few weeks after his meeting with Brown, hints at what Powell was capable of at the time, but Brown says that, three years earlier, Powell's appearances with Cootie Williams's big band displayed a pianist as strikingly original in that context as Dizzy had been with Calloway or Parker with McShann.[23]

"Everybody was talking about him, when I saw him play theater dates with Cootie back in Pittsburgh. He used to play behind a tap dancer they had on their show, a guy named Ralph Brown who wore a hat and was kind of smooth and talked and sang a little bit. While he tapped, Bud would play 'Cherokee' to accompany him. But he played so good that everybody started watching him and not watching the dancer, so Brown got mad. 'Whoa! Cool it down a little bit back there,' he shouted, 'I'm the star here you know!' "

Rehearsing alongside Powell and Roach, Ray Brown found himself playing a very different style of music from the kind he had performed with Snookum Russell. Yet he had exactly the right type of stamina to keep a solid beat moving along behind Dizzy and Parker and to play chorus after chorus of the flying tempos they demanded. In addition, he had the ability to play solos. He combined this with an unparalleled curiosity about harmony and getting exactly the right note in his bassline for each chord change. "After I'd been with Dizzy about a month and figured I had everything down, I cornered him after the gig and said, 'Diz, how'm I doin'?' He said, 'Oh fine. Except you're playing the wrong notes.' That did it. I started delving into everything we did, the notes, the chords, everything. And I'd sing the lines as I was playing them."[24]

Although Milt Jackson was not hired in quite such a dramatic way, he joined Dizzy's group shortly after Ray Brown, as part of the lineup who were to travel to California, in which the quintet's former Three Deuces pianist Al Haig and Dizzy's old colleague from Philadelphia, Stan Levey, were drafted to replace Roach and Powell. Dizzy knew that his contract with Billy Berg's club required a five-piece band. He also knew, from his experience of the Earl Hines Orchestra, that on the road Parker was sufficiently erratic when it came to matinees and early evening starts that it would pay him to recruit an additional member of the group so that there would always be five musicians on stage. The extra man was Milt Jackson.

"I first met Dizzy in 1943 with Earl Hines," Milt told Charles Fox. "He came through Detroit, where I was working with local bands, and he came by this particular club. Well, when you came to Detroit you couldn't go no place without going by this club to jam, because it was noted for that. So, naturally, all the musicians who came into town came by the club. Dizzy came by, and he heard me play and he encouraged me to come to New York.

"So I said, 'Maybe I'll leave Detroit and go to New York.'

" 'When you do,' said Dizzy, 'look me up.' And he gave me a card.

"Now when I came out of the service in 1944, I went to New York for a weekend on a pass. I just ran around, stayed up for over forty-eight hours, didn't even get no kind of sleep, and went from club to club.

Because all the musicians I'd always heard about and dreamed about seeing, suddenly here they were, right here in the flesh—and I just went completely nuts!"

Milt recalled his first encounter with 52nd Street with just the same awe and wonder as Ray Brown. "It was just remarkable and totally unbelievable," he said. He met Dizzy briefly on that trip, but then returned to Detroit, only coming back to New York in the fall of 1945.

"I got what little money I could, packed my clothes and came back to New York," recalled Jackson. "And in three weeks after I had gotten back to New York, I had a job with Dizzy. I went to Washington with him for two weeks, in a night club. Then shortly thereafter, when we returned to New York, we turned around and with the six-piece band, including Charlie Parker and Ray, we went to California. And I was in seventh heaven, three times tripled over. Man, I was getting the best education. I was going to the best conservatory in the world, every single night for eight solid weeks, and I loved every second and every minute."[25]

Jazz histories in general have promoted the idea that Dizzy's arrival at Billy Berg's club in Hollywood was a milestone in the spread of bebop and that in some way the arrival of this quintet on the West Coast marked the point at which the new jazz broke free of Manhattan and spread across the nation. Equally significant in this myth is the idea that the gig at Billy Berg's club was an unmitigated disaster. Leonard Feather, for example, wrote: "The booking was an unhappy one from the start . . . there were adverse comments about the presence of two white musicians, Al Haig and Stan Levey. [It was] a superb musical combination and a commercial disaster. . . . Business was miserable at Berg's. Except for a small in-group of young musicians, hardly anyone in California understood or cared about bebop, and the clique in question had so little money that it couldn't help much. Dizzy was further hampered by the reactionary local critics and disc jockeys, who were not merely passively disinterested in his work, but actively hoping to see him fail."[26]

The reality is that bebop was already a familiar sound on the West Coast, that similar music had been featured at Berg's over the previous months, and that the engagement was far more successful than Feather suggests. The band also broadcast on the popular AFRS "Jubilee" show, as well as appearing on the Rudy Vallee show.

On February 1, 1945, ten months before Dizzy's arrival, Billy Berg had featured the Coleman Hawkins Quintet at his club on Vine Street, a short distance from Sunset Boulevard. Hawk had assimilated the compositions and many of the harmonic ideas of Thelonious Monk (who had been his pianist) into the band's repertoire, and, with Howard

McGhee on trumpet and Oscar Pettiford on bass, the band had many of the identifiable characteristics of the new music. Singer, multi-instrumentalist, and humorist Slim Gaillard was leading the second band at Berg's during Hawk's stay (which lasted until mid-April), just as he was to do during Dizzy's residency. Hawk's transitional brand of bebop caused no problems with audiences, since, as John Chilton put it, "neither Hawkins nor anyone in his group was modern enough to be offensive to the ears of patrons at Billy Berg's Club." McGhee, equally succinctly, said, "California people knew about Coleman Hawkins but they didn't have the slightest idea what the band was like. And so when they came they said 'Oh Man! What a band! We haven't heard music like that, ever!' So I guess Coleman was the one who opened the West Coast up as far as modern sounds in jazz."[27]

The discs that Hawkins made for Capitol during his group's stay on the Coast (despite the addition of guitarist Allan Reuss, which gives the rhythm section an anodyne swing-influenced feel) suggest that McGhee was only a pace or two behind Dizzy in developing the Eldridge approach to the trumpet, and his leaps into the upper register and controlled flurried of notes on Hawkins/Monk collaborations like "Rifftide" and "Stuffy" are decidedly bebop in style.

Local California musicians agreed. Drummer Roy Porter, who had toured the United States with Milt Larkins's band, and heard McGhee with Andy Kirk and Charlie Barnet, believed that "Maggie" was the real catalyst for bop on the West Coast, especially when he remained there after Hawkins went back East. We know already that McGhee had learned firsthand from Parker and Dizzy when he saw them on the road with Hines, and he combined his experience of their work with the influences of forward-looking West Coast musicians in setting up his own band, to play at the Down Beat Club on 42nd and Central in Los Angeles. "Howard was playing bebop, *hard* bop, and that was exactly where I wanted to be," said Porter. " 'Maggie' was truly the 'Bearer of Gifts,' being the one who brought bebop to the West Coast as far as that's concerned."[28] Porter had visited New York in 1943 and absorbed some of the rhythmic innovations of Kenny Clarke and Max Roach. He noted that when he joined McGhee's new band on the Coast in mid-1945, other drummers were still playing the swing style "rudiments, paradiddling and ratamacuing. They just weren't happening."

Porter makes clear that McGhee's group got widespread exposure in California, both in terms of club bookings and radio broadcasts. Its press included the predictable quota of hostile reviews, "from people that were not capable of understanding what we were doing musically," suggesting that the change in psychological attitude that prevailed in the bop bands of 52nd Street was also gaining ground in the West. After appearing at several local clubs (including Billy Berg's) McGhee's band was working nightly at the Streets of Paris on Hollywood Boulevard when Dizzy's band arrived to open at Berg's on December 10, 1945.

Charlie Parker, almost as keen to discover where the after-hours action was in any city he played as he was to find a source of heroin, soon arrived at the Streets of Paris and strolled up onto the bandstand. Although McGhee's band included tenorist Teddy Edwards, one of the most forward-looking players on the Coast, Parker made an immediate impact when he sat in. "The people there were spellbound when Bird got through playing," recalled Porter. "They had never heard anything like that in their lives. I knew I hadn't!"[29] This and other comments made by Porter support the view that the impression made by all the members of Dizzy's group was in their individual improvisatory ability, of which Parker was the outstanding exponent, rather than in introducing a style that was already established in the West.

Dizzy's band's journey to California is well documented in Ross Russell's *Bird Lives*, as is the depressing realization among the musicians that away from New York and a ready supply of heroin, Charlie Parker was a liability. Parker's system now required daily doses of the drug, or a substitute such as morphine, and his usage had transformed from the high-spirited experimentation of his days on the road with Hines to a much more full-blown habit. His occasional missed sets that had dogged the first few weeks in Hines's band became *de rigueur* with Dizzy's group, and even on the band's opening night Parker only made it to the stage for the final set of three. Dizzy's shrewdness in hiring an extra musician protected the band contractually, but those who turned up to hear Parker could well end up disappointed. This, and the hostile press notices the band received, contributed to the view that the Berg's engagement was a disaster.

Older musicians, who were among the crowds that packed Berg's on the opening night, sided with the critics. "I was out at Billy Berg's the first night that Dizzy Gillespie came out there with Charlie Parker," recalled trumpet veteran George Orendorff, a man who had joined the 1920s exodus of Chicago musicians to Los Angeles and made a good living with bands like Paul Howard's Quality Serenaders.[30] "I got in early and had me a complete dinner. I went out of curiosity. Eddie Heywood had just left there. He had a nice band with Vic Dickenson. Dizzy came on with his 'Salt Peanuts! Salt Peanuts!,' and the people said, 'What's happening?' They wasn't used to that stuff, they didn't understand it. Other guys came in to listen like [trumpeter] Ernie Royal, who came down from San Francisco where he was in the navy. He loved that kind of stuff because he was used to what was happening in New York. Me, I like to hear the melody sometimes."

Many of those who felt hostile to the new music supported Orendorff's view, and in his history of the West Coast scene Robert Gordon wrote, "Overwhelmed by the complexities of the new music being played by Gillespie and company, the club's regulars stayed away in ever increasing numbers."[31] However, well before this was written, and supported by interviews with musicians who were either in Dizzy's group or in the audience at the club, a different attitude started to emerge.

It began as early as 1968, when saxophonist Sonny Criss was interviewed for the British periodical *Jazz Monthly*. "If you want to think of it as a total flop, you would be mistaken," he told Bob Porter and Mark Gardner. "I don't recall it that way because the club was packed every night . . . contrary to the reports, Bird and Dizzy did not play to audiences of ten or twelve people. Billy Berg's was a unique club, in the sense that it was in the center of Hollywood, and it was the first really cosmopolitan club with a good deal of publicity behind it where negro and white people mixed without any pressure. It was a groovy atmosphere, an atmosphere that embraced people from all walks of life."[32] Ted Gioia's admirable history of West Coast jazz, published six years after Gordon's, investigated further, and includes an interview with Harry "The Hipster" Gibson, who shared the bill with Dizzy and Slim Gaillard. "We were packing them in. The place was packed."[33]

Gioia advances the idea that Parker's subsequent nervous collapse, which happened a short while after the rest of Dizzy's band returned to New York, in some way colored history's view of the whole sequence of events and unjustly tarred the Berg's engagement with the stigma of failure. Certainly, bassist Ray Brown felt that this was the case when he spoke to the author. He agreed that the band had had to include some hastily written arrangements of more commercial pieces into its sets, including a few vocal numbers, but he did not feel there had been any compromise.

"When we got to Billy Berg's, the newspaper said after the first night: 'Men from Mars Playing at Billy Berg's!' They thought we were the most outrageous thing they had ever heard. They didn't understand a note of it. But all the musicians were in there every night, because they knew. Art Tatum used to come in there every night even. If you had been a musician and you had heard Charlie Parker and Dizzy Gillespie play at that time, you would know. It would be like, whoever is the best in your own chosen profession, if you suddenly ran across them, you would know that they were exceptional. The movie *Bird* said that we got fired, but we didn't get fired. The guy said if you want to finish out this engagement, you're going to have to be more commercial, so Charlie Parker wrote out a couple of arrangements where we sang—the whole band were singing—and later they added another guy, Lucky Thompson. He was a great saxophone player but he didn't match up to these guys, but we finished out the engagement."[34]

The Berg's booking was to be the last occasion for some time when Parker and Dizzy worked together. Toward the end of their run, which finished on February 3, 1946, Parker became increasingly erratic and failed to appear when the rest of the band flew back to New York on February 9. He remained in California and was subsequently admitted to the Camarillo State Hospital for six months between August 1946 and January 1947.

Parker and Gillespie did make some commercial recordings in California with Slim Gaillard, plus one track with Dizzy's own band for Ross Russell's fledgling Dial label, and appeared together on Norman Granz's poll winner's concert at the Philharmonic Hall, which was a prototype session for Jazz at the Philharmonic (a concert package that Dizzy and Bird would both benefit from in years to come). The music they made is discussed in the next chapter, but it is worth noting here that the band's most vital and interesting playing comes in their broadcast work. The recordings that survive give a clear impression of the band that appeared at Billy Berg's and benefit from neither being constrained to the three and a half minutes of a 78-rpm disc nor having the lineup diluted with other musicians.

Dizzy's announcements with MC Ernie Whitman reveal a man who was already jovial and relaxed at the microphone and no longer the inept presenter of his "Hep-sations" tour. Perhaps he had learned from appearing opposite Gibson and Gaillard at Berg's. "Who's gonna do the singing here? Who's gonna tell the jokes?" ran drummer Stan Levey's account of the expectations of the Berg's audience, and Dizzy found himself falling into the role of genial host-cum-bandleader. But Levey noted that behind the persona Dizzy's business edge had sharpened. The southern tour with the big band had been salutary, and Dizzy no longer countenanced slackness from his men. "Dizzy had his act together," recalled Levey, "[and he] was voracious in his drive to succeed."[35] Parker's behavior was not acceptable to Dizzy and, admirer of Bird's playing that he was, Parker's erratic habits no longer fitted Gillespie's will to achieve. The year 1946 was to be one in which Gillespie again pushed forward the development of the new music unaided by Parker.

11
1945—The Records

The year began with the first of the large number of free-lance sessions that Dizzy and Charlie Parker were to make for small specialist labels. Clyde Hart's All Stars gathered with blues singer Henry "Rubberlegs" Williams to make a session for Continental on January 4. As it turns out, although Williams had had a busy career in vaudeville and had made a film "short" for Vitaphone in 1933, this was his first recording session.

A large imperious man, tending in his late thirties to be somewhat overweight, Williams had made his reputation and acquired his nick-name as a specialty dancer on the variety circuit. From winning provincial dancing contests in his early teens to a string of appearances as a hoofer in shows like *Cotton Club Parade* and *Blackbirds of 1933*, Williams had added singing to his act in the early 1930s, appearing with Fletcher Henderson's band and at several New York clubs. He briefly operated his own club, was chosen to sing at Bessie Smith's funeral, and his non-smoking, teetotaling, genial personality made him a much-liked favorite in Harlem and the New York black community. Unfortunately, either as the result of a practical joke or an accident, Williams's debut on wax was something he would later prefer to forget.

Charlie Parker was in the habit of sharpening his senses for per-forming by dropping the contents of a benzedrine inhaler into a mug of coffee and downing the contents to ward off the somnolent effects of drink or drugs. The Williams recording took place in the small hours of the morning after all the participants had finished their various club dates, and so Parker was in need of one of these special coffee cocktails. Another musician had brought some rough whisky called "Joe Louis" to the session, and, despite his customary abstinence, Williams swigged a considerable amount of it. Accounts vary as to what happened next, and whether Rubberlegs accidentally drank Parker's drink or Parker spiked Rubberlegs's coffee. Whichever is the case, listening in sequence to the the five masters that were cut at the session shows Rubberlegs degen-erating from the smooth baritone blues singing of "What's the Matter Now" to the ranting and raving of the vocals on his final effort, "4f Blues."

The backing to Rubberlegs's set involved some hasty arrangements with no organized ensemble playing and a string of solos, either obbligatos behind the singer or, as his contributions became increasingly sparser and less coherent, between his vocals. By contrast, the second half of the session involved some well-organized charts to back up the rather saccharine singing of trombonist Trummy Young, and in these there were some formal solo opportunities for Parker, Gillespie, and tenorist Don Byas, all of whom produced some cogent and well-rounded playing.

Dizzy takes only two solos on the Williams sides, a self-parody on "GI Blues" that hovers round the flattened fifths of the twelve-bar blues sequence before one of his cliché high-register figures, and a more formed solo on "4f Blues" that has Rubberlegs shouting "Open it up! Open it up!" as Dizzy plays a succession of boppish figures. He makes no attempt to emulate the conventions of trumpet accompaniments to the blues either here or in his obbligatos behind Williams, but remains comprehensively outside the blues idiom throughout the session. Bird, on the other hand, takes a succession of sublime blues choruses on several of the Rubberlegs tracks, from an outstanding obbligato on "That's the Blues" to a lyrical chorus on "What's the Matter Now."

Despite his southern background, Dizzy displayed an antipathy to blues in much of his work and in many interviews confirmed that this was deliberate. Bird, put into a blues context, could not help himself. He was, as Ray Brown told the author, "the best blues player you ever heard. He grew up playing the blues."[1]

According to Trummy Young, Rubberlegs was upset by Dizzy's resolutely bop solos, and through his whisky and benzedrine haze accosted Dizzy with his characteristic mode of address: "Miss Gillespie, if you play another of them bad notes, I'm gonna beat your brains out."[2] This antipathy was preserved for posterity in a small number of photographs of the two of them (though it is not clear whether these were taken at the session) that show Rubberlegs holding Dizzy threateningly by the lapels.

Characteristically, for a man who, as Billy Taylor recalled, had intellectualized the bop revolution, Dizzy was not prepared to deviate from his chosen path to emulate the sounds of the blues. "I am not the type to have followed the blues," he said. "I wasn't a blues follower. But Hot Lips Page and Charlie Parker had come from what was really a blues area, where the guys really did that. Now there was nobody playing anything in my hometown. I was listening to Roy Eldridge and Chu Berry and I was more inclined to that. I heard the blues all my life, so I knows it when I hears it—that's very bad grammar, but you see with the blues you have to say things like that. But anyway, Charlie Parker was really a blues player. Played a mean, low-down blues."[3]

This interview reveals a number of things: Dizzy's consistent reiteration of the myth that he heard Eldridge and Berry before he left Cheraw; his ability to intellectualize his reaction to blues even to the extent of parodying its grammar; and his nonetheless grudging admiration for Parker's intuitive blues ability.

When the musicians turned their attention to the tightly scored charts for Trummy Young's half of the session, after an increasingly violent Rubberlegs had been ushered away, their natural big band instincts emerged in a beautifully balanced reading of Sy Oliver and Jimmie Lunceford's "Dream of You." This was clear common ground for all the musicians present, and the style, unsurprisingly, settled into something akin to that of John Kirby's little group. After a magnificent opening solo from Parker, Dizzy's eight bars are a perfect example of the modified bop playing he had used with a swing rhythm section on Leonard Feather's New Year's Eve date, four nights earlier.

Many musicians who frequented 52nd Street at the time have made the point that in 1945 the "bebop" label was still meaningless to the majority of musicians. In just the same way as Art Tatum, Roy Eldridge, and even Benny Goodman had been sitters-in at Minton's in 1940–41, swing and bop musicians mingled constantly in the studios and on 52nd Street during the mid-1940s. "Although the fans at the time were totally divided, the musicians were not," wrote Bob Wilber, of the era when he was a starstruck teenager, hopping from club to club on "the Street."[4] Although he and Dick Wellstood were playing traditional jazz (music that Dizzy once described as "so far in, it's far out"), Wilber listened avidly to Bird and Dizzy and remembers jamming with Howard McGhee and Stan Getz during a stay in Boston a year or two later. Clyde Hart's band, on this date with Trummy Young, is the epitome of the swing-bop transition, with musicians from both sides of the supposed divide represented.

On "Seventh Avenue" and Trummy Young's own "Sorta Kinda," Dizzy takes the type of tightly muted solo that was to be a hallmark of his bop quintets and sextets, but does so over a backdrop of Al Hall's walking bass, Specs Powell's light brushwork, and Hart's prodding chords, a swing setting more redolent of Basie's Kansas City Five and Seven small groups than the swirling bop of Max Roach and Oscar Pettiford. Only on "Oh Oh, My My," the closing track of the set, does the rhythm section start to break up the beat, with some sharp rimshots from Powell. Ironically, the soloist he chose to back in this way was neither Parker nor Dizzy but Don Byas.

Five days later, in rather more overtly modernist surroundings, Dizzy was back in the studios, this time for Manor. The session again broke into two halves, the first involving an eighteen-piece band under Oscar Pettiford's leadership and the second a sextet led by Dizzy in what was to be the very first session under his own name. In a perverse twist of fate, the vocalist on Pettiford's session was none other than Rubberlegs Williams.

Pettiford's big band set was nearly a disaster. Although he had hired the musicians successfully (not all their names can now be reliably confirmed), he had omitted to furnish them with any arrangements.[5] Fortunately, drawing on his experience with the Eckstine band, Dizzy roughed out a head arrangement based on "Max Is Making Wax," called "Something for You," which provided a raucous, exciting, uptempo backdrop for some dramatic solos by Don Byas and Dizzy himself.

The rhythm section is anchored by Pettiford's restless bass and the offbeat accents of drummer Shelly Manne, who also used his bass drum pedal effectively in echoing some of the front-line phrases in the opening head arrangement. The chords at the end of the channel in the first chorus have some of Dizzy's typically adventurous voicing, as have some of the brass figures behind Don Byas's opening solo. Some critics have felt that Shelly Manne's attempts to drum in the bop style were not altogether successful, but he punctuates the chart here with feeling for both the style and the arrangement, adding some propulsive rimshots and accents.[6] Dizzy's own solo begins dramatically with a high-note scream and then floats over a bed of brass riffs and rhythm before the brass fall back, leaving him to finish his solo with a dramatic flourish as the trumpets reenter for the closing riff. There is a sense here of how the Billy Eckstine band might have sounded, had it been recorded more often in its short life, blowing freely on one of Dizzy's impromptu charts.

"Empty Bed Blues" (beginning with Rubberlegs singing, ironically in the circumstances, about waking up with an aching head) is divided into two parts. The first features yet more first-rate backing from Don Byas and some growling blues trumpet from someone other than Dizzy, whose own contribution is limited to a few plangent phrases toward the end. The second section has some boppish underpinning from Dizzy behind the vocal, which is probably about as far as Dizzy was prepared to go in the direction of blues at this point in his career, recalling his work with Pete Brown for Leonard Feather, backing Norah Lee King. (Perhaps his most effective work as a blues player came in the session with Albinia Jones, a few months later, in April 1945. He builds the opening of his solo on her "Evil Gal Blues" around the traditional flattened third of conventional blues playing, and turns in a splendid outchorus in Eldridge style for "Don't Wear No Black." But the underlying point that Dizzy was not keen to involve himself in an authentic blues style could hardly be better reinforced than on "Albinia's Blues" when his boppish intervals collide stridently with clarinetist Gene Sedric's conventional phrases on the final twelve measures.)

The four sextet pieces that Dizzy cut under his own name immediately after Pettiford's eighteen-piece set are far more significant, with three staples of the bebop repertoire—Tadd Dameron's "Good Bait" and Dizzy's own "Salt Peanuts" and "Bebop"—plus Dizzy's definitive version of a ballad that was to become a regular part of his repertoire: "I Can't Get Started."

This last tune, by Vernon Duke to lyrics by Ira Gershwin, had been a swing era standard, recorded, among others, by Billie Holiday. But what became the accepted approach to the song was set out in Bunny Berigan's big band version. (Berigan also cut an impressive alternative with a small group.) Berigan included a vocal as well as a trumpet solo that was much imitated (among others by Nat Gonella in England).

Dizzy, by contrast, treated the entire piece as a trumpet solo and played throughout—an eight-bar introduction, the thirty-two-bar "AABA" main theme, a two-bar tag, and a brief coda—the whole thing taken at a slow ballad pace. Trummy Young and Don Byas supplied long notes for the opening and a clever riff under the "A" section of the theme, underlining as they went some subtle reharmonization by Tadd Dameron at the end of the second eight-bar section as it leads into the central "channel," which has subsequently become the most widely adopted jazz harmonic sequence for the tune. "That was Tadd Dameron's arrangement," said Dizzy. "I figured that a new idea on it wouldn't take anything away from Bunny Berigan but show there were possibilities for the tune. Later I used the ending of that version of "I Can't Get Started" for the introduction of 'Round Midnight.' "[7]

Dizzy plays the main theme almost as written when it first arrives, but then produces an elegant paraphrase, before the bridge section, that combines long high notes with some quicker flurries of notes almost in double time. It was one thing to produce the fast, flowing trumpet that dominated "Something for You" by the Pettiford eighteen-piece band at the start of the session and quite another to reinterpret the most familiar trumpet ballad of the Swing Era in so immediately authoritative and fresh a way that it became impossible to listen to Berigan's version without feeling that, however well played, it was harmonically shallow and intellectually stale. Dizzy could hardly have chosen a better vehicle for his first session as leader to announce that he had arrived at full maturity as a soloist. As the year went on, he was to restate this again and again, with a series of ever more accomplished solos, although few manage the delicate balance of imagination, modernity, and beauty that he achieved here.

The second piece that Dizzy cut with his sextet, Tadd Dameron's "Good Bait," was to become central to his big band repertoire, and this prototype compares interestingly to the far more developed version cut by the big band in December 1947. The sextet employs a series of trombone pedal notes in the opening chorus—a Basie-style vamp—that is absent from the big band chart. The overall effect of the sextet arrangement is closest to a Kansas City small group (unsurprising, given Dameron's arranging experience there for Harlan Leonard), with Shelly Manne producing a passable Jo Jones impression on the hi-hat, and Trummy Young turning in a trombone solo that accurately catches the nuances of Dicky Wells's playing in Basie's band. The composer credits for this piece, when it was eventually copyrighted, include Basie, whose band did not add it to their repertoire until 1948.

Dameron had known Dizzy since 1940, almost certainly meeting him at the same time as Gillespie first met Charlie Parker when the Calloway band was in Kansas City, although Dizzy once suggested that it may even have been slightly earlier that year when Harlan Leonard's band was briefly in New York.[8] From the time of Dizzy's Onyx Club residency in 1943–44, the two men had gotten to know one another better. Dizzy recalled that Tadd spent more time writing than looking for opportunities to play, and Budd Johnson observed that Dizzy would be keen to demonstrate different voicings to Tadd as they clustered round the keyboard to work out new arrangements.[9] In early 1945, Tadd and Dizzy were still enjoying their cooperative association, as is obvious from the two Dameron arrangements included in the session.

Later, in 1946, when Dizzy founded his second big band, their relationship cooled when there was a squabble over money. Because Tadd did not play regularly but expected to make a living from writing, he charged Dizzy for his arrangements for the big band.

"I taught Tadd, you know," recalled Dizzy. "You can tell that his writing was very much influenced by my harmony, by what I had worked out on the piano myself. So I'd say to Tadd, 'How much is this arrangement?'

"He'd say, 'Seventy-five dollars.'

"I'd say 'Seventy-five dollars? Do you think I'm gonna pay you seventy-five dollars for my shit?' You know what I mean. I had shown him, and so I'd say: 'You can't charge me what you charge Jimmy Dorsey and Tommy Dorsey and all those people. Because I'm the one that *caused* your music!' So in the end I didn't pay him anyway."[10]

Gil Fuller suggested that Dizzy failed to pay Tadd because in 1946, when he set up his next big band, he simply didn't have the money.[11] But one way or another, the productive relationship that lay behind the first record date under Dizzy's own name was not to endure for much more than another year.

The last two pieces at the sextet record date were Dizzy's own. "Salt Peanuts" is again a prototype, showing the skeleton of the treatment that the tune would receive both in his small groups and later big bands. It is notable for a flowing high-register solo by Dizzy that extends over slightly more than two full choruses as well as for Pettiford's expert shadowing of the opening riff in the head arrangement. "Bebop" has an even lengthier solo from Dizzy, which is a more fluent piece of extended thinking than many of his solos from the period, no longer consisting of the sequence of separate chorus-length "architectural" ideas noted elsewhere, but a genuine development over ninety-eight measures. Because Trummy Young did not solo on this track, it has been assumed by most discographers that he was not present, but his trombone bass notes are clearly audible backing up Dizzy on the opening sections behind Don Byas's muscular tenor sax.

Dizzy's first session under his own name was an unqualified success. The rhythm section of Pettiford, Hart, and Manne did not perhaps have the fluidity that Max Roach might have brought to it, but the sound was convincingly different from most earlier bebop small groups and had a homogeneity that was absent from, for example, Coleman Hawkins's sessions from the year before. Above all, Dizzy demonstrated a confidence and assurance in every aspect of his playing that breezes out of each track, suggesting a man who had arrived at the formula he wanted as the showcase for the style he had been developing for so long.

Three days later, he was to show that he could impose the same breezy confidence on a very different type of band, one that, indeed, proves perfectly Bob Wilber's point about the lack of stylistic boundaries between 52nd Street musicians. Clarinetist Joe Marsala was highly regarded as a fluent Dixieland player and, after moving from his native Chicago, had fronted the band at two of New York's best known jazz clubs, Adrian Rollini's Tap Room and the Hickory House, during the 1930s. Dizzy would assuredly have known Marsala by reputation and, in his thirst for nightlife following his initial arrival in New York, it is quite probable he had sat in with Marsala at various points over the years.

Marsala, too, was open to ideas well beyond the hidebound Dixieland stereotype, and had employed Roy Eldridge for his Delta Four discs in 1935 and Henry Allen as his front-line partner for club work. When he went into the studio to cut four sides for the Black and White label on January 12, 1945, he invited Dizzy to fill the trumpet chair. "I liked Diz and a lot of the things he did," Marsala told Leonard Feather, "I never could do it, but I liked it."[12] The repertoire they selected was for the most part sufficiently mainstream to be an easy meeting of styles. The opening "Perdido" has a hint of the approach Dizzy was to bring to the many dozens of times he was to jam on this sequence for Jazz at the Philharmonic, a well-structured bop-inflected solo that would have sounded just as coherent in the context of his own more fluid rhythm section, but that glides over the even four-to-the-bar laid down by Buddy Christian's drums and stride pianist Cliff Jackson (born in 1902 and, at forty-seven, virtually a veteran, and a representative of the first generation of jazzmen).

It is Jackson who starts off the most stylistically archaic of the pieces they recorded, a version of "My Melancholy Baby," in which his stride introduction would not have disgraced James P. Johnson or Fats Waller, but is followed abruptly and effectively by an uncompromisingly modern solo from Dizzy. While Dizzy was, it seems, unwilling to adapt his playing to add an air of authenticity to blues sessions, his confidence in his solo style was such that in company with jazzmen he respected he could adapt just enough to find common ground, while retaining his uniquely identifiable character. Equally for his part, Jackson was a wily enough accompanist to know when to drop back and simply provide basic chords to support the trumpeter. The most awkward moments in the session come in "Cherokee," when, apart from an excellent solo, Dizzy finds himself on a collision course with guitarist Chuck Wayne, whose unbending iteration of the melody leaves little room for a trumpet obbligato.

In terms of its overall importance, this session is, as suggested in the previous chapter, insignificant. Yet it is a pointer to Dizzy's growing adaptability in a variety of contexts. When, in subsequent years, critics were overcritical of the inclusion of swing players like Cozy Cole and Sid Catlett on Dizzy's own discs from later in 1945, they would have done well to reflect on the broad range of Dizzy's own recording activities at the time and the general lack of stylistic pigeonholing they represent.

Dizzy's tenure with Boyd Raeburn is a case in point. The highlight of this association is the studio recording of "Night in Tunisia," cut with the big band on January 26, 1945. We can assume that this is the arrangement Dizzy wrote for Earl Hines that was traded with Raeburn at the birth of Billy Eckstine's orchestra, since a virtually identical chart was played by Raeburn's band in a recorded broadcast from the spring of 1944, featuring Roy Eldridge in the solo trumpet role. Eldridge's treatment is straightforward swing trumpeting, one of his famous breaks that spirals through the whole register of the trumpet ushering in a behind-

the-beat relaxed solo. Equally, Don Lamond anchors the rhythm section
in an easy swinging four-to-the-bar. For the studio date, Dizzy's presence
seems to have galvanized both the lower reeds (who provide the opening
ostinato) and the rhythm section into a more Latinate feel, and the drumming of Shelly Manne is more overtly modern in style, with some sympathetic accents behind Dizzy's miraculous solo. The trumpet enters in
a rush of short phrases, tumbling over one another, and never settles
behind the beat in the way Eldridge did, maintaining a dramatic tension
for the whole solo, spiced up by some unusual harmonic intervals. This
is yet another example of how well Dizzy was playing in January 1945,
and his energy, power, and effortless high register work is, if anything,
more at home in the big band context than in the various small groups
he recorded with. He produced another accomplished solo on Raeburn's
"March of the Boyds," and also featured in broadcast versions of "Bare-
foot Boy with Cheek" and "Jumpin' for Maria." The only doubtful exercise from Dizzy's period with Raeburn is a dire broadcast vocal version
of "Night in Tunisia" as "Interlude," similar in structure to the Sarah
Vaughan version cut on New Year's Eve. Raeburn's singer Don Darcy
was not the same caliber of vocalist as Sarah, and even Dizzy's short solo
fails to relieve the tedium of the track.

Patti Powers, who sang with Georgie Auld's studio band, was only
marginally better, but her version of "Sweetheart of All My Dreams"
includes a good example of Dizzy's ability to "play in the cracks," his
sinuous trumpet solo snaking through the full power of the other sections
in an early February session. His most acclaimed work with Auld is the
version of "In the Middle" from the same date, which also features some
stylistically transitional piano from Erroll Garner.

Two days after Auld's session, which, like Dizzy's own recordings,
was made for Guild, Dizzy was back in the studios for the same company
to cut another pair of sides under his own name. These were his first
recordings of "Groovin' High" and "Blue 'n' Boogie." His front-line partner was a veteran of the Eckstine band, tenorist Dexter Gordon, and the
piano chair was occupied by the man who was to share copyright in a
number of Gillespie compositions in return for transcribing Dizzy's solos
on them, Frank Paparelli.

At the time, Guild decided not to issue "Groovin' High," so the
version of the tune that is best known came from the collaboration three
weeks later with Charlie Parker (this later version was issued on the back
of "Blue 'n' Boogie"). Structurally, the two attempts at "Groovin' High"
(a piece built on the chords of "Whispering" and officially attributed to
Dizzy and Kirby Stone as joint composers) are almost identical: the in-

troduction, unison opening chorus, bridges between sections, and slow ending are all similar, with the chorus after the opening saxophone solo given to the guitar on the earlier take and to Slam Stewart's bowed bass on the second. Gordon's solo is a strong statement, even if it lacks the bite of Parker's chorus. The real surprise in the earlier version is the strength of Dizzy's solo. He plays open horn (in contrast to the muted instrument in the take with Parker) and scrabbles into his solo with a repeated high phrase during his two-bar break. He then plays right through to the end of the disc (whereas he falls back for a short guitar solo on the later version), leading the ensemble clearly into the slow coda with a sequence of beautifully hit high notes.

There are, perhaps, two inferences to be drawn from this. First, that, following Gordon's solo playing, which was less assertive than Parker's, Dizzy felt it incumbent on him to provide the touch of drama that he instinctively knew the arrangement needed. Second, having heard how this sounded, for the subsequent recording Dizzy chose to alter the timbre and shape of the arrangement by muting his horn, bringing in the guitar before the coda, and featuring Stewart's bowed bass. The underlying arrangement was, as Thomas Owens has pointed out, "the most complex jazz melody superimposed on a pre-existing chordal scheme." In his survey of bebop, Owens also notes that the piece "was atypically elaborate for bebop performances, with its composed six-measure introduction . . . its modulations . . . its choruses of varying lengths and its dramatic half-speed coda."[13] Yet it would appear that it was precisely his search for this kind of structure (as in his setting of "I Can't Get Started," or its sequel, " 'Round About Midnight") that set Dizzy apart from Parker and the other boppers. His efforts to refine "Groovin' High" into a varied and interesting three-minute 78-rpm disc are evidence of his compositional thought.

"Blue 'n' Boogie" was the only track to be issued at the time from the session with Gordon and Paparelli. Both men take accomplished solos, but it is again Dizzy who holds the attention with a brilliantly conceived chorus. He is effectively backed by some inventive drumming by Manne, who once more proves that he had assimilated the style of Clarke and Roach more thoroughly than most.

The session on February 28 is the first of two (the second was on May 11) that are the crowning achievement of Dizzy's work from 1945 and that set down for posterity the high watermark of the unique and fruitful collaboration he enjoyed with Charlie Parker. The seven tracks made at these two dates reveal Dizzy's earlier recordings under his own name to have been paving the way for this collaboration. They defined the bebop small-group style once and for all, and they mark a turning point in jazz history. Surprisingly, this was far from obvious, especially in the United States, at the time.

The way the tracks were originally issued, "Blue 'n' Boogie" (with Dexter Gordon) and "Groovin' High" formed Guild 1001, while "Salt Peanuts" and "Hot House" from the May session were issued back to back as Guild 1003. ("Shaw 'Nuff" and "Lover Man" became Guild 1002.)

One of the longest running critical feuds in jazz history, as James Lincoln Collier put it in his monograph on the subject, is the "myth which has clung like a burr to jazz history," namely "the idea that it was first taken seriously by Europeans."[14] Irrespective of the merits of this argument in terms of early jazz, it is indisputably the case that the dramatic importance of these Parker–Gillespie sides was first illustrated by a European critic. Perhaps because the impact of World War Two was such that Europeans had to catch up on five years of listening that had been denied them, this telescoping of time sharpened their critical faculties. Perhaps the routine issuing of yet more minor label material by former swing band stars bypassed the attention of the main U. S. writers. The reviews of Guild 1001, 1002, and 1003 in the United States were lightweight compared to the double-page article "Toward a Renewal of Jazz Music?" that André Hodier produced for the French magazine *Jazz Hot* in the May 1946 issue.[15]

Typical of the U. S. reaction, *Down Beat*'s regular "Diggin' the Discs with Don" feature was dismissive. On "Blue 'n' Boogie" and "Groovin' High" it read, "neither side exhibits Dizzy's horn or style to the best advantage. Riffs are not new, except to one who has not dug Dizzy's work before; they're obvious but still interesting. Both sides except during the ensemble parts, sound a little forced."[16] "Lover Man" and "Shaw 'Nuff" were damned with faint praise in the same column. "There's a lot to this style—it's exciting and has plenty of musical worth, yet for lasting worth must rid itself of much that now clutters its true value. Dizzy's and Charlie's solos are both excellent in many ways, yet still too acrobatic and sensationalistic to be expressive in the true sense of good swing."[17] Perhaps the most disparaging comments of all were reserved for Dizzy's first session of the year (without Parker) when the original version of "Salt Peanuts" was cut: "The arrangements are too affected and overdone, so much that it's hardly good swing."[18]

There is no such dismissive writing in Hodier's piece, which also includes extended transcriptions of sections of "Groovin' High," "Salt Peanuts," and "Hot House."

Immediately after the war, Hodier was depressed to find that jazz appeared to have stood still since 1939. "The Liberation, with its black and white G.I.s and their tons of V-Discs did nothing to change my opinion. . . . In truth there were some new names, but it didn't seem that even King Cole, Don Byas and Oscar Pettiford, despite their incontestable talent, were much more than followers, who brought little new to the art of Teddy Wilson, Hawkins and Blanton." He goes on to say that news of the annual *Esquire* awards, with many new names and some new ideas, sowed the seeds of hope that jazz would find a new and happy direction to take it into the 1950s. "That hope has become a certainty in the form of two black discs with red labels, in which is inscribed the future of African-American music."[19]

Hodier had noticed Dizzy's work in his contribution to Lionel Hampton's "Hot Mallets" in 1939. He points out that Dizzy had not stood still in the interim, but that the success of the new records lies almost entirely in the inspired collaboration of Parker and Gillespie. "We are in the presence of what we have awaited for a long time, two original creative talents whose closely allied ideas go together as effectively as those of Armstrong and Hines or Johnny Hodges and Duke." On "Groovin' High," he found Parker's solo the main attraction: "the manner in which this marvellous improviser treats the theme, ornamenting it without giving the impression of rambling, never overdoing it, and indeed, by contrast, brightening up his melodic phrases by the use of silences between them in a way that only Johnny Hodges knows how to do, will ravish the listener and confound the critic. I have set out these eighteen measures in the hope that committing them to paper will not too greatly obscure the subtle thought of their creator, even if, alas, it is impossible to capture the beauty of his sound."

On this piece, Hodier finds Gillespie's own muted solo an effective development of his "Hot Mallets" ideas, but given to cliché and minor technical errors that obtrude in an otherwise intelligently worked out solo. But Hodier rightly commends Gillespie for his grand coda, pointing out that this is a new departure in a grand tradition of trumpet finales pioneered on record twenty years earlier by Armstrong.

Hodier reserves his highest praise for the May 11 tracks (even though he inadvertently transposes the names of Curley Russell and Al Haig): "I believe that the history of jazz will remember as an essential date the point in May 1945 when five black musicians recorded 'Hot House' and 'Salt Peanuts.'" He sees Dizzy and Parker as trying to escape the past, in a miracle of creation the equal of the great age of jazz in the 1920s, but "at the start of a new and valuable aesthetic." He hails Parker's talent as "diabolical," and correctly assesses Dizzy's outstanding contribution to jazz trumpet: "More powerful and sure than Armstrong, more rapid than Eldridge, he seems to laugh at difficulties . . . he climbs into the highest register with derisive ease, and his ample tone and heat are something to marvel at."

By any standards, Hodier's writing gets directly to the essence of his subject. It is by far the most informed and analytical of any criticism written about Parker and Gillespie at the time, and he adroitly seizes on the very aspects of their work that made them great individual musicians but, briefly, an even greater partnership. Hodier's analysis of Parker's natural improvisatory ability notes how it differs from Gillespie's more technically flamboyant virtuosity and "architectural" solo structure. He also catches the point so quickly dismissed by the *Down Beat* critic— that Dizzy's and Parker's best soloing derived from the very creative environment of Dizzy's compositions and arrangements. Hodier's description of Tadd Dameron's "Hot House" (based on the chords of "What Is This Thing Called Love?") has hardly been bettered: "It is almost entirely built on augmented fifths and dissonant sevenths, which confer a peculiar character on it. Without going over completely to atonality, the melody invokes sufficient tonal uncertainty to baffle insufficiently informed listeners, but to charm all others."

If ammunition were needed to prolong the debate over the European critical reaction to jazz, this would seem to constitute a well-stocked magazine. To be sure, Dizzy and Bird would attract a lot of press in America, but the majority of column inches devoted to their work in the two years or so that followed would be given over to the sartorial and linguistic innovations of the boppers: berets, horn-rimmed spectacles, and goatees in an atmosphere of jive-talk. Few writers would so astutely focus on their contribution to the development of jazz and so accurately pinpoint the recordings that charted the change.

Before moving on to the remainder of 1945, it is worth noting that "All the Things You Are" from February 28 has a shared ballad chorus from Dizzy and Parker at the start, along with a brief muted solo from Dizzy at the end, which builds around a riffed countermelody. This piece, like all the others, has a closely arranged introduction and coda, suggesting a relatively fixed approach to how the pieces would normally be played during the quintet's gig at the Three Deuces. "Dizzy Atmosphere" also has just such an opening figure, leading naturally into the first chorus and picked up by Dizzy in a stunning open solo that reuses in their mature form many of the devices noted in their infancy in his Cab Calloway solos. Finally, "Lover Man," from May 11, is the most successful recorded collaboration up to that point between Dizzy and Sarah Vaughan. The song would have been familiar to Dizzy from vocalist Willie Dukes, who sang it as a feature while billed opposite Dizzy at the

Onyx. It had been recorded in a nonvocal version in 1944 by Doc Chea-
tham with Eddie Heywood's band, but Sarah's version with Parker and
Gillespie was one of the first recordings of a full vocal treatment of Ram
Ramirez's beautiful song.[20]

One of the pitfalls of working for the tiny Guild company was that
it folded before all Dizzy's discs had been issued. "All the Things You
Are" and "Dizzy Atmosphere" did not emerge until all the company's
masters had been transferred to Musicraft the following year, so, in addition to the time taken to issue the sides Guild did manage to release,
there was a further delay before all the material from these productive
sessions was able to have a full impact on the listening public.[21] Hodier's
criticism was restricted to the two discs that initially made their way from
the United States to France in late 1945, and even in America the majority of the community of musicians would not have become aware of
all of this part of Dizzy and Parker's output until the first phase of their
association was more or less over.

However, as the discs filtered through to their intended audience,
they had a remarkable effect, even if jazz critics themselves were slow to
realize it. Pianist Lennie Tristano, writing in *Metronome* two years later
in 1947, described the extraordinary effect the records had had in spawning a whole host of imitators: "Artistically, the situation is . . . deplorable.
These little monkey-men of music steal note for note the phrases of the
master of the new idiom, John Birks 'Dizzy' Gillespie. Their endless
repetition of these phrases makes living in their midst like fighting one's
way through a nightmare in which bebop pours out of the walls, the
heavens, and the coffeepot. Most boppers contribute nothing to the idiom. Whether they play drums, saxophone, piano, or glockenspiel, it still
comes out Gillespie. Dizzy probably thinks he's in a house of mirrors,
but, in spite of this barrage of dead echoes, he still sounds great. They
manage to steal some of his notes, but his soul stays on the record."[22]

After a further session with Sarah Vaughan, at which the regular
Three Deuces Quintet was augmented by the addition of Flip Phillips
on tenor and Bill De Arango on guitar, with Nat Jaffe and Tadd Dameron taking turns at the piano, Dizzy and Bird gathered on June 6 at the
unearthly hour of nine in the morning for a remarkable recording session
that marks, more effectively than almost any other, the transition in jazz
that they had brought about. Red Norvo's *Fabulous Jam Session* was cut
at the WOR studios on 38th Street and Broadway. It brought together
a collection of Swing Era giants and bebop pioneers, and is exceptional
because (in yet another example of the free-for-all recording jamboree
enjoyed by the small companies in 1945) it was one of only three sessions
made by the Comet label, a company backed by a jazz enthusiast called

Lee Schreiber that put jazz onto 12-inch 78-rpm discs, which allowed a longer playing time than the conventional 10-inch format. This format was ideal for the loose jam-session style Norvo had in mind, but without the efforts of Ross Russell, who ultimately collected the masters and issued the material on his Dial label, and Tony Williams, who preserved it in a splendid documentary issue from his English Spotlite company, the music might have disappeared without a trace. Comet's 12-inch discs were notoriously fragile, and the company only issued four sides from the date, even though eight further masters (albeit of the same tunes) had been saved.

The Comet sides did not have anything like the same impact as Dizzy's Guild records, especially since musically they did not present anything radically new, apart from Dizzy and Bird's solos, and their distribution was, to say the least, limited. But they are an extraordinary document of the final stages of the transition from swing to bop, with unreconstructed swing musicians like Red Norvo, Teddy Wilson, and Slam Stewart (who were with Benny Goodman at the time) creating exciting, swinging jazz alongside Phillips, Dizzy, and Bird. In many ways, especially since bebop in its purest form lasted only a few years, this session is the harbinger of the 1950s and beyond, illustrating the loose mixture of styles that carried over into the great concert touring shows like Jazz at the Philharmonic and George Wein's Newport packages.

Dizzy and Bird were working at the Three Deuces the night before the session, finishing there at 4 A.M. Press reports show that the band was still doing good business. ("Dizzy Gillespie, 'the young Louis Armstrong' whose sensational trumpet fills the Three Deuces nightly with swarms of hot jazz fans" ran one piece.[23]) They apparently were not too concerned about getting any sleep and went directly to Hector's Cafeteria on 49th Street for an early breakfast before heading downtown to the session. Red and his Goodman colleagues were just in town for a day or two, during a tour of one-nighters with Benny's Sextet, and Phillips similarly had some time off from Woody Herman's current road tour. Drummer J. C. Heard was still a member of Cab Calloway's band at the time.[24]

It took several takes of most of the tunes to arrive at versions with which Red Norvo was satisfied. The opening "Hallelujah!" went through six, "Get Happy" through four. Three complete versions of "Congo Blues" plus two false starts survive, as do two versions of Stewart's feature " 'Slam Slam' Blues." Comparing Dizzy's contribution to the various takes, it is clear that he worked hard to develop his ideas from one to the next. It seems almost impossible that anyone could better his inspired solo on the first take of "Hallelujah!," which bursts into life with an

Eldridge-inspired opening phrase that crackles up to a repeated high note, picking up from Teddy Wilson's laid-back piano chorus in which Specs Powell drops out, reentering explosively to add even more drama to Dizzy's solo. Yet the second take shows Dizzy's experimenting to produce an improved slant on his ideas, announced in the head arrangement where he rephrases the middle eight (which he leads on muted horn) and confirmed when he opens his solo in an entirely different way with a phrase subtly borrowed from "The Peanut Vendor." The "architecture" of his solo is consistent, with the same downward-running figure in the final eight. Interestingly, in the final (and originally issued) take Gillespie abandons this figure and much of the structure he had developed in his second solo.

It is intriguing to reflect on the thinking that went into the three missing takes in between, and to ponder whether there was a continuous compositional development of Dizzy's ideas. This is certainly the case on "Congo Blues," where Dizzy's first full-length effort, moving from muted to open horn, is abandoned, and the latter two takes have elegant high-speed muted solos, redolent of his later trumpet battles with Roy Eldridge from the 1950s. Even here, Dizzy develops ideas from take to take. The opening bugle-call motif gains shape across two aborted and three final versions, ending in an obliquely abstract idea that is all the more fascinating for the documentation of how Dizzy arrived at it.

Whereas "Congo Blues" is a fast series of improvised choruses on the twelve-bar blues sequence, it has very little to do with "blues" playing as such. The slower " 'Slam Slam' Blues" is, however, another insight into Dizzy's attitude to slow blues playing. His muted solo on the first (originally unissued) version offers some angular modern phrases, in contrast to Bird's heartfelt blues choruses; but despite his bleak tone and boppish intervals, Dizzy cannot help himself from interpolating a quote from "The Irish Washerwoman" that completely shatters the mood. He keeps himself in check for the issued version, but his contribution once again holds back from the genuine emotional power displayed by Parker.

The roles are reversed on "Get Happy," where, on the originally issued take, Dizzy produces some high-speed playing that shows his unerring accuracy at what, for most players, would be a bewildering and impossible tempo. Against the swing setting offered by the rhythm players, this is unquestionably Dizzy's most dramatic and startling contribution.

The prolific recording activity of early 1945 was then interrupted by Dizzy's road tour with the "Hep-sations" package. His return to the studios with Parker was in almost a cameo walk-on role. The "Koko" session of November 26 has become one of the legends of jazz history, not least because of the way in which, for Charlie Parker's first session under his own name, Savoy Records chose to obscure the facts surrounding the date. In John Mehegan's note to Savoy MG 12079, the first complete issue of the material recorded that day—billed as "the greatest recording session made in modern jazz history in its entirety!"—he was given to understand that the pianist on the date had been Bud Powell, recently released from the hospital and, as we know from Ray Brown, rehearsing regularly with Parker and Gillespie at around that time. Mehegan's incredulity that some of the less competent playing on the date could possibly have been the prodigiously gifted even if recently hospitalized Powell was apparent from his writing: "The piano intro is completely chaotic rhythmically, and harmonically: I just can't believe it is Bud. Who is playing piano?"[25] The answer, of course, is that the player was not Powell, but for some of the tracks an obscure musician called Argonne Thornton and, on the rest, none other than Dizzy Gillespie, who was called in to support Bird's regular trumpeter of the time, Miles Davis.

The sheer brilliance of Parker's playing on much of this session has tended to give it a vastly overrated position in the history of bebop overall. Ross Russell, in *Bird Lives*, called it "the definitive session toward which bop had been striving,"[26] and the majority of writers have gone along with that view. Certainly, the inclusion of Parker's one-time Three Deuces colleagues Max Roach and Curley Russell provided a less archaic level of rhythmic support than Sid Catlett or Cozy Cole on Dizzy's earlier sessions, but the absence of a strong harmonic texture on piano was a severe restraint, especially under Miles's solos, which lack both confidence and fluency.[27]

The one classic that was produced, "Koko," which gave its name to the session, is a glimpse of one of Dizzy and Bird's old Three Deuces routines, altered and reshaped for the playing time of a normal 10-inch record. For this, Miles surrendered the trumpet chair to Dizzy, who joins Bird for the head arrangement and the coda, both of which include some unaccompanied flurries for the two principals. On the take that was eventually released, the piano chording behind one of Parker's most accomplished recorded solos is Dizzy's. Missing from that take is the original opening chorus from their standard 52nd Street arrangement, which reveals the tune as "Cherokee." This does survive on the aborted first take, but, as Tom Owens suggests in his analysis of the session, it is likely that the arrangement was truncated to allow room for Parker to have more solo space. A half-chorus drum solo leads to a short off-center tag.[28]

Various accounts of the Savoy session (which, like Red Norvo's, took place at the WOR studios) tell of Parker's reed problems, his send-

ing out for more reeds from a midtown music store, of Miles's nap in
the studio, of the producer Teddy Reig dozing behind the glass, of the
party atmosphere as friends came and went, and of a lengthy overrun
beyond the prescribed three hours. What seems certain is that Parker's
first record date under his own name was a curious reflection of his own
personality: random, disorganized, occasionally touching genius, but ultimately reliant on his own spur-of-the-moment instrumental and improvisatory prowess to illuminate a group of fairly unsophisticated head
arrangements. Compare this to Dizzy's systematic attempts (with or
without Parker) to document his core bebop repertoire, and it is significant that the session's most enduring piece was cobbled together from
one of the Gillespie quintet's more structured arrangements of Ray No-
ble's standard song.

The Savoy tapes are a fascinating document, and in their more recent and scholarly releases it has been possible to piece together the true
story of the session.[29] But in an attempt to understand the unique place
in jazz history of the Gillespie–Parker collaboration of 1945 they are less
valuable than the recordings made for the AFRS Jubilee radio show by
the group that went to the West Coast.

It was not until 1975 that all the known surviving numbers from
Dizzy and Bird's West Coast broadcasts were collected together and
issued, so these recordings had no impact on the development of jazz at
the time, other than on those who heard them in the flesh or on the air.
Just over two weeks after Dizzy's band arrived at Billy Berg's they were
guests on the AFRS Jubilee program. The producer, Jimmy Lyons, recalled: "They were late. All the studio musicians were already on risers
on the stage. And we had a live audience, composed of injured guys from
the hospital. Dizzy turned and kicked off the first tune on the roster with
his heel, "Hot House." The place went up in flames. The studio guys
just threw their instruments up in the air. They started laughing and
holding onto themselves, watching these strange youngsters playing their
funny music."[30]

No recording of "Hot House" survives, but the three tracks that do
betray nothing of that apparent derision from the studio band. The audience is enthusiastic in its applause, and MC Ernie Whitman's only
hint at unseen reaction is his comment after "Shaw 'Nuff," "I just blew
my gasket!" But this is consistent with his usual line in appalling banter,
every bit as much as his subsequent introduction of Dizzy as "Professor
Rebop and his whole class of cats."

These airshots are important because they are the best example of
Dizzy and Bird's quintet (with Milt Jackson added on "Dizzy Atmosphere") playing as they might have done in a club, with none of the

length constraints of 78-rpm discs to worry about. The band is consequently both relaxed and inspired, with Parker at his best, Dizzy at his
most breathtakingly spectacular, and the remainder providing a perfect
accompaniment. Al Haig's nonchalant echoes of the head arrangement
in "Groovin' High" and his aggressive chording behind Dizzy's "Shaw
'Nuff" solo are matched by Levey's powerful punctuations and Brown's
rock steady pulse. The stylistic steps from the swing-based rhythm sections on the Guild sides to this quintet are not huge—certainly not as
dramatic as many past critics have suggested—but the cohesion of this
regular working band, captured in what was more or less its natural
environment, gives the listener half a century later a glimpse of just what
a remarkable group it was.

The version of "Groovin' High" from these broadcasts underlines
the difference between the band playing "live" and in a studio. The com-
pact and complex nature of Dizzy's arrangement still acts as a taut framework for the performance, but the slightly more relaxed pace, the inter-
action between the front line and the rhythm section on the head
arrangement, and the extended solos stretch over five and a half minutes.
Parker grapples with a minor reed problem in his first few bars, but
produces a flowing solo that leads naturally into a couple of choruses
from Dizzy. Instead of the split choruses of the Guild recording, each
player is able to develop his ideas in far greater space, and Dizzy's second
open chorus with its high notes and final flares gives a sense of the
extroverted showmanship that he brought to his playing.

Even though many of the figures he used were sufficiently well used
to be on the point of becoming clichés (his first chorus on "Dizzy Atmosphere" reuses note for note the last eight-measure figure he incorporated
in the first and second takes of Red Norvo's "Hallelujah!," in itself one
of Dizzy's stock phrases notated by Thomas Owens in his study of bebop), Dizzy placed them with the instincts of a sure dramatist. Parker's
seamless flow of invention is less cliché bound but conveys less of a sense
of playing to the gallery. Dizzy's long training in the bands of Hill,
Calloway, and Millinder was already lending a showman's flair to his
work in this pioneer bebop group. Listening to those airshots made so
long ago, and especially the audience reaction to the band, a description
of Dizzy's playing by Gene Lees comes to mind: "There is a gesture he
has, a motion, that always reminds me of a great batter leaning into a
hit. He has a way of throwing one foot forward, putting his head down
a bit as he silently runs the valves, and then the cheeks bloom out in the
way that has mystified his dentist for years, and he hits into the
solo. When that foot goes forward like that, you know that John Birks
Gillespie is no longer clowning. Stand back."[31]

Milt Jackson joined the group for some inspired soloing on "Dizzy Atmosphere," and the Berg's contingent is completed by Lucky Thompson on their other surviving broadcast from their West Coast sojourn: a brief "Salt Peanuts" from the Rudy Vallee show. Perhaps the most extraordinary thing about this lightweight tune is that, like "Groovin' High," it has a complex arrangement. In its brief two-minute broadcast slot the band managed to fit in virtually all of it, complete with breaks for Levey's drums and Brown's bass and solo spots for most of the others.

After the band closed at Berg's they made two attempts at recording for Ross Russell's new Dial label. The first, with several of the group absent but Charlie Parker in attendance, produced a solitary side, "Diggin' Diz." The second featured all the band except Parker as the "Tempo Jazzmen," and it was a highly productive session under Dizzy's leadership, every bit the equal of his work almost exactly a year earlier with Don Byas and Dexter Gordon as his front-line partners.[32] (The Tempo date included a vocal version of "When I Grow Too Old To Dream" that is almost certainly one of the vocal numbers the band added to its sets at Berg's. It also saw Dizzy's first recordings of " 'Round About Midnight," which sketch out the plan for the big band's version the following year.) However, during the Berg's residency, Bird and Diz made one other collaboration on disc, this time featuring their support act at the club, Slim Gaillard.

From a comment during one of the sides, it is generally assumed that Slim Gaillard's Orchestra cut its four tunes shortly before Dizzy and Bird's appearance on the AFRS Jubilee show and probably contributed to their late arrival there. During the residency at Billy Berg's, Gaillard and Dizzy had a scuffle, apparently prompted by Gaillard's wife's unfounded accusation that Dizzy had called him a "Tom." Accounts vary as to whether this took place before or after the recording session, but it would seem that in addition to the personal tension between Gaillard and Dizzy there was another quite unexpected outcome from this date.

Born according to older reference books in Detroit, but by his own account a native of Cuba who later ran away to sea and was abandoned in the Mediterranean, Gaillard was an entertainer of the old school, a man whose handsome looks and minor Hollywood roles had earned him the nickname "Dark Gable." He spent most of his last years in Europe, and the author recalls with affection his party trick of playing complex piano solos with the backs of his fingers, his guitar strumming, scat-singing, and talking in a nonsense language of his own invention called "vout," as well as surreal jokes like asking members of the audience to walk up to the bar and order him a vodka and peanut butter. He had formed a successful musical and comic partnership with bassist Slam

Stewart, and "Slim and Slam" enjoyed a brief hit in the late 1930s with their version of "Flat Foot Floogie."

The session with Diz and Bird was to involve a remake of this song as well as another of Slim's novelty vocals, "Poppity Pop." On "Flat Foot Floogie," the band joins in on the vocal, and there are brief solos from tenorist Jack McVea, Dizzy (producing a passable imitation of a muted Charlie Shavers), and Bird, before Slim's guitar ushers the ensemble back in. More remarkable for its relaxed low-key atmosphere, a slice of Slim's inimitable patter, and some loose solos over a simple vamp backing, is "Slim's Jam," in which the punctual Dizzy is clearly getting more and more worried about getting to his next gig, finally blowing some sour notes on the last riff chorus.

Musically, the session was unexceptional, but at the time it obviously captured something of the image the popular and music press wished to convey about the "men from Mars" playing at Berg's, especially since all the main participants (with the exception of Harry "The Hipster" Gibson) were present. Three months later in March 1946, KMPC, the local Los Angeles radio station, created a flurry of press interest by banning bebop. This has shades of the 1960s moves to ban the subversive music of the flower-power generation. A report in *Time* magazine showed just how off-beam press appreciation of bop actually was: "Hot jazz overheated, with overdone lyrics full of bawdiness, references to narcotics and double talk." A perfect description, perhaps, of the act that had made Cab Calloway one of the most popular and wealthy stars in the United States. Equally, it might just qualify as a description of Gaillard's stage act. Could it be that Slim's low-key record date for a minor Los Angeles label had actually fed the flames of this pointless and misguided ban?[33]

The last days of Dizzy and Bird's California association are preserved in two other recordings: Norman Granz's January 29 concert at Philharmonic Hall and a private jam session in a friend's apartment, captured by the redoubtable Bob Redcross. It should come as no surprise that Bird produced his most spectacular playing not on the concert platform but on the version of "Sweet Georgia Brown" played after hours in Freddie James's apartment.

Dizzy's band prepared to fly back East. "There was no mysterious reason why Bird didn't come back to New York with the rest of us," recalled Stan Levey. "He missed the plane. I had all the tickets and I spent $25 in cab fares trying to find Charlie on the morning we were due to leave. I couldn't find him anywhere and in the end I had to leave his ticket at Burbank Airport in case he showed up after we had gone."[34] The next stage of Dizzy's career, without Bird, was about to begin.

12
The Big Band, 1946–50

People who have never seen Dizzy in front of a big band have no idea," said Milt Jackson in 1976. "They have never actually seen Dizzy. Once you see him standing out there in front of that big band, he is really phenomenal and very dynamic and it's just like, well, he should never be without a band. He should have a band sponsored by the Government if necessary, for what he means, because he's second only to Duke Ellington, who was fortunate in keeping a band [together]. The same thing should happen with Dizzy, but the media of course can ruin you. You see Dizzy lost a hundred thousand dollars, like that first year."[1]

Back from the West Coast and in New York once again, Dizzy's medium-term objective was to try to form another big band and have a second attempt to transfer the new music to a bigger ensemble. First of all, however, he started work again with his sextet. The Three Deuces job was open for him to return to, but he chose instead to move to a relatively new venue called the Spotlite, a few doors away along 52nd Street. This club was operated by Clark Monroe, who had already moved his Uptown House from Harlem to "the Street" and opened the Spotlite as an additional venue. A day or two after he reached New York, Dizzy started making phone calls.

"He called Milt Jackson and I," remembered Ray Brown, "and said he had gotten a big band the year before and it lasted about three months and it went belly up, and then he'd got the quintet that we were in. But he told us: 'I'm gonna get a big band. It's gonna be different, but if you guys wanna stay, you're welcome.'

"So we said: 'Yeah!' "[2]

With Ray and Milt on board, the personnel was initially very similar to the group that had gone to Berg's. Al Haig and Stan Levey remained for a while, and saxophonist Leo Parker took the chair that Lucky Thompson had temporarily occupied in the West.[3] Clark Monroe had suggested to Dizzy that if an initial period of eight weeks at the club was successful, he'd be prepared to back launching a big band at the same venue for a further eight weeks. Dizzy was billed at the club by the end of the first week in March,[4] when his group took the place of Henry "Red" Allen's band, playing alternate sets opposite Coleman

Hawkins. Soon, helped by some judiciously targetted publicity from Billy Shaw, the Spotlite was doing what *Down Beat* reported as "sensational business."

The Guild label had gone out of business late in 1945, leaving Dizzy temporarily without a recording contract, but he intended to sign with Musicraft, the company that had bought up the assets of Guild and was about to issue his remaining 1945 sides. Musicraft had established itself as a classical label, but under the aegis of producer Albert Marx moved into jazz. It had better and more established distribution than many of the myriad minor labels that flourished at the time and carried the work of its bebop pioneers, like Dizzy and Sarah Vaughan, to a wide audience, although its reach still fell far short of the major labels.

Only a matter of days before Dizzy signed up with Musicraft, he got a call from Leonard Feather. "Just in time, I corralled him for an album I was recording at Victor, to be called *New Fifty-Second Street Jazz.* . . . Victor wanted an all-star group featuring some of the *Esquire* award winners, so we used J.C. Heard on drums and Don Byas on tenor, along with three of Dizzy's own men—Milt Jackson, Ray Brown and Al Haig—and the new guitarist from Cleveland, Bill De Arango. Thanks largely to Dizzy's name we outsold every jazz album of the last few years."[5] (The album consisted of four 78s, eight sides in all, packaged together. In his account, Feather fails to mention that the other four sides in the album were by Coleman Hawkins, and this no doubt contributed to the discs' success.)

"Dizzy Gillespie and Coleman Hawkins have had a lot of popularity recently, and here they are in a new album," reported the *New York Times*. "[They] take four sides apiece and they make them mighty warm."[6] Although J. C. Heard was a sympathetic drummer (by his own account far looser than Cozy Cole, his Calloway predecessor[7]), he adopts what might be thought of as a Sid Catlett approach to bebop, failing to "feed" the soloist as effectively as Stan Levey on the evidence of the Berg's airshots, but providing a sensitively swinging accompaniment that works to perfection behind Byas's solos. De Arango brings little to the ensembles except a brisk staccato on "52nd Street Theme" that combines with Jackson's vibes to create a strangely futuristic sound.

The first take of this piece has an unusually flawed solo from Dizzy that sounds as if he is experiencing some lip problems and contrasts with his exceptional playing from his West Coast recordings. (In his autobiography, Dizzy suggests that this is when he consulted Dr. Irving Goldman about a minor split on his lip, but in an interview with Stanley Dance he dated this more persuasively to late 1942 when he left Millinder.[8] In any event, Goldman's treatment, which involved lancing the lip and putting "white powder" around it, appears to have cured Dizzy's problems for good, and he said repeatedly that nothing similar occurred after 1946 for the rest of his career.) The subsequent takes betray no further trouble, and Dizzy's playing on a new arrangement of "Night in Tunisia" is simply breathtaking in its clarity and power.

The discs had an immediate impact, especially on other musicians: "I was in junior high school with Eric Dolphy," remembered pianist Hampton Hawes. "One day he asked me to come to his home to hear some new stuff. Then I heard Dizzy Gillespie and that did it. I said, 'This is what I want to play!' It was the hippest music I had ever heard in my life. Dizzy, Don Byas and J. C. Heard playing bebop. I knew that was the way I wanted to go."[9]

It is probable that Dizzy signed to Musicraft at the beginning of March, because his next session, on the sixth, was for Tony Scott and featured vocals from Sarah Vaughan, for the Gotham label. Sarah (later a Musicraft artist herself) used her own name, but Dizzy used the pseudonym B. Bopstein, suggesting his new contract had come into effect.

As March and April went on, Dizzy continued to do good business at the Spotlite. Clark Monroe, true to his word, agreed that Dizzy could start a big band, based at the club. The decision, when it came, was quite rapid, and Dizzy and his arranger Gil Fuller found themselves scurrying round to assemble the band in a matter of days. At this point Sonny Stitt took over from Leo Parker, who moved in due course to the big band's baritone chair. The other alto player was Howard Johnson, who had been working with pioneer drummer Harry Dial at Small's Paradise in Harlem. On his night off from Small's, he went to another Harlem venue, the Club Sudan, on the site of the old Cotton Club. "Billy Eckstine had the band there, and Dizzy Gillespie was sitting in. He came over to my table and said, 'If you have time, come on down tomorrow.' He was putting a big band of his own together."[10] The next morning a somewhat hungover Johnson was rounded up by Gil Fuller and brought along to Dizzy's rehearsal, together with trumpeter Kenny Dorham, who had been in the Savoy house band alongside a Texas friend, Henry Boozier, who may also have spent a short time in the band. Dorham recalled: "[Dizzy] was going to start a big band, and invited us to audition for it. The next day we went to the big band rehearsal at Minton's Playhouse and we got the gig."[11] Dorham stayed for some months.

There was also Kenny Clarke, who'd just come out of the army after actually being a regimental trombonist. "I'd been away three years. That was a lifetime then, believe me. Such a lot was happening in music in New York," he remembered, when reminded that Dizzy had summoned him to join the new orchestra. "When I got back I didn't think I was up

Dizzy and Sonny Stitt recording for Musicraft, 1946. (Frank Driggs collection)

to it. I thought I'd been away too long and couldn't absorb it fully. I thought I wouldn't be capable enough to play for Diz. But he encouraged me. He said: 'I don't care how you play, man. You're gonna join the band. We want your spirit.' I joined and after a few months it was like I'd never been away. It was a good feeling."[12]

His arrival brought a previously unknown degree of professionalism to the rhythm section. Ray Brown told the author: "He was a kind of special guy. I'd never seen anybody take this kind of care. He would go into work when we were with Dizzy's big band (this is 1946); he would go in early and take a cloth, a wet cloth and wipe down his bass drum. And I would go in and he would say: 'Now I want you to stand here and point your bass this way.' Because he wanted the bass notes to go through the bass drum, you know. And I don't find guys taking that much care about sound."[13]

Clarke's arrival had an immediate impact on Dizzy's music. Ray Brown believes this was because "Kenny Clarke was the only guy he could find that played drums to fit in with the stuff he wanted to do . . . so it was perfect." Just as significantly, no other bandleader, according to Ray, actually wanted Kenny to play in his natural style, "so here Kenny could get in a band where he could do all of *his* stuff, and Dizzy was like, 'Yeah!' You know."[14]

Kenny felt the same: "[Dizzy] was really good to me. His encouragement and interest helped me feel I'd never been away. When I came home I knew a great change had taken place. The development of music then was phenomenal. The whole approach was different. It was nothing like it had been in the years before the war." Within a few short weeks, Dizzy's band had moved the pace on even faster. The band developed an extraordinary spirit. "The power, the rhythm, the harmonies of that band were like something I'd never heard before. You can't imagine what it was like to play in. It was a wonderful part of my life," Clarke continued. "Diz was the pivot. We got to a point where there was nothing we couldn't do."[15]

So just what was so special about that band? In a perceptive article written as long ago as 1969, the critic Jack Cooke summed it up very eloquently: "The performances of the group . . . remain the most articulate and valuable extensions of big band thinking for many years, the last attempts within a conventional format to push the concepts of orchestral techniques into line with solo techniques."[16] His analysis is echoed by Howard Johnson: "It was a rewarding experience because I was in that new group, playing stuff that was very interesting and exciting. I was playing first chair alto, playing what somebody had written, and I more or less had to get in the spirit of what they were doing."[17]

The first inklings of what the band was capable of came in a small band record Dizzy cut in mid-May. With Sonny Stitt taking the alto solos and Kenny Clarke back in the drum chair, the session has much the same cohesion as the broadcasts with Bird from California. But nothing is preparation for the dramatic impact of the big band itself on its first record: "Our Delight." Apart from a short tenor solo, the only soloist is Dizzy himself, but the brass and reed sections wind their way through melodic lines of a complexity seldom heard before, echoing, exactly as Cooke suggests, the improvisatory lines of a bop saxophonist. Brown's strong basslines, Clarke's dynamic shading, and some complex chordal comping from Milt Jackson on piano add to the impression that small-group bebop is genuinely making the transfer to a larger orchestra.

The feeling is confirmed in Gil Fuller's breakneck arrangement of "Things to Come," first recorded in a broadcast performance from the

Spotlite and then cut formally in a studio session in mid-July. This is playing of staggering virtuosity, with all the sections (and Milt Jackson on vibes) achieving a precision at a speed previously only attained by small groups, not to mention the extraordinary unison glissandi at the end of the arrangement. "The music wasn't really danceable," wrote Howard Johnson. "Bebop didn't have any beat or anything to make people want to try to dance to it."[18] Sammy Lowe, with Erskine Hawkins's Orchestra at the time, noted a month or two later as Dizzy took to the road: "I went by to hear Dizzy's band at a ballroom. Everything was at uptempo and they were just doing their thing. When I looked around I saw that nobody was dancing. A few people were standing round the bandstand. What the band was doing should have been at a concert, where the people were sitting down."[19]

Although the Spotlite was one of the largest clubs on 52nd Street, it was barely big enough to offer dancing space. Dizzy was, in effect, playing to a concert audience at the club, and his band's habits were formed in that environment, turning what had been a disadvantage of the "Hep-sations" tour into a conscious policy for the band. As ever, Dizzy himself was quite happy to dance to the band's sounds, and he is to be seen in several numbers from the film *Jivin' in Bebop*, made in the second half of 1946, spinning around and mugging in front of the band in a way that immediately recalls Louis Armstrong's "soundies." At the very time his orchestra began to revolutionize big band music, Dizzy's own performances retained much of the elements of black show business that he had experienced during his apprenticeship.

Yet even on these filmed numbers, mimed to a prerecorded soundtrack, the band's extraordinary spirit comes across. "We had a bunch of musicians who loved music, and the musicians, they loved each other," said Milt Jackson. "Now in the daytime, we're sitting about and everybody's on edge as a matter of fact. It may even have been a little bit hostile, because they could not wait until night time came. They would be just overjoyed when it turned dark and we knew it was approaching time to go to work. 'Cause we couldn't wait to sit down and get to that band and hit the first note. From the first note to the last you could hear everything. You could hear that happiness, that togetherness, you can hear it all in that music."[20]

Dizzy had at one point hoped to get Bud Powell for the piano chair in the band. When that idea fell through, he persuaded Thelonious Monk to join, and, despite habits almost as erratic as Powell's, Monk is to be heard on the band's initial broadcasts. Monk had been playing at the Spotlite with Coleman Hawkins's band, taking the sets opposite Dizzy's small group for much of March and April. Then, during the week of April 23, Hawkins left the club to join Norman Granz's Jazz at the Philharmonic tour on the West Coast. Monk did not make that journey and ended up joining Dizzy instead.

Critical opinion was still undecided about Monk. As a pianist, his jagged, idiosyncratic style with its overtones of stride seemed at first to have little to do with the fleet linear improvisations of bebop horn players. Yet, as a composer, his questing exploration of underlying harmonies had been, and remained, a major influence on Dizzy, both inspiring and consolidating many of Dizzy's own harmonic experiments at the keyboard. A *Metronome* reviewer in January 1946 was clearly unmoved, and wrote that Hawkins's rhythm section, which had also included Al McKibbon on bass and Denzil Best on drums, was "hampered not a little by pianist Thelonious Monk."[21]

When he arrived in the ranks of Dizzy's big band, Monk clearly had no intention of conforming to the usual role of the comping piano player. Ray Brown, doubling up with laughter at the memory, explained to the author how Monk would sit stock still as the big band ran down one of its charts: "Monk is a subject in itself. I mean, most piano players in most big bands sit down and they play with the band, you know. But Monk would just sit there like *this*. And all of a sudden there'd be a pause from all the trumpets and everything, and Monk would go 'plink!' like that. And everybody would go 'Yeah!'

"He really was wild, really different. But he didn't stay because most of the time he would come an hour late, and sometimes he wouldn't show up at all. So we really wanted someone who was there all the time—and playing all the time, too! Dizzy was always on time himself, and he knew that it doesn't tend to get any better—it usually gets worse."[22]

Monk's tenure with the band lasted about a month, and early in June Kenny Clarke introduced Dizzy to an army acquaintance of his called John Lewis, whom he thought might be a suitable replacement. Although Monk was already established as a composer, and his " 'Round Midnight" was a regular part of the band's repertoire, he did not contribute original pieces or arrangements to Dizzy's band. Lewis, on the other hand, was both a competent composer and arranger, as well as a natural teacher. His instincts dovetailed exactly with Dizzy's.

"I met Dizzy through Kenny Clarke," he recalled. "We were all a group of people who were interested in making music in this way as opposed to what had gone on in small groups before. . . . Certainly, I had a very good time in Dizzy's band. He's a natural leader. I wrote for that band, and I'd done quite a bit of jazz writing previously, because, see, most of my thinking or self-training was . . . on the jazz side."[23]

The arrival of Lewis, alongside Brown, Clarke, and Milt Jackson, had an additional benefit to Dizzy, which was ultimately to create one of the longest lasting institutions in jazz, the Modern Jazz Quartet. In the beginning, the rhythm section simply began playing together for a few numbers to give the brass and reed players a break from their unremittingly demanding charts. Listening today to the band's initial broadcasts, through the combination of Clarke's inventive drumming, Brown's rock-steady basslines, and the harmonic punctuations of Lewis, one hears that the rhythm section seems to represent a marked break with tradition and to have transferred successfully into a large band format many of the rhythmic nuances of bebop small-group playing.

At the time, as Ray Brown explains, they were barely aware of this, and certainly unaware to start with of their potential as an ensemble in their own right: "For that time, that period, and we're talking about the forties, the rhythm section had a definite function. There was a lot of different things going on with the horns, so somebody had to lay down something for them to do that over. There were very few soloists in the band to do the bulk of the soloing. We didn't have a prominent trumpet soloist besides Dizzy, and in the saxophone section [for much of the time] we really only had James Moody. So most of the 'All Stars' were in the rhythm section, and there were enough of us there to write things to feature us.

"As well as that, the brass players, especially the trumpets, had high notes and lots of 'em. Just screaming figures and more and more high notes. And after about half an hour of that, you'd look over at the trumpet section, and everybody's lip's hanging down, looking like some ground meat, you know.

"It wouldn't be time for an intermission, so Dizzy would say 'OK, band off!' and we, that's the rhythm section with Milt, would play for fifteen minutes and give the guys a rest. So since we got to doing this every night, we started putting some stuff together."[24]

Clearly, from Brown's account, these quartet sets began very early in the life of Dizzy's big band. Milt Jackson corroborated this: "The music Gil Fuller wrote was sort of difficult, especially for the brass section. So one night Dizzy suggested, 'Hey, why don't you and John and Ray and Klook play a little bit—give the guys a rest!' Which we did and it immediately became a spontaneous reaction. From that night on it became a regular part of the band, and we enjoyed it so much that we decided on that same type of group, with the same personnel, once we'd left Dizzy."[25]

The Milt Jackson Quartet (or "MJQ," the forerunner of the Modern Jazz Quartet) did not come into being formally for another few years, but by the spring of 1947, less than a year after the Spotlite gig, Dizzy's rhythm section was being billed as an attraction in its own right, with publicity focusing on the fact that Jackson and Brown were both recipients of *Esquire* awards that January.

They made one of their first appearances independently of Dizzy (whose name nevertheless appears in large lettering in the advertisements) at Small's Paradise in Harlem, billed as "The Atomics of Modern Music" and sharing the program with them was "Dizzy's New Winning Rave Tenor Saxophonist" James Moody.[26] Other saxophonists were to come and go over the years, but when Moody arrived in Dizzy's big band in 1946, for the opening night of the first month at the Spotlite, one of the most enduring relationships in jazz was born. (Moody recalled the circumstances in detail for the author, confirming that Monk was on piano when he joined and that Clark Monroe put pressure on Dizzy to fire his unreliable pianist. "One night Monk was there, and the next night John Lewis was there in his place."[27])

"I was with Dizzy on and off for forty-five years," Moody recalled. "Never a day goes by when I don't think about him. I have his picture in my wallet and in my prayer book. It seems that almost everywhere I went in the world, I went for the first time with Diz. And he stayed close to me right up to the time he died. When I'd be touring as a solo, in the 1980s, the phone in my hotel room would ring and a little falsetto voice would say, 'Hello, is this James Moody?' And I'd say, 'Diz! How'd you know it was me?'

"When I came into the big band, right from the opening night at the Spotlite on 52nd Street, I took the saxophone solos. I came straight out of the air force and joined Diz. The reason I come to be called 'Moody' rather than any other name goes back to the air force. People there would say, 'Moody do this! Moody do that!' and when I got into Dizzy's band the name stuck.

"I didn't know anything, and when I joined Diz I found I *really* didn't know anything. Monk was the piano player, Kenny Clarke was the drummer, Ray Brown was the bass player, Milt Jackson vibes and Howard Johnson—'Cap' we called him—was the alto player. 'Cap' played a little piano too; he was from Boston and was a really fantastic musician.

"People always say to me, 'It must have been exciting!' Well, it was groovy to be with Diz and all, but you don't realize what it is because you're young. That famous phrase sums it up for me: 'It's too bad, youth is wasted on the young!' If I had known then what I know now, I'd have been a much much better player. But if you don't know what it is you don't know, then you don't know how to ask for it."[28]

With the benefit of hindsight, perhaps Moody might have made even more of the relatively few solo opportunities he had in the band, but this was not a band that was really about soloists in the more accepted modern sense of a big band. Its strength was its massive ensemble power and energy, coupled with its leader's athletic trumpet playing. Those who heard the band had never encountered anything similar.

"To be in that little club, the Spotlite, with its low ceiling and hear that band play 'Things to Come.' It would take your head off. Incredible. Definitely one of the most exciting experiences you could ever have," recalls critic Ira Gitler. Sleevenote artist and designer Robert Andrew Parker heard them a little later: "I was in Chicago, and they came through town and played a smallish club. I'd never heard anything like the power of that brass."

Critic Ralph J. Gleason was a determined follower of the band: "The energy that blasted out . . . was sensational. They had only a microphone for the vocalist to sing into and be heard over the house public address system. They had no amplification for the band itself and no electrical instruments at all, not even a guitar with a pickup. But they had the volume of the Cream or the Who and with that band I discovered a truth about loud music. If it's good it turns you on and makes you feel good . . . I never left a performance of that band anything but sky high on its sound and feelin' no pain."[29]

Ray Brown has often related that he felt in some ways the least experienced member of Dizzy's small group that immediately preceded the big band, but that Dizzy's patient tuition and the attitude he engendered in the band made Brown a better and more mature player. For him, the heady mixture of youthful inexperience (like Moody's) and the raw power of the new big band was irresistible: "In those days everything was exciting. At that age everything is an experience, and you can't wait to get up, you can't wait to get to the bandstand, you can't wait to play. It's a great time in your life. The music is new, it's exciting, and we all know somehow that this music is beginning to catch on, it's just starting and like a snowball it's getting bigger and bigger and bigger."[30]

Brown produced some compositions of his own, which were eagerly added to the group's repertoire in what Gil Fuller recalled as a constant search for charts. Again, this is an example of Dizzy's harnessing the energy of this extraordinary band in a constructive direction. To hear Brown describe the opportunities he was given is similar to hearing Dizzy on his earliest and happiest days with Calloway, when he produced "Pickin' the Cabbage" and "Paradiddle." Brown told the author: "I used to do some arranging for Snookum Russell's band, but I never did anything original. I just would work on something that had already been written. I didn't start writing originals until after I joined Dizzy's band,

and then although I wrote music for it, I wasn't one of the arrangers. Walter [Gil] Fuller and Tadd Dameron did most of the arranging."[31]

As far as can be ascertained after all the time that has passed since the Spotlite period, Fuller was charged with the responsibility of organzing the band and adding to its library. From Brown, he took thematic ideas and worked them into arrangements, such as "Ray's Idea," "One Bass Hit," and "Oop Bop Sh'bam," doing the same for other members of the band including Dizzy himself (who gets co-composer credits on the last two titles). Fuller and Dizzy both maintained that by this stage they were not receiving more new charts from Dameron because they could not afford them. Yet Dameron's charts, which reached their zenith in the pieces he wrote for this band, were in many ways responsible for the orchestra's unusual sound. "What I admired about Tadd," wrote tenorist Frank Foster, who was rising twenty at the time, "was not his unconventionality, but the fact he wrote so pretty. His voicings were very beautiful."[32]

Benny Golson, later a stalwart of Dizzy's band, worked with Dameron in Bull Moose Jackson's band in the early 1950s. "Tadd was my very first influence as an arranger. He was an exceptional 'dearth' writer, his voicings could make just a trumpet, saxophone, and trombone sound full. He knew how to exploit the piano, and all the range of pitches from top through medium to the bottom. He would specify when a drummer should use a particular cymbal—to him everything meant something. I don't know how academic he was, but for me, having just gotten started and to be thrown into the situation of working alongside him: Lo and Behold! It was like being thrown into heaven."[33]

There does not seem to have been much love lost between Dameron and Fuller, and clearly the warmth of Tadd's early relationship with Dizzy cooled as the big band got started. Fuller recalls in Dizzy's autobiography that he was unhappy about the dismissal of Monk because of Monk's promise as a composer. (Setlists from their many broadcasts, however, do not reveal, as mentioned previously, that more than one of Monk's actual compositions made it into the band's general book of arrangements.)

John Lewis, in due course, contributed complete arrangements, rather than melodic ideas that were turned into charts by Fuller, and the band's 1946 arrangement of "Emanon" (with composer credits to Dizzy and the band's agent, Billy Shaw) is generally regarded as by Lewis.

Late in the Spotlite engagement, Dizzy was helped by the generous support of Billy Eckstine, who had decided to curtail his own touring activities. As historian Grover Sales put it in a letter to the author, "Billy eventually gave Dizzy the band book and music stands and said, 'Take all this shit and God bless you!' "³⁴ Armed with the band's own original charts and the Eckstine book, and equipped for the road with the rest of the Eckstine paraphernalia, Dizzy was ready for Billy Shaw to have a second attempt at booking the band out on tour.

Before leaving the Spotlite, Dizzy made a guest appearance with Norman Granz's Jazz at the Philharmonic troupe when it arrived at Carnegie Hall on June 17, following up on his brief appearance with a similar show on the West Coast back in January. He was teamed with fellow trumpeter Buck Clayton, who had been with the package since its tour began on the West Coast in April. After starting out in the West with a host of stars, including (prior to his stay at Camarillo) Charlie Parker, Granz had slimmed down the package for most of the provincial dates to Coleman Hawkins, Lester Young, Clayton, and the rhythm section of Kenny Kersey on piano, Al McKibbon, bass, and J. C. Heard, drums, with vocalist Helen Humes appearing as his "surprise star."

The New York concert added Illinois Jacquet on tenor, Trummy Young on trombone, and Chubby Jackson on bass, as well as Dizzy. Nevertheless, despite the extra guests, the core of the concert was the item that had thrilled audiences since the tour began. "Every night was something that everybody had been waiting for, to see Coleman Hawkins and Lester Young battle it out," wrote Buck Clayton. "We would begin with all of us playing together with the rhythm section. Hawk would blow his own beautiful solo and bring down the house, then it would be my turn to get into it. After me came Lester with his own unique style of playing, which was totally different from Hawk."³⁵ With Jazz at the Philharmonic, Dizzy held his own in some of the country's fastest jazz company and set the seal for a long-term relationship with Granz that was to bring him to the attention of international concert audiences for many years to come. For the immediate future, he was to focus less on his own career as a soloist than in fronting his own big band, but occasional guest appearances for Granz from 1946 onward allowed him to maintain an independent solo career of sorts.

The tour with his own band began gently, and Dizzy's orchestra left the Spotlite for a week at the Apollo Theatre, starting on Friday, June 28. His "stage career" was launched with a one-off on-stage jam session at the theatre, and the following week's *Baltimore Afro-American* showed pictures of Dizzy mugging with guitarist Tiny Grimes and clarinetist Buster Bailey. Compared to later billings, when Dizzy was dubbed the "Merry Mad Genius of Music," the Apollo simply referred to him as the "New All-American Trumpet Star." As for the previous year's Hepsations tour, the band was again the center of a revue, this time featuring

Eddie Cantor's radio co-star Thelma Carpenter, the "suave star" Bob Evans, and two novelty acts, "Spider Bruce" and "Moni and her dance of serpents."

Once the band left the Apollo, it was out on its own, for appearances in Pennsylvania, Ohio, and Indiana en route to Chicago, where it played opposite a singer who was to become a feature of the band for much of the last part of the year. Ella Fitzgerald and her trio, with Raymond Tunia as her pianist and musical director, were billed as the Regal's "Twin Stage Treat!" opposite Dizzy, with her "throbbing, vibrant and electrifying swing voice."[36] A few days later, Ella was voted winner of the *Chicago Defender*'s "Queen of Swing" award in a readers' poll, and she and Dizzy were photographed during her "coronation" on stage at the Regal, with MC Eddie Plicque and Raymond Tunia.

Ella continued to tour with her own group during August and September, ending up at the Apollo for the week of September 21. Meanwhile, Dizzy also continued to travel with his big band, taking in St. Louis and Peoria before headlining a dance at Chicago's Savoy Ballroom in September. Not long afterward, he appeared as a soloist in an all-star jazz session at the Chicago Opera House, sharing top billing with Sidney Bechet, who was taking the night off from appearing in a stage play in New York. Billy Shaw's office continued to produce strong press releases to advertise Dizzy, and he was described in one paper as the person "who has influenced jazz playing more than any man since Louis Armstrong."[37]

Shaw's next idea was to present Ella Fitzgerald as the featured vocalist with Dizzy's big band and have another go at selling the band in the South. In fact, the band traveled a very different route for this new tour and only played in four venues (San Antonio, Galveston, Birmingham, and Atlanta) that had been visited by the earlier "Hep-sations" show, avoiding the Carolinas, most of Georgia, and Florida altogether.[38] Shaw had learned that it would be unwise to repeat the errors of the previous year, and, as well as steering clear of several cities where Dizzy had had a poor reception, he began the new tour with visits to the main East Coast centers of Washington and Baltimore. He saw to it that there and in the subsequent week's visit to Norfolk, Virginia, the black papers ran glowing reports of the band's performances.

"The two-star combination of Dizzy Gillespie's band of bebop music dispensers and Ella Fitzgerald's plaintive swing singing style created such a furor here last weekend," ran a dispatch from Norfolk, "that it became necessary to supplement the original night's engagement at the Palais Royal Ballroom with a two-day appearance at the Booker T. Theatre in order that the tidewater music fans could all get an earful of the twin rhythm makers."[39]

It was a shrewd combination from Shaw's point of view, since Ella was an established big star. The black press hummed with gossip about her, but instead of this gossip being salacious (as it frequently was concerning other singers, notably Billie Holiday and June Eckstine, who both featured prominently in articles published during the tour[40]), it was all good wholesome stuff.

During the week before her tour with Dizzy began, Ella was photographed with Louis Jordan (her ex-Chick Webb band colleague, with whom she had once had a romantic entanglement) to coincide with the success of their joint disc "Stone Cold Dead in de Market," recorded the previous year. As the tour progressed, she took part in civic events such as the dedication of a memorial to naval hero Dorie Miller at the Austin Auditorium in Texas. Ella's strong image was beneficial in selling a band that had had a mixed press and where the grapevine of the booking circuit would still be buzzing with news of how badly Dizzy's previous big band had fared with southern audiences. James Moody confirmed that in the bulk of their programs she headlined the show, coming on to sing her most famous hits for the last five or six numbers of a set, a familiar palliative for audiences that grew restive and uncertain during the powerhouse arrangements by Dameron and Fuller. He also confirmed how easily Ella, accustomed to big band life after her apprenticeship with Chick Webb's Orchestra, which later became her own band, fitted in naturally with the other musicians, especially recalling an occasion when she was holding the salary of several musicians and it was stolen. She made up the difference herself.[41]

Ella also enjoyed Dizzy's company, renewing their association from his brief stay in her band after he was fired by Calloway. Both bred in the 1930s show tradition, Ella loved to trade a few dance steps with Dizzy, and their common heritage of the Savoy Ballroom surfaced in their stage act. It is also from Ella that we get a brief glimpse of the band's domestic life.

It was common for black orchestras touring the South to cook their meals backstage, rather than face the ignominy of being refused service in "whites only" restaurants. Ella traveled with her cousin Georgianna, who had a deft hand at producing backstage meals for the band, and many of Dizzy's sidemen recalled her culinary efforts with affection. Ella noted that Dizzy, however, had Lorraine traveling with him, and she alone was allowed to fix his special style of eggs.

The tour with Ella continued until January 17, when she was replaced for a week at the Apollo by Sarah Vaughan, perhaps a more musically sympathetic singer for Dizzy's ensemble, but whose name was not nearly well enough known to have ensured a comparable level of success out on the road. Ella moved on to join Cootie Williams's band at the Paramount Theatre.

It is hard to see in terms of Ella's long-term output that there was really any lasting effect on her natural style from the tour with Dizzy's band of boppers. Claims have been made on the basis of one or two airshots that her harmonic language was irrevocably altered by the experience, but, with the exception of one or two passing notes, the main contribution of the tour was to add overtly bebop lyrics like "Oop Bop Sh'bam" to her repertoire, and for her to shadow Dizzy's horn during scat choruses on "Lady Be Good." Ella's quick ear and facility for singing back a phrase of great complexity on first hearing would have been a strong aspect of her stage act with the band, but (and this must remain speculation unless more recorded examples of her work with the band than the handful that exist should come to light) she does not seem to have acquired the inner understanding of bop harmony that Sarah Vaughan had. Vaughan was, of course, a pianist as well as a singer, and had shared the formative experiences of the Hines and Eckstine bands with Dizzy.

"[Ella] lent Dizzy her prestige," said John Lewis, confirming that "at the time, in '46, along with the rest of the band I was more interested in Sarah. My appreciation for Ella wasn't as great as it should have been, although after Dizzy kept pointing it out to me every night, I got the message!"[42]

Perhaps the most lasting effect for Ella of the tour with Dizzy was that she began a romance with Ray Brown, culminating in their marriage in late 1948. Initially, the affair was low key, but in due course, after Ray had moved out of the YMCA and into Ella's apartment, it was to cause tensions in the band. "I met her on the tour, riding a bus all over the country for two to three months. But later on it was, I think, bad for the band for me to show up in a $400 suit and a big Cadillac to come to the job, and the guys are making $67 a week," Ray Brown told the author.[43] Ultimately, by the autumn of 1947, the problems in the band caused by the affair were to lead to Ray's being fired by Dizzy, with Al McKibbon taking his place. Before Ella's career took a different direction in 1948, when she went on the road backed by Ray Brown's group featuring Hank Jones, she was nevertheless featured on several more concerts and traveling dates with Dizzy following the 1946–47 tour.

It would seem that, even with Ella's bankable presence on that tour, Dizzy was not making money. "On three different occasions, Ray Brown, myself, and Joe Harris, who replaced Kenny Clarke as the drummer in the band, we had to lend him money to pay the rest of the band off," said Milt Jackson.[44] Whether the losses were as great as the $100,000 quoted by Jackson is a matter for conjecture, but it is certain that the band finances were uneasy. "If you've got enough money to play for yourself . . . you can play anything you want to," Dizzy was quoted as saying. "But if you want to make a living at music, you've got to sell it."[45] It took an extra special effort from Billy Shaw to keep things going, and he chose to do it by creating an image for Dizzy that had little to do with the music itself. Instead he focused on bop clothes, culture, and language, creating a cult of modernism. The beret, goatee, and horn-

Dizzy in 1946. (Frank Driggs collection)

rimmed spectacles fueled a Dizzy fashion, and cartoons appeared showing shops with signs "bebop spoken here," while mail-order firms offered
bebop garb. A series of increasingly silly articles culminated in a *Time*
feature that ran photos of Dizzy and Benny Carter indulging in a "bebop
greeting."[46]

"From the Gale office," wrote Barry Ulanov, "streamed reprints of
articles about Diz, a steady diet of Gillespie food for editors, columnists
and jockeys. Stones were not to be left unturned, they were to be bull-
dozed out of the way. By the end of 1947, Dizzy and Billy and the men
who played Dizzy's music could breathe more easily, could smile expectantly, could look forward to more folding money. Maybe Dizzy wasn't
a threat to Sammy Kaye or Stan Kenton, but he . . . was proving that a
colored band with difficult music could make enough sense to enough
people to pay off."[47]

Ulanov, who produced two broadcast "band battles" in September
1947 that featured Dizzy and Charlie Parker pitted against a band of
traditionalists assembled by Rudi Blesh, was very much a part of the
movement to create a positive press for Dizzy. His tangles in print and
on air with Blesh crystallized into the polarization of critical positions
for and against modern jazz, summarized in a piece (by Ulanov) called
"Moldy Figs vs. Moderns" in the November 1947 *Metronome*. This article and similar pieces from Blesh's side of the critical divide contributed
to a schism in public taste and critical opinion from which jazz has never
really recovered.

Bob Wilber, once able to move freely around the groups on 52nd
Street and sit in with modernists, mainstreamers, and traditionalists alike,
found himself marooned in the restricted camp of the revivalists, and he
has noted many times in interviews and articles his concern that lack of
public enthusiasm in the United States for great musicians who did not
pigeonhole easily into one group or another ended many careers pre-
maturely and left musical giants of the 1930s and early 1940s scuffling
for work as the 1950s began. In due course, Wilber and a handful of
other musicians refused to be hidebound; his experiments in bands like
"The Six" show how wrongheaded it was to categorize players into
"moldy figs" or modernists.

Yet the damage was done, and with it came a set of economic circumstances that gradually swept away forever the great swing orchestras
in which Dizzy had risen to musical maturity. In the wake of the war,
public tastes changed. If it was no longer possible to dance to bands like
Dizzy's, then why bother? If the public would respond to a smallish band
playing a different kind of music, rather than an expensive eighteen-piece
swing orchestra, why should bookers continue to risk their profits by

hiring large bands people might not dance to? Instead rhythm and blues took hold, and, as the jazz camps battled it out on the spurious lines drawn between traditionalist and modernist, the public slipped away.

Experienced leaders like Charlie Barnet, who was himself open to many of the bebop innovations, started to lay the blame for the migration in taste at the door of the modernists: "Outside of the top exponents of the music like Charlie Parker and Dizzy Gillespie and a few others, the boppers were a bunch of fumblers who were obviously incapable of handling the new idiom. . . . This effectively delivered the death blow to the big bands as we had known them."[48]

Ironically, Dizzy's resolve—and his growing success at the hands of Shaw's publicity machine—allowed him to continue to keep his large band going at the very time that other leaders like Cab Calloway were forced to scale down to much smaller forces. A record contract for the big band with Victor on the back of the small group *52nd Street* album gave him a much stronger distribution for his music than Musicraft had

Dizzy's 1947 big band recording for RCA, on August 22. (Left to right) Ray Orr, Cecil Payne, Elmon Wright, Bill Shepard, James Moody, Dave Burns, Taswell Baird, Howard Johnson, Matthew KcKay, John Brown, John Collins (obscured), Joe Gayles, Ray Brown, Dizzy Gillespie. (Frank Driggs collection)

The 1947 big band. Dizzy, Elmon Wright, Joe Gayles, John Lewis, John Brown.
(Photo: Popsie Randolph; Frank Driggs collection)

achieved, and, amid the grind of incessant touring broken by weeks at the Apollo or the larger regional theatres, Dizzy continued his occasional appearances as a soloist, fronting a couple of benefit concerts with Charlie Parker and guesting with Lionel Hampton at Carnegie Hall.

Shaw and Leonard Feather also presented Dizzy's big band in a Carnegie Hall concert, where Ella topped the bill and Charlie Parker was briefly reunited with Dizzy for a small-group set. One other memorable occasion pitted Dizzy's big band against the octet of Illinois Jacquet in a "Battle of Swing" at White Plains when his powerhouse band had the wind knocked out of it by a smaller band. Sir Charles Thompson, on piano for Jacquet, remembered: "When we got through it sounded as if we had fourteen pieces and he had eight. We were Shadow Wilson, Al Lucas, Joe Newman, Russell Jacquet, J. J. Johnson, Leo Parker, Illinois and myself."[49]

This was a relatively unusual event, since the stream of airshots and formal recordings that survive of Dizzy's band show a group that was truly remarkable in its consistency and power. In due course, there was professional recognition of this, when the country's disc jockeys voted the band the best big band of 1948, with Dizzy as top trumpet soloist. (He beat Fats Navarro into second place by a massive margin.) Dizzy

Cornell, 1948. James Moody, Chano Pozo, Dizzy. (Frank Driggs collection)

and the band were rewarded with a Christmas concert at Carnegie Hall during which Leonard Feather presented their trophies.

Despite the critical war that sprang up around him, Dizzy's big band managed two very significant achievements during the years before economics eventually forced it to disband in 1950. The first was to extend the new territory it had marked out in 1945–46 by going on to add the Cuban rhythms of an extraordinary genius called Chano Pozo. The second was to take its exciting brand of orchestral modern jazz to Europe, where the ground had been prepared by the arrival of his Victor discs and the writings of men like André Hodier.

Dizzy's love affair with what became known as Afro-Cuban music goes back to his earliest days in New York. His introduction to Cuban bands through Mario Bauza and Albert Socarras is discussed in Chapter 6, and it was an interest that did not disappear, even during the heady days of his small groups with Parker.

Bubbling away behind many of Dizzy's own compositions from "Pickin' the Cabbage" to "Night in Tunisia" was the apposition between a four-four swing beat and a Latin rhythm. The logical next step for Dizzy was to see if it was possible to combine these rhythms with the powerful sound of his big band and balance the off-center accents of Kenny Clarke's drumming with the genuine sound of Cuban percussion.

"I was looking for someone to put into that spot," recalled Dizzy, "and Mario Bauza cut me into Chano Pozo. 'I got the guy for you if you want the real stuff,' said Mario. Chano Pozo couldn't even speak English. He was just staying around New York, working Russian theatres, behind dancers, and things like that."[50] Pozo's real name was Luciano Pozo y Gonzales, and he was thirty-two when he made his formal debut with Dizzy at Leonard Feather's Carnegie Hall concert on September 29, 1947. A huge mystique was constructed around Pozo, who was a strangely exotic character. He belonged to the Cuban *lucumí* faith, which drew on West African rituals, and he introduced the idea into the band of adding primal chanting to some of their numbers. He also used to hand out percussion instruments to members of the band on the bus, and encourage jam sessions, based around Cuban rhythms. He spoke a kind of pidgin English, and his catch-phrase, quoted on many occasions by Dizzy, was "Dizzy no peaky pani, I no peaky engly, but boff peak African."

Pozo's contribution to the Carnegie Hall concert was a piece called "Cubana Be–Cubana Bop," combining his melodic and rhythmic ideas with Dizzy's and arranged into a suite by the up-and-coming composer George Russell. "It was the most successful collaboration I ever seen with three people," said Dizzy. "Because I could see what I wrote and I could see what George wrote and I could see the contribution of Chano Pozo. George Russell came back and spread out what I had written and what Chano had done and it was beautiful."[51]

Russell, the son of a professor of music at Oberlin, had spent some considerable time in the hospital with tuberculosis, and in the fall of 1947 was lodging with Max Roach's family in Brooklyn. He had started to study music seriously through a rehabilitation program run by the New

York welfare department, and had begun to work on his lifetime's pre-occupation with a harmonic system based on modes while still hospital-ized. Talking about the period still awakes sensations of experiment and discovery in him, and he told trumpeter and author Ian Carr that his ideas grew as he worked his way out of poverty, first in the Bowery area and then with the Roach family. "I had this experimental feeling about everything. Things that people would think were horrible to me weren't. They were adventures like romancing reality. I knew I was experiencing it all for some reason, like having to step over people frozen to death under the Third Avenue El. All this was shaping something in me, and I had the fundamentals of the Lydian concept worked out.

"Diz and Miles and everybody used to come to Brooklyn to visit Max, and when I got out of the hospital and stayed there, I guess it made me a member of the inner circle. Dizzy approached me one day and he said that he was getting very interested in Afro-Cuban drumming and there was a wonderful drummer in town, Pozo, and he had a theme and would it be possible for me to put a suite around it.

"It was a beautiful theme, so it didn't take long for me to get the idea of what to do with it. The whole introduction was modal. I didn't base it on a chord. I based it on a scale giving the sound of C 7th: augmented ninth, flat five chord. I used the appropriate parent scale, and the whole piece, the harmony and everything is coming out of this scale or environment for this chord, which I think is actually B♭ auxiliary di-minished. I gave this scale the name of auxiliary diminished because it wasn't directly a member of the Lydian family.

"People had begun to use that scale, but they hadn't named it pre-cisely. So we premiered 'Cubana Be–Cubana Bop' at Carnegie Hall and people were really surprised and impressed. After Carnegie Hall, we had Boston Symphony Hall, and I went with the band. Going up on the bus, Chano, in the back, started doing this African black magic chanting. Heavy mysterious folk music. So I said to Dizzy: 'You should open the whole middle section up, bring Chano out in front, let him do this. We build a whole thing out of it.'

"We tried it that night at Boston Symphony Hall and, to show the temper of the times, the black people in the audience were embarrassed by it. The cultural snow job had worked so ruthlessly that for the black race in America at the time its native culture was severed from it com-pletely. They were taught to be ashamed of it, and so the black people in the Boston audience were noticeable because they started to laugh when Chano came on stage in his native costume and began."[52]

Russell's account is interesting for three distinct historical reasons.

He confirms that Dizzy was working with concepts of modal harmony years before Miles Davis followed a similar path. He confirms how the chanting sections of the suite came to be added, and he confirms that Dizzy was starting to pursue a conscious Afro-centrism in the way in which Pozo's music and personality were presented. Later, Dizzy himself adopted African clothes and stressed the connections in his music with the Afro-Cuban rhythmic tradition, but, far from being a product of the 1950s and 1960s as is often maintained, it had its origins in the 1940s.

Not all the band were convinced. Ray Brown told the author: "Chano Pozo just started not long before I left. Matter of fact, one of the things I never really got adjusted to was having conga players, although he [Dizzy] had some of the best ones. Chano playing on 'Manteca' or another Latin tune I thought was great, but playing on our arrangements I didn't think was great. It didn't sit real good with me on every song. I mean this guy's doing all this when we're just trying to swing straight out, and it seemed to inhibit us. I guess I just hadn't got used to doing it."[53]

Trumpeter Benny Bailey came into the band shortly after the Carnegie Hall concert. "By the time I joined, Chano used to sing on 'Cubana Be–Cubana Bop' every night, and I guess it was my first taste of anything like that. It was almost abstract, he would take a long solo on the conga drums and be singing this chant, which I guess was African, or derived from Africa, and we would chant along after him, but we didn't know what in hell we were singing."[54] With the cynical professional optimism of brass players the world over, Benny and the trumpet section happily joined in and sang nonsense for night after night. For them it was nothing to do with Afro-centrism, but just part of Chano's act that was a bit of fun in an otherwise lengthy and demanding suite.

On the other hand, Benny was far from dismissive of Chano's talents. He recalled that, when he first heard Chano, he assumed everyone from Cuba probably played that way and only gradually realized that Pozo was a very unusual and talented musician. Pozo's nightly preparations carried an air of mystique and so did his drums: "He made them himself, burning them out of sections of tree trunk and covering them with goatskin. Nowadays you can buy conga drums, but in those days you couldn't, and the ones Chano played were nothing like the modern variety. His were very thick, and he had to heat them up with Sterno before each gig; of course nowadays they have tuning things on them to do that.

"But those things were loud, man. You could hear them far away, and the ones they make now sound like toys in comparison. And Chano's hands were all calloused, very hard. So he was just as loud as Kenny Clarke. Those drums were really formidable, and he was a strong guy, his hands were almost like wood."[55]

There is no doubt that the exotic figure of Chano Pozo made a great impression on audiences, especially in Europe during the band's 1948 tour. He also did much to help Dizzy formalize a basis for incorporating a rich vein of polyrhythm into the language of modern jazz. Other musicians, notably Stan Kenton, took hold of the idea, but few collaborations capture the heady mixture of excitement, virtuosity and the exotic that can be found in "Manteca," "Cubana Be–Cubana Bop" (also known as the "Afro-Cuban Suite"), and "Guarachi Gauro" from the first fruits of Pozo's tenure with Dizzy's band.

Exceptional as his musical contribution was, what elevated Pozo to legendary status was his tragic and untimely death before 1948 was out. On the second of December he was shot dead in a Harlem bar. As the press reported at the time, "Pozo, rated as one of the nation's greatest bongo drummers, was shot and instantly killed Thursday night, while drinking at the Rio Bar on Lenox Avenue at 111th Street. Rumor had it that the incident that led to the slaying was an argument over narcotics. This angle has not been confirmed by the police department."[56]

In due course, some, but never all, of the truth has emerged. Pozo was indeed killed in a drug feud, and his death seems to have kindled a sense of even greater responsibility in Dizzy. In the years that followed, he was to become an ever sterner disciplinarian, firing musicians whom he suspected of indulging in drugs, and at least once humiliating Charlie Parker when he sat in with the big band in a condition that made him unable to play. Throughout the rest of his life, Gillespie would pay homage to Pozo's talent and never took away from his achievements in helping to define Afro-Cuban jazz, but he was deeply wounded by his colleague's death. A succession of other Latin percussionists (including Candido Camero and Pozo's cousin Chino Pozo) joined the band, but none made the same kind of evolutionary contribution to jazz history and Dizzy's own development that Chano Pozo achieved in just over a year.

The 1948 European tour by Dizzy's big band turned out to be one of the most important seminal events in the history of modern jazz in Europe. There is little doubt, both from recorded evidence and the accounts of musicians and listeners alike, that the tour was a musical triumph, matched only by the saga of managerial incompetence, financial skullduggery, and frayed tempers that underpinned it.

"It affected the consciousness of all musicians," wrote Maurice Cullaz of the band's first French appearance, "but also of the public in general. . . . I think most of today's French jazz musicians who were at the concert discovered their vocation for jazz then and there, and particularly for bebop. They'd already had contacts with the music via discs and Voice of America broadcasts, but I believe it was at this [Salle Pleyel] concert that the music really clicked for them."[57]

The tour, which was originally intended to encompass Sweden, Denmark, and Belgium, had been booked by Billy Shaw, who appointed his son Milt to travel to Europe with the band as Dizzy's manager. A Swedish entrepreneur called Harold Lundquist set up the concerts and had been asked to deposit a bond of half the band's guaranteed earnings with the Shaw Agency in New York. It appears that when Dizzy set sail, the money had still not been received in the United States and that, once on board ship, the contractual conditions were further eroded, as the band found itself in third-class cabins, despite a stipulation that it should travel first class.

The *Chicago Defender* of January 31, 1948, printed a picture of the band crowding the rails of the *S. S. Drottingholm* ten days or so before, as she sailed from New York bound "for the Scandinavian country for an unlimited engagement." Warmly wrapped in overcoats and hats, the band members were still unprepared for the full force of the January storms in the North Atlantic. Virtually all the musicians were seasick, especially crowded into their third-class cabins in the bowels of the ship. Yet with the help of John Lewis and Dizzy, the band's morale was kept up in a series of onboard rehearsals. These were largely for the benefit of some recent recruits who had come into the ranks alongside men who had been with Dizzy throughout 1947. Among the newcomers were Benny Bailey on trumpet and drummer Kenny Clarke, back in the fold after his original replacement Joe Harris had been fired by Dizzy in an altercation over money. Harris had demanded payment for a rehearsal at which Dizzy was (uncharacteristically) two hours late.

In late December 1947, the majority of the touring band had assembled in the Victor studios for a recording session, which had been hastily convened as the AFM had called a recording strike from January 1, 1948. This gave the touring group a brief opportunity to work together on new material, although Benny Bailey recalls Gil Fuller putting the finishing touches to the charts in the studio, and that the overall sensation was one of rushing to get some material on disc before the ban. Rehearsals on board ship gave the new members of the band a better chance to work their way in and for all the musicians to take their mind off the rolling seas and appalling weather. Despite minor injuries all round and seasickness, which most affected Lewis and Chano Pozo, an astonishing amount of work got done and a real *esprit de corps* developed. Kenny Clarke was to recall this as the most accomplished of the various lineups of Dizzy's band with which he played.

"Gil Fuller did not travel with the band, but John Lewis had written some wonderful arrangements," recalled Benny Bailey. "And he used to come in and teach us theory on the boat. It was a long trip anyway, but made even longer because of the stormy seas. So to use this time, every day he'd come in and teach all of the trumpet players things about harmony. They were theory lessons, because everybody wanted to know more about the structure of the music. And then Dizzy would come in and give us tips on how to play fast passages. It was like a school. He used to say, 'The first ten years you have to practice like hell, and then that's it. You should have got it by then.'

"That was his theory, because by that time he hated to practice. When I went on tour with him years later in the Clarke-Boland band, he was our guest, and he still hated to practice in the hotel room. He was never one of those guys who liked to do that, but he would do it on the bandstand. When he was not in form he didn't care. He never pushed it. He'd look at his horn like it was a person, and say to himself, 'If not tonight, then tomorrow night.'

"But he was a harmonic and technical genius, and for us in the brass section of that 1948 band, he was the guy to look up to. When I talked to other trumpeters like Fats Navarro and Kenny Dorham, they felt far, far beneath Dizzy actually. Because Diz was doing everything with the horn and harmonically that you could possibly do."[58]

Yet, despite the close musical relationship the band developed, troubles were bubbling under the surface. To a large extent, these centered on the strained relationship between Kenny Clarke, already a seasoned traveler, and Milt Shaw, whom Kenny suspected of having pocketed the difference between the cost of first-class travel and the poorer quality cabins in which the band ended up. Subsequent events, when Shaw's father, Billy, crossed over the Atlantic to sort things out with Lundquist (during which both men were briefly arrested), proved that it was the band's Swedish booker, not its American agent, who was at fault. Nevertheless, Clarke's suspicions prompted Dizzy to engage his wife Lorraine as his personal manager thereafter, a position she held (informally at least) for the rest of his life. In due course, Dizzy managed to sustain an uneasy truce between Milt Shaw and Clarke, even though Shaw apparently attempted to push Clarke overboard when they eventually arrived in Europe.

The storms delayed the band so severely that they docked in Gothenburg around the time they were supposed to be on stage for their first concert on January 26. The state of the tides meant that they had to be ferried ashore and ended up beginning their show well over two hours late. By all accounts, this, and the subsequent dates they played in Scandinavia up to and including February 9 were riotously successful.

In Stockholm, extra concerts were arranged to allow the crowds of fans who turned up for the chance to hear the band. "America's latest jazz phenomenon, bebop music, has taken this jazz music hotbed by storm . . . as devotees of popular music packed every nook and cranny of the Vinterpalaset to hear the dispensations of Dizzy Gillespie, great American trumpeter," ran one dispatch. "Every attendance record ever established has been broken to smithereens as the goateed American and his amazing aggregation have played to capacity crowds on three different occasions. Originally, the band was to play a single concert but there were so many patrons unable to gain admission that an encore was arranged only to have the same situation develop, thus necessitating a third date. Once again there was a sellout, enabling Diz to set a record of 26,749 paid admissions for the three concerts."[59]

Critics were just as enthusiastic about the band as the crowds. "There is no doubt that the bebop style will influence the music of the future," ran a review in the local jazz magazine *Estrad*, by Rolf Dahlgren. Yet despite the critical acclaim, not to mention the public's enthusiasm, the band was scuffling for accommodation (no hotels had been booked by their agent), and, even more worryingly, attendance records or not, there was no sign of any money. Dizzy took to sleeping in the corridor outside Lundquist's hotel room so he could not escape in the night with the box office takings, and finally an advance on the band's earnings was secured before the whole ensemble set off for Belgium on the next leg of the tour.

Nevertheless, just over a week later, the band became stranded in Antwerp without any further money, and, with no clear guarantee that anything they had earned would find its way to them from Lundquist, even the funds for their return to the United States looked in jeopardy. At this point the French critic Charles Delauney stepped in to rescue the situation. In a contribution to Dizzy's autobiography, and in his own memoirs, Delauney gives the impression that this was an impulsive act of generosity. In fact, he had rather gloomily predicted as early as the January issue of *Jazz Hot* that in the postwar recession it was unlikely that the band would ever find its way to France. "Dizzy Gillespie and his orchestra arrived in Scandinavia on 16 January [*sic*]. Negotiations are taking place with a view to presenting the orchestra in Paris. But latest indications seem to be that travel costs for this 17-piece aggregation, allied to the country's present economic crisis, are likely to foil any such plans."[60]

The unexpected double-dealing of Lundquist, and a panic phone call from Willy de Cort, president of the Belgian Hot Club, put things in a different perspective. Delauney no longer had to negotiate via Lundquist, and he could ask a band with no money to share the risk of the enterprise with him. He underwrote the travel costs and organized a series of concerts, plus a lightning (and extremely effective) publicity campaign. By coincidence, the publicity coincided with plans for the first postwar Nice jazz festival, at which American bands led by Louis Armstrong and Mezz Mezzrow were booked to appear. At least one critic took advantage of the opportunity to talk up Delauney's bold move in bringing bebop to Paris, by writing: "Just when Nice is going to give us an idea of what jazz has been, it's wonderful that Paris is presenting what it is now. We can thank Charles Delauney, who, unlike the 'technocrats' in Nice, is not subsidized."[61]

Writing in *Combat*, the day before Gillespie was due to arrive in Paris, critic Boris Vian was typical of those who shared a sense of nerve-tingling excitement at the prospect of Dizzy's French debut. "Young American musicians copy everything about Dizzy, including his physical mannerisms—the beret . . . pulled down to ear level, horn-rimmed glasses, moustache, goatee . . . and his stage manners which involve directing his band with his entire body. But they cannot copy the consistency of his attack, his confidence all over the trumpet, from the very bottom up to screech-level, his infallible harmonic instincts, and the purity of his dry, clear sound—as well as the dizzying complexities of his phrases."[62]

The first of Dizzy's Paris concerts was due to take place the very evening of the band's arrival in the country, on February 20. The train arrived at the Gare du Nord at 8:30 and the musicians took over an hour to clear customs. It took a further hour before the band was able to go on stage, replacing the anxious warm-up act, Jacques Danjean's trio, who had kept a restless crowd sufficiently entertained to stay in their seats, pending Dizzy's arrival.

As the band went on stage there were gasps from the audience, who realized that this seventeen-piece band was about to play entirely without sheet music. Somewhere on the journey the charts had gone astray and there was no time left to find them. "What the hell are we gonna do now?" Kenny Clarke remembered asking Benny Bailey backstage. "No trouble—we just hit!" replied Benny. "We've been playing the same music for a month already now. We know it ass-backwards."[63] Charles Delauney noted that after the first piece there was complete silence; the audience was so carried away by the raw energy and power of the music that it forgot to applaud.

The concert was so successful that it was repeated at the Salle Pleyel on February 22 and 29 (the recording of the latter is discussed in the next chapter), and there were other appearances out of town, plus further Parisian shows at the Club des Champs Elysées and at a cinema in the Place Clichy called the Apollo. There could be only one conclusion about Dizzy's performances, and it was most elegantly summed up by Boris Vian: "Bebop, the most recent evolution in the history of jazz, has conquered Paris. Thanks to Dizzy Gillespie."[64]

Yet Dizzy's pioneering appearance in Paris appears to have deepened a critical schism in France every bit as divisive and ultimately damaging as that which Barry Ulanov and Rudi Blesh had begun in the United States. For a time, Delauney and Hugues Panassié had been regarded as the "twin Popes" of the French Hot Club. As Panassié left the Salle Pleyel, he is widely reported as having dismissed Dizzy's music: "I love jazz—but that's not jazz!" His antipathy toward bebop did little to heal the scars that Gillespie still felt from what he regarded as his unfair exclusion from Panassié's 1937 record dates involving the other members of Teddy Hill's band. Delauney, perhaps despite his own real instincts, found himself inevitably aligned with the modernists, at the start of a bitter dispute between the two critics and their followers whose only real benefit, as Boris Vian subtly observed a year later, had been to keep jazz in the headlines far more than would otherwise have been the case.

Kenny Clarke remained behind in France when the Gillespie band returned to the United States. He was to become a central figure in the group of expatriate American jazzmen who created a lively postwar musical life in Paris and settled in the city because of its general openness and racial tolerance. It is ironic that there were violent scuffles outside the last of Dizzy's Salle Pleyel concerts, during which the gendarmerie beat back the hordes of jazz fans who were queuing for autographs; in the auditorium itself a voice was heard heckling Dizzy to "Go back to Timbuktu!"[65]

The odd such incident aside, the tour had been a musical success. Furthermore when their liner *De Grasse* docked at New York, the somewhat impoverished musicians discovered that Billy Shaw had finally received a substantial part of their money for the tour. "I was paid $600, which may not sound much today, but it was a fortune in 1948," recalled Benny Bailey. "I left the band, and I took a long, long time slowly spending that money in and around New York, and soaking up the jazz scene that was going on there. Dizzy briefly broke up the band, and I didn't join him again when it re-formed."[66]

After a party at the Ebony Club to welcome the band home, Dizzy seems to have followed Bailey's example and taken some time off to live on his tour earnings. But by the end of April he was ready to go back on the road and, following a week at the Apollo, he prepared some new charts (billed as a "Swedish Suite," based on his tour experiences) for a late night concert at Carnegie Hall. The Shaw office used stories of the European tour to fuel the continuing bebop cult, which was kept alive by articles in various of the quality U. S. weeklies. Audiences were encouraged to appear in berets, beards, and horn-rimmed spectacles, and in a widely publicized move to combat any critical press adverse to the sound of bebop itself, the New England Conservatory invited Dizzy to talk to students about the structure of the new music.

Throughout 1948 and 1949, the band continued on the road, its personnel shifting gradually, with newer talents like Paul Gonsalves, Jimmy Heath, and John Coltrane appearing in the ranks as 1950 dawned.

Although the goatee, glasses, and beret cult helped bring in the crowds, notably on a late 1948 trip to California, where once again the band played at least one concert without charts as its luggage caught up with it, the gradual audience desertion from big bands and dance halls became a factor impossible to ignore. In Dizzy's case, the problem was more acute because the band had not seriously attempted to cater for dancers since 1946.

In New York, this was not really a problem, as promoters and club owners were sympathetic to the idea of "jazz for listening." Even the New York Times grudgingly admitted, in a piece headed "Bop: Skee, re or be, it's still got to swing," that "the young crowd, while it is more than willing to listen, seems to have forgotten how to dance fast tempos." It went on: "One result is a new kind of nightclub—notably the Royal Roost (with a roped off section labelled 'Metropolitan Bopera House' where for a small fee, a crowd gathers in the Götterdaemmerung gloom to bend an ear without having to buy drinks.). . . . In these spots there is no dance floor, no lavish review, just tables and the shattering blasts of twenty-odd musicians."[67] The Roost, where Dizzy was resident for much of late 1948, took the same attitude as Clark Monroe, when he launched the band at the Spotlite a couple of years earlier. If patrons were prepared to listen rather than dance, then more people could be squeezed in and they could pay for the privilege. The Roost's ads parodied those of the Met itself, announcing Dizzy as "the distinguished conductor" and billing the support acts as "chamber music by the Tadd Dameron ensemble" and "the renowned diva, Anita O'Day, soloist."

But away from New York and on the touring circuit that most agents reckoned was still essential to maintain the earnings of a sixteen- or seventeen-piece orchestra the underlying problem of the 1945 "Hepsations" tour remained unsolved. Fans attracted by the bebop cult clustered around the bandstands, but the traditional dancing public, who were the mainstay of the provincial audience, were either confused or stayed away.

In addition, an attack on the band arrived out of the blue in the pages of *Down Beat* from a very unexpected quarter. "That big band is a bad thing for Diz," railed Charlie Parker in an interview with John S. Wilson. "A big band slows anybody down because you don't get a chance to play enough. Diz has an awful lot of ideas when he wants to, but if he stays with the big band he'll forget anything he ever played. He isn't repeating notes yet, but he is repeating patterns."[68]

In a welter of contradictory statements, clearly designed to try to promote the idea of Parker as the originator of bop, Bird accused Dizzy of not being aware of playing bop changes before 1942, of putting his name to tunes written by Parker "to give him a better commercial reputation," but above all of sacrificing the rhythmic flexibility of bop. "The beat in a bop band is with the music, against it, behind it . . . it pushes it, it helps it. Help is the big thing. It has no continuity of beat, no steady chug-chug."

Clearly stung by his old colleague's comments, Dizzy hit back, with a surprising softening of his attitude, compared to earlier comments. "Bop is part of jazz . . . and jazz music is to dance to. . . . We'll use the same harmonics, but with a beat so that people will understand where the beat is. We'll use a lot of things which are in the book now, but we'll cut them and splice them together again like you would a movie so as to leave out the variations in beat."[69] Dizzy also admitted that, as Lorraine mingled with audiences on tour, she had realized how impossible the majority of people found it to dance to the band.

This revision in Dizzy's thinking underpinned the start of a new recording contract, as the band transferred from Victor to Capitol. Shorn of much of its rhythmic impetus and excitement, and no longer with the catalyst of Chano Pozo to add an extra dimension to the band's rhythm, the Capitol sessions are among the most anodyne recordings the band ever produced and give a hint as to Dizzy's desperate bid to compromise his original ambitions in favor of public taste, simply to keep a working big band going.

By early 1950, he was finally persuaded to give up the struggle, prompted, as ever, by Lorraine. "My wife said: 'You got a hundred musicians or me! Make up your mind.' So I broke up the band."[70]

With the end of this big band, Dizzy changed direction for good. He experimented in other ways, notably in bringing Afro-Cuban percussion into his small groups and with the repertoire and approach of the succession of occasional big bands he fronted from the mid-1950s until his final United Nation Orchestra in the 1980s. Yet he never went back to the cutting edge of modern jazz development. He largely abandoned the shifting beats and dynamic rhythmic excitement of the 1940s band and in much of his work adopted something far closer to the swing rhythm sections he had grown up with. In his countless sessions for Norman Granz, he fitted happily into the mainstream environment of Oscar Peterson's accompaniment. There were, of course, odd exceptions, notably the brief periods when he was reunited with Art Blakey, first in his own 1950s band, and then in the 1970s Giants of Jazz.

For the majority of his later career, however, Dizzy turned his back on many of the innovations that had made his 1940s big band the high point of his own creativity as a soloist and unquestionably his greatest overall musical achievement—successfully transferring the energy and vitality of small-group bebop to larger forces.

13

The Big Band Records

ot long after its debut, the 1946 big band began to be recorded at a rate unprecedented in Dizzy's career. From a mixture of studio sessions, transcriptions, and airshots by the band, notwithstanding Dizzy's own guest appearances as a soloist, the sheer amount of recorded material that survives makes it virtually impossible to continue the kind of disc by disc survey that has been used to chart Dizzy's early development. For much of the remainder of his life, with only a few fallow patches, Dizzy's career is thoroughly documented on disc, and to note his continued development it becomes necessary to highlight only the most significant records.

Also, the 1946–50 big band tended to play a repertoire so similar from one live session to the next that it was hardly more varied than that which straitjacketed Louis Armstrong's All Stars for over twenty years. Dizzy's commercial discs of some of his core arrangements are not necessarily his best, and many highlights of the band's work can be found by sifting through its impressive legacy of live recordings.

When Dizzy's sextet cut its May 1946 session for Musicraft, the big band was on the point of being launched. As mentioned earlier, this record date hints at the direction in which the big band would move, and in particular offers the first example of Dizzy's reunion with Kenny Clarke after the drummer's spell in the army. The most modernistic of the tracks, from a rhythm section point of view, is "That's Earl Brother," where beneath a fluent solo from Dizzy, Ray Brown lays down the basic pulse, Kenny Clarke shadows him on cymbals with some dramatic snare and bass drum punctuations, while Al Haig adds some chords that seem almost to hang above the underlying meter of the piece in suspended animation.

In a number of sessions from this period, Dizzy included rather unconvincing blues vocals from Alice Roberts, not helped by his own continued lack of sympathy for the genre. On her "Handful of Gimme" from the sextet date, Dizzy parodies a blues trumpeter's shake and vibrato at the end of her first chorus, and it is left to the plaintive alto of Sonny Stitt to inject any depth of blues feeling into the piece. By contrast the joyous ensemble vocals on "Oop Bop Sh'bam" give a foretaste of the kind of nonsense scatting that would become a feature of the full orchestra's live concerts. "One Bass Hit" is a prototype of the subsequent big band arrangement, with Dizzy counterbalancing the nimble basslines of Ray Brown with a solo break that was later to be shared among all the members of his trumpet section.

Alice Roberts sang on one of the big band's two debut recordings for Musicraft, and although the brass writing, Dizzy's own solo, and some prodding piano work from Milt Jackson on "Good Dues Blues" hint at what the band might be capable of, it is only on the other track from that session, "Our Delight," that there is any real evidence that a new and vital voice had arrived on the big band scene.

The real impact of the band is measurable from the surviving recordings from the Spotlite, which are the only document of Thelonious Monk's tenure with Dizzy. Monk always had an affinity with the stride style of Fats Waller and James P. Johnson, and he displays similar links to Count Basie on the set opener, "Our Delight," taken a little slower than the commercial recording. Monk's piano punctuations interject dramatically at the end of the brass and reed phrases in the opening choruses of Dameron's Kansas City–style chart, and later he worries away at a single note in characteristic style. Of the uptempo pieces, the band is at its powerful best on a breakneck "Things to Come" and on a throwback to Dizzy's time with Hines and Eckstine, "Second Balcony Jump," which is the finest example of the Monk/Brown/Clarke rhythm section in action. Brown's dependable pulse creates the freedom for Clarke to punctuate with more freedom than on any other recording of the band in its early months, and Monk's sporadic chording, full of stimulating voicings and thoughtful effects, spurs Dizzy on to an exceptional solo that never flags from a parody of "Honeysuckle Rose" at its inception.

Although Clarke moves the beat around dramatically, the band is so firmly anchored by Brown that it seems hard to understand why dancers found it so difficult to move to. It is only in comparing this band to other contemporary big bands, with their four-square swing rhythm sections, smooth guitar chords, and simple offbeat drum accents, that it becomes obvious just how revolutionary Dizzy's band sounded and how effectively (especially in a full-band arrangement of "Groovin' High") the nuances of small group bebop had been transferred to a larger force.

Two other recordings from the Spotlight stand out. One is a version of "One Bass Hit," complete with falsetto voice effects by Dizzy in the famous D to B♭ clarion call, which echoes round the brass section. The film of this number in *Jivin' in Bebop* shows how Brown would be featured at the front of the band on this piece, but the Spotlite recording captures his most accomplished playing. Before an audience in the lively atmosphere of the club, Brown is more daring than on the commercial studio recordings of the piece; his secure intonation, quarter note figures, and neatly executed breaks give some hint as to the unique chemistry that he brought to Dizzy's rhythm section. It is only with such a powerful and dominating personality on the bass that Clarke was able to achieve such freedom in his playing, and, although Brown's replacements Al McKibbon and Nelson Boyd both later made valiant efforts to play this piece, neither so effectively combined Brown's fluent solo voice with the ability to anchor a band.

The other outstanding recording is a lengthy (and incomplete) "'Round About Midnight." (This is the title that Dizzy gives it in his announcements, rather than the truncated "'Round Midnight," the name under which Cootie Williams had first recorded Monk's composition in 1944.) The band runs through the extended introduction (with its strong affinities to Dizzy's 1945 disc of "I Can't Get Started"), but the effect is radically different from the band's other recordings of the tune, owing to Monk's outlandish chording behind the reed figures. Monk's piano chording adds dramatically to the density of the arrangement, both behind the full band and Milt Jackson's daringly slow chorus, before his own brief solo, which cascades into a rapid sequence of descending broken chords like a disintegrating chandelier. Dizzy's own chorus is a masterly statement, showing his full maturity as a ballad player. Throughout the six minutes or so of the track, there is cause for regret that Monk did not remain longer with the band or record with it more.

By the time of the band's July Musicraft session, John Lewis was installed on piano. Although by his own accounts James Moody had begun to play with the band by this time, he is apparently on neither of the orchestra's first two formal sessions, including the staggeringly accomplished "Things to Come" referred to in the last chapter and the commercially issued full band version of "One Bass Hit."

Moody's official recording debut was on a September 1946 session under Ray Brown's leadership that brought a small band contingent from Dizzy's orchestra together with Brown's old colleague Hank Jones. Apart from the fun of trying to spot which trumpet solos are by Dizzy and which by his section leader Dave Burns, who had assimilated Dizzy's style remarkably effectively, these four sides are notable for Moody's Lester Young–influenced solos on "For Hecklers Only" and "Moody Speaks."

Moody's prowess is the more surprising in that he came late to the saxophone (despite growing up in a musical family). He did not take up the instrument until he acquired an alto in 1942 at age seventeen.

Although he had enjoyed listening to Jimmy Dorsey and Charlie Barnet, he did not really get down to serious work on the sax until he was drafted into the air force in 1943. Then, he heard Lester Young for the first time, and not long afterward Charlie Parker. "Then there wasn't any more Charlie Barnet or Jimmy Dorsey," he recalled.[1] "Not that I didn't appreciate them, but I just felt something else inside, especially when I first heard Lester."

Moody had met Dizzy when the ill-fated "Hep-sations" big band came to the air force base at Greensboro, North Carolina. Contrary to accounts that he played with Dizzy at that time, Moody confirms that he was simply a tenorist in the air force band at the base and it's unlikely Dizzy even heard him. Nevertheless, they got to talking. "I'm going to be regrouping," Dizzy told Moody, evidently already aware that the 1945 band was not a long-term prospect. "You'll be discharged in a few months, and when you get out, come to New York and try out for my band. So I did." Gil Fuller, among others, was less than kind about Moody's prospects,[2] but he was soon installed alongside his fellow ex-Air Force colleague Dave Burns, who had also been in the Greensboro band.

A few weeks after his appearance on Ray Brown's session, Moody made his recording debut with Dizzy on the John Lewis arrangement of "Emanon." Although there had been brief solos by other reed players in Dizzy's band before that point, Moody's contribution to "Emanon" was a sufficiently definitive statement that it came to be widely copied by other saxophonists. "It was my very first recording with Dizzy's band," recalled Moody, "and that opening phrase from the solo still tickles me."[3]

Not simply because of this chorus by Moody, which seems effortlessly to combine the speed and dexterity of Charlie Parker with the wistful tone and spacious feeling of Lester Young, "Emanon" is a interesting piece. It is one of the few charts from the mid-1940s that anticipates the style of the State Department big bands that Dizzy was to head in the 1950s. Partly this is due to its relaxed tempo, which is less frantic than some of the band's other showpieces. Equally, the reed figures that follow Lewis's almost rhapsodic piano introduction have a lot in common with the kind of phrasing Quincy Jones was to write for the 1950s band, although the brass punctuations are a constant reminder of the visceral energy of this band. Lewis's chart may seem relatively unexceptional today, but seen in context it is a strong modernist statement that would have been much noticed by other musicians. For this reason, as well as its innate grace and balance, Moody's solo crept into the consciousness of a generation of saxophonists.

From late 1946 until the middle of the following year, Dizzy's band was touring, with intermittent periods in New York, including lengthy stays at the Savoy and the Downbeat Club. No recordings survive from that period, which marks the end of Dizzy's association with Musicraft. In the wake of the success of his small group sides for Victor, Dizzy signed his big band to that label, and their first session was made in August 1947, with a characteristic mixture of straightforward bop charts and more commercially orientated material.

"Ow!" starts with the band's typically brash and urgent brass attack, giving way to a medium tempo piece, in a comfortably danceable groove, with an unexceptional solo from Dizzy and a rather better one from baritone saxophonist Cecil Payne, who was becoming one of the band's unsung heroes as a solo player. If "Ow!"is pretty standard fare from the band, then "Oop-pop-a-da" mixes a catchy nonsense scat vocal with some disciplined section playing and first-rate solos from Dizzy and Moody. It epitomizes the band's ability to play uncompromisingly in its own style, while making the material approachable for a general public through vocal horseplay.

"Two Bass Hit" almost certainly marks Ray Brown's recording swan song with the band and is another perfect demonstration of his ability to blend flexible soloing with metronomic underpinning of the band's overall pulse. Some sources give Al McKibbon as bassist here, but the RCA archives (borne out by the quality of the playing itself) list Brown as the bassist, with Joe Harris replacing Kenny Clarke on drums. Dizzy's own playing for this session is at its best on Tadd Dameron's relatively conventional chart, "Stay on It." The rhythm section resists the temptation to tear up the beat (reinforcing the view that it is the comparatively restrained Harris rather than the innovative Clarke on drums), and the section writing is neither particularly harmonically nor rhythmically developed from a standard swing band model. It is the band's aggressive attack and Dizzy's own fleet solo that stamps the band's personality over the piece. Entering during a two-bar break, Dizzy phrases attractively behind the beat, moving easily throughout his range and including some rapid downward spiraling phrases in a solo that is excellently shaped and balanced. The band sounds less unconventional than on its earlier Musicraft discs and appears to have tailored its approach to the commercial demands of a major label with wider distribution. Ironically, the playing from this inaugural Victor date that most closely resembles the raw excitement of the big band's earliest work is to be found in the most overtly commercial "Oop-pop-a-da," in the passages that separate the vocals.

By mid-1947, Charlie Parker had returned from California, looking, by all accounts, fitter, slimmer, and younger than he had for a long time. The cure in the Camarillo had temporarily cleared out his system and, although he was not slow in resuming many of his former habits, he produced some remarkably assured playing in a small number of one-off reunions with Dizzy that fitted in and around the big band's busy schedule.

Barry Ulanov's Modernists, the band that competed with Rudi Blesh's traditional lineup on the *Bands for Bonds* broadcasts, saw Parker and Dizzy reunited for two successive sessions in September. Despite Ulanov's extravagant claims for his rhythm section, Billy Bauer's dated and stilted guitar playing sounds out of place, colliding hopelessly with Lennie Tristano's piano on his solo feature "I Surrender Dear," and inhibiting the natural flow of the full band tracks. Tristano himself turns in some exciting locked hand phrases, notably on "Hot House," and manages to avoid slavish dependence on either Bud Powell or Thelonious Monk's approach to bop piano. The only glimpse of Diz and Bird's real empathy and solo skill comes on their successive choruses on "Fine and Dandy," which are as accomplished as anything from their 1945 collaborations. A ghastly rendition of "Tiger Rag" from the second session, enlivened only by Roach's relentless bass drum counterrhythms, shows just how pointless the whole exercise of pitting modernist and traditionalist against one another was.

Dizzy and Bird's first recorded public appearance from this period was a Carnegie Hall concert from late September. They fronted the big band rhythm section as a quintet for part of the second half of a concert that had already featured the big band, introduced Chano Pozo, and displayed Ella Fitzgerald singing a number of standards. Parker's old habits nearly prevented this reunion from happening. Producer Teddy Reig discovered that Bird had passed out in a bathtub. "We went to his room and broke down the bathroom door. We got him out of the tub, dried him, dressed him, got him in a cab, stuck the horn in his hands and pushed him from the wings on to the stage."[4]

The audience bursts into spontaneous applause as Bird produces a magisterial statement of the theme of the channel on the opening chorus of their first number, "Night in Tunisia." The same happens as he launches into a fluent and logically developed solo on the subsequent chorus, urged on by Dizzy shouting and, no doubt, mugging alongside him. Joe Harris and Al McKibbon set up rather a relentless beat, which threatens not to swing at times, but backing Bird, and subsequently Dizzy, on inspired form, the rhythm section's deficiencies are easily overlooked and the recording of the concert accurately captures what must have been an electrifying event.

Harris switches to brushes to set up the rapid-fire introduction to "Dizzy Atmosphere," in which Dizzy and Bird successively play the opening phrases before launching headlong into the main riff of the head arrangement. Harris's transfer to sticks leaves him, as Ross Russell put it, "scrambling frantically" to keep up with Bird, who sustains his inspiration through an exceptional solo. Following him, Dizzy rises magnificently to the challenge, the more remarkable because he had already been responsible for most of the trumpet pyrotechnics with his own big band earlier in the concert. The combative aggression of Bird's playing inspires all those around him.

Although it was some time since they had worked regularly together, by "Groovin' High," the third number, Bird and Dizzy lapsed back into the telepathic understanding of one another that had marked their best playing from 1945. "They fit just like a hand and a glove," recalled Ray Brown (although he had left Dizzy's band by this time). "They sounded like one horn. If somebody could put one mouthpiece on two horns and play it at the same time, that's what they sounded like. Bird used to play with Red Rodney and Miles, but it was never like with Dizzy. And Dizzy had bands with a lot of saxophone players, including Sonny Stitt, but nobody ever sounded like Bird did with him."[5]

Dizzy paraphrases his own recorded solo on this piece, a technique he often used with material he had committed to disc. Bird, by contrast, plays with a flow of original ideas that make little more than passing references to any of his earlier work. Both men execute the introductions to "Confirmation" and "Koko" with no hint that Bird's condition had barely allowed him to get on stage and no rehearsal had been possible. Their understanding is intuitive, and one feels privileged to eavesdrop on the empathy between them, as well as on the inspired solo that Parker produces on "Koko" that clearly brings the audience to its feet in cheers and whistles as Harris's thrashing drum solo takes over from the alto.

Inspired as the Gillespie/Parker reunion clearly was, it did not alter Dizzy's unswerving commitment to his big band, especially since the arrival of Chano Pozo had started a whole new level of musical cross-fertilization in Dizzy's own work. A concert from Cornell allows us to hear the changes that were beginning as a result of Chano Pozo's debut in the band, but it is in the last two sessions of the year for Victor that the Afro-Cuban ideas that Dizzy had been toying with for some time were finally converted into commercial recordings.

In the weeks preceding these two apparently rather hastily convened sessions, a number of changes had occurred in the band's personnel, notably among the trumpets. One player who never managed to record with the band but who was in the trumpet section during late 1947 was Joe Wilder. Four and a half years younger than Dizzy, he had grown up in Philadelphia, where his father had been a member of Frankie Fairfax's band. Joe recalls hearing Dizzy with Fax while still a schoolboy and relished the opportunity to play in what he considered to be the most exciting big band of the day.

Joe recalls that, during one of the band's 1947 Apollo weeks, Dizzy castigated the trumpet section for looking too serious and leaving all the comic entertainment to him.

"He told us we looked like a bunch of mummies, sitting up there," recalled Joe. "He said, 'I'm the only one showing any signs of life!'

"Well, Elmon Wright, the lead trumpeter, and I went out and we got some giant lollipops that were popular at the time called 'All Day Suckers.' They were about as big as your hand, and so, when Dizzy announced the brass section that night to take a bow, we all stood up and licked these giant lollipops. And that had some effect on the audience.

"The next day, we looked around backstage and we found a little truck that they used for pushing luggage around, and we also found some costumes, including a policeman's cap and tunic. So during the show, while Dizzy was out front doing his act, I dressed up as a policeman, and

Strand Theatre, 1948. Dizzy's full band and revue showing the context in which the band was performing on many of its stage shows. (Frank Driggs collection)

Elmon lay down on the truck and I pushed him right across the stage. Then, we turned right around, and stood up. I'm just a short guy, and Elmon was quite tall, so he grabbed me by the scruff of the neck, on my uniform jacket, and marched me out across the stage, like one of those old time musical comedy walks, with me virtually on tip toe and him hanging on to my collar. The audience were in fits.

"So, finally, after that show, Dizzy comes round to see us. 'OK, guys, enough!' he says. 'Really, you don't have to do any more.' "[6]

Joe left Dizzy at the very start of December 1947 to join Lucky Millinder, and his place was taken by Benny Bailey. Perhaps because, ever since he first discovered Europe as a member of Dizzy's 1948 tour, Benny spent the majority of his career there, he has failed to get comparable critical recognition in the United States to many inferior musicians who remained in the States. Benny's path to becoming a major individual voice on the trumpet began in his hometown of Cleveland, where his mentor was a slightly older entertainer and musician called Hubert Kidd. It was through Kidd that Benny first met Dizzy, when the Eckstine band arrived in Cleveland before Benny was out of his teens.

"Hubert knew Dizzy. He was a trumpeter and a fluent musician himself, who died tragically young," recalled Benny. "He took me to a jam session at the Eckstine band's hotel, which was where Dizzy's playing first really knocked me out. At that jam session I remember Bud Powell was there as well, and Tadd Dameron came in. All the musicians stayed in the Majestic Hotel, and I guess there may have been two or three bands in town when Eckstine arrived, and the practice was for everyone to get together in a room and just play. Because I was a trumpeter, I really just remember Dizzy's playing and how incredible it was.

"Then I went on to a career in music, and by late 1947 I was with Jay McShann. We were in Chicago, and so was Dizzy, when Joe Wilder left his band. I heard about it, so I went to one of the rehearsals Dizzy had in a hotel basement, where I just sort of sneaked in and started playing. See, the trombone player in the band was from Cleveland also—his name was Bill Shepherd—and so he was instrumental in helping me get into the band. He knew me, and he got me into the rehearsal. I was very shy in those days, I didn't say much, so I just got my horn out and began. Well, soon Dizzy came into the room, hears me, and says: 'Who's this guy?'

"Shepherd says: 'That's Benny Bailey from my hometown.'

"So I got the job. I knew that the chair was empty, because Joe Wilder had already gone back to New York, and I was determined to get the job by hook or by crook. It was a wonderful band, a wonderful experience and I learned a lot. I wasn't interested in the money, even, I didn't care, because I was near Dizzy, and I had never heard anything like what he was doing on the trumpet. I didn't even know it was possible to play the trumpet like that. So it was a joy going to work or going to rehearsal.

"Elmon Wright did all the lead playing, and he didn't bother about playing solos. Because it was quite a job playing lead. The other trumpets were Dave Burns, and Lammar Wright Jr., Elmon's brother, who was a high-note specialist. They were the two sons of Lammar Wright, who'd played in Calloway's band. I saw both of them again around New York in 1980 not long before they died, and they'd both more or less given up playing, but back then in the 1940s, they were great players. The music was so new, and challenging. Dizzy used to come around and help us, give us tips on how to play certain passages, because a lot of the things you hear that band do were not written. Gil Fuller might just write down eight bars or so of what he wanted, and Dizzy would come along and show us how to develop it. Even that long line the horns play on 'Things to Come' was never properly written down. Like one trumpet would have the phrases written, but not all the others would have their parts, and we had to hear what we had to do. Some nights it came out right. But that made it a very fast and exciting business.

"But to cap it all, to hear Dizzy himself was amazing. He was a great musician later on, but in later years he didn't have to prove anything. Back then he was something else. He was all over the horn, and then he'd go up high. He was moving around at the top of his range, which was just unheard of then. And the people went wild!"[7]

Back in New York just over a week after the band closed at the Regal in Chicago, Dizzy took the orchestra into the studios for Victor. In the first of the two sessions, on December 22, Chano Pozo's presence dominated the proceedings, from his insistent presence on "Algo Bueno" (formerly known as "Woody 'n' You)" to the two-part "Cubana Be–Cubana Bop."

"Algo Bueno" has a very different feel from the earlier version Dizzy made with Coleman Hawkins, mainly because the absent Latin rhythm on that first version is more than compensated for by Pozo, who is almost too enthusiastic. The band feels as if it is being held back a little and strains like a greyhound on the leash at the start of the brief saxophone solo, where there is suddenly a break into a four-square swing rhythm. At this point, the unease expressed by Ray Brown over Pozo's contribution was clearly inhibiting many members of the orchestra, since on familiar and more secure ground the band really lets rip on the swing rhythm of Tadd Dameron's "Cool Breeze," the only track cut at this session that was not overtly Afro-Cuban.

In contrast to Dizzy's first Victor big band session, when the orchestra appeared to hold back from its instinctive style, "Cool Breeze" is far more characteristic of its best work, and only a very brief scat chorus by Dizzy and Kenny Hagood nods at Victor's commercial demands; the rest of the piece sounds uncompromisingly modern and pugnacious. In particular, the new trumpet section is brashly assertive, punctuating the opening chorus dramatically as the trombones blast a countermelody to the massed reeds. Dizzy's solo following the vocal is consistently aggressive, and Pozo adds some dynamic effects behind John Brown's alto before Dizzy returns to float over the whole ensemble.

This track alone demonstrates both the band's originality and why it presented dancers with a dilemma. It is undoubtedly rhythmic, but it is too fast and the section work too brash and aggressive to be comfortable dance-hall fare. It is, on the other hand, undoubtedly the right heady mixture for the European concert audiences to whom the band played just over a month later. In contrast to the large swing bands that had crossed the Atlantic in the late thirties, this orchestra sounded so new and exciting that it would simultaneously help to create and satisfy the taste for modernism that overtook Europe in the period of reconstruction after World War Two.

The most significant achievement of this December Victor session, however, is that the Afro-Cuban element of the band's work is brilliantly captured in "Cubana Be-Cubana Bop." Pozo's introductory rhythms create a dark and somber mood, picked up in turn by trombones, reeds, and muted trumpets, with Dizzy's open horn blazing over the top. Dizzy's phrasing has strong Hispanic elements, and it makes an interesting comparison to the Miles Davis/Gil Evans collaboration on "Sketches of Spain" over a decade later, having a passionate intensity both in the solo playing and ensemble charts that is entirely absent from that later work. The rhythmic density of the piece is matched by the strength of George Russell's writing, in which the voicings maintain the somber mood, while demonstrating his modal preoccupations. After a trumpet-conga exchange, Pozo starts his chanting, with shout-backs from the band. The effect is African, exotic, strange, and intensely modern. Pozo brings commitment to his own chanting, so that even if the responses are, as Bailey suggested, merely nonsense once they become simple repetitions of the title, there is a depth and seriousness about the piece generally lacking from most preceding Latin jazz records. After the chanting, Lewis's jangly piano chords and the wave after wave of reed and brass figures that pile in behind them are equally unfamiliar ground for jazz of the period. This studio recording of a piece that was already a central part of the band's concert repertoire is a landmark in the history of modern jazz every bit as important as the Parker/Gillespie collaborations two years before.

The Afro-Cuban mood is sustained on the highlight of the second December session with "Manteca," a Pozo/Gillespie composition. The word allegedly means "greasy," and the band slips effortlessly from the strong Latin groove of the head to the more swing-inflected rhythms of the saxophone and trumpet solos. The out-choruses have a swaggering Latin swing worthy of Machito or any of New York's other leading Latin orchestras, and Dizzy's soloing retains its authentic Hispanic feel, which carries over into his tone and phrasing in the studio version of Dameron's orthodox swing chart "Good Bait."

In addition to Bailey, several other members of the band have mentioned in interviews that the band was light on material for this second session and that Gil Fuller was finishing charts in the studio. One of them was "Ool-Ya-Koo," yet another scat vehicle for Dizzy and vocalist Kenny Hagood. Credited to Dizzy and Gil Fuller, all the brass section knew that the riff was actually penned by Joe Wilder during his tenure with the band.

"I used to play it as a blues thing, like a solo on blues, or as a background riff behind a singer like a preacher with a plunger mute," recalled Wilder. "Gil needed a riff for the session and he adopted it, both as the vocal and as the brass figure behind the sax solos. I was never given credit for it, and nobody ever mentioned me when it was played. But the fellows in the band knew I was the one that had put it together."[8]

The band's next recordings were made on the other side of the Atlantic. In the remarkably faithful sound quality achieved by Swedish radio, they document the extraordinary impact of bebop in Scandinavia at one of the Stockholm Vinterpalatset concerts. The opening theme, "I Waited for You," has some occasionally scrappy section work, but Dizzy's confident and assured ballad playing hovers over the kind of densely textured voicings that can seldom, if ever, have been heard in Europe before. As the band romps into "Our Delight," the contrast between Kenny Clarke's live and studio work is immediately obvious; his drums not only convey all the light and shade in the arrangement, but his fills and accents are both more daring and accomplished than anything he cut in the studio, especially in Dizzy's second solo on the piece, where Chano Pozo's congas add to the arsenal of percussion effects.

"Ool-Ya-Koo" from this concert is a further example of how the band was able to extend and develop its studio work, with Fuller's impromptu version of Wilder's tune having taken on a newer and more complex personality after the first week of the European tour. The same is true of "Oop-pop-a-da," where the unison glissandi behind the opening vocal are vigorously taken up by all the trumpets (and even at one point the trombones) in a novel extension of the chart that makes it sound like a field of Roman candles, and the presence of both Wright brothers in the trumpets allows the section to pitch the riff behind the tenor solo one, if not two, octaves higher than on the original disc.

The band's repertoire from Stockholm and the subsequent recording of a Paris concert are nevertheless predictable, with little variation from the setlists of the preceding months, except for a poised and authoritative ballad version by Dizzy of the Rose/Youmans song "More Than You Know," which because of its very unfamiliarity is more effective than the by now overused "I Can't Get Started."

The infectious mood of enthusiasm and excitement from Stockholm was intact almost a month later in Paris, where several of the pieces recorded at the Salle Pleyel are given in far more extended versions than their original recordings as the band loosened up the charts written for the constraints of 78-rpm three-and-a-half-minute discs. An incomplete "Oop-pop-a-da" runs to just under five minutes, with a storming and extended tenor solo from George "Big Nick" Nicholas. Although Nick's phrasing and harmonic sense veers intuitively toward the Swing Era, he and fellow swing veteran altoist Howard Johnson both sat happily in Gillespie's bebop ensemble. In Nick's case, this had much to do with his time in Earl Hines's 1942 band alongside Budd Johnson, who was always notably sympathetic to Dizzy's ideas and (following the partnership established on 52nd Street) later spent short spells in Dizzy's own orchestra. Nick clearly also felt comfortable with the Salle Pleyel crowd, later commenting: "Right from the beginning I fell in love with European audiences: I found them to be so knowledgeable and enthusiastic."[9]

The highlight of the Paris concert is the "Afro-Cuban Drum Suite" ("Cubana Be–Cubana Bop" in slightly altered form). Russell's chart seems perfect for the concert-hall atmosphere, and Pozo's theatrical chanting and playing obviously created a magical rapport with his Parisian audience.

This aspect of Pozo's work is also a highlight of the other major concert recording that survives from his brief stay in the band, cut for the indefatigable promoter Gene Norman at the Pasadena Civic Auditorium. It combines the excellent acoustics of the hall with a high-quality recording, giving the best sound of the band's live sessions from the period, even though the mix favors Pozo at the expense of Dizzy's new drummer, Teddy Stewart. The congas are in evidence from the opening bars of "Emanon," dominating the piano solo and setting the mood for successive choruses by Dizzy and Moody, the latter back in the band after a period in Europe on his own and playing in a much more boppish style than on the earlier record of the piece, albeit never sacrificing the Lester Young overtones in his work. Pozo's dominance of this track leads by way of an assertive presence on almost every piece to his most dramatic concert recording of "Manteca."

The concert shows how a piece like "Ool-Ya-Koo" had developed even further through seven months as a regular item in the band's concert programs. Here it begins with the vocal over just bass and piano with a light dusting of rhythm from Pozo's congas. A relaxed Dizzy and altoist John Brown play the scat vocal for laughs, using microphone technique to add an absurd emphasis to syllables like "oo" and "shoo," deliberately popping the mike before embarking on a hushed series of "shab-a-dooby-ooby-doo" phrases. Given the overwhelmingly accomplished sound of the band overall, along with its outstanding instrumental soloists, it would be easy to dismiss the vocals of Dizzy and his regular accomplices from the late 1940s—Kenny Hagood, Joe Carroll, John Brown, and occasionally James Moody—as mere crowd-pulling stunts, helping to sell unpalatable or unfamiliar music to the public. Yet closer examination shows that there is more to Dizzy's vocals than that, despite his relatively limited timbre and range. No writer has put it better than Barry McRae in his short life of Gillespie: "[He] organized his wordless gibberish with a draftsman's hand. . . . He was a prisoner within the confines of an extraordinarily limited vocal situation and had no alternative but to extricate himself from melodic cul-de-sacs by sleight of voice creativity. To do so he demonstrated amazing dexterity, disguising the limited number of sounds he used by the shaping of the solo and by the unpredictable direction of his melodic line."[10]

Despite his accomplished vocal horseplay, Dizzy's own solos had taken on a certain predictability. In his poised and elegant solo from the Pasadena concert on " 'Round About Midnight," one phrase is mirrored by a unison orchestral vocal, and other elements of his playing sound more predetermined and less spontaneous than in his earlier work. This is hardly surprising, given the way in which a touring band settles into its repertoire and into certain familiar stage routines, but it does add a certain justification to Charlie Parker's attack on Gillespie in the following year's *Down Beat* article. Only Cecil Payne's extended baritone solo on Dameron's "Stay on It" from Pasadena has the kind of adrenaline-inducing novelty of the band's best work, although the band roars through several of its uptempo warhorses with great verve and better-disciplined overall section playing than on the European concerts that began the year.

The band's stay in California following the Pasadena concert suggests that it was universally warmly received, with the trappings of bebop "fashion" helping to achieve "standing room only" signs at Pasadena, a house record at Los Angeles's Million Dollar Theatre, with a gross of $18,000, plus extended stays at both the Cricket Club and Billy Berg's.

The trumpet section had undergone one or two changes by mid-1948, reducing from four to three trumpeters with Lamar Wright Jr.'s departure. Elmon Wright and Dave Burns remained, although Burns was to be replaced by Benny Harris before the year was out. Benny Bailey's place was taken by the future Ellingtonian Willie Cook.

Cook, like Bailey, had spent some time in Jay McShann's Orchestra and had also been among the ranks of Earl Hines's band, to which he was recruited by Hines's one-time musical director, the veteran band-leader, arranger, and talent scout, Jesse Stone. From there he went to the Lunceford band, which was jointly run by Ed Wilcox and Joe Thomas, and it was from that orchestra that Dizzy hired him. "After I got there I didn't want to leave," Cook recalled. "I stayed with Dizzy until the band broke up in June 1950. Working in that band, I really learned a lot. It was out of tune and everything, but there was so much spirit you didn't even notice that."[11]

Judging from the band's many airshots from the Royal Roost, the tuning problems were not as severe as Cook remembered. The spirit and attack of the band are not quite as vibrant as on its very first 1946 records, but there is some aggressive and attacking playing on some of their air-shots, notably the AFRS sessions, in which, during the late 1948 set, the brass riffs and flared long notes behind Ernie Henry's alto on "The Squir-rel" are played with burning passion, and Dizzy produces some strato-spheric trumpet in his own solo. Another interesting development in the perennial "Oop-pop-a-da" from that broadcast is the band's unison chant of "I know how to do it!" at the opening, proving that even the rappish unison vocals favored by late-twentieth-century groups like the Dirty Dozen or the Rebirth Brass Bands from New Orleans had their origins in the late 1940s Gillespie orchestra.

There had been some developments among the band's arrangers as well, and Erroll Garner's brother Linton (also a pianist and a fellow bandsman of James Moody at Greensboro) produced a number of charts, including "Minor Walk" and "Duff Capers," which were recorded for Victor and then became regular parts of the band's live sessions. Gerald Wilson also contributed compositions and arrangements to the band, both in his own right and in collaboration with Dizzy.

Dizzy appeared on a January 1949 all-star recording session orga-nized by *Metronome* magazine that offers a brief, but generally rather uninformative opportunity to compare his playing at the time to that of Miles Davis and Fats Navarro, each of whom takes some short solo vignettes in a recording dominated by the presence of Charlie Parker in top form, at a time when, according to his biographers, he was far from consistent in his public appearances.[12]

Dizzy's own recording sessions for Victor continued during the first half of 1949 but generally show a decline from the band's earliest work for the label, and a growing proportion of lightweight novelty tracks or vocal ballads for Johnny Hartman. Undistinguished versions of the "Swedish Suite" and "St. Louis Blues" were recorded alongside two Hartman songs in April, and the May session that followed is most notable for Dizzy's poised and delicate solo playing on the ballad "Katy" retitled "Dizzier and Dizzier." The band regains something of its former fire on "Jump Did-le-ba" from the same date, with Dizzy's old "Bye Bye Blues" stock phrase played in unison by the trumpet section on the final chorus, yet a novelty vocal dominates the first half of the track. This trend continued into the final session the band cut for Victor, where "Hey Pete Let's Eat Mo' Meat" is redeemed only by first-rate solos from Dizzy and J. J. Johnson on trombone. Yet, amid the ghastly vocals, the section playing is as tight as ever and the band was clearly still capable of producing electrifying live performances.

By the time the band began to record for Capitol, later in the year, the personnel had undergone a major reshuffle. Faced with a number of departures from the reed and rhythm sections, Dizzy looked to his previous stamping ground of Philadelphia for replacements. The pianist was his old colleague from the very first band Dizzy had led in the city, Johnny Acea. On drums was Specs Wright, and the two alto saxophonists were from the group of players at the forefront of modern jazz developments in Philadelphia, Jimmy Heath and John Coltrane.

A year or so before they joined Dizzy, these two sax players had been working with trumpeter Calvin Massey in their hometown. "We helped each other advance musically by exchanging musical knowledge and ideas," recalled Heath, a process that continued once they were installed in Dizzy's sax section.[13] Saxophonist Bunky Green, catching the band on tour in Milwaukee, noticed the two altoists during the intermission: "They were standing in a corner playing Charlie Parker solos note for note. One would play a line and the other would counter with a complementary line. What they were doing, I guess, was playing Bird duets with each other."[14]

The young Coltrane had been recruited to Dizzy's band by tenor player Jesse Powell. "Trane" had earlier had a short-lived job with the saxophonist and blues shouter Eddie Cleanhead Vinson, but this was his first long-term job with a high-profile band. The strong tenor of Powell was to be a musical influence on Coltrane when he switched from playing

Dizzy's big band, Orpheum Theatre, Los Angeles, 1949. (Frank Driggs collection)

alto to tenor himself after the big band broke up in 1950. Powell's compatriot in the reed section was Yusef Lateef during the first few weeks of Coltrane's tenure with Dizzy, and, if Powell influenced Coltrane's playing, then Lateef influenced his spiritual side, introducing him to religion and philosophy. Dizzy would get drawn into some of these discussions, taking an active interest in reading matter and thinkers on religious subjects, although such talks often ended with Coltrane accepting Powell's invitation to go and get drunk.

The alto book called for Coltrane to take many of the solos that Ernie Henry or John Brown had formerly played, and those who heard him on " 'Round Midnight," "Night in Tunisia," and "Manteca" were impressed. Journalist Franklin Power saw Coltrane appearing with Dizzy at Philadelphia's Earle Theater and felt that his playing was sufficiently noticeable that he was moved to write a profile of the young saxophonist that appeared in the *Baltimore Afro-American*.[15] According to other eyewitnesses, it was not just the press who began to notice Coltrane's potential as a soloist: "In Pittsburgh, [Dizzy's] band was playing an arrangement of 'Minor Walk.' Dizzy was in front of the band pleasing the audience with his showmanship when John charged into a solo. Dizzy snapped round and stood with his mouth hanging open as if hearing something he'd never heard before. That was only one of several nights that John took over."[16]

Coltrane and Heath brought more than musical prowess and ideas into the band. They and drummer Specs Wright were already interested in heroin, and in their time with Dizzy they became addicted. "Using heroin was fashionable, when the big blowers like Bird were using," wrote Art Pepper about Coltrane. "Working in Dizzy Gillespie's band, playing lead alto, he became a junkie."[17] Dizzy allegedly fired Heath and Wright when he discovered their getting high and they returned to Philadelphia for a time.

Coltrane was also fired, but for drunkenness, although Dizzy later relented and rehired him. Several of Trane's biographers suggest that he drank excess whisky to try to suppress his drug problem, but lacked Parker's indestructible constitution. On at least one occasion in a hotel room on tour, Coltrane was saved from a near fatal collapse by mouth-to-mouth resuscitation from Heath.

Despite the narcotics, all accounts suggest that this last version of Dizzy's big band, with its coterie of Philadelphia boppers, was one of his best, recapturing some of the vigor (in live performance at least) of the 1946 orchestra. Dizzy himself was clearly proud of it, and tenorist Paul Gonsalves, who replaced Powell, recalled that, when he was asked to join, "I wondered about myself, because I didn't consider myself a 'modern' artist, but if Dizzy saw something in my playing . . . well, maybe I ought to go. It was one of the best [bands] Dizzy ever had."[18]

Unfortunately, the recordings the band made for Capitol offer no indication of the band described by its members. Even full-scale instrumental numbers like the Chico O'Farrill arrangement of "Carambola" have a superficial veneer of Latin percussion and sound more like a half-hearted Latin band trying to inject some jazz feeling into its playing than a top-flight jazz orchestra. And it is hard to disagree with bebop's British apologist Steve Race when he wrote this epitaph for Dizzy's first big band period in 1950: "Even Dizzy could not resist the ravages of commerciality . . . the final blow fell when he moved over to Capitol and made 'You Stole My Wife, You Horse Thief,' a hunk of pure Mickey Mouse music. Dizzy, the pioneer, like so many men before him had succumbed."[19]

14

Dee Gee, Paris, and Massey Hall

The first few months of 1950 saw the big band play out its final engagements. It headlined at the Apollo for the last time in March, where it still retained the full entourage of a touring revue.[1] Even though the economics of bandleading made it harder and harder for Dizzy to keep the orchestra going, he remained surprisingly cheerful. John Coltrane, whose own personality was far less exuberant than Dizzy's, watched from the saxophone section as Dizzy clowned for his audiences. Trane was also genuinely impressed by his off-stage manner with the musicians: "I don't make a habit of wishing for what I don't have, but I often wish I had a lighter nature. Dizzy has that beautiful gift. I can't say, 'Be happy, people!' It's something I can't command."[2]

Dizzy's cheerfulness was the more remarkable since he was suffering the after effects of a fall from his bicycle in New York. A car had hit him, scarring his arms and affecting his ability to play high notes. A meager compensation award eventually arrived, but meanwhile, not long after the Apollo week, the big band finally broke up, having played the Silhouette Club in Chicago.

The first recording Dizzy made after this suggested that he was to return to the music he had played before starting the big band. In June, Norman Granz assembled an all-star group for a studio session in New York, and for the first time managed to get Dizzy, Charlie Parker, and Thelonious Monk together in front of the microphone. By this time, Granz had become the controlling element in Charlie Parker's recording career, and was also risking the possible problems that could arise from Bird's erratic behavior to book him as a featured artist on Jazz at the Philharmonic concert tours.

One such tour had just finished, and, despite an incident in which Parker and his young white trumpeter, Red Rodney, had missed a scheduled flight from Kansas to St. Louis and ended up being ferried there in a fellow musician's private plane, Granz was aware that Parker was not only playing close to the top of his form but was a highly bankable asset—

his legendary reputation pulled good audiences wherever the touring show appeared. Granz had also successfully recorded Bird with a string orchestra, late in 1949, and this shrewd marketing ploy was also fueling the Bird legend in the wake of the disc's release in early 1950.

Red Rodney left Bird's touring quintet when the Jazz at the Philharmonic tour ended in May, and Granz applied his usual keen marketing mind to the problem of replacing him. On record, at least, Dizzy was the automatic choice, and while Granz's enthusiasm for Buddy Rich brought a less than sympathetic drummer into the group, the combination of Gillespie, Parker, Monk, and bassist Curley Russell was inspired. Parker's personal manager at the time, Teddy Blume, who had been charged with the arduous responsibility of getting all the musicians (including Parker) into the studio on time, was commemorated in "Bloom-dido," an outstanding twelve-bar blues, in which Monk's eccentrically angular solo catches nuances from Bird and Diz's preceding choruses. Five other tunes were cut, all but one of them in two versions. Both takes of the hell-for-leather "Leap Frog" show that the intuitive radar by which Dizzy and Bird navigated through the most complex of bebop lines was still intact.

Rich was on record as disliking bebop and only agreed to the session because of his admiration for Parker. His biographer, singer Mel Tormé, has pointed out that Buddy stuck relentlessly to a four-to-the-bar bass drum because he thought most bop drummers were too "busy" behind the soloist: "He was willing to bow to the new wave up to a point . . . [he] was critical of the current crop of drummers who, in his opinion, were hamstrung in the bebop bag and did not swing."[3] The success of the session, however, is largely in spite of, rather than because of, Rich, whose concept of swing is firmly rooted in the pre-bebop era and who lacks the lightness and fluency of Max Roach or the ability of Blakey or Clarke to move the bass drum pattern around. Any of these three bop drummers might have further enhanced an already accomplished session, providing an even better springboard for Dizzy and Bird's ideas. A week or two later, the two musicians were billed opposite one another at Birdland, when Dizzy's new group joined Coleman Hawkins's quartet as a backup attraction to "Bird with Strings." During this engagement, Diz and Bird occasionally shared front-line duties.

Yet, tempting as it might have been for Dizzy to pick up his small group playing where he had left it in 1946, he chose a different route. By late August, his new sextet was sharing the billing at the Apollo with Billy Eckstine, who was returning to the Harlem theatre after a three-year absence. Given Dizzy's overall lack of affinity for the blues in most of his recorded work up to this point, it was a surprise to all concerned that, instead of continuing to develop the fractured rhythms and angular phrasing of pure small group bebop, Dizzy elected to combine his solo style with the riffs and shuffle beat of the rhythm and blues craze.

The Apollo blurb praised Dizzy as "a standout as one of jazzdom's most creative musicians and one of show business's most colorful personalities."[4] Yet the band's debut recording, made for Prestige by producer Bob Weinstock (who was recording a wide roster of bebop players), reveals an uncertain feeling about the group's general direction, across a set of discs with no sense of homogeneity. The "old" Dizzy is apparent in a poised ballad performance of "Thinking of You," with his open horn recalling his exemplary playing on "I Can't Get Started" or " 'Round About Midnight." A foretaste of the kind of muted playing he was to adopt later in the 1950s, obtaining a characteristic "thin" tone with a stemless harmon mute, can be heard on a neat arrangement of Gershwin's "Nice Work If You Can Get It"; his muted horn is counterbalanced by some well-constructed saxophone countermelodies and riffs.

Unfortunately, neither of these styles prevailed, and the track that set the tone for the next three years of Dizzy's work was "She's Gone Again," with a rambunctious shout-back vocal: "One, two . . . she's gone again!" Milt Jackson had been a perfectly capable occasional pianist for the big band, but here his keyboard talents are barely up to the task. He comps a shuffle beat behind the vocals and under Dizzy's solo, but his own single-line piano solo is hesitant and has none of the natural fluency of his vibes playing. Dizzy alone plays in his natural style, happily accommodating his bop phrasing to a beat more usually associated with trumpeters like Louis Prima and reminding us of his skill at adapting to non-bebop rhythm sections from the mid-1940s.

Once the band took to the road, the same paradox continued, especially when the group arrived on the West Coast, where the bebop beret and goatee movement had been such a feature of previous visits by the big band. The goateed hipsters felt shortchanged by trivial rhythm and blues numbers like "Hey Pete Let's Eat Mo' Meat," and on one occasion in Los Angeles a group of them began making faces at Dizzy during the tune. Bassist Bill Crow recounts the story: "After the vocal Dizzy put his trumpet to his lips and played three of the most brilliant, explosive, difficult choruses ever played by any trumpet player. When he finished he leaned over to the hipsters and said pointedly: 'Seee?' Then he went right back to singing 'Hey Pete.' "[5]

On Dizzy's first West Coast tour after breaking up his big band, he was reunited with the Johnny Richards Orchestra to record an album with strings. He had first done this in 1945 and 1946, although the results lay unissued, and so it seemed in 1950, to those who were unaware of his earlier attempts to front an orchestra, as if he was seeking to cash in on the "Bird with Strings" idea pioneered by Norman Granz. Several critics have pointed out that Dizzy's session exposed his naturally thin tone, and this was one occasion where his ability to use the microphone to flatter his sound did not pay off. In contrast to Bird's rhapsodic flow of ideas over a pedestrian string section, Dizzy was also inhibited from playing in his natural style, and, although he was to continue to flirt with various orchestral settings, none of them managed the extraordinary success of Parker's discs, either commercially or artistically.

The period from 1950 until 1953 was to be an artistic low point in Dizzy's career, redeemed by a few examples of his technically brilliant playing on record or in concert and with a few glimpses of the future direction he was to take. Nevertheless, he was generally eclipsed by Parker's successful promotion at the hands of Norman Granz and the emergence of Miles Davis's individual voice following his 1949–50 *Birth of the Cool* discs. Miles's nine-piece band may not have been a commercial proposition as a touring ensemble, but its album, with arrangements by Gil Evans, Johnny Carisi, John Lewis, Gerry Mulligan, and Davis himself, showed that it was possible for jazz to develop in a very different direction from Dizzy's incursion into rhythm and blues.

Essentially the Miles Davis Nonet tackled the question of large ensemble jazz from an angle entirely dissimilar to Dizzy's late 1940s big band. Whereas Dizzy's starting point had always been the sinuous horn lines and visceral excitement of a prototypical small group, with each section in his big band representing the linear improvising voice of a solo trumpet, saxophone, or trombone, Miles looked at a different area of jazz history for inspiration—the orchestral tonal palettes of Duke Ellington and Claude Thornhill. While Dizzy's arrangers Gil Fuller, Tadd Dameron, and John Lewis built the invigorating harmonies of bop into the voicings for each big band section, such tonal experimentation as there was took place within the conventional swing orchestra instrumentation. Gil Evans and Miles Davis, who had met in 1947, first put together Miles's Nonet for a couple of weeks at the Royal Roost in September 1948 and followed this up with a series of three record dates for Capitol, adding trombone, French horn, tuba, and baritone sax to the conventional bop quintet of trumpet, alto, piano, bass, and drums.

Interestingly, some of the arrangements were by John Lewis, whose chart for "Move," recorded on January 21, 1949, places a cameo of small group bebop into an orchestral setting: an exercise in contrast rather than an attempt to transfer the entire content of the music to larger forces. Miles and altoist Lee Konitz replicate the Parker/Gillespie bebop front line, set in a feather bed of tonal effects from the additional horns—

sustained long-note harmonies and brief flurries at the end of phrases, with some particularly effective downward moving figures from tuba and baritone together. The arrangement may have been Lewis's, but the concept owes most to Evans, whose earliest nonet charts include "Why Do I Love You?" (a vocal vehicle for Dizzy's one-time vocalist Kenny Hagood) that survives from a Royal Roost broadcast. This opens with an orchestral flourish, complete with trills, and closes with a ravishingly beautiful full chorus, with the parts moving against each other in poised slow motion, an effect typical of Evans's work for Claude Thornhill's big band, but totally justifying Miles's observation that Evans "can use four instruments where other arrangers need eight."[6]

The relationship between Miles and Dizzy has always been hard to pin down. Clearly, when Miles worked in the Eckstine trumpet section and later joined Charlie Parker's quintet, he and Dizzy fell into master/pupil roles. Miles seems to have retained this feeling well into the 1950s, both at a conscious level (agreeing to sub for Dizzy at Birdland in May 1953: "I needed the money and I would do anything for Dizzy"[7]) and a more subconscious one, choosing to use four of Gil Fuller's charts based on Gillespie material for the Blue Note sessions by his sextet in May 1952 and April 1953. Yet he was frequently critical of Dizzy's stage persona: "As much as I love Dizzy and loved Louis 'Satchmo' Armstrong, I always hated the way they used to laugh and grin for the audiences. I know *why* they did it—to make money and because they were entertainers as well as trumpet players."[8]

For his part, Dizzy initially rationalized Miles's new direction and the birth of the cool school as a logical development from his own music. "It came right out of what we'd been doing. . . . it was still based on bebop. A lotta guys started copying that instead of copying what we had done . . . I never felt eclipsed by it all because knowing what my contribution was I knew it would pass."[9] Yet it is possible to discern in Dizzy's attitude for much of the 1950s and 1960s a latent suspicion—a hostility even—to some of Miles's work that dates from *Birth of the Cool*. It seems no accident that Dizzy should follow Gil Evans's collaborations with Miles on *Porgy and Bess* and *Sketches of Spain* by producing *Gillespiana* with Lalo Schifrin in 1960, and obvious critical comparisons were drawn (not always to Dizzy's advantage) when both men appeared at their respective Carnegie Hall concerts in the spring of 1961. It was only with the relative security of old age, long venerated as an elder stateman of jazz, that Dizzy became more forthcoming, and then only to underline the major (and very obvious) difference between himself and Davis: "It's a principle Miles has adopted: never to play again what he already played. It's difficult and very courageous on his part. Plenty of people want him to go back and play his old pieces—but you'll never hear that happen! He's always trying something new. It's a choice Miles imposed on himself. For myself, I do play what I've played before—even material from the 1940s. Always to be striving for something new isn't so vital for me."[10]

At the beginning of 1951, Dizzy's small band played a season at Birdland, and surviving airshots reveal that it reverted to scaled-down versions of the big band's best known numbers from the late 1940s. "Good Bait" was a popular feature, as was Dizzy's treatment of "I Can't Get Started." Milt Jackson settled back on vibes, alongside John Coltrane, who had by this time finally traded his alto for a tenor sax. Billy Taylor appeared on piano on some broadcasts, and Jimmy Foreman on others, and the band had the benefit of Art Blakey on drums for almost two months.

Conscious that he needed to take some kind of initiative to kickstart his career, Dizzy then made a surprising move. Just as his contemporaries Parker and Davis were beginning to cut discs for major labels, Dizzy decided to start his own, and he chose Detroit as the unlikely location for both the label and his first session. His business partner was a former trucker, Dave Usher, who had been a regular attendee at Dizzy's concerts in the area and who became (and remained, even after the label's demise) a friend of Dizzy's. "We were friends for many years—in fact when I went on my State Department tour of Latin America in 1957, Dave came along," recalled Dizzy.[11]

The business side of the label was left to Usher, and at first Dizzy did little more than to lend it his initials, calling the imprint Dee Gee Records, and bringing in a band to cut an inaugural session every bit as stylistically mixed as the previous record date for Prestige. The discs were cut as 78-rpm singles, with labels designed by Lorraine Gillespie, who had recently enrolled in art school.

Commercially, Dee Gee's decision to stick with the 78 format was unwise. The new LP and EP era had begun, and for a band that wanted to be identified as cutting edge, it might have been a better marketing ploy to embrace the 33- or 45-rpm formats. The real problem, however, was artistic. Although the new band cut definitive versions of two of Dizzy's most enduring standards—the Gil Fuller/Chano Pozo "Tin Tin Deo" and Dizzy's own "Birks' Works"—the style had not settled. These suave, sophisticated arrangements, redolent of the soundtracks to many a 1950s B-movie evocation of a jazz club, sit uneasily alongside the eight-to-the-bar shuffle of "We Love to Boogie," despite a strong tenor solo from Coltrane and a powerful solo from Dizzy that paraphrases well-known blues licks and sounds more like Louis Armstrong in its on-the-beat timing and high-note style than almost anything Dizzy had ever recorded. Kenny Burrell was brought in on guitar to add to the rhythm section, and Jackson played vibes on the more bebop arrangements plus his usual brand of blues piano on the boogie.

Coltrane's one solo appearance betrays little of his future style, or of the formidable reputation he had built up among his fellow musicians even during his stay with Dizzy's final big band. "At that time," recalled Dizzy, "his phrasing resembled Charlie Parker's. It wasn't until later that he worked on finding his own style. You know, you can begin to build your own style on a single measure—and then everything starts to change in the way you perceive your music. Each time you pick up the horn again to play, this strange thing, this 'style' comes back: it's always there. Coltrane had been gone from me for quite a while before he was really able to construct his own style."[12]

Back in New York at Birdland, Dizzy's band was joined briefly by John Lewis, who otherwise spent most of 1951 accompanying Lester Young.[13] John Coltrane left for good during late March or early April: "Slowly but surely his addiction to heroin preoccupied his mind . . . Dizzy finally had to get rid of Trane," wrote his biographer Bill Cole.[14] Coltrane's departure was most likely to have been on March 21, when the band came to the end of its run at Birdland. Shortly afterward, the club played host to an all-star group of beboppers under Dizzy's nominal leadership, which also featured Charlie Parker.

This quintet was one of the most talented groups ever to have played together and fulfilled Dizzy and Bird's ambition to work regularly (albeit briefly) with Bud Powell. Tommy Potter joined them on bass, with Roy Haynes, later one of Powell's most successful trio partners, on drums. The quintet worked as a unit during one of four weeks in which Charlie Parker's "Bird with Strings" package was appearing at the club.[15] We know just how exceptional a group it was because a section of the performance of March 31 survives in an airshot recording, as does a fragment of another evening that appears to have Billy Taylor on piano in place of Powell.

The spring of 1951 was a turning point in the careers of both Parker and Powell, following which both disappeared from the New York club world for some time. Parker had recently moved into an East Village apartment with his partner Chan, who seems to have been a stabilizing influence on him, temporarily curtailing his erratic habits. He had successfully appeared with his strings package in Detroit, Pittsburgh, and Buffalo, and was financially better off than he had been for a considerable period. In June, however, on suspicion of his drug use, but with no firm evidence to prove possession or dealing, the New York authorities removed his cabaret card, making it impossible for him to continue to appear in the city's nightclubs. Consequently, although there were to be get-togethers on concert platforms and in a television studio, this 1951 reunion with Dizzy was the last to take place in a club setting before their 1953 concert at Massey Hall in Toronto.

Powell, by contrast, had largely been prevented from appearing regularly in public with musicians like Dizzy and Bird because of his own fragile mental health. The spring of 1951 marks a brief period when a burst of creative brilliance coincided with a sufficiently stable phase in his life for him to appear in public and in the studio before he disappeared from view for almost two years. In May, he was to make his historic trio session for Blue Note, from which three exploratory takes of "Un Poco Loco" show his fluent right hand technique at its most imaginative, coupled with Latin rhythms from Max Roach that reexamine the Afro-Cuban ideas pioneered by Dizzy and Chano Pozo. The Birdland date displays him in the same devastating form alongside Dizzy and Bird, recalling the brilliance that Ray Brown remembers from their brief alliance during the fall of 1945. *Jazz Hot*'s New York correspondent Larry Quillingan noted that Bud's Birdland appearance followed "his last 'nervous depression,'" and by October that year the magazine noted that "Bud Powell has been hospitalized in a sanitarium."[16] Powell was also the victim of a trumped-up drugs charge in June, framed by a teenage informant called Lynn Messier, who begged him to sell her marijuana; with the authorities on the offensive, it was probably no coincidence that his arrest coincided with the decision to revoke Parker's cabaret card.

In these circumstances, it is indeed fortunate that the Birdland management was able to present the All Star Quintet and that the results are as exceptional as the Massey Hall concert of 1953. This is a bebop band in full maturity, and the relentlessly probing piano of Powell, coupled with Potter's rhythmically stable bass and Haynes's questing, restless drum punctuations, offers a dramatic contrast to the simplified beat and shuffle rhythms that Dizzy was introducing into his own work. Dizzy and Bird's playing, as so often was the case when they were together, seemed to stimulate both men to achieve more than usual, and their extended phrases in respective solos on "Anthropology" show a more relaxed and drawn-out approach to the narrow quarter-note patterns that are a hallmark of their earlier collaborations. There are joyful interpolations of riffs here and there, including a repeated quote from "Royal Garden Blues" in "Blue 'n' Boogie" that has an intriguing downward motif added at the end. The four numbers that survive are evidence that, despite the different directions he had taken in his big band and small-group work, Dizzy remained the preeminent bebop trumpeter and still the most evenly matched front-line partner of Charlie Parker's career.

Despite this, less than two weeks after the all-star group closed at Birdland, Dizzy's own group went back into the studio and for its very first track, cut a rhythm and blues treatment of "Lady Be Good." (The same lineup had moved into Birdland after Parker's eventual departure, broadcasting a couple of days before the session.) Gershwin's song is sung by Joe Carroll after an introduction of offbeat handclapping, with Art Blakey demonstrating his credentials as a backbeat drummer.

However, just as the first Dee Gee session had mixed a couple of pieces that were to be future planks of Dizzy's core repertoire alongside similar rhythm and blues material, this April 16 date produced a two-part minor classic, originally issued on both sides of a 78-rpm disc: "The Champ." In the four decades that followed, Dizzy was often to record this piece, but this first version is definitive and, according to critic Alun Morgan, became something of a hit at the time.[17]

Whereas in the All Star Quintet Haynes and Powell played fragmented rhythms that relied on momentum from both soloist and bass player to move forward, Dizzy's rhythm section achieves something closer to the driving power of a late 1940s swing big band. Indeed, the disc is a prototype of the Norman Granz Jazz at the Philharmonic style of mainstream performance, with Blakey's hard-swinging drums and Percy Heath's strong bass providing a fierce momentum for all the soloists in turn, more remarkably because the piano chair is occupied, respectively, by Dizzy and Milt Jackson, with Dizzy backing the vibes solo before returning to trumpet for five brilliantly constructed solo choruses. Budd Johnson also anticipates Jazz at the Philharmonic with a roaring tenor solo that owes more to Illinois Jacquet than Charlie Parker. Although it was made at the time when Dizzy's career was in something of a rut, this exceptional disc shows the degree to which he was capable of anticipating the future.

By the time of his next studio session, he had surrounded himself with a small group that paired him with baritone player Bill Graham and an unexceptional rhythm section (apart from Milt Jackson), and he settled into his "rhythm and blues" period for a couple of years. Nevertheless, "The Champ" shows how, as early as 1951, Dizzy was laying the groundwork for his many vital contributions both to Jazz at the Philharmonic itself and for his own next generation of big bands.

In some ways, the session that followed "The Champ" typified the problem that confronted him when recording for Dee Gee records. Dizzy cut versions of two pieces that were to be regular parts of his good-natured concert repertoire, but had none of the musical challenge of his best work of the 1940s. These are "Schooldays," Gus Edwards's vaude-ville song, shoehorned, as Leonard Feather pointed out, into the twelve-bar blues format, and "Swing Low Sweet Cadillac," a title based on a simple pun around the traditional spiritual title that was stretched, over the years, further than its lightweight subject matter could bear.

Why, when he could produce such direct, hard-swinging jazz as "The Champ," setting a course that distinguished him musically from both Par-ker and Davis, did Dizzy elect to play such shallow pieces in a blues-inflected style that he had always admitted was not his natural forte?

The answer lies in the waning fortunes of Dee Gee records. In his autobiography, Dizzy grandiloquently claimed, "I really tried to show that art could be popular and make money," but in an interview with one of his earliest biographers, Michael James, he said less guardedly: "I'm not interested any more in going down in history, I want to eat."[18] The firm was not achieving distribution comparable to even the minor labels for whom Dizzy had recorded before. Dave Usher was not only inexperienced, he was being drawn into his father's work in the oil in-dustry and failing to devote adequate time to the record business. In an admirable resumé of the label's problems, Leonard Feather summed up the difficulties of this "turbulent situation." Usher's output was failing to get acceptance among the retail trade or broadcasters, the switchover from 78- to 45- or 33-rpm standards further complicated matters, and Detroit was the wrong place from which to try and run a label in the early 1950s (in marked contrast to its importance to the burgeoning soul movement a decade later).[19]

There were signs, too, that Usher had extended the label's activities too widely for a start-up company. He had issued discs by tenor saxo-phonist Billy Mitchell and recorded a big band led by pioneer third streamer Bill Russo, replete with French horns, tubas, and orchestral woodwind. He had recorded Shelby Davis on a quartet date, and was soon to record the singer again, alongside a pioneer group of West Coast cool musicians, led by Shelly Manne and featuring Conte Candoli, Art Pepper, and Bob Cooper.[20] Perhaps the most successful commercial de-cision Usher made was to offer Milt Jackson two sessions with the fledg-ling Modern Jazz Quartet. "Milt Meets Sid" and "D and E" became landmarks in the rapid ascendancy of this group and were among the very few titles to feature the original lineup with Ray Brown and Kenny Clarke, who was back in the United States from France for a period of just over a year.

All this activity cost money, and, although the label's receipts ap-peared adequate to cover the costs, Usher had made no provision for taxes. This was eventually the label's downfall. Dizzy's reaction, before the tax position became clear, was to make the most overtly commercial discs he could, to try to hike up the level of sales.

The Milt Jackson Quartet sides were cut only days apart from Dizzy's "School Days" session, which is musically notable in only two respects: it displayed Milt Jackson's most accomplished piano playing on record and spotlighted Dizzy turning his back on bebop and playing a series of choruses that might just as easily have been the work of Roy Eldridge.

In the months leading up to this August 1951 studio date, Jackson had been doubling regularly in Dizzy's small groups at Birdland on both piano and vibes. Compared to the hesitant playing on the year's earliest recordings, he was beginning to show real ability as a pianist and in some accomplished chordal work had started to break free of his usual vibraphonist's standby, the "two-finger" emulation of mallets pioneered by Lionel Hampton. Yet with the advent on disc of the Modern Jazz Quartet, Jackson's days as a pianist were numbered.

"I started on the guitar when I was seven," he says. "I took private piano lessons between eleven and twelve. In high school I was mucking around, off and on, with five different instruments, which included piano, bass, drums (which at the time was my major instrument); I was playing violin in the orchestra and first tympanist in the concert band. . . . By process of elimination I just decided that I would play the vibes instead. One of the reasons that hampered me from actually becoming a pianist was that I couldn't separate these last two fingers and I felt handicapped, so I said, 'If I can't do it right, until I can really play it, then I won't.' It took me a long time [to put it right], and even today [1976] I can't really very successfully do it. That's what led me to adopt the Lionel Hampton type two-finger style . . . but that's also what stopped me from actually playing the piano professionally."[21]

It is on "Bopsie's Blues," behind the Eckstine-influenced singing of Melvin Moore, that Jackson's piano work starts to show the signs of a really individual voice. In a further session he was also to experiment on organ, but before long he would give up the piano for good, and focus on vibes and on the Modern Jazz Quartet.

Two versions of "Bopsie's Blues" survive, with solos from Dizzy continuing the conservative swing style of "School Days." Quotes abound, as do stock blues phrases, and there is a strong sense of a player going through the motions rather than playing with the genuine conviction and creativity to be found on "The Champ." Even Dizzy's startling break on "Swing Low Sweet Cadillac" is a throwback to a much earlier stage in his career, echoing Shorty McConnell's high-note contribution to Billy Eckstine's "Stormy Monday Blues," recorded with Earl Hines almost a decade before.

Other musicians noticed Dizzy's stylistic regression, including violinist Stuff Smith—the surprising choice of guest on the next session in October. He had no time for the bebop style of Dizzy and Bird. "At that time I thought they was very, very foolish," he said. "They were playing notes that didn't fit in the cycle of chords. They was just playing all around the chords, in the chords, out the chords . . . I'd fall back in that chord somewhere, you see, these cats would get out of that chord and stay out there you know. And they called it bebop. I never did like it.

"Dizzy came after me. I knew Dizzy in New York . . . but Dizzy didn't play no bop . . . when I recorded with him. Cause I made the arrangement on 'Caravan' that I made with him, and they played very fine. He had the bass player with the Modern Jazz Quartet [Percy Heath] and then he had this other guy who plays vibraphone, yeah, Milt Jackson was playing piano."[22]

The only concession to Dizzy's 1940s work in "Caravan" is the crash of Latin percussion that begins the track and reappears at various points throughout. Stuff Smith doubles the backing riffs with Bill Graham's baritone and contributes a swing solo comparable to his own 1930s small group playing. Dizzy's solo continues his resolutely un-boppish approach, phrased over the conventional barlines, with the kind of punchy attack he would have heard from his Calloway section mates, like Smith's erstwhile partner Jonah Jones.[23]

Many accounts of Dizzy's career in 1950 and 1951, following the demise of the big band, suggest that he spent much of this time as a soloist, without a permanent band of his own. However, the Dee Gee dates and a regular stream of bookings at Birdland, plus the occasional week at the Apollo or out of town, indicate that Dizzy kept his small group working fairly consistently until early in 1952. Nevertheless, critics noticed a decline in his playing.

With the benefit of hindsight, some were inclined to write Dizzy's work off from this moment onward. One was Max Harrison, who noted: "Gillespie's rarely swerving downward path from the classic small combo recordings he made during the immediate post war years was among the most saddening features of the jazz landscape in the 1950s."[24] Yet even those writing at the time were aware that things were not as they had been and, during one stint at Birdland opposite Lester Young's small group during September 1951, *Metronome* critic Bill Coss singled out Lester's trumpeter for special praise: "Jesse Drakes cut Dizzy to my mind, if only in the consistency of his solos." Pointing out that Young's band was playing strongly with the opportunity for soloists to play as they pleased, the article noted that Pres was in the run up to yet another Jazz at the Philharmonic tour, where his contribution would be the usual endless battles with other leading tenorists, Coss added: "Lester without Granz is a good combination."[25]

Shorn of the surroundings in which his playing flourished best, either a big band or a full-fledged bebop quintet, Dizzy focused more and more on the novelty vocals he shared with Joe Carroll and on a jump band repertoire that had more in common with Louis Jordan and King Curtis than with Charlie Parker and Thelonious Monk. He kept his small band going until the end of February, appearing for brief seasons opposite his former boss Cab Calloway and also the rising star Dave Brubeck. "My first meeting with Diz happened to be in Toronto," Brubeck told the author, "when we accidentally ran into each other in the hotel where we were both staying. Soon after that we were working together."[26]

Dizzy himself realized that he was in need of something that would alter his prospects, revive his playing, and earn him some real money, so he accepted an offer to visit Europe as a soloist. In his absence, Bill Graham took over the group, billed (significantly) not as beboppers but as "The Bill Graham Swing Band."[27] Dizzy's first port of call was Paris, where he was helped by the fact that Lena Horne was also appearing there. "Lena and Dizzy in Paris Halls on Concert tour" ran one press report, mentioning Dizzy's imminent debut at the International Jazz Salon in Paris. Conveniently, when he arrived in France Dizzy was able to work often with Lena's rhythm section of Arnold Ross, Joe Benjamin, and Bill Clark.[28]

The impact of Dizzy's 1948 big band had not been forgotten by a French public starved for modern jazz. In the meantime, aided by a number of expatriate U.S. settlers, the Parisian jazz community itself had developed a number of musicians highly competent in the new style. Finding himself lionized by the French concert- and club-going public, Dizzy embarked on a creative spell of recording activity, both with fellow Americans and some of France's rising stars.

To the surprise of many who heard him, particularly the French enthusiasts for the "new jazz," Dizzy did not rush headlong into recreating the sounds of mid-1940s bebop, despite teaming up with his old 52nd Street partner, Don Byas, who had settled in France. Perhaps because of the naturally more conservative style of Lena Horne's accompanists, he adopted a predominantly ballad repertoire and a lyrical, straightforward approach to his first recorded appearance at the Théâtre des Champs-Elysées on March 25. "Dizzy leaned back on a rhythm section [in a style] a long way removed from the orthodoxy of bebop," wrote critic Alain Tercinet[29] about the string of delicately played and gracefully balanced standards recorded on that date for Blue Star.

Notable among these is the former Herschel Evans feature from Count Basie's repertoire, "Blue and Sentimental." Byas pays homage to Evans in a full-toned tenor statement of the theme before ushering in Dizzy, playing in a style hardly recognizable from his big band days. There is light and shade in the dynamics, from gentle twists and turns in the opening phrases to some rounded swelling long notes preceding two eight-bar sections in which the high notes are punched out in a style close to that of Buck Clayton, himself a popular visitor to Paris in the early 1950s. Only the nimble cascade of notes in the phrase Dizzy uses to descend from this high passage betrays this as his work, but he sounds otherwise for all the world like a seasoned Kansas City ballad player, vying with Don Byas to tug at the listener's heartstrings. Bassist Joe Benjamin and drummer Bill Clark were joined for this first session by a U.S. expatriate, pianist Art Simmons, and together with Humberto Canto Morales, who contributes his conga drumming on a couple of sides, they form a perfect and unobtrusive background to the ballad playing of the horns.

On "Blue and Sentimental" and the equally measured "Cocktails for Two," Dizzy is consciously working on his tone and displaying a maturity as a soloist that contrasts dramatically with his lightweight and unsatisfying efforts for the Dee Gee label not long before his departure from the United States. As he moved on to his second Parisian session, for the Vogue label, it became clear that this contrast was no mere flash in the pan.

The British expatriate and long-term observer of the French jazz scene Don Waterhouse wrote: "With the big band a thing of the past and bop well beyond its first flush of youth, his audiences were in for a fresh, very different sort of surprise. Dizzy had bop, but he also had roots, and his style had begun to mellow into an amalgam of his entire jazz experience to form the basis of a new classicism."[30] There is no evidence to show that Dizzy had attempted this kind of consolidation before leaving the United States, yet Waterhouse's astute comments mark almost the exact point that Dizzy began to groom himself for his eventual "elder statesman" role. It would take some years of touring with Jazz at the Philharmonic and the revival of his career as a big band leader in the middle to late 1950s for this grooming to be complete, but the opportunity that Paris offered Dizzy to stand aside from the grind of regular tours or dates at Birdland with his quintet, to think about his own playing, and to put himself on the international stage as a soloist, is a land-mark in his development as an individual musician.

The Vogue sides are not quite as consistent as the Blue Star discs from this 1952 period in Paris. Of the surviving takes of "Afro-Paris," for instance, the first breaks down and the second only narrowly avoids disaster as Byas loses the train of thought in his solo. The final and originally issued take has an extended muted solo from Dizzy that looks forward to his later trumpet battles with Roy Eldridge. The end result is a balanced mainstream performance, reinforcing the impression of Dizzy digging into his knowledge of the very tradition he was so keen to rebel against a decade before.

Perhaps one reason for focusing on ballads and developing his tone was that Dizzy intended to have another attempt to record over the lush backing of a string orchestra. However, Dizzy and his "Operatic Strings" are far less satisfying than his work with Lena Horne's trio either with or without Don Byas. The way in which the microphone flatters Dizzy in a jazz context seems once more to elude him in the recording envi-ronment of a large orchestra. Partly, just like the sides with Johnny Rich-ards, this is likely to have been a side effect of the available technology in the early 1950s, but there is no disguising Dizzy's thinness of tone and breathiness on the quieter close-miked passages and his transition to a rasp as he stands back from the mike and opens up his volume.

The contrast is obvious between Dizzy's uneven performance over these lumbering orchestral arrangements, and the glowing, incandescent playing from his second small-group date for Blue Star at the Théâtre des Champs-Elysées. On it, his horn floats above the rhythm section in a brisk version of Louis Armstrong's theme "When It's Sleepytime Down South" (complete with a suitably sleepy snoring sound from Dizzy) and the muted "Blue Moon."[31]

Away from an American rhythm team, and paired with Don Byas among an all-French group for his second Vogue session, Dizzy domi-nates the proceedings. His confidence and strong musical personality create much the same effect as when Roy Eldridge was recorded a couple of years earlier for the same label and with the same pianist, Raymond Fol. Even the most accomplished locals sound hesitant and unconvinc-ing. In Dizzy's case, there are two honorable exceptions to this, altoist Hubert Fol (the pianist's brother and leader of the group that formed the nucleus of Dizzy's backing band) acquits himself admirably, and, more important, bassist Pierre Michelot plays at a standard equivalent to his very best United States counterparts. It is easy to see why Kenny Clarke regarded him as the doyen of European bassists. Dizzy's inability

244 | Groovin' High

to resist the temptation to quote passages of the "March of the Tin Soldiers" and the "Irish Washerwoman" during "Somebody Loves Me" does not mar a dazzling quartet performance, with trumpet and bass effectively trading fours at the end.

The oddly named "Cripple Crapple Crutch" (a misheard phonetic title based on Dizzy's lyric "I wouldn't give a blind sow an acorn, I wouldn't give a crippled crab a crutch") shows Dizzy embracing the blues style with more authenticity than earlier in his career, especially in his vocal, but this is an exception among his French recordings, whereas it would surely have been a mainstream part of his contemporary U.S. output.

One curious impression from this session is that it sounds remarkably like some of the work of the emerging U.S. West Coast cool school.[32] Dizzy's playing, particularly on the quartet tracks, presages Chet Baker's quartets from the following year, although the range of pitch and dynamic variation on "Somebody Loves Me" that Dizzy achieves, particularly on his second chorus, is dramatically more varied than anything Baker produced in the early 1950s. In some interviews and commentaries written about Dizzy's work during this period, it is proposed that he resented the emergence of musicians like Baker and Art Pepper, appropriating bebop and, it is suggested, packaging it as a "white" and more commercial variant of his 1940s innovations.[33] These recordings demonstrate that, had he wished, Dizzy could easily have eclipsed anything produced by the West Coast school, but the evidence of his return to the United States and the first discs he made on that return, is that he resolutely turned his back on this approach and continued, for the time being, to flirt with rhythm and blues as well as send up well-known popular songs in the time-honored manner of Fats Waller and Louis Armstrong.

One of Dizzy's first dates on his return to the states (after his one and only brief television appearance with Charlie Parker) was in Chicago, at the Capitol Lounge, where he was reunited with what had temporarily become the Bill Graham Swing Band. Milt Jackson was billed on piano, Percy Heath on bass, Al "Junior" Jones on drums, with Graham himself on alto and baritone and Joe Carroll once more on vocals. Clearly audience demands were different back in the United States. While French crowds had marveled at Dizzy's technical mastery of the trumpet, and the majority of his recordings emphasized his growing depth and maturity as a player, Americans wanted something different. The Capitol Lounge made much of "The Baron of Bebop . . . considered one of the greatest showmen to front a band. His gestures, mimicry and contortions are the delight of every audience before which he has worked, including the crowds which flock to the Capitol every time he works there."[34]

While he was still in Chicago, Dizzy cut what turned out to be his final session for Dee Gee. Milt Jackson was replaced by the up-and-coming pianist Wynton Kelly, a Jamaican-born musician who combined the experience of playing in rhythm and blues bands with a fine jazz sensibility developed through accompanying Dinah Washington and touring with Eddie "Lockjaw" Davis. Bernie Griggs came in on bass for Percy Heath, who, like Jackson, forsook Dizzy's band to make the Modern Jazz Quartet a reality. The Modern Jazz Quartet had recorded for Blue Note (with saxophonist Lou Donaldson) during Dizzy's sojourn in Paris and by year end had become firmly established.

Only a measured version of "They Can't Take That Away From Me" cut at the Chicago recording date offers any clue about Dizzy's recent Parisian experiences, showing just a glimpse of the musical depth of the Blue Star set of ballads. Otherwise, the session is an unashamed attempt at show-biz tunes, including "Umbrella Man" and "Oo-shoo-be-doo-be." No critic has ever summed up this lowest of all points in Dizzy's recording career more succinctly than Max Harrison: "Only a deaf man or a fool would deny Gillespie's very exceptional musical gifts, but only a fool or a deaf man could fail to regret the uses to which he has chosen to put them throughout what should have been his musical maturity."[35] Harrison was writing more specifically about Dizzy's European concerts with this band the following year, but this final Dee Gee session preserved for posterity much of what they were to play.

One track from the date that caused a mild furor, fanned into a conflagration in some quarters by the entrenched position of the critics on both sides of the Atlantic who pronounced themselves "for" or "against" modern jazz, was Joe Carroll's vocal parody of Louis Armstrong, complete with Dizzy's equally effective takeoff of his playing, called "Pops Confessin'." Louis was to get back in April 1954 with his recasting of the lyrics of the "Wiffenpoof Song" and its attack on the boppers—"Let them beat their brains out/until their flattened fifths have gone/they are poor little cats that have lost their way"—but the irony of the whole situation was that Dizzy's stage demeanor, show business instincts, and by the early 1950s much of his repertoire, were unashamedly moving closer and closer to Armstrong's.

Virtually all U. S. press accounts of Dizzy's work from the period dwell on his "mugging," while his own group's rhythm section and his own ballad playing had little or nothing to do, as Tercinet pointed out, with the "orthodoxy of bebop."

Dizzy's group made no more formal recordings in 1952, and the following year the Dee Gee label was wound up; its assets were acquired by Savoy. For a few months in late 1952, Dizzy (with his quintet and Joe Carroll) returned to the old circuit, with the odd week at the Apollo and a late fall residency for some weeks at Birdland.

One exceptional event in that latter part of 1952, during one of Dizzy's Apollo weeks, was a concert at Carnegie Hall promoted by Birdland to feature their artists alongside a number of jazz legends and billed as "the Greatest Musical Attraction This Side Of Heaven."[36] It was nominally to celebrate the twenty-fifth anniversary of Duke Ellington in show business and brought together the entire Ellington band, Billie Holiday, Charlie Parker (complete with string orchestra), Dizzy, Stan Getz, and Ahmad Jamal. There were two houses, and during the second set in the early hours of November 15, after Dizzy's work at the Apollo was finished, there was a brief but inevitable reunion between Dizzy and Parker. Earlier, Dizzy had scuttled between venues and briefly resumed his former place in the Ellington brass section as the band played "Body and Soul."

It was an emotional occasion for Ahmad Jamal to appear on the same bill as a number of musicians who had changed his life, he told the author. He recalled seeing Ellington's band in his youth and also going as a teenager to hear the Gillespie big band appearing at the Savoy in Pittsburgh, at the time when Hen Gates ("a great pianist no one knows, except those who've been around like I've been around") and fellow Pittsburgh native Joe Harris were in the band. "What a change Dizzy and Bird's records 'Salt Peanuts,' 'Groovin' High' and so on, with their red labels, brought in my life," recalled Jamal, who had been leading a trio for only two years when he was selected to appear on the Carnegie bill, playing a set that included "This Can't Be Love" and "It Ain't Necessarily So." Bird and Diz revisited many of their earlier triumphs, including "Night in Tunisia" and "Ornithology." *Variety* condemned the evening's hybrid of "standard and progressive" jazz, reserving its praise for Billie Holiday's "impressive" performance, but to Jamal and other eyewitnesses it was an evening never to forget.[37]

In the spring of 1953, hoping to build on his success the previous year, Dizzy set off once more for Europe, this time taking his quintet and Joe Carroll with him. Within days of their arrival in France, via Scandinavia and Germany, the band returned to the scene of Dizzy's 1948 triumph, the Salle Pleyel, where they recorded for Vogue, obviously in front of an audience who were wildly enthusiastic to hear Dizzy. After a protracted introduction from the French compere, Dizzy walks on stage, and with his knack for winning over an audience, cuts through the shouts, claps, and whistles with the single word "Silence!" pronounced in an impeccable French accent. There is an intriguing eyewitness description of him "wearing a light suit with a corned-beef tartan beret that made him look like a twenty-four handicap golfer on his first trip to St. Andrews."[38] From their opening notes there is an immediate difference between this group's playing and Dizzy's work with Lena Horne's rhythm team. Dizzy's quintet is a regular working band, united after weeks of playing together at Birdland and on the U.S. circuit, and they attack "The Champ" with devastating force. The initial momentum is not maintained, with a meandering vocal from Carroll drawing in everything from Slim Gaillard's "Motor Cycle-Poppity Pop" to "Ool-Ya-Koo." However, Dizzy's own playing is exemplary and he regenerates the band's momentum after a wide-of-the-mark drum solo from Al Jones.

The repertoire is an intriguing blend of Dizzy's 1940s big band standards (scaled down for quintet) and the more blatantly commercial of the Dee Gee output. Bill Graham, unfortunately, is no Charlie Parker, and his vapid solos (combined with Carroll's vocals) detract from the overall quality of the concert. Yet Dizzy's masterly playing, with its behind-the-beat swing and empathy for Wade Legge's relaxed piano, is further evidence of his deepening maturity as a soloist. The presence of bop pieces like "Good Bait" give him the chance to display his continued mastery of that style alongside his newfound depth as a ballad player. He also attacked the bongos with great vigor, introducing "Swing Low Sweet Cadillac" and demonstrating that it was not necessary to tour with a full-time Latin percussionist in attendance.

But in just the same way as the critical establishment frowned on Louis Armstrong's "crowd-pleasing," few jazz writers found much good to say about the concert. Max Harrison made the trip from London and wrote on hearing the recording of the evening: "Joe Carroll and the leader's vocal antics sounded almost as boring and silly then as they do now, and I realized how undistinguished the sidemen were . . . [it is] incontrovertible evidence of just how bad his band actually was."[39]

Even Vogue was not convinced by the quality of all that its engineers had recorded, and it became a great critical game during the 1950s and 1960s to work out which choruses had been edited out of the various releases of material from the concert.[40] Unfortunately for him, it was mainly Bill Graham's solos that ended up on the editing room floor, and even the fully restored versions of the concert that have emerged with the CD age tend to omit his feature "Ghost of a Chance."

Graham was also omitted from the studio recording session that Vogue arranged almost two weeks after the Salle Pleyel concert, when his place was taken by the New York–born Paris resident, trombonist Nat Peck. Peck had been at the Paris Conservatoire until 1951, after working in a range of U.S. jazz orchestras. He flitted between France and the United States in the 1950s, but remained a frequent member of the Parisian jazz scene thereafter, with periods in London and Berlin and a long association with the Kenny Clarke–Francy Boland band. On the Vogue session, his harmonic backups to Dizzy are often thoughtful and occasionally unusual, but the star of the set of discs is Dizzy himself. Here his soloing moves a step closer to what would become his Jazz at the Philharmonic style, with bop phrases easily integrated into his train of thought, but sitting happily in the generic swing phrasing of his own opening and closing choruses and the rhythm section. His extended solos in "Fais Gaffe," "Always," and "Mon Homme" are good examples of this integration at work, and this is probably the most successful material from his second 1950s trip to Paris, since nothing redeems a further attempt with his "Operatic Strings."

Back in New York in March, Dizzy's well-traveled quintet opened at "the World-famous Birdland Bistro," where they were to remain until the beginning of May. Their weekly broadcasts reveal much the same repertoire as they had played throughout the European tour, blending occasional ballads with Dee Gee pieces like "Blue Skies," "Oo-shoo-be-doo-be," and "Umbrella Man." Some extra publicity was achieved with the release of a curious band battle recorded for MGM at Birdland be-tween Dizzy's musicians and Jimmy McPartland's Dixielanders called *Hot vs. Cool*, but the signs were that Dizzy was settling in to continue the regular work and uninspired routines of the past two years and was not immediately going to develop the promising directions shown in his playing from the first Paris trip.

Inspired by a group of Canadian jazz fans, however, one event took place in May that shook Dizzy out of this environment and placed him once more among a group of the greatest bebop innovators. Much has been written about the New Jazz Society of Toronto Poll Winners' Con-cert at Massey Hall, which featured Dizzy, Bird, Bud Powell, Max Roach, and Charles Mingus. Amid over forty years' worth of writing about the event, three common misconceptions abound. The first, prom-ulgated by Ross Russell in *Bird Lives*, is that Powell was well below par, had only just emerged from a mental hospital, and, already suffering from drink when the concert began, rendered himself virtually unable to play by visiting a neighboring bar during the interval. The second, also stem-ming from Russell's account, is that there was a coolness between Dizzy and Bird because of the "feud" between them that went back to their parting of the ways in California during the early weeks of 1946. The third is that the musicians involved were somehow not performing to their own best standards, but were indulging in vulgar crowd pleasing. As Owen Peterson put it: "Their performance shows . . . a constant battle of aesthetics is being waged, not only between the soloists and the audience but between the soloists and each other."[41]

The background to the event is that, in an accident of planning, the Toronto enthusiasts booked the Massey Hall for the same night as a heavyweight boxing title fight between Rocky Marciano and Jersey Joe Walcott. Consequently, only about a quarter of the hall's 2,500 seats had been sold. Nevertheless, the event went ahead, with three sets—a big band of local musicians, Bud Powell's trio (with Roach and Mingus), and the "Quintet of the Year"—the last two being recorded.

Because Russell's account ignores Bud Powell's own highly competent set, and (it would appear) the evidence of his playing on the recording of the quintet, it can be discounted. Powell had, in fact, been released from the Creedmore Hospital well over three months earlier and had been working regularly since, as demonstrated in a series of recorded broadcasts and one particularly inspiring club session from Washington with Mingus and Roy Haynes, cut six weeks before Massey Hall.[42] His playing at the concert itself is frequently dazzling, and almost always an intelligent and immediate response to what is going on around him. His dissonant approach to "All the Things You Are," a track that suffers badly in virtually all reissued versions from excessive "wow," and which caused some critics to suggest he was "in a different key," was summed up eloquently by Max Roach: "When I listen to Bud, he was so honest you could tell in his playing, although he didn't play anything wrong, that he was depressed, because everything was dark, in a sense. . . . When he played 'All the Things You Are' he was so expressive he could speak with his instrument."[43]

This was the final track of the quintet set, and in it Powell is daringly experimental. The performance is very loosely based on the February 1945 Guild recording by Dizzy and Bird, complete with its familiar opening riff picked up both by Mingus's bass and Parker's alto, but then opened up for much longer solos. Dizzy's initial statement of the theme is straightforward—a muted paraphrase of the earler disc—but, as Parker enters, Powell inserts a rising whole-tone scale behind him and proceeds to create an extraordinary texture that involves changing chord on every beat. A flurry of quotes and some extraordinarily inventive playing from Parker over Powell's strange backdrop never lose sight of the piece's underlying structure, and Powell prompts Bird with a fragment of the melody at the end of his first chorus. Behind Dizzy's sensitive muted solo, which opens up for some high-note fireworks in the middle, Powell produces a more conventional accompaniment, but reserves his most daz-zling playing for his own solo, in which he constantly refers back to the melody in his left hand while producing a complex linear improvisation with his right. Although this is not as easily approachable as some of Powell's trio work and the recording quality makes it a difficult piece to listen to clearly, it does not represent the work of an incoherent drunkard.

The set had begun with "Wee" ("Allen's Alley") in which the theme is taken at a fairly measured pace. After a lengthy solo from Parker, Dizzy's own solo shows him feeling his way into the setting. In contrast to Parker's fluent phrases, Dizzy imposes an overall shape on his cho-ruses, almost losing the plot in the first as he unconsciously quotes "Night in Tunisia" in the middle eight. His second chorus, with repeated high notes, is redolent of Roy Eldridge and gives only a few hints of the inspired soloing that he was to produce later in the set. On this first piece it is Powell who produces the most miraculous solo before Roach's drums take over.

Accounts from Dizzy and Roach suggest that the band thrived on the near hysterical reaction of the audience, despite the small numbers present. It is folly to suggest, as Peterson does, that "they are too good for their audience" and that Bird and Dizzy in particular are "brought down" to the audience's level, by introducing quotes and crowd-pleasing devices into their playing. Any examination of the dozens of live club sessions that include any of these players will show that such playing is part of the stock-in-trade of the bebop musician and that the warm reception of this audience drew some exceptional performances from the band. No better example survives of the intrinsic difference between Bird's spontaneous ability to conjure endless variations in a jam-session environment and Dizzy's to construct architecturally thought-through choruses in which his stock phrases are carefully integrated. Yet Dizzy was acutely aware of his surroundings and, even though his solos have an overall shape and form, he caught every nuance from those around him. When Parker threw in a quote from Bizet's *Carmen* in "Hot House," Dizzy picked it up in his own solo a chorus or so later on, and then booted it up by an octave to dramatic effect, never deviating from his solo line, and also managing a healthy quote from "All the Things You Are."

Dizzy's finest solo comes in "A Night in Tunisia," stretched over three imperious choruses that create plenty of space for his ideas but have an inexorable sense of construction, drama, and poise. The Hispanic figures of the opening chorus are matched by the on-the-beat phrases of the second, with a high-note paraphrase of the melody coming exactly at the center of the solo. The crowd's wild applause is obvious, here and

Massey Hall, 1953. Charles Mingus, Max Roach, Dizzy. (Frank Driggs collection)

in the subsequent "Perdido," where Dizzy again produces a masterly construction over four choruses. There is no doubt that everyone in the band was having a thoroughly enjoyable time, and the grandstanding, such as it is, is all good-natured. Dizzy dispelled any notion of a rift between himself and Parker in numerous interviews, but never more forcibly than when he told Charles Fox "We loved one another, man. I mean all those stories about the rift . . . there was no question of a rift between Charlie Parker and me."[44]

Ironically, the musicians themselves remembered the event for entirely different reasons, mainly financial. The poor crowd meant that the organizers' costs were not covered and all but one of the musicians received a check that subsequently bounced. Only Parker had the wits to cash his immediately.

Mingus, however, angered Dizzy and Bird more. He quite openly recorded the concert, but did not at the time announce to the others that he intended to issue the results on the Debut label that he and Max Roach co-owned. Parker allegedly offered the tapes to Norman Granz for $100,000, split five ways, but, when this was understandably declined, no comparable deal was arrived at in advance by Mingus.[45] "It was [already] a financial fiasco because all our checks bounced," recalled Dizzy. "Charlie Parker cashed his at the box office, so he was 'in.' Then the master tapes were taken by Mingus and put out, and we didn't receive any money for years and years and years and years!"[46]

Roach, perhaps defending the integrity of his former partner (although incorrectly recalling that Mingus was a last minute replacement for Oscar Pettiford) is quick to point out that Mingus had had a very difficult time musically during the concert itself. "We never rehearsed, we just got to the stand and said 'Salt Peanuts' or this or that. 'Cos we knew among ourselves what we had been playing on 52nd Street. . . . He was from the West Coast and he had a different repertoire that they played with Buddy Collette and that crowd, and of course we had a repertoire that we dealt with. [When] Oscar broke his arm, we got Mingus 'cos he could deal with the instrument, but we hadn't even thought about the repertoire he hadn't played with us . . . and Mingus's feelings was hurt, quite frankly, because we didn't give him a chance. We just went right into it, assuming that Mingus knew what we were going to do anyway.

"During the intermission he complained. While we were leaving the stage for the intermission Mingus left and asked us to have a meeting in the band room, and he explained to us, he said: 'You know, you guys are playing things that I can play if I knew them.' It's not that they were difficult."[47]

Given that Mingus had been working with Powell for about seven weeks prior to the concert, this seems slightly far-fetched, even if Mingus had never played the repertoire from the Parker/Gillespie Guild sessions in public before. It is, however, incontrovertible that dissatisfaction with his own playing was one of the main reasons Mingus doctored the tapes before issuing the results and added in a new bass part. "When we got back to New York, a lot of it had been recorded so you couldn't hear the bass anyway," recalled Roach, "so on some of the pieces he just dubbed himself in. I think it's one of the earliest times that a person overdubbed themselves."[48]

The Massey Hall concert has become one of the most celebrated events in jazz history and is especially valuable because of the relative scarcity of collaborations between Dizzy and Bird after 1946. In taking Dizzy out of the rut of his usual quintet it showed that he was still a performer of the first order who thrived in the concert hall. Before 1953 was out, his career had taken a dramatic new turn, and his prowess in a concert setting was exploited by Stan Kenton in a touring package show. Close on Kenton's heels, Dizzy was signed up by Norman Granz, and his career underwent a remarkable revival, both through Jazz at the Philharmonic and Granz's prolific recording activity.

15

International Soloist

Nothing surpasses my performances with small bands," wrote Dizzy, "especially with Charlie Parker. A small band doesn't forestall creativity. I'd make the route and go on tour with Jazz at the Philharmonic, alone. I'd break up the little band . . . go out with Jazz at the Philharmonic and make some money, then come back and organize another small band."[1]

Up until 1954, Dizzy's contribution to Jazz at the Philharmonic had been restricted to that of an occasional guest soloist. When the troupe arrived in or around New York, if Dizzy's own bandleading duties allowed, he would join in for a handful of dates on the spring or autumn all-star tours arranged by Norman Granz. Also, in the early 1950s, after the demise of Dee Gee records, Dizzy was without a proper recording contract. From 1954 onward, he began to be a regularly featured member of the Granz package shows and recorded on Granz's Norgran and Clef labels, the precursors of the famous Verve catalogue, to which he in due course transferred. At almost the same time as he became more visible as a soloist, Dizzy added to the effect by beginning to use his characteristic upswept trumpet, with its bell angled at 45 degrees above the body of the horn.

The start of Dizzy's more active association with Norman Granz dates from December 1953, when he recorded with Stan Getz and a rhythm section led by Oscar Peterson in Hollywood. But either side of this date, Dizzy briefly found himself a star soloist in a very different environment, not directly connected to Granz. This was a package tour featuring Stan Kenton's orchestra and its star guests in what was grandiosely titled "The Festival of Modern American Jazz."

Very few of the many large-scale projects led by Kenton from the moment he formed his first band, the Artistry in Rhythm Orchestra, in 1941, were without a strong whiff of the grandiose or the pretentious. Although he fostered the careers of many excellent soloists as well as a higher-than-average number of composers and arrangers (required to feed the hungry maw of his oversized bands), many of his "progressive jazz" experiments have not stood the test of time well. The lumbering, dated feel of many of these are a sharp contrast with the Gillespie big bands of the 1940s and 1950s, which still, for the most part, sound fresh and modern today.

In 1953 and 1954, in the public's view at least, Kenton, a gaunt figure with pointed features and slicked-back greying hair, was a significant figure in modern or progressive jazz. His approach was not unlike that of another white bandleader, Boyd Raeburn, but whereas Raeburn had been something of a prophet without honor, Kenton was determined not to suffer a similar fate. He threw himself into self-promotion on a scale matched only by the outsize proportions of his band. "Kenton is tireless," wrote critic Ralph J. Gleason at the time. "He works hours that would kill a stevedore. Riding all night in a bus he'll catch a few hours sleep and then tear around all afternoon to disc jockeys and record dealers before the night's performance. Capitol Records . . . for whom he has sold almost three quarters of a million albums in the last decade, considers him one of its best public relations projects. . . . Stan is always the center of a storm in the music business, being hailed as a savior of jazz (a recent traveler following Kenton's concert route said it was like following a religious pilgrimage to observe the devotion and faith in Stan that his fans have) or being attacked for his opinions. . . . You either love him madly or hate him just as madly. Apparently those who love him outnumber those who don't."[2]

Dizzy himself was not one of those who fell sharply into either of Gleason's love or hate categories, and remained ambivalent about Kenton. He enjoyed the enthusiasm and approval for his own writing and playing that he received from Kenton's sidemen, but, apart from one or two harsh words in various interviews, he was lukewarm about the man himself. This seems to date from the late 1940s, when critics reviewing Dizzy's own big band suggested that it might have been influenced by Kenton's much-hyped concept of progressive music. Dizzy was adamant: "There's not one note that I play that was influenced by anything that Stan Kenton has ever done. Not one note. Stan Kenton was the copyist."[3]

Kenton, of course, was equally unlikely to admit that his own Afro-Cuban experiments were in any way attributable to Dizzy's. He had his own firm views about when and how he had discovered the background to his famous discs like "Peanut Vendor" and "Cuban Carnival": "At the beginning of 1947 was when I first heard genuine Afro-Cuban music . . . a band by the name of Noro Morales. I went to this place called the Embassy Club, in New York . . . and there was this back room where the band was playing where people were dancing and it seemed at first I heard things that sounded like Woody Herman, and then I heard music that sounded like us, and then like Ellington. . . . One guy was dancing by the band and he said 'If you think this is good, you go hear Machito!' "[4]

Kenton did not acknowledge Dizzy's 1947 experiments that took place a few months ahead of his own, and he also took a similarly exclusive view of another aspect of jazz history, telling interviewers (whom he perhaps believed were unaware of Dizzy's 1948 triumphs) that the reason his 1953 European tour was a success was because "we were the first American band in after the war."[5]

Various accounts tell of band battles during the late 1940s when Dizzy's band, with its sophisticated concept of Afro-Cuban time, its magnificent brass section, and ingenious arrangements, outplayed Kenton. Yet in late 1953, with the highlights of Paris beginning to fade in his memory and his working quintet covering little new ground, Dizzy swallowed what antipathy he might have felt toward Kenton and accepted the offer to become a solo star in Kenton's new package. There were to be a few dates in late November and then a nationwide tour early in 1954.

The original guest stars were Erroll Garner (and his trio), singer June Christy, Dizzy, Stan Getz, conga player Candido Camero, and Slim Gaillard. This lineup took to the road, playing among other places to sellout houses in Chicago, at the Opera House, on November 30. Nine days later, at the end of this first tour, Norman Granz teamed Dizzy and Getz together in the studios, quite probably with the idea that their collaborative album would sell well in the United States as a result of Kenton's impending nationwide New Year tour that was again planned to feature both soloists. Unfortunately, Getz, who had been a heroin user for several years, was arrested for drug use after a gig at Zardi's in Los Angeles in the early morning of December 19.[6] Convicted in January, he was recalled by the court for sentencing in February, with the almost certain likelihood that this would involve a prison term (which proved to be the case). Because his repeat court appearance fell right in the middle of Kenton's national tour, Getz pulled out, and was replaced, ironically, by an even more confirmed narcotics user: Charlie Parker. Altoist Lee Konitz was drafted to replace Gaillard.

Musically, this made for a very stimulating package, with Dizzy and Bird potentially reunited in front of a big band that—despite the coolness between Dizzy and Kenton—always responded to backing soloists of such caliber. However, even when the package played at Massey Hall on February 12, the scene of the previous year's triumphant Quintet of the Year, each soloist was restricted to playing his own routine with the band. As Dizzy recalled: "I did my spot; Charlie did his spot, the band did their spot, all of us. Yard and I didn't play together, each of us had his own music with the band. It was beautiful, you know, because there was such a great deal of respect from the musicians in the band."[7]

Keeping the different sections of the show separate on stage was more or less replicated in the band's travel arrangements. Kenton's trumpeter Buddy Childers remembered: "There were two buses. All the guys that came in were mostly black. It wasn't a segregation thing, but they just naturally gravitated together onto one bus because they had been friends for so many years. I rode on their bus so I could hang out with Dizzy. I got to be as close as someone like me could get with Charlie Parker. Bird was so beautiful. His spot on the program came right after the bit where I played 'Solo for Buddy,' the Bill Holman chart. He loved that. When you're that good you don't have to be jealous of anyone, and he enjoyed everything. There's a lesson to be learned there. If you get good enough at what you do, part of getting there is enjoying what other people do and learning from it. If you enjoy it enough you're bound to learn something."[8]

From Texas, where it began in Wichita Falls on January 29, the Kenton tour wound down to New Orleans, then up through Alabama and Georgia to the Carolinas, and eventually to New York. After a number of East Coast dates, it headed north to Ann Arbor, Toronto, and Detroit before returning to Chicago where the earlier tour had been so successful. The final leg took in the West Coast, where at the first of these dates the band was recorded in Portland, Oregon, and the results eventually issued. Although Dizzy and Bird did not play together, this is one of the last moments when both were in the same place at the same time. They only worked one official engagement together thereafter, at Birdland for three weeks in August 1954, when Dizzy's regular group appeared opposite "Bird with Strings."

There was a sharp contrast between the way in which Dizzy and Bird each appeared in front of the Kenton band. Dizzy turned up for the tour with a caseful of Gil Fuller's charts, expecting to integrate his playing as fully with Kenton's men as he would have done with his own orchestra. He was helped also by the presence of his own former drummer Stan Levey in Kenton's ranks, ensuring that, even though the band had experience of Kenton's Afro-Cuban experiments, the rhythmic element of the charts would be capably handled by a musician he had trained himself. Bird, on the other hand, turned up with nothing more than his alto, to play extended solos over what ended up being merely atmospheric backing charts for "Night and Day" and "My Funny Valentine" (arranged by Lennie Niehaus) and "Cherokee" (arranged by Bill Holman).

Dizzy's feature usually began with a medium-paced version of "On the Alamo," and then proceeded to either "Oo-shoo-be-do-be" or "Manteca," to which Candido applied a liberal dose of conga drumming. The recorded version of "On the Alamo" that survives shows Dizzy at his most athletic, with his trumpet zooming into the stratosphere above the band's brass section and then taking off on a solo cadenza. The Kenton brass section follows him avidly through Fuller's charts and does a competent job of recreating Dizzy's own big band brass on "Manteca." Levey and Candido set a thrilling backdrop of Latin rhythms, and Dizzy's horn, plus his occasional shouts of encouragement and sung scat phrases, rides over the whole performance. It is a good example of total musical integration; Dizzy involves the entire band and also plays alone over the barrage of percussion.

The audience clearly loved it, and Dizzy's showmanship is evident from the recording as he says, "Ladies and gentlemen, you're so wonderful I'd really like to do two or three hundred more numbers for you, but I don't want to take up the time of any of the other superb artists on the bill, and I'm not taking up any of their money either. But I think I do have time for just one more short one." He then stamps off four beats with his foot, and he and the band play one single deafening chord, before he leaves the stage to tumultuous applause and laughter.

Parker's playing, in direct relation to his poor health, underwent constant problems throughout the tour, and Dizzy recalled urging him to forgo his increasingly high doses of alcohol and narcotics for the sake of his playing—in particular so that he was not shown up by Lee Konitz. Apparently Parker did pull himself together, on Dizzy's advice, and played much better as a consequence. "That's a story I always tell when people say Yard played better while under the influence," wrote Dizzy. "That's the biggest lie they ever told."[9] The Portland concert, near the end of the tour, catches Bird on good but not inspired form, and the sense of excitement and drama of Dizzy's set is largely absent. As far as can be discerned from the recording, the audience is involved but not so caught up in events as during Dizzy's set.

Ross Russell, in his account of the tour in *Bird Lives*, besides omitting any mention of Parker's presence on the East Coast sections of the tour, also produces a description that has become part of Parker folklore: "When Charlie appeared with the twenty-piece Stan Kenton Orchestra, he would walk onstage holding his saxophone and, without recourse to the public address system, begin his solo, cutting through the screaming brass section with its five trumpets and four trombones and the huge reed choir. 'His sound was so strong,' one observer remarked, 'that it cut through all that triple forte background.' "[10] The Portland concert was obviously recorded through a feed from the public address system and gives the lie to this description. Not only was Parker firmly on microphone throughout, entering in a carefully prepared break after an eight-bar band introduction on "Night and Day," but the "triple forte" background that had so enlivened Dizzy's appearance was muted to a gentle purr behind Parker's lengthy and mellifluous solos.

Once the Kenton tour was over, Dizzy reverted to working with his own small group, which now included tenorist Hank Mobley and drummer Charlie Persip alongside his old stalwarts Wade Legge on piano and Lou Hackney on bass. Nat Hentoff, reviewing one of the band's frequent 1954 Birdland appearances, described them as "adequate, but hardly up to Dizzy," who himself was described as "at the peak of his powers as a soloist—his ideas when he's concentrating on playing are mindful of an exceptionally adventurous firework display."[11]

This is the first press piece in which Dizzy's upswept horn is referred to, and despite the involved tale that appears in Dizzy's autobiography about the horn having been damaged during a party in January 1953, no mention of it appears in Hentoff's *Down Beat* article. Instead, Dizzy takes entire credit for the revolutionary design, having "gone to work on changing the instrument itself." Hentoff reported four tangible benefits of Dizzy's new horn:

"1. Acoustically, the sound is more pleasing in a club. You don't blow straight at the customers. The sound gets up into the air and spreads.

"2. With the bell not in the way, the new horn makes reading very much easier for the player.

"3. The trumpeter now can really hear himself. Before, when he played fast, Dizzy says, it seemed to him that more notes went by him than he could hear.

"4. Tone is improved, he says."

Because the upturned trumpet was to become a symbol of Gillespie as immediately identifiable as his spectacles and goatee, he was to offer dozens of evasive and generally unhelpful answers to the many interviewers who asked him about this trademark. Typical was the experience of Roy Plomley, on the long-running British radio show *Desert Island Discs*, to whom Dizzy never really answered the question as to why his horn was upturned, but simply said, "It's an acoustical thing. When people ask me why my horn's like that, I say 'Why don't you ask a French horn player why the bell curves backwards, and he's got his hand up in it and he's playing with his left fingers?' My horn's not nearly as weird looking as a French horn. . . . In music, it seems rather strange if you're playing to somebody and your music's going in the opposite direction . . . so I'm playing it up in the air and they're putting it in the back. . . . I've been doing it twenty years . . . quite a number of people have copied the idea especially in marching bands. It's fine for reading too, because some people hold their horns down in the stand."[12]

If the question could be sidestepped, it usually was. What was a novel and publicity-pulling idea in the mid-1950s clearly palled over time, although Dizzy never abandoned the upturned horn. The likelihood of its having been created by accident is remote: "It would be nearly impossible to get a bell bent at that angle as a result of a trumpet being knocked," wrote trumpeter John Chilton.[13]

So how did Dizzy come to adopt the upturned trumpet? One clue goes back to the events mentioned in Chapter 3 when Dizzy sat in with the band at the Ritz ballroom in Manchester, England. "Drummer Alan Pilling was playing there in 1937 when Dizzy was playing a week at the Palace with the Teddy Hill Band in the 'Cotton Club Show,'" wrote English journalist Pat Brand. "On Monday afternoon, the boys noticed a few colored folk in the ballroom. Between sessions, two or three of these wandered into the band room and one went up to the lead trumpet, Billy Perkins.

" 'Boy, that horn's a killer!' he said.

"Because . . . Bill had his trumpet bent upwards to carry the sound out over the music stands. Pulling out a mouthpiece, he fitted it into the horn and, as Alan puts it, 'proceeded to blow about the best trumpet ever to be heard in the Ritz tunnel.'

"Not surprising since 'he' turned out to be Dizzy Gillespie . . . soon the bandroom began to jump as the other boys joined in."[14]

Dizzy had met Brand in the mid-1950s between sets at Birdland with his quintet, while playing his new-angled trumpet, and mentioned that he'd had "some great times" in Manchester. He accurately recalled the Ritz ballroom, in a way that led Brand, and the members of the band that played there in 1937, to wonder if he had just as accurately remembered playing Bill Perkins's angled horn, only to store away the memory and use it to create a visually exciting instrument at the very time his own role as an international soloist was about to begin.

We know from photographs that he was still using the straight trumpet with Getz in December 1953, but by June 3, 1954, when he cut a studio disc with a Latin rhythm section, the new horn had appeared and Hentoff's piece ran in the following month's *Down Beat*. In these early photographs, Dizzy aligns the index finger of his left hand with the upturned section of the instrument, emphasizing the angle. He often used this pose in photographs over the next couple of years, but then went back to a conventional left-hand grip. Perhaps this pose gives another clue as to why Dizzy chose to adopt his very unusual horn, as his protégé Jon Faddis suggested in an interview when he said unhesitatingly "I think it's a phallic symbol."[15]

The first instrument Dizzy had made for him had a detachable bell that incorporated the angle and fitted into a specially made socket in the body of the horn with a tightening screw to hold it in place. The author has examined one of Dizzy's earliest horns (which later belonged to trumpeter and pianist Joe Bushkin, who brought it to Britain at one point), and it had obviously been made to a very precise specification. The intention behind the detachable bell was that the horn could be packed into a conventional-sized traveling case. Later, Dizzy opted for one-piece horns; their oddly shaped cases added immeasurably to the complexities of his already elaborate luggage whenever he went on tour.

The collaboration between Norman Granz and Dizzy happened at a mutually beneficial time for them both, and the relationship between Dizzy and this mercurial entrepreneur one year his junior was of critical importance in reviving his fortunes. Granz needed stellar musicians of Dizzy's caliber whom he could accommodate in his Jazz at the Philharmonic tours, record for his labels, and promote aggressively alongside his other key musicians, such as Ella Fitzgerald, Oscar Peterson, Lester Young, Stan Getz, and Roy Eldridge. Dizzy's showmanship and concert skills, backed up by his years in the ranks of big bands, made him an ideal sparring partner for the other soloists, with a clearly identifiable individual sound.

Dizzy himself needed a dramatic career turnabout to rescue him once and for all from the doldrums where he had been since his big band broke up in 1950. This was not least because, as the 1950s wore on, in addition to the threat to Dizzy's preeminence from the cool jazz of Miles Davis, the most consistent poll-winner became the clean-cut, T-shirted, brooding figure of Chet Baker, whose moody vocals and elegant Davis-influenced playing captured the public imagination far more readily than the founding father of bebop trumpet, who had begun to seem just a little old hat.

Granz pioneered a style of management that was as apposite for the 1950s as that of Duke Ellington's and Cab Calloway's agent Irving Mills had been for the 1930s. He recognized the global market for his musicians, he was able to think beyond the shores of the United States, and he put his advertising to work in a way never previously seen in the jazz world. He never stinted on his advertising budget, but also realized that spending to promote one activity, such as concerts, could bring more than marginal benefits to another, such as disc sales. Amid the welter of individual designs adopted in the press ads of the period, his 1950s panel advertisements for Jazz at the Philharmonic and his record labels adopted a uniformity of appearance, linked to the powerful line drawing of a trumpeter that became his motif. In consequence, over a four- or five-year period, they stand out from the crowd as strong design statements, portraying an image for his music captured by no other organization save perhaps the Blue Note record label, which had begun to use Bauhaus ideas and Reid Miles's sleeve designs to similar effect.

Granz recognized that there was a healthy national and international public for jazz who would pay handsomely to see their idols in the setting of a concert hall rather than in smoky clubs or outdated dance halls, and who would also pay to acquire discs that contained similar music. His instincts pushed his musical policy toward the adrenaline-charged forum of the Swing Era jam session complete with "cutting-contests" and "battles," and this became the key feature of his live presentations. At the same time, even his studio recordings captured something of this thrill of the chase and were issued alongside discs of his concerts themselves. With a tour of Japan in late 1953 (on which Dizzy was not present), Jazz at the Philharmonic had expanded to add an international dimension to what had previously been annual and then twice-yearly ten-to-fifteen-day barnstorms across the United States. "Going to Japan was the biggest thing that had ever hit there, jazzwise," recalled Ray Brown. "We had a two- or three-hour tickertape parade through the streets from the airport in open cars. We went to Europe as well, but going to Europe doesn't set you up for going to the Orient, because everything was different. And the Japan of 1953 wasn't the same thing as Japan in the 1990s. But we didn't have any adjustment problems, when people are eager to see you, it doesn't matter who they are—it's always comfortable to go somewhere where people want to see you."[16]

Between this dramatic and successful expansion of his tours in 1953 and 1957, when Granz decided to abandon the U.S. concert circuit (although continuing to promote concerts in Europe where he settled in 1959), Jazz at the Philharmonic became a touring roller-coaster, offering several weeks of employment a year and considerable financial rewards to its stars.

For musicians like Dizzy or Ella Fitzgerald, who came from an underprivileged background riven with prejudice, Granz also offered a level of backup that boosted their self-esteem and helped them feel important and valued as artists. "Jazz at the Philharmonic was 'the elite,' " recalled Dizzy. "Norman Granz hired the best musicians and made them fight one another on stage, musically. He paid them top money, and they traveled first class. He was the first one for whom musicians always traveled that way, lived in the best hotels and so on, and he was the first one to insist that we played in Texas for a nonsegregated audience."[17]

Granz was a man every bit as complex and contradictory as Dizzy, but at the heart of his long-term relationships with his key players was an instinctive level of trust. He did not have formal contracts to represent Ella Fitzgerald (whom he managed for years) or Duke Ellington, yet he achieved great things for both of them as well as for many of the other musicians he employed, recorded, or promoted. In Dizzy's mind, what came across in many interviews was his regard for a man who, drawing on his own experiences as a member of a Jewish minority in Long Beach where he spent part of his childhood, not only set aside most of the ingrained social mores of the whites Dizzy had encountered in the South as a child but actively worked to demolish such barriers of prejudice and unfairness. "He was a very strong-willed individual," Dizzy said. "He had this idea about how jazz musicians should be treated, first class, and he demanded that for everyone around him."[18]

One of the most acute pen portraits of Granz is by Leonard Feather, who was perhaps uniquely qualified to understand a man who operated so successfully in the areas of concert promotion and record production that Feather himself knew so well: "To the musicians . . . Granz was a paterfamilias, a benevolent giant who strode through the world in seven-league boots, knocking down Jim Crow pygmies as he went. To competing promoters, night club operators trying to buy talent, booking agents and other businessmen who needed him more than he needed them, Granz was a petulant grudge-bearer and a hard man with a buck."[19] Feather sketches in a detailed background of Granz's upbringing in Los Angeles, from Long Beach (where his father ran a store) to the less affluent area of Boyle Heights, where Granz's family moved after his father lost his shop during the Depression. He captures Granz's appetite for work in a description of the young man laboring in a brokerage house to finance his studies at UCLA while committing what little spare time he had to play basketball for his college.

Granz does not seem to have been a man of passing enthusiasms—his youthful penchant for jazz records turned to serious collecting just as speedily as his later keenness on the visual arts led him to acquire a significant body of paintings and sculpture. Granz's career as a jazz promoter began in the early 1940s with weekly jam sessions at Billy Berg's (at which racially mixed audiences were *de rigueur*) and quickly progressed to the fledgling Jazz at the Philharmonic concerts that were in progress when Dizzy and Bird visited the Coast in 1945 and 1946.

The first such concert, characteristic of Granz's views about social equality, had been a benefit for the liberation of a group of Mexican detainees sent to San Quentin after a killing. To many of those in the arts and film worlds this was perceived as the racially motivated imprisonment of a more than reasonable number of suspects, and so Granz hired Philharmonic Hall to stage a concert in aid of the "Sleepy Lagoon Defense Committee" in July 1944. What took place was clearly recalled by its chief protagonist Illinois Jacquet: "It was a benefit show in Los Angeles, 1944. [We] did it for the army. They walked in there when we had a record strike and recorded the band. Jimmy Lyons, who promotes the Monterey Jazz Festival, was the engineer in the army. They were setting up mikes for this benefit concert in the Philharmonic Auditorium and we saw all these mikes there. 'Why are they using such high mikes?' we asked ourselves. We couldn't make no records, because there was a record strike. But that was the army—making a command performance for the soldiers on the ships and so they could hear American Jazz over in Europe. And after the war they released those records—and Phew!— they sold like the *Daily News*!"[20]

Jacquet's solo on "The Blues" "had the kids wild with the screaming high notes of his tenor sax," wrote *Down Beat*. By and large, critics (unaware of Jacquet's skills as a ballad player, arranger, and composer) dismissed this display as shallow and crowd pleasing. Yet Granz's astute promotion, first of the record of the event that was eventually issued and then of concert tours promising more of the same, played to the very aspects the public adored and the critics so derided. "We started touring, packing auditoriums all over the United States," remembered Jacquet. "Everywhere we'd go, even Carnegie Hall, the packages began to get bigger and bigger. There's Ella Fitzgerald, Gene Krupa, Buddy Rich, Dizzy Gillespie, but you know it all came from my solo on Jazz at the Philharmonic, 'The Blues Part Two.' All the high notes. Hell, I didn't know what I was doing! I was just having fun. I'd been with Cab Calloway, and he was busy every night singing 'Hi-de-ho,' and then they'd feature me. So that got me started, but when I got to play on this concert, Nat King Cole on piano, Les Paul, Lee Young on drums, J. J. Johnson, Jack McVea—we had a jam session. The place was packed. We had the kind of audience that was glad to see this, and whatever I did, it was okay. If I'd stopped and whistled, it would've been okay, 'cos once you hit 'em, and you got 'em, you gotta know how to hold 'em. So I started playing like that then to please the audience."[21]

When Dizzy joined the touring fold in late 1954, the Jazz at the Philharmonic pattern was well established and Dizzy soon fell in to a comfortable, profitable, and musically fairly limiting routine. He would be featured on a ballad in "the ballad set," usually "Star Dust" or "My

Old Flame," he would play one of his own standards in "the modern set"—generally "Ow!"or "Birks Works"—and he would trade endless blues choruses with whoever else was present—more often than not his one-time idol Roy Eldridge.

Dizzy appeared on Jazz at the Philharmonic tours each year until Granz forsook the United States circuit. In late 1955 there were forty-two dates in a row, and in the spring of 1956 an international tour lasting eight weeks, following an opening concert in Oslo on February 18. The package used Oscar Peterson's trio as its anchor, and featured Ella, Roy Eldridge, Dizzy, and Illinois Jacquet, visiting thirty cities in eleven different countries, including Sweden, Norway, Denmark, Holland, France, Germany, Switzerland, Austria, Yugoslavia, and Italy.

By that fall, for the U.S. tour, Granz had added the Modern Jazz Quartet, veteran Basie Band drummer Jo Jones, tenorists Stan Getz, Flip Phillips, and Sonny Stitt, plus multi-instrumentalist Eddie Shu (who played in Gene Krupa's quartet). Dizzy also appeared in the valedictory Jazz at the Philharmonic all-stars tour of October 1957. He went on to play in the overseas packages that Granz subsequently managed.

One or two concerts in each tour were recorded and the results issued by Granz. With the benefit of hindsight, the routines seem hackneyed after hearing just one or two examples, and few players dip further than surface deep into their repertoire or imaginations. Yet it is evident from the recorded sounds of the wildly enthusiastic audiences that something rather special was taking place, and the modern listener needs to imagine how this music must have been received at the time, on both sides of the footlights. "That was really the high point in jazz improvisation, the Jazz at the Philharmonic," Dizzy once said. "Because Norman Granz would get the best guys, put them together and just sit back in the corner and wring his hands, waiting for one of those guys to kill one another on stage. He loved to see fighting between two tenors. He'd always put two tenors together, two altos, two trumpets, you know, so that they could fight it out with one another. It leads to a great deal of creativity. You know somebody was before you, and somebody's going to come after you, so you're sort of on your p's and q's."[22] In retrospect, the "creativity" was limited, but these remarks give a clue as to the prevailing level of adrenaline among the musicians themselves.

English journalist Barry McRae heard the tour in London in 1958 and remembers being bowled over just by the list of names that would be appearing. "One was prepared to be uncritical, but it was unnecessary," he wrote. "Few of the giants had feet of clay and Sonny Stitt and Coleman Hawkins played quite superbly. Stan Getz was something of a disappointment, and, in restrospect, it must be said that Dizzy produced a set that did little to tax the musical imagination of the audience."[23]

Jazz at the Philharmonic in Scandinavia, 1956. (Photo: Popsie Randolph; Frank Driggs collection)

Many thousands of people first heard Dizzy and his fellow Jazz at the Philharmonic musicians in the context of these touring packages. Their consistent commercial success, and the part they played in turning each participant into a household name (or maintaining the reputation of those who had already achieved their fame), was the backdrop to Granz's other activities on behalf of his roster of artists, in effect financing many less profitable ventures, one of which was the first studio recreation of Dizzy's big band. Granz is reported by Leonard Feather as having spent $5,000 on this one disc alone. "Who needs that album I just made of Dizzy Gillespie with his big band?" Granz asked him, rhetorically. "It can't possibly make money, but Dizzy wanted to do it. He's happy."[24] Given that most of these Gillespie sessions are still in catalogue, over forty years later, there must be some doubt as to whether the recordings were unprofitable overall, but the principle is plain—Granz was prepared to put himself out for his artists and to allow them an unprecedented measure of artistic freedom on record. In return he obtained their services for his international touring shows.

Another aspect of Granz's complex personality relates to a moment in Houston, in October 1955, when a group of Jazz at the Philharmonic musicians, including Granz himself, was arrested by the Texas police, in what clearly appeared to be a setup, for playing dice backstage in a state where such gambling was illegal. Granz put up a bail bond of $10 each for himself, Ella Fitzgerald, Dizzy, Illinois Jacquet, and singer Georgina Henry, who were detained. But to keep the show on the road, they skipped bail. Granz ended up spending nearly $2,000 to get the cases dismissed and their names cleared. To his musicians, this was the kind of loyalty they came to expect from Granz, but it also shows a streak in his character that challenged needless shows of authority and the pointless or unfair.

At the time, the whole incident seems to have been a minor offense blown up out of proportion, with the police even waiting "until the first show was over before taking the performers to the police station." However, it took place in Texas, where Granz had insisted on a nonsegregation clause in his contracts, and this explains why his troupe was targeted for what seems a minor infringement of the law by factions whose blood ran high after he had simply offered money back to any white customers who complained about having to sit in an integrated audience for what (in many cases) was the first time.

Jacquet, who grew up in the state, was reported in the papers at the time as "nonchalant," telling reporters his name was Louis Armstrong (something Dizzy later claimed he had done), while Ella, according to the Associated Press report, "dabbed tears from her eyes with a wispy handkerchief as she was being booked. 'I have nothing to say,' she told reporters. 'I was only having a piece of pie and a cup of coffee.' Asked if she was actually taking part in the dice game, she blotted another tear and shook her head." Then, lest we forget this was 1955, the report continues: "Miss Fitzgerald was wearing a décolleté gown of blue taffeta and a mink stole."[25]

So how did Granz build on the foundations of Jazz at the Philharmonic to rebuild Dizzy's career? An examination of the records he produced supplies the answer. He put Dizzy into a context as a solo recording star that allowed him to challenge head-on the rise of Miles Davis and Chet Baker while firmly linking his name to already established trumpet kings like Roy Eldridge and Harry "Sweets" Edison. He revived Dizzy's greatest achievement, the big band, and was helped along by a stroke of luck when the State Department underwrote overseas tours by the band, putting Dizzy back in the limelight both as an innovative leader and an ambassador of the United States. Finally, he made a small number of discs by Dizzy's regular working band, or permutations thereof, adding status and cachet to a group that badly needed to be drawn back into the jazz mainstream. Overall, he gave the trumpeter a setting that was—for the most part—appropriate for what turned out to be his best years as a soloist.

The December 1953 session with Stan Getz was an auspicious start, not least because Dizzy's lack of a record deal in the early 1950s had made him almost invisible to the record-buying public, especially overseas. This new high-profile collaboration with Granz and Getz delighted his fans, such as English writer Steve Voce. "I remember the excitement I felt when the *Melody Maker* announced that Gillespie and Getz were recording together and printed a photograph of the participants. They were such major figures it seemed so obvious that they should appear alongside one another on disk, but nobody had teamed them up before. I had something to celebrate at the time and decided to buy myself a small number of the best available records, and this was the automatic choice."[26]

The session itself can best be described as only partially successful, although it would be hard to disagree with Nat Hentoff's impression that Dizzy had reached a new high point as a soloist. However, Getz's porcelain tone, poise, and clarity of thought do not naturally sit alongside Dizzy's convoluted muted lines or high-register flurries, and many of the introductory and closing ensembles are messy, rather than having the spontaneous jam-session inspiration Granz was obviously hoping for. The presence of Max Roach on drums further complicates matters. On the uptempo "It Don't Mean a Thing," Roach plays his natural style, punctuating aggressively behind Dizzy's muted solo, but elsewhere he is constrained to playing swing-style drums that restrict his inventiveness. One reason for this is that he is crowded out by the guitar of Herb Ellis. Switching uneasily between comping and adding an extra solo line, Ellis never really sounds at home and makes an already dense rhythm section more so, compounding Oscar Peterson's tendency to be busy at all costs.

The most successful elements of the album are the ballads, and a long, well-planned two-part version of "Siboney" that gives Roach the freedom to explore Latin meter and offers plenty of space to the main soloists, especially Dizzy, who opens the proceedings, dominates the first part and returns for a dynamic conclusion to the second section. On "It's the Talk of the Town," Dizzy produces a ballad performance that comes close to his 1945 reworking of "I Can't Get Started," showing the kind of mature playing that Granz was eager to display in Dizzy's cameo slots in the touring concert packages. The feeling here is altogether more abstract than in his playing of the previous decade, and Dizzy subtly leaves some phrases to the listener's imagination, especially when he sets up what might be thought of as the "question" in a question-and-answer routine, but leaves a pause where the response might be. This is obviously a deliberate ploy and occurs more than once in the final sixteen bars of his first chorus, before he soars magnificently into his higher register for a second chorus over sustained notes from Getz.

One pattern of behavior as a soloist that was to recur repeatedly during the Jazz at the Philharmonic years is established in "Impromptu" from the Getz session, in which the horns solo extensively over an up-tempo blues sequence. It is obvious how things will progress when Peterson begins with fifteen straight choruses of introduction, leading in due course to Dizzy producing a solo that might just as easily have come from Charlie Shavers or Roy Eldridge (both of whom were frequent Jazz at the Philharmonic participants). The reasons for this anachronistic element in Dizzy's playing are straightforward. Although the tempo is no less daunting than those set by his own 1940s big band, the chugging momentum of the swing rhythm section, with Ellis's guitar reinforcing the beat, leaves no room for Dizzy's characteristic rhythmic mobility. Despite Roach's presence, there is no chance of establishing the looser, more accommodating backdrop that Dizzy required for his most effective high-speed solos. Instead he falls back on his big band apprenticeship and produces an arsenal of repeated high notes, stock phrases, and swing clichés. Because of his outstanding ability to negotiate the trumpet's high register at speed, this is never less than brilliantly executed, but it is a pale shadow of the innovation contained in his 1940s big band solos. This type of playing however, was to become the familiar sound of the Dizzy that many fans all over the world saw and heard for the first time in a Jazz at the Philharmonic context, battling it out with Eldridge, Shavers, or one of the tenor saxophone giants, and perhaps did much to accelerate his popularity by removing most of the rhythmic and harmonic aspects of bebop that were hardest for uninitiated listeners to understand or appreciate.

It would, however, be misleading to suggest that Dizzy in any way disliked the rhythm section he was given for his Jazz at the Philharmonic work. Indeed, he had been so impressed on first hearing Oscar Peterson sit in with his big band in Montreal late in 1948 that he telephoned Leonard Feather long distance in New York to tell him about the phenomenal pianist he had just heard. In his eagerness to get Peterson to play for him at an after-hours club shortly after their first meeting, Dizzy walked straight through an ornamental fountain on his way to the piano, soaking his clothes and shoes before he gestured at the keys and invited Peterson to begin. He often said that Peterson was one of the greatest accompanists he ever worked with. Nevertheless, the effect on his own playing was, in the broadest sense, conservative and out of kilter with the direction he had taken with the majority of his own bands.[27]

Fortunately, Granz was sensitive enough to Dizzy's requests and his own jazz instincts to know that there would be mileage in reviving a proper bebop big band for Dizzy to front, but he also knew that the public at large would be well satisfied with the more approachable side of Dizzy's work as an uptempo swing player, and so continued to feature this aspect of his playing, both in concert and in the next significant solo album from October 1954—the first of a pair to team Dizzy with Roy Eldridge and Oscar Peterson's rhythm section.

For this session, there was no pretense about the style of accompaniment. Max Roach was replaced by Louis Bellson, who provides exemplary swing drumming and helps to create a scaled-down studio version of a Jazz at the Philharmonic band. There is nothing scaled down about either trumpeter's contribution, and an open-ended "Trumpet Blues" romps through thirty-five choruses of alternated solos and (eventually) swiftly traded four-bar segments. No doubt because of the immense respect between mentor and protégé, the results are far more even than those of the Getz session, and the far wider range of material covered, while only dipping a cautious toe into bebop territory in "Algo Bueno," includes the wryly humorous "Pretty-Eyed Baby," the delicate "I Can't Get Started" (in which Dizzy takes a different tack from his 1945 version), and the battleground of the hitherto innocuous "Blue Moon."

The latter has been the subject of some study by musicologist Dr. David Aaberg, who has transcribed much of the most quickfire exchange between the protagonists as a means of analyzing the fundamental differences between the two men's styles. Although his conclusions are predictable, they nevertheless help to demonstrate why the chemistry between Eldridge and Dizzy was so potent, since "while Gillespie's command of the trumpet might seem superior to that of Eldridge, Eldridge contributes greatly to the intensity and direction of the battle." We can see laid out before us many of Dizzy's stock phrases and fingering patterns that go back to his Calloway days, but Eldridge's playing is packed with surprises: the creative use of space to reinforce the dramatic placement of his notes, the amazing ability to conjure a high G out of nowhere (to shouts of amazement from Dizzy), and the ability slowly but surely to push Dizzy into a higher and higher range as the solos progress. Given Dizzy's earlier comments about Roy's competitive nature, few better examples exist of it demonstrated in practice.[28]

Granz was apparently so convinced by the on-stage and in-studio musical friction between the two men he was genuinely surprised to discover (as Dizzy put it): "We'd *never* fight! We were friends."[29] They were sufficiently close that they were often last to come on stage for their concert sets, after having a good time backstage. This so irritated Oscar Peterson and Bill Harris that on one occasion they swapped the mouthpieces between the two men's trumpets during the intermission. Dizzy could not get a sound from Roy's mouthpiece when he picked his horn up to play, and Roy, stepping valiantly into the breach created by Dizzy's silence, produced only a few sad moans.[30]

A follow-up album with Harry "Sweets" Edison on two extended tracks was cut the following year in 1955, with Buddy Rich blending in perfectly to the background. His presence here in what are essentially swing surroundings is as natural and unforced as it seemed out of place on Dizzy and Charlie Parker's only recorded collaboration for Granz five years earlier. The highlight of the second meeting between Dizzy and Eldridge is once more a measured and tasteful set of ballads.

Another aspect of Granz's plans for Dizzy in this period was to make sure he was a guest on albums by other members of his artists' roster, and so Dizzy dutifully appears, playing in his modified Eldridge style, on a couple of tracks on Benny Carter's *New Jazz Sounds* album from September 1954. It is amusing to reflect, despite a poised and well thought-through solo on "Just One of Those Things," that this is likely to have been far more musically conservative than Dizzy's work in Carter's regular band back in 1941–42.

Just how much of a straitjacket was applied to Dizzy by the Jazz at the Philharmonic house rhythm section of Oscar Peterson, Herb Ellis, Ray Brown, and either Buddy Rich or Louis Bellson on drums, only becomes apparent when Dizzy is allowed his head with an entirely different rhythm team. The first clues appear in a 1956 album called *For Musicians Only* in which John Lewis takes the piano chair and Stan Levey appears on drums, backing Dizzy, Sonny Stitt, and Stan Getz, but even here the continued inclusion of Herb Ellis on guitar is a restrictive presence. The subsequent album with Stitt, which also includes tracks with tenorist Sonny Rollins, dates from 1957 and is a revelation.

On Stitt's own tracks, the rhythm backing provided by the Bryant brothers, Ray on piano and Tommy on bass, plus Charlie Persip on drums, seems almost so understated as to need reinforcement. The bass ostinato on "Con Alma" is relentless, with an array of Latin effects from Persip in the forefront, but it provides a platform on which both soloists can develop ideas with tremendous freedom. Because the backing is so clear and minimal, Dizzy and Stitt do not get tangled up in the ensembles as he and Getz did over the fussy accompaniment of Peterson's quartet. Stitt (experienced in playing alongside Dizzy from the days of their 1946 collaborations) is a far more balanced and dramatic partner than Getz, mixing Eldridge's combative spirit with a genuine bebop vocabulary.

The opening of "Haute Mon'" is even looser than "Con Alma," with the rhythm accelerating slightly as they establish a groove and almost falling apart during the unfocused entry by the horns. But as Dizzy and the ever more aggressive Stitt move into solo gear, the performance grows to a level of intensity that is as intellectually stimulating as it is viscerally exciting. Dizzy's open solo is focused and brilliant, his phrases dancing across the beat and displaying his uncommon bond with Persip's natural rhythm.

Add the provocative presence of Sonny Rollins to the mix and the fireworks start to fly in a way quite unlike the swing grandstanding of Jazz at the Philharmonic. On "I Know That You Know," Rollins kicks off with a stop-time solo that is simply breathtaking in its complexity of thought and simplicity of execution, but Dizzy and then Stitt follow him with equally stunning solos. The whole thing is made possible by Tommy Bryant's insistent bass, Ray Bryant's decision to play simple prodding chords and otherwise stay out of the way, and Persip's stabbing off-center drumming that perfectly carries forward Max Roach's innovations into a new decade. Both Rollins and Ray Bryant had been regular associates of Miles Davis, and this session shows how each reacted to the provocative challenge laid down by Dizzy, Stitt, and Persip, all the time retaining the logic and instrumental control required by Davis, but adding a new combative ingredient that may well be a positive benefit of Dizzy and Stitt's time in Jazz at the Philharmonic.

The inclusion of Ray Bryant on these sides is no accident. He was a regular member of Dizzy's big band at the time, which by 1957 was— with help from Granz and the State Department—once more a working unit. The discs made by this revitalized and rejuvenated band will be examined in the next chapter, but the use of its rhythm section with Bryant and Persip on a small-group recording shows that, while Dizzy was being exposed to a vast concert audience across the United States, Europe, and Japan in front of the swing-based Oscar Peterson trio or quartet, he was simultaneously managing to retain regular contact with the rhythmic innovations of his 1940s band in a setting that suited his personality and playing better than the cameo role he played in Jazz at the Philharmonic.

Bryant (born in Philadelphia in 1931) had known Dizzy since the late 1940s, when he was a promising teenage pianist. He had gotten to know him better in the early 1950s when he led the house trio at a club in Philadelphia called the Blue Note—a rhythm section that also included Dizzy's one-time drummer Specs Wright. "I remember Dizzy once calling my house at that time to ask my parents if I could go on the road with him, and although it didn't work out, my mother still talks about that to this day, saying 'What's the name of that man who called here that time to ask if you could go on the road with him?'

" 'Dizzy Gillespie!'

" 'Yeah! That's right.'

"The way I got to be in the big band was that Dizzy's small band was playing in Birdland one night, and I happened to walk in just to hear the band, and the piano player was late. So Dizzy spotted me in the crowd and says: 'Come on up! Play with us, because the piano player's not here yet.'

"So I went up just to play a couple of numbers with him, and to cut a long story short I stayed for four months, just as he was in the process of forming the big band, and so I went on to play dates with him in both bands.

"During the big band tour, Dizzy had a commitment to record for Norman Granz, and he pulled me and Charlie Persip out of the orchestra to make the date. He asked me who I'd like to have on bass, and I suggested my brother. Dizzy told me we were going to have a couple of saxophone players—and they turned out to be Sonny Rollins and Sonny Stitt. So we got together, and everybody knows what happened on that date—people are still playing those records!

"Originally it came out in two LPs—the first was called *Duets*, with 'Con Alma' and 'Wheatleigh Hall,' but the other LP with both saxophonists came out about six months later, and it was called *Sonny Side Up*. Right around that same time, Benny Golson, who was with me in the big band, called and said: 'Dizzy's gonna make a recording, and I'm putting together an eight-piece band of guys to work around him.' He and Dizzy fixed for me and my brother to play on that session too."[31]

Tenorist Benny Golson was another Philadelphia musician, a couple of years older than Bryant, who shared much of the same musical background. He and drummer Philly Joe Jones, like the Bryants, had spent their formative years listening to the generation of Philadelphia musicians half a step older, which included John Coltrane and the Heath brothers, and, like many a would-be modern jazz saxophonist, Golson had then divided his time between managing to play his chosen form of music and earning a living in the rhythm and blues bands of Bull Moose Jackson and Earl Bostic. Like Bryant, at the time of the Verve small group recordings, he was a member of Dizzy's 1957 big band.

Several of the charts for the December 1957 octet date were Golson's, the rest were by altoist Gigi Gryce. Golson had learned his craft at the hands of Dizzy's one-time arranging colleague Tadd Dameron, who had worked alongside him with Bull Moose Jackson and later convened his own modern jazz group to include Philly Joe Jones, Golson, and trumpeter Clifford Brown. Dameron had made an enormous impact on Golson, who was to go on to become as celebrated a composer as he was a tenorist. "It's much more difficult to write for a small group than for a big band," recalled Golson. "When you don't have all those voices there, you have to work hard to make trumpet, saxophones and a trombone sound full. You have to learn a lot about the instruments themselves, their technical limitations and how to exploit their strengths. Tadd showed me how to exploit the piano—where to pitch certain figures at the top, middle or bottom of the range, and even which cymbals to specify—they all mean something. He knew how to use all these things strategically. By the early 1950s, he'd certainly learned how to write for small groups, including those with Fats Navarro and Charlie Rouse, so that they never sound abbreviated or too short of parts."[32] Golson's charts for Dizzy, including "Blues After Dark" and "Out of the Past," show the Dameron influence very clearly and are the main delight of this one-off recording session that put Dizzy for one of the very few times in his career into a medium-sized studio band with proper arrangements rather than a hasty assemblage of Jazz at the Philharmonic personnel relying on impromptu versions of standards.

Gryce's charts are fussy and rather unfocused. Using the piano to simulate rippling water in "Sea Breeze" simply clutters the ensemble, while the convoluted form of "Shanbozz" over a Latin meter only becomes clear in the three central solos from Golson, Dizzy, and Bryant. Dizzy's solo on this is muted, in much the same spirit as in his Eldridge collaborations, though with more double-time figures and rapid runs.

Golson's "Blues After Dark" is, by contrast, a model of clarity in its arrangement. It falls firmly into the Kansas City small-band style of Dameron charts like the 1945 "Good Bait" discussed in Chapter 11: muted trumpet and tenor alternating with a choir of alto, trombone, and baritone sax over the opening vamp. Dizzy's muted solo over this slow-medium tempo is a model of restraint, showing a kind of economy not often present in his work from this or any other period, and he nods in the direction of Basie's trumpeters of the time, Thad Jones and Joe Newman, just as Ray Bryant pays homage to Basie himself. But it is Golson's "Out of the Past" that is the highlight of the session.

The theme is one of Golson's clever, memorable tunes, woven into an ensemble head arrangement that features first Dizzy and then trombonist Henry Coker over some gently moving harmonies. Pee Wee Moore's baritone sax has a prominent role in anchoring the parts, which finish with a flourish on a deft downward run that launches Golson's own solo. Dizzy himself takes two extended solos, the first with a harmon mute between Coker and Ray Bryant's choruses and the second on open horn, which he picks up using the same downward run from the opening arrangement. His muted playing offers an interesting contrast with Miles Davis, who favored the harmon mute in his band of the time (his quintet with John Coltrane and its successor with altoist Cannonball Adderley added to the lineup). Although Miles's harmon playing is cool, detached, and cerebral, Dizzy's is sufficiently structured to stand up to detailed analysis and is much more overtly rhythmic. There are dance, funk, and blues inflections scattered all through it, and he also demonstrates a formidable technique in his evenness of tone in the lower register before blasting up into the stratosphere for his final sixteen measures. His opening solo is like nothing Miles could have produced—a darting high-register chorus that has all the effortless grace, showmanship, and underlying sense of form to be found in his Massey Hall solos. The rhythm section provides an interesting halfway house stylistically, with a fundamental swing pulse from the Bryant brothers combined with sensitive bop snare drum punctuations from Persip, who follows every contour of Dizzy's solo like a hawk. This is the kind of playing foreshadowed by the April 1951 version of "The Champ" with Art Blakey and Milt Jackson.

A handful of minor Verve sessions by Dizzy with his regular working small band round off his 1950s recording activities for Norman Granz, with the exception of what must now be regarded as his major achievement of the decade: the rejuvenation and rebirth of his big band. It came about initially with one of Granz's ideas for a "concept" album. This was *Afro*—what he called "another attempt of mine to fuse Afro-Cuban music with jazz. I think you will discover, as I have, that there are enough common denominators to be found within both types of music to make this fusion logical and practical. The qualities of excitement and the qualities of improvisation, both within the Afro-Cuban rhythm and the American jazz solos make, I feel, this idea a sound one. In the past we have tried it with Charlie Parker, Flip Phillips and Buddy Rich with Machito's Orchestra; Chico O'Farrill later attempted it successfully, with his *Second Afro-Cuban Jazz Suite* in which he used soloists Doug Mettome and Flip Phillips; and this is our third effort with Dizzy Gillespie and Chico O'Farrill."[33]

One side of the *Afro* LP is a relatively unspectacular session that pits Dizzy against an arsenal of Latin percussion, aided by flautist Gilberto Valdes and pianist Alejandro Hernandez. The other is the first studio session organized by Granz to put Dizzy back where he belonged—in front of his own big band.

16
The 1950s Big Bands

When Norman Granz set up the big band recording session for Dizzy and Chico O'Farrill on May 24, 1954, in a week when Dizzy was nearing the end of a run at Birdland with his regular small group opposite his newest rival Chet Baker, few of the participants would have had any idea that this would set in motion the train of events that produced Dizzy's most enduring and successful work of the 1950s. In many ways the session itself is not a particularly memorable one, and O'Farrill's four-movement suite *Afro* based around "Manteca" is a hybrid between Cuban rhythms and instrumental voicings that floats dangerously close to cliché on the one hand and the natural uninhibited swing of Dizzy's small group (which was the core of the band) on the other rather than a genuine fusion of styles. Yet it is clear from the first few bars of ensemble playing, as the trumpets flare out over a dense carpet of baritone sax and trombone figures mingled with Latin percussion and Dizzy's horn swirls dramatically upward through the melée, that, compared to Jazz at the Philharmonic or even his own small groups of the time, the big band is Dizzy's natural home.

Arturo "Chico" O'Farrill was a trumpeter himself, born in Havana in 1921, who had studied composition as a young man in Cuba, where he also dabbled in bandleading. He came to the United States in the 1940s and studied composition with Bernard Wagenaar, Stefan Wolpe, and Hall Overton. Wagenaar was a Dutch composer who taught his students the elements of neoclassical style at the Juilliard School for many years from the 1920s to the 1960s, but both the other men were more directly involved in jazz.

Wolpe was a Berliner who escaped Nazi Germany in 1933, via Vienna, where he studied with Anton Webern, and then via Jerusalem where he began to devise a theory of atonality while simultaneously exploring local folk music traditions. This open-mindedness made him an exotic and magnetic addition to New York's musical life when he arrived there in 1938. Among his pupils, modernist composers like Morton Feldman and Isaac Nemiroff mingled with jazz musicians like Lee Finegan, Johnny Carisi, Eddie Sauter, and George Russell. Along with O'Farrill, these jazz pupils explored with him the territory where jazz met twentieth-century composition, the interstices between score and improvisation, and the application of modal theory to the creation of textures in scoring. It is no accident that almost all this group went on to be among the most innovative and influential arrangers of the late 1940s and early 1950s.

O'Farrill's other influence, Hall Overton, was his contemporary, still studying with Vincent Persichetti at Juilliard when the two men knew one another. But Overton was that rare bird among composers: an improvising jazz musician who played alongside Teddy Charles and Stan Getz and produced arrangements for Thelonious Monk. Together with Wolpe, he provided O'Farrill with the beginning of a compositional language that could unite the underlying *clavé* rhythms of much Cuban music with jazz instrumentation and a truly original sense of orchestral texture.

O'Farrill's first efforts were for his own New York–based Cuban band, and he went on to write for Benny Goodman on the one hand and Machito on the other. He was the composer of several of Stan Kenton's Afro-Cuban experiments, and to some extent Kenton's overweight orchestra was the ideal band for O'Farrill's sense of orchestral color mixed with Hispanic rhythm.

The problem with *Afro* is that the four movements (five if one counts the reprise of the "Manteca" theme at the end) never really integrate into a satisfactory whole as, say, George Russell managed in his score for Dizzy and Chano Pozo's "Cubana Be–Cubana Bop." Instead, O'Farrill parades a sequence of accomplished Latin effects, several of which are individually brilliant but, because they do not inhabit a coherent structure, end up being indigestible. At its best, such as the angular brass figures that begin "Jungla," or Dizzy's cadenza over percussion later in the same section, which leads into some stimulating orchestral chording, this disc contains music that marks a halfway house between his 1940s big band and what he went on to produce in the following couple of years.

The most important features of the disc, apart from Dizzy's uniformly inspired soloing, are the maturity of the section work and the relatively unfussy rhythm playing in the non-Latin parts of the piece. The bridge section between "Jungla" and "Rhumba Finale," for example, has a romping four-four beat for the rhythm section, a strong riff for trombones, baritone, and tenors, with trumpets overlaid above and Dizzy soloing over the top. Yet, spurred on by Charlie Persip, the rhythm is never as fragmented as it would have been in the 1940s band, and the punctuations from his snare are almost an understatement of the Max Roach style. This is the first evidence that Dizzy had begun to devise a new rhythm section style for a bebop big band that did not compromise on heat or excitement, but provided the kind of strong and compelling beat that he alluded to in his 1949 *Down Beat* diatribe against Parker: "We'll use the same harmonics, but with a beat, so that people can understand where the beat is."[1] This was to be the hallmark of almost all his 1950s big band discs, and it was this rhythmic development, rather than O'Farrill's orchestral textures, that was carried forward from *Afro*.

That same *Down Beat* piece reported that Dizzy's old Calloway colleague, arranger Buster Harding, was producing charts for the big band. Given that 1949 was very late in the first big band's life, few of Harding's arrangements were ever recorded by Dizzy at the time, but, just four months after the *Afro* session, a studio big band was convened under Granz's stewardship to cut a set of Harding originals. The band itself was partly organized by Quincy Jones, who at that stage in his career as an ex-Lionel Hampton trumpeter had begun to make a name for himself as a freelance arranger.[2]

This recording group was to be the genesis of a band that gradually took shape over the next year and a half and became a genuine working orchestra by early 1956. Ironically, in much the same way as the most perceptive writing about Dizzy's small band discs with Charlie Parker came from the French critic André Hodier, it was again a contributor to *Jazz Hot* who was among the first accurately to sum up the essence of this group. "In two words, this present group of Gillespie's doesn't have the fire of his earlier big bands. This isn't to say that swing is absent, from time to time there's a genuine feeling of exultation, but the wild tradition of the band's predecessors is missing, because, simply, of the nature of the arrangements . . . these insist in their writing, on the simple swing of Count Basie, coupled with the New York school of 'funk.'"[3] Alfred Appel Jr. goes on to regret Dizzy's new style, but makes the point that it is "the distinctive trumpet of Dizzy" that gives the orchestra its undeniable character.

He also singles out Charlie Persip: "He has become a great big band drummer. He swings the whole band, punctuates the breaks excellently, and . . . takes the minimum of solos. After spending several years with Dizzy, he's constantly improving. . . . He was once just a continuation of the Max Roach tradition, without the master's imagination. But he's proved that now he has plenty of taste." Appel was writing a couple of years or so after the 1954 date when the band cut Harding's charts, but his observations are acute. It is undeniable that Dizzy was no longer leading an all-out bebop big band with a point to prove about its new music. Instead, he accurately gauged the tenor of the times. For the overall style of his new band, rather than looking toward Miles Davis's "cool" experiments or the similar movement gaining ground on the West Coast, he took note of one of the most successful of the Swing Era bandleaders who had creatively reinvented his own style for the new decade.

The mid-1950s Count Basie band, the so-called "New Testament" group, was the most influential group Basie had led since he first burst onto the New York scene with his original band in 1937. Formed out of an octet that he led in 1950–52, the new band pioneered a pared-down, clearer version of his earlier work, which could also accommodate bebop harmonic thinking into the swing band formula. With Gus Johnson, and later Sonny Payne, on drums, the rhythm section had a flamboyant counterpart to the even swing of Basie and guitarist Freddie Green; the sections played with exceptional discipline and control because of the rehearsal efforts of altoist Marshal Royal; and the soloists included trumpeters Thad Jones and Joe Newman, trombonists Henry Coker and Benny Powell, and tenorists Frank Foster and Frank Wess. The arrangements were mainly by Neal Hefti and Ernie Wilkins, with quite a number of charts by Buster Harding as well, and their writing had much to do with the distinctive sound of the Basie band.

Dizzy had toured briefly in California alongside Basie in September 1953.[4] He would have heard the band every night on that tour and was clearly impressed enough to take into the sound of his own group much of what he heard, eventually recruiting Ernie Wilkins to play and arrange for him alongside Quincy Jones. The four Buster Harding tracks cut by Dizzy's 1954 band exhibit the first evidence of this stylistic amalgam of Basie's New Testament sound with Dizzy's immediately identifiable bebop soloing.

This is in no small measure due to the judicious choice of personnel, many of whom were to stay involved in Dizzy's subsequent 1950s big bands. The full lineup was Quincy Jones, Jimmy Nottingham, Ernie Royal, and Dizzy himself on trumpets; Leon Comegys, J. J. Johnson, and George Matthews on trombones; Hilton Jefferson and George Dorsey on altos; Hank Mobley and Lucky Thompson on tenors; Danny Bank on baritone; and Dizzy's regular rhythm team of Wade Legge, Lou Hackney, and Charlie Persip.

Three of the four pieces are characteristic of the Basie band's habitual medium-tempo groove, with only "Pile Driver" having the all-or-nothing dash of Dizzy's earlier big band. There is an immediate sense of that earlier band in the first ensemble chorus, when Dizzy plays the opening an octave above the other trumpets, adding an aura of drama and excitement that is carried forward in a magnificent tenor solo by Lucky Thompson. Under Dizzy's own solo, the rhythm threatens to run away from him, but Persip's powerful punctuations haul everything back in line. Had this been a Gil Fuller arrangement, there might have been more to the final choruses than the repeated brass figures plus a question-and-answer routine between reeds and brass that Harding provides. The writing is closer to the measured control of Neal Hefti than to the wild abandon of Fuller at his best.

The other three charts, although similar in tempo, are far from dull and include many devices new to a Gillespie big band. In "Cool Eyes," for example, the whole trumpet section is muted, playing the kind of phrases familiar in Basie charts but seldom previously used by Dizzy, apart from the unison glissando toward the end. "Confusion" is harmonically an extension of some of the ideas in Dizzy's earliest writing from the days of "Pickin' the Cabbage," also bringing to mind the writing of Don Redman in "Cupid's Nightmare" for the Calloway band in the way Dizzy solos over a densely harmonized bed of reeds and trombones that moves (for part of the time) chromatically. This is Harding's most adventurous writing; its complex harmonic texture is relieved by some compelling blues piano from Wade Legge and the clever way in which Dizzy's solo squeezes out from among the brass to make space for itself.

Most commentators agree with Brian Priestley's view that the un-credited arrangement of "Begin the Beguine" from Dizzy's next big band session a year later "sounds very much as if it is the work of Dizzy himself [and] exploits the ambiguity between 3/4 and 6/8 and refers back to his late 1940s arrangement of 'Lover Come Back to Me.' "[5] It is a piece that contains many of Dizzy's characteristic ideas, especially the bass ostinato that sets the underlying rhythm at the outset and the band chording that alternates with Dizzy's casual, almost dismissive, statement of the theme. With this number (which stands out from the rest of this session in which Quincy Jones, Ernie Wilkins, and Ermet Perry simply develop Harding's template), the stylistic jigsaw for Dizzy's regular touring big band became complete. It showed how Latin rhythms could be accommodated into Dizzy's new formula, created the right solo conditions for Dizzy (both against the band and over a backdrop of percussion alone), and had all the sense of shape missing from Dizzy's earlier collaboration in a similar vein with Chico O'Farrill.

In late 1955 and early 1956, Dizzy was still only able to assemble his large band for the occasional studio session. Much of the fall of 1955 was taken up by a Jazz at the Philharmonic tour, following which there was a one-off studio session with a ten-piece band for Verve, cut on the West Coast, featuring "Sweets" Edison and altoist Willie Smith (both favorites of Norman Granz) and reuniting Dizzy with trombonist and arranger Melba Liston. She had met him in the late 1940s when she was in Gerald Wilson's short-lived band and had then briefly played in one of Dizzy's late-1940s big bands.

Back in the East, Dizzy re-formed his sextet, playing opposite Kai Winding and J. J. Johnson at New York's Basin Street in November, and starting 1956 as the headliner at Birdland.[6] He also played the Showboat in Washington, and it was at this point that Adam Clayton Powell recommended to the International Exchange Program of the American National Theatre and Academy (ANTA) that Dizzy, leading a big band, would be a suitable candidate to pioneer a proposed series of overseas tours by American musicians. The idea was simple—by actively promoting one of America's most visible and internationally popular assets, jazz, through a budget underwritten by the State Department, a positive image of the United States would be conveyed to audiences across the globe. Indeed, given the racially motivated arrest and imprisonment in Houston that Dizzy had undergone with Jazz at the Philharmonic as recently as October 1955, the image conveyed by a multiracial big band under a black leader was substantially more positive than the reality in many parts of the United States.

Dizzy's band was selected to inaugurate the program in April by visiting South Asia, the Middle East, and Eastern Europe. He subsequently undertook a second major tour in August 1956 to South America, paving the way for Benny Goodman's band to visit eight nations in the Far East in December. Rather like Gillespie, Goodman had only been able to keep a big band going sporadically since the end of the 1940s, and State Department funding offered both leaders the opportunity to go back to fronting an orchestra with far less financial risk than would otherwise be the case. With this unexpected kick-start Dizzy managed to keep his band going more or less intact from mid-1956 until the end of the following year.

To begin with, however, there were problems. Dizzy was committed to a Jazz at the Philharmonic tour in Europe from February 8, 1956, until April 15, and so it was proposed that his big band leave for Asia and meet up with him en route in Rome.[7] As he left for Europe, Dizzy placed the task of assembling and rehearsing the band in the capable hands of Quincy Jones, while he entrusted the diplomatic dealings with Washington to his personal manager—his wife Lorraine. There were two quite distinct political problems to be dealt with. The first was to ensure that the personnel included a suitably representative mix of musicians to convey the kind of positive image of the United States that the State Department required. In a predominantly black band, white musicians including altoist Phil Woods and trombonist Rod Levitt were also added. (Levitt recalling that being Jewish caused some problems in entering the predominantly Arab states of the Middle East section of the tour and that U.S. officials employed a certain amount of guile in dealing with his visas.[8]) To ensure a female presence in the band, Dizzy saw that, in addition to singer Dotty Saulter, Quincy Jones asked his recent West Coast colleague, Melba Liston, to join the trombone section, bringing with her a number of arrangements.

The second problem was that, despite all outward appearances, there was a strong propaganda element to the tour. "Our tour was limited to countries which had treaties with the United States, or where you had U.S. military bases," wrote Dizzy. "Wherever we went the political question was definitely involved."[9] As a consequence, the plans to open in Bombay, India, fell through because of Nehru's policy of nonalignment. India had been squabbling with the United States over aid given to Pakistan for military purposes since 1953 and had repeatedly attempted to establish its own position of remaining free from close alignment with or interference from the United States, the USSR, and the Chinese. One of Nehru's "five points" enshrining these principles, first codified as the introduction to a treaty with China, was that there should be "no interference in internal affairs." It was clearly felt that an American band on a propaganda mission at a time when India objected strongly to the U.S. arms trade to its neighbor would not be acceptable under such a principle, and so the tour was rescheduled to begin in Abadan, Iran, close to the Iraqi border.

The band was based there for a week, playing three formal concerts at the Taj Theatre, plus a number of additional "benefit" appearances. There was no doubting the seriousness with which local officialdom treated the visit. Despite Abadan's being five hundred miles away from the capital, Tehran, the Shah himself was on hand, together with his sister, in whose honor the first concert was billed as "In the Gracious Presence of Her Imperial Highness Princess Shams Pahleve."

Although there had been no opportunity for Dizzy to be formally "briefed" by the Washington department who sponsored the tour because of his absence with Jazz at the Philharmonic, he seems to have reveled in the diplomatic role every bit as much as when he won over Swedish, French, and Belgian audiences at the head of his earlier big band in 1948. "He did much more than just introducing American style music over there," reported one U.S. paper. "He accomplished, perhaps better than all the ambassadors and envoys and ministers combined, the almost impossible feat of making genuine friends on an intimate personal basis."[10] In addition to projecting bonhomie, he had devised a program that cruised gently through the history of jazz before arriving at the band's regular arrangements. (The historical approach was not entirely coincidental as Marshall Stearns, founder of Rutgers' Institute of Jazz Studies, was on hand to deliver some lectures between concerts on the story of the music.)

"It was an improbable spot for American Jazz," ran one report from the small posse of reporters whom the State Department had brought along. "Most of the Moslem audience had never heard this strange music before. Some looked with disfavor on girl trombonist Melba Liston and vocalist Dotty Saulter, whose very appearances violated orthodox Islamic tradition."[11] There were some odd looks, too, at the printed program, in which attempts had been made to translate "Dizzy's Blues" and "Shoo-be-Doo-be" into Arabic.

The band opened with the Iranian national anthem and then that of the United States, before Charlie Persip demonstrated African rhythms, singer Herb Lance "poured his heart" into some spirituals, and Dizzy did his time-honored impression of Louis Armstrong's "I'm Confessin'" as part of a traditional set that included the "Saints Go Marching In." After that, there were pastiches of various swing styles as the band played some Goodman, Basie, and Lunceford charts.

"Then a miracle began to unfold," ran the report. "These Arabs, who were completely ignorant of what jazz was and how to act at a jazz concert, started to catch the beat, awkwardly clapping in time with the music. Soon, whistles and screams reached the stage. By intermission . . . the theater was as hot as any American spot where Dizzy performed for long-standing fans." This began to be the pattern throughout the tour as uninitiated audiences were "educated" and swiftly converted. One of the organizers, the official spokesman for ANTA, said, "I've never seen these people let themselves go like this."[12]

The tour went on to Karachi in West Pakistan, where over a thousand people crammed into the Palace Theatre. It was here that Dizzy posed for photographers while trying his hand at snake-charming. "The cobra remained uncharmed by bop," according to one dispatch, "because he lashed out at Dizzy a moment after the picture was taken. Even though the poisonous fangs were removed, Diz vowed 'never to try that bit again.'"[13] Other photographs taken in less risky circumstances show Dizzy examining various local ethnic instruments and hobnobbing with comedian Danny Kaye, who was also on a goodwill tour.

Karachi was one of a number of venues where Dizzy undertook the distribution of concert tickets himself—going and giving them to the poor and underprivileged when he realized that many of the people at whom the goodwill mission was aimed would never hear the band if he did not take steps to help. A similar situation arose in Ankara, Turkey, on the final leg of the tour: "An instance of Dizzy's diplomatic technique took place . . . one afternoon when he had been invited to give a concert at the swank Turkish-American Club," reported the *Pittsburgh Courier*. "As the concert was about to begin, Gillespie noticed a gang of raga-muffins outside the wall, peering in. Before he would give his downbeat, Dizzy leaned over the bandstand and asked a USIS official about the kids. The official explained that this concert was only for 'invited guests.' And Dizzy characteristically said, 'Man, we're here to play for all the people.' He won his point. The kids came swarming in to the toney club, went berserk about the music and spread the word about town that 'dis American's OK.' A few days later, in Istanbul, the crowd became joyously hysterical as the Gillespie band really opened up. Only a 'non-bop' ren-dition of the Turkish and American national anthems could quell the pandemonium."[14]

After Karachi, the band crossed the subcontinent to Dacca in what was then East Pakistan (now Bangladesh) and then returned to the east-ern Mediterranean. In Syria the band was photographed in Arab head-gear near the scene of its concert in Aleppo; it also played in Damascus, where Dizzy managed one of his characteristic *coups-de-theatre*. He re-membered that in Ramadan, the month of fasting that is part of the Islamic calendar and was in progress during his visit, the fast lasts until dusk. As the sun went down behind the hall in which they were playing, he stopped the band and shouted "Food!" Band and audience alike made for the buffet that had been set out to take place after the show.

In Beirut, in those pre–civil war days still a glittering and glamorous city when Lebanon itself was a popular tourist destination, the band played for President Camille Chamoun at a dance. From there, the itin-erary took them to the Balkans, to Zagreb in Yugoslavia, to Ankara and Istanbul in Turkey, and finally to Greece, where, despite political cool-ness over U.S. support for Turkish Cypriots, Dizzy once more broke through to his public. After a dramatic concert in Athens during which he fell through a makeshift stage to the amusement and concern of his band, he was carried shoulder high through the nearby streets by cheering crowds. Returning to New York via London (where the band did not play) must have seemed an anticlimax after such a warm reception throughout the tour.

The State Department pronounced itself pleased: "It is felt that the Gillespie orchestra is more than serving its purpose to promote goodwill in [this] tense area."[15] In terms of Dizzy's own career, something far more significant had happened. It was not simply a question of "serving" a purpose. Dizzy had found the purpose that was to guide him through over three more decades of professional music at a time when his inno-vative contribution to jazz was largely over. He had discovered that the combination of his immediately identifiable image, "dizzy" behavior, clowning, upswept trumpet, sometimes bizarre clothes, sense of social justice, and natural ability to be himself in front of any crowd, together with the power of his music, made him the ideal ambassador, not just for the U.S. State Department, but for jazz itself.

During the tour, Dizzy had conducted himself with impressive dignity among presidents and potentates. He had also worked amicably with the majority of the U.S. and British diplomats who organized his tour on a local level, but was perfectly prepared to rewrite the rules if he felt it within his overall brief from the State Department. His vision of the role was encapsulated in the wire he sent President Eisenhower after the tour: "Jazz is our own American folk music that communicates with all peoples regardless of language or social barriers. I urge you to do all in your power to continue exploiting this valuable form of expression of which we are so proud."[16] To Dizzy, writing in such terms to the president, or his behavior on tour, like swapping places with his rickshaw man and pedaling the driver around, or insisting that "ragamuffins" be allowed into a show, or offering free tickets to the underprivileged, was no mere affectation. It was a natural part of what he felt the job to be.

Part of his success with the public was that he unerringly found a level on which to relate to his audiences—just as he had at the Salle Pleyel in the early 1950s when he caught their attention by shouting "Silence!" as his concert was about to begin. This was not least due to the fact that, despite his sophisticated playing, fast talk, and ready wit, he could still be the gauche boy from Cheraw. A perfect example comes from one of the press reports of the tour: "Invited to attend a cocktail party given by the high brass of the U.S. Sixth Fleet at the plush Istanbul Hilton Hotel, Dizzy noticed polite aides passing round trays of Scotch, rye, bourbon and bottles of soda. While conversing with the Admiral of the Fleet, Dizzy was suddenly confronted by one of these trays. He tried to explain that he never drank before a concert, but the aide and the Admiral insisted that 'one drink can't hurt.' So Diz lifted a bottle of soda to his lips and proceeded to drink. Everyone was aghast except Dizzy, who continued the conversation as if nothing had happened."[17]

Yet, however talented a natural diplomat Dizzy was, he would not have succeeded if the music itself had not been exceptional. Marshall Stearns, traveling with the band, wrote, "This is probably, right now, the best modern jazz band in the world. Literally. They are playing with a fire, cohesion and impact that is unbelievable, and the team spirit is soaring."[18] Even when one of the band's key members, Charlie Persip, caught the inevitable stomach bug in Karachi, Dizzy's decision to include a local percussionist in his place simply fired up the band still further.

Dizzy's own playing was challenged by the presence of the twenty-eight-year-old Bostonian trumpeter Joe Gordon, a soloist who, but for his premature death in a fire in 1963, would have become one of the most significant players to develop the Gillespie style. In the State Department band, Gordon inspired Dizzy's own playing to greater heights, but he was also one of the first young players whom Dizzy regularly featured instead of himself. In the 1940s band, Dave Burns had occasionally soloed in a style indistinguishable from Dizzy's, but for the most part Dizzy took all the trumpet solos. Now he realized the wisdom of encouraging younger players and began another trend that was to become a significant element of his "jazz ambassador" role—singling out and fostering the talents of up-and-coming trumpeters.

Quincy Jones, who as well as organzing the group was also a member of the touring band's trumpet section, appreciated the encouragement given to Gordon, but he also saw the wily side of Dizzy's character in the idea, especially on the band's August tour to South America. "In the Middle East it had been hot, but it hadn't interfered with our playing," he told Dizzy's biographer Raymond Horricks. "In the South Americas it was winter. In Quito, at an altitude of 5,000 feet, there was bad intonation and breathing on account of the rarefied atmosphere. Dizzy was smart and let Joe Gordon show off on all the trumpet solos. Joe almost killed himself. He was really ill after the concert and had to drop out of the band. In Buenos Aires we used a trumpet player called Franco Corvini, but after that we made do with the four trumpets."[19]

Before the South American tour, the band recorded a substantial part of its repertoire for Norman Granz on three dates: May 18 and 19 and June 6. These yielded at least seventeen issued sides, although research into Verve's archives suggests that these were not all the product of just one of the sessions, as Dizzy was fond of telling interviewers. "We went into the studio for Norman Granz, and Norman wasn't there. Norman used to give me permission to go and get a studio and go and record in one, you know, to keep the band in. Norman does that, you know, if the guys in Basie's band got a week off, Norman gave them a record date. On one session I made seventeen sides. That was a World Statesman album, *Dizzy in Greece*. They came out different times, but that was unprecedented, seventeen sides in three hours, that was going some, because it would take you an hour to tune up, so it was in two hours."[20]

In looking at the "take" numbers (the numbers from the recording log that used to be issued to each 78-rpm matrix and remained the standard means of identifying recorded performances), there is evidence that every piece ran to two takes and some to three, suggesting that the band may well have produced seventeen takes on one of the three sessions, but that these were not all issued, as implied in Dizzy's claim. What the sessions did, however, was to capture a working band at the peak of its magnificent form. After over a month away from New York, the band had gelled into a tight unit, with a characteristic style of its own.

The very first track, "Dizzy's Business," despite some intonation problems from Nelson Boyd's bass, has Dizzy soloing in splendid form before urging on Phil Woods during his alto chorus with shouts of encouragement that can clearly be heard over the roar of the band. Persip's control, dynamics, and ability to swing the whole ensemble are little short of sensational. Charts by all the band's arrangers were cut over the duration of the three sessions and there is a considerable unity of approach between them, perhaps best epitomized by Dizzy's own "Tour de Force," during which his own solo adds a layer of harmonic and rhythmic complexity over what is, in essence, a very simple swing chart, with a catchy three-note riff on the head arrangement. This exactly demonstrates French critic Alfred Appel's point that the band's bebop feeling emanates almost entirely from Dizzy.

The best opportunity to assess the extent to which this is the case is offered by Quincy Jones's composition "Jessica's Day"—a piece that was recorded by Count Basie's orchestra using virtually the same chart just three years later.[21] For Basie's band, Jones rescored the opening to make use of Frank Wess's flute playing, in a subtle duet with Eddie Jones's bass and subsequent solo. The rest of the chart is identical, with a trumpet solo for Joe Newman and an alto solo for Marshal Royal, before the only new element, a fragmented ending that continually repeats a paraphrase of one of the motifs from Gershwin's *American in Paris*. The Gillespie band treatment of the same music sounds entirely different, apart from the obvious similarities of melody and tempo. Virtually the entire piece becomes a vehicle for Dizzy himself: he takes the opening theme in harmony with the saxes and Boyd's bass, he leads the head arrangement after Billy Mitchell's tenor solo and at the end, and he produces a solo that combines all his trademarks, high notes, tumbling phrases, intricate double time, and harmonic complexity into a spellbinding mix that leaves Newman's solo with Basie sounding dull and uninspired. Through his ensemble lead playing and soloing, Dizzy is unquestionably the entire bebop ingredient of his band's performance of the piece.

His musical personality is so strong that, even where he is not the main trumpet soloist, his presence draws the listener's attention—Joe Gordon turns in a highly commendable solo on "Night in Tunisia," with a clearer tone than Dizzy's and a string of faultlessly executed high notes (even if some are a little off-mike), but what remains in the memory from Quincy Jones's reworking of Dizzy's old arrangement is Gillespie's own inimitable timing in the opening choruses. More notes are implied rather than played: there are half-valve effects and momentary hesitations or speed-ups, all of which personalize the playing to a far greater extent than Gordon could manage. It was not until Lee Morgan came into the band in Gordon's place that Dizzy had a trumpeter of comparable individuality to his own, and Morgan's contribution to the following year's "That's All," despite a furious tempo, proves that it was not necessary to play similarly to Dizzy to hold down a trumpet chair in his band. Morgan's buzzier embouchure, squarer phrasing, and entirely different approach to the building-block motif that ends his solo displays a new kind of musical imagination at work. It is one that draws on Dizzy's approach, to be sure, but does not depend on it for survival.

Melba Liston's contribution to the 1956 session, in addition to her own extended solo on "My Reverie" (adapted from Debussy's "Reverie"), is a lush "Stella by Starlight" and another classical adaptation, in this case derived from Grieg's "Anitra's Dance." This is her outstanding chart, which blends Persip's Latin drumming with some dense chording. It offers another chance to compare Dizzy's highly developed individual solo style with Joe Gordon's less adventurous approach, although once again Gordon's effortless high register is technically remarkable.

During May, June, and July 1956, Dizzy was able to keep his band together between State Department tours. They were featured at Birdland, Basin Street, and the Apollo in New York, and also undertook a small amount of traveling in the United States before they were again sent abroad for the South American tour, which began in late July.

The personnel remained almost constant, except that Benny Golson replaced Ernie Wilkins in the tenor saxes. Benny recalled: "I was with them less than two years, maybe a year and a half, but it was a concentrated period of playing. We didn't make a lot of money during those days, but the knowledge that I gained and being able to listen to Dizzy playing every night was great. In the beginning it was quite discouraging, as you come to grips with somebody that can play so much. It can either inspire you or really make you feel terrible. And to start with I felt terrible. I joined the band without a rehearsal, while it was playing at the Howard Theatre in Washington, D.C., and we opened up and he was standing just about four or five feet in front of me. That's where he'd stand, right in front of the saxophone section, and when he started to play, I just felt, my goodness, I'll never ever be able to play like that! And you feel sorta depressed.

"But at the end of the show I felt that I was compelled to say something to him. So the curtains closed, and everybody started leaving the stage, and he was one of the last ones there, picking his trumpet up and whatnot, and I went over to him, not knowing what I was going to say, but knowing I had to say something. He had touched me so. And I can't believe the corny words that came out of my mouth—I walked over and said, 'Diz! You sure did play!'

"He was just as embarrassed, but he had so much humility that he turned to me and said, 'Aw shucks! It was nothing.' And in fact it was everything!

"He was so well versed in rhythms and harmonic concepts. When you played something and it wasn't right, it was as though there was a knife in his heart. He'd say, 'No! No! No!' like it really was painful. And he did this every time he'd hear something wrong, so you had to always try to play it right. I learned so much from him it was worth it.

"When I joined, Quincy Jones was still there playing fourth trumpet, and he did most of the writing and was the musical director of what was going on. It worked out great for me. Billy Mitchell and I were the tenors right through until the band broke up."[22]

The South American tour took in Ecuador, Argentina, Uruguay, and Brazil. In Brazil, Dizzy encountered samba and bossa nova firsthand; in Argentina, he played and recorded with a number of tango musicians. In addition to four sides cut with a local band in Buenos Aires, Dizzy collected tango themes for an arrangement of his own called "Tangorine," which became a regular part of the big band repertoire.

The principal legacy of the South American tour, however, grew out of the meeting between Dizzy and a young Argentinean pianist, composer, and arranger, Lalo Schifrin. Theirs was to be a strong musical relationship that in due course fostered Dizzy's large-scale works for concert hall; it also provided him with one of the most original pianists to hold the chair in his 1960s small group.

Schifrin was twenty-four when the Gillespie band came to Buenos Aires. He had been born into a family in which his parents played string quartets rather than bridge. His father, Louis Schifrin, was a professor at the local conservatory and concert master of the Buenos Aires Philharmonic Orchestra, for whom his uncle Roberto was the first cello, and so the house was always full of musicians, discussing, playing, and listening to music. Schifrin's first piano teacher was Daniel Barenboim's father, Enrico. Amid this predominantly classical background, Lalo discovered jazz through imported American recordings and the activities of the local Hot Club. He describes his discovery of Dizzy and Parker on disc as being like "a religious conversion," but when he and some of his fellow teenage musicians tried to play bop in a Hot Club concert, fights broke out, and small change was hurled onto the bandstand in a gesture of disapproval. In a remarkable parallel to the schism in the French Hot

Club, a new association was formed called the Bop Club of Buenos Aires. It was there that the young Schifrin played to audiences on a regular basis for the first time.

It was almost accidental that Schifrin was in Buenos Aires in 1956 when Gillespie's band came through. Some years before, he had won a scholarship to study at the Paris Conservatoire, where his main subject was composition. Although he angered his professor, Olivier Messaien, by admitting to playing jazz—so much so that the great composer took to addressing Schifrin only by notes passed via another student—he qualified with good grades and took an apartment in Paris, intending to pursue his career in Europe. Besides specializing in composition, both for concert hall and films, an addiction that was well served by the movie-houses on the Champs-Elysées, where Schifrin remembers seeing every new film up to fifteen times in order to remember the score, he had become a professional pianist in the burgeoning postwar Paris jazz scene. In addition to jamming with many visiting Americans and seeing touring packages (including Jazz at the Philharmonic and the Basie band as they passed through France), Schifrin became a member of saxophonist Bobby Jaspar's quintet. In this group he played some of the most avant-garde jazz to be heard in Europe at the time, alongside guitarist Sasha Distel and bassist Pierre Michelot.

In 1956, he returned to Buenos Aires for a holiday and to see his parents. While there he re-formed a group of Bop Club members to play jazz and was invited to direct the Argentine Radio Orchestra; this is what he was doing when the news broke of Gillespie's State Department tour. "American or European jazz musicians never came to Argentina before this," he told the author. "There were professional Argentinean musicians like guitarist Oscar Aleman, but I knew from Paris how important it was to see American musicians playing rather than just hear them on record. What does a certain drummer do to make a particular sound? You can tell more easily by watching as well as hearing. This was the first time that such a band came to Argentina.

"When Dizzy came, I felt such affinity for the band. They were playing exactly the way I felt music should be done. They were in town for a week and I went to all the concerts, which were completely sold out. That week I didn't sleep—I still remember all the great players in the band: Quincy Jones, Phil Woods, Benny Golson, Carl Warwick, Charlie Persip, and Dizzy out front as the major soloist. It was fantastic!

"One night we played for him after his concert. When Dizzy heard my band, with me playing piano, he said, 'Did you write these charts?'

"I said, 'Yes.'

"He said, 'Would you like to come to the United States?' Well now, of course, here I am—the rest is history. I couldn't believe such a Cinderella story, especially as I'd made up my mind to return to Paris.

"It took me one and a half years to get the papers through the U.S. consulate to become a legal immigrant, and some time after that to get my Green Card. By the time I finally arrived in the United States, Junior Mance was playing piano in Dizzy's band. In time he decided to leave, but when I first arrived and made contact with Dizzy, he said, 'Why don't you write something for me?' So I did, and what I came up with were the first sketches for *Gillespiana*."[23]

Dizzy's sixth sense had somehow identified the man who would create a series of pieces for him that suited his personality as effectively as the creations of Gil Evans suited Miles Davis. Their 1960s collaborations saw the creation of yet another large orchestral setting for the Gillespie trumpet, but, as Dizzy returned home from South America, the days were numbered for his outstanding big band of the 1950s. He temporarily broke up the orchestra for most of September and October 1956 to take part in a Jazz at the Philharmonic tour, but it was back together in November for several weeks at Birdland, followed by a New Year's engagement at Philadelphia's Blue Note Club. Photographs from Birdland picture the group squeezed onto the stage, with the band members wearing smart tartan jackets. A number of airshots from the club survive that show the enthusiasm and power of the group was undiminished; this continued into the spring of 1957, when another series of studio sessions were cut for Norman Granz, first in Los Angeles and then New York.

The personnel underwent a number of changes. Talib Dawud came in on fourth trumpet in place of Quincy Jones, while Joe Gordon had been replaced by the teenage Lee Morgan. Al Grey entered the trombone section for Frank Rehak, and, although Rod Levitt stayed for these recordings, he was replaced in time by Chuck Connors. Ernie Henry replaced Phil Woods, and Billy Root joined on baritone in place of Marty Flax (Root in turn was replaced by Pee Wee Moore). More significant, the young Wynton Kelly took over the piano chair from Dizzy's longtime associate Wade Legge, and (after a somewhat hairy audition) Paul West took over on bass from Nelson Boyd.

The studio sessions, with tracks like Ernie Wilkins's "Left Hand Corner," Benny Golson's "Stablemates," and Dizzy's own "Tangorine," produced yet more compelling evidence that this was one of the finest big bands of the mid-1950s, although the discs of their live appearances capture even more of this orchestra's particular character. The 1957 Newport Jazz Festival is perhaps the best example, with the band's virile reading of "Manteca" (starting with the chant "I'll never go back to Geor-

Dizzy's State Department band, at Birdland in 1957. Note the upswept trumpet, and the band uniforms. (Photo: Popsie Randolph; Frank Driggs collection)

gia") comparing well with the 1940s band, while Dizzy's heartfelt extended solo on Golson's "I Remember Clifford" shows how the band could still a festival crowd to silence with such a moving ballad.

"Manteca" is a much more open-ended reading than the earlier band might have produced, with plenty of space for each section to have their say, including an extraordinary saxophone glissando, a figure caught onto by the trombones. There follows plenty of rhythmic percussion over Wynton Kelly's solo and a splendid parody of a tango in the chart as the whole band reenters. As a new recruit, trombonist Al Grey noted: "Dizzy let everybody play, regardless of how well you could play or how badly. He would give you a chance and let you blow. He brought me back to life really because I'd been hidden away down South for so long [with Arnett Cobb]. It was a family band, really together, and everybody hated to see it break up."[24]

The band struggled on until the end of the year, with the usual pause for Jazz at the Philharmonic in the fall. At times the wages were a dismal $30 per week, and English drummer Ronnie Verrall, on a U.S. tour with Ted Heath's Orchestra, sought out Charlie Persip and was amazed to discover he was managing to play the Birdland gig with a split snare drumhead he had no money to replace. Dizzy remained philosophical and jovial, but he knew the band could not last indefinitely. The State Department initiative had shown that he could once more front a big band; he had reinvented his musical style to do it, and he had in the process once more become a major jazz figure on the world stage. Like all seasoned troupers, his stage patter included an element of the well rehearsed alongside the spontaneous wit. Perhaps, given that the band had survived through thick and thin for a second year, there was more than a little irony in the greeting he offered to those who made the trek to Birdland during the band's final weeks: "Ladies and Gentlemen, I'm sorry we are a little late getting started this evening, but we just came from a very important benefit. The Klu Klux Klan was giving a party . . . for the Jewish Welfare Society. It was held at the Harlem YMCA so you can see we were lucky to be here at all this evening."[25]

17

Gillespiana

Ever since he started to become the subject of high-profile magazine articles in the 1940s, Dizzy had been in the public eye. The State Department tours, the revived big band's appearances at Newport and at the New York Jazz Festival at Randall's Island, his recording contract for Norman Granz, and his frequent appearances with Jazz at the Philharmonic moved him much more firmly into the spotlight than ever before. Press articles emphasized his ambassadorial role and drew attention to the paradox that he was a shrewd musician and leader despite his zany image. Typical was this extract from the press release for his January 1957 Philadelphia residency with his big band at the Blue Note: "His new role as ambassador of jazz fits Dizzy as well as his famous berets. He has always been known as a spectacular showman because of the beret and other trademarks that have spread the Gillespie name, such as his goatee, horn-rimmed glasses, up-tilted trumpet and bop singing. Although all these so-called trademarks could give the idea that Gillespie is a sort of off-beat character, the exact reverse is true. He has one of the sharpest minds in the music business and has developed all the other things solely in the interests of good showmanship."[1]

Despite this accurate summary of Dizzy's own public image, it did nothing to prevent his sounding off in a feature in *Esquire* magazine about the decline of standards in jazz and the folly of an American public prepared to listen to "a mongrel music made up of the strains of Presley, Liberace, Tennessee Ernie and Sh-Boom." He directed particular venom at Lawrence Welk for "his zany hats, cuckoo clocks, tramp costumes and other gimmicks that have absolutely nothing to do with good music."[2] Undeniably, Dizzy's own musical standards were exceedingly high, but he readily employed all the gimmicks listed in the earlier press piece to sell his music to the public, and in the hat and costume department gave Welk a good run for his money. It seems as if the precarious state of his big band and its finances had goaded him into a series of defensive actions, and he began to use the legitimacy bestowed on him by his recent State Department funding as a platform for speaking out about the state of jazz as he saw it. In the same *Esquire* piece, for example, he called for jazz to be included in the curriculum for schoolchildren and for the U.S.

government to set up a national collection of working materials and archives of jazz and endow a national jazz collection. A few months later, he agreed to become one of the tutors on the newly formed jazz summer school to be run annually by his former pianist, John Lewis of the Modern Jazz Quartet, at Lenox, Massachusetts, using the facilities of the Boston Symphony Orchestra's Berkshire Music Center at Tanglewood.[3]

Although economics forced him to retreat to a small group for most of 1958 and 1959 (and to do ever more touring as a soloist for Norman Granz's packages), this was not always immediately evident in the way the press represented him to the general public. He was selected to headline a special jazz event in April 1958 promoted at New York Town Hall by the *Village Voice*, aimed at a general audience, ostensibly to celebrate the career of veteran trumpeter and composer W. C. Handy, which presented him at the head of an all-star aggregation as "a titan of the trumpet" opposite Miles Davis.[4] In addition, his big band was reconvened for occasional special events, including a brief flurry of activity in 1959 with a week in Chicago followed by the Randall's Island Festival in New York. For his appearance there, Dizzy took part in the presentation of a check for $1,000 to New York's Special Committee on Narcotics, and the press coverage emphasized that he "has long been a leader in the fight against narcotics," one of the first moments when newspaper reports connected Dizzy directly with good causes or humanitarian work.[5]

All this helped to ensure that Dizzy was one of the few jazz musicians to have a sufficiently strong image to be recognizable to the general public as well as the jazz-loving audience. In the late 1950s and early 1960s, a gentleman's agreement subsisted between the press and public figures that drew a discreet line between their public images and the realities of their private lives. Nothing more forcibly demonstrates the tenor of the times compared to today's climate than the press treatment meted out to significant politicians. President Kennedy's philandering, for example, was well-known to many in the press corps, but never referred to, whereas no contemporary public figure could expect to be so fortunate. It was a time when popular icons were treated as such by the media and investigative journalism was only in its infancy.

Just such a gentleman's agreement protected the careers of jazz musicians, especially that handful who had risen to a level of national public prominence. By the time of the State Department tours, Dizzy had been with Lorraine for eighteen years. She handled his business affairs with determination and prudence, and their marriage, although childless, was viewed as an institution in the jazz world (and remained so for Dizzy's lifetime), as were one or two others that dated from the Calloway days, such as those of Milt and Mona Hinton or Danny and Blue Lu Barker.

Lorraine had plenty of show-business experience and knew what marriage to a musician would involve: "I know musicians. I didn't like them at first, not for boyfriends, just for friends, because I know the dear boys and all about what they'll do."[6]

Danny Barker was more specific. He told the author: "Musicians rarely had a problem with the ladies. It was a very monotonous deal sitting on a stage playing one-and-a-half-hour stage shows four, five, sometimes six times a day, seven days a week, for months and months at a time. Playing the same songs over and over under the hot stage lighting. When the stage show was over, you went to the small crowded dressing room, always near the roof of the theater. You practiced, worked with your hobby and wrote letters. Many musicians could not take the daily routine, blew their tops and quit. Others waited till after the show and went to a restaurant, cabaret, or joint. But in all honesty all these places all over the land were just about the same . . . whisky was available, food and music (juke box, piano) and, if you were in the mood, the owner could always call some girls who were not long in appearing."[7]

Barker, like almost all his generation of big band musicians, was tempted from time to time by what such places had to offer, but this never threatened or compromised the stability of his marriage. This was a morality commonplace among musicians and accepted without question by all parties involved. Dizzy, too, took advantage of the abundance of female company that was available during his life on the road. His musicians commented on it, especially noticing the difference in his behavior on the relatively rare occasions when Lorraine decided to leave home and accompany the band on tour—a typical example being the State Department trip to South Asia and the Middle East. Vocalist Herb Lance compared the "other Dizzy" the band knew and "the Dizzy" who accompanied his wife: "He was like a Sunday school teacher on that tour. See, Lorraine was there. No funny business *at all*!"[8]

In any press reports that turned attention to Dizzy's personal life, he was quick to stress the importance of his marriage to his career, of the relaxing life he and Lorraine enjoyed at their new home on Long Island, where he "tried to spend four or five months a year," and of the investments the pair had made in property in New Jersey. "She's the cause of any little success I have," he told one reporter. "She's the influence of all my virtues. My vices I made up myself. . . . Anything that's nice about me is directly contributable to her. She's remarkable. I'd rather talk about her than myself. . . . First of all she was a dancer, and now she's a sculptor, painter, weaver. She handles all my business. . . . She's my two marriages—my first and my last."[9]

The marriage had, however, been put under some strain when Dizzy was the subject of a couple of paternity suits in the early 1950s, both of which were successfully rebutted by his astute Philadelphia-based lawyer Charlie Roisman. Little or nothing about this appeared in the U.S. press of the time, and Dizzy maintained a publicly untarnished reputation. In Europe, however, his fondness for female company attracted some attention, and Norwegian writer Randi Hultin remembers after a 1958 Jazz at the Philharmonic concert in Oslo that he was "looking for a couple of girls." Instead she lured him to a jam session at her home with promises that there was a beautiful, young blonde girl waiting for him, not mentioning that the girl in question was her babysitter and several months pregnant. Dizzy had no hesitation in tiptoeing upstairs to seek out the young lady's bedroom—only, on this occasion, to be rebuffed.[10]

In France a year or two later, journalist Philippe Adler attempted to interview Dizzy during the Juan-les-Pins festival. In his first attempt, a boxer-shorted Dizzy, trumpet in hand, was chatting up two bikini-clad girls.

" 'Can we have seats for tonight?' they asked.

" 'Of course, because I want to flirt with you.'

" 'What, both of us at once?'

" 'Yes! Yes! And you can also bring your mother.' "[11]

Later, Adler's attempts to talk to Dizzy during the breaks in a recording session were frustrated by a beautiful woman in shorts who terminally distracted his interviewee. Adler gives us a good glimpse of Dizzy's technique.

"He ran across the room after the woman, finishing by catching her and pulling her firmly back behind him. 'I love this woman!'

" 'You're mad!'

" 'Me? Mad? Never!' . . . You know who I am?'

" 'Yes—but let me go! And anyway, stop trying to embrace me!'

" 'I am Dizzy Gillespie and I love you!' "

The woman does not leave, and their embraces grow fonder in each break, as Adler tries in vain to ask some serious questions.

Published in French and Norwegian, such accounts would not have made any impact on the English-speaking world, but they do show that Dizzy had never given up the flirtatious habits of his 1937 trip to Europe, and that while on the road he still sought female companions despite his long and stable marriage. He was always witty and funny company, and many women were charmed by his attractions.

Surprisingly, one of his longest-lasting liaisons from the 1950s, and the one that would have stirred up most press interest if it had become public at the time, remained under wraps until the very last years of

Dizzy's life. It was not until 1990 that it became publicly known that singer Jeanie Bryson was the daughter of Dizzy and songwriter Connie Bryson.

"Since her mother and father were never married," ran one of the earliest press pieces, "[Jeanie] Bryson's relationship with Gillespie is 'a very difficult situation. But he keeps in touch with me,' she says. 'He knows my phone number. I would like him to come around and acknowledge me more, but I wish him well regardless and I don't feel angry. As a teenager I used to chase him around a bit, but I'm not trying to force his hand any more.'"[12] During the last three years of Dizzy's life, he maintained a discreet silence on the subject, although in the weeks immediately after his death in January 1993, which by a bizarre irony coincided with Jeanie's first major-label CD release, his press office and lawyer issued statements denying that Dizzy was indeed her father. "I've known Dizzy for a long time and to my knowledge he has no children," said his New York lawyer Elliott Hoffman.[13] Gillespie's publicist, Virginia Wicks, stated: "We have no reason to believe this is true. It's a heartbreaking thing for this to come out."[14] It is indeed curious then that Dizzy should have quietly paid a modest amount to support Jeanie from the age of seven until she was twenty-one.

It is even more curious, were she not very close to him, that on one occasion when she had only just graduated in anthropology and ethnomusicology from Rutgers, and had not made firm plans to become a professional singer, Dizzy should have singled her out from the crowd at a concert in Salem County near Atlantic City and asked her up on stage with his band, where she sang "God Bless the Child." " 'I was barely singing then,' Ms. Bryson said, 'I was just beginning. So I'm disappointed it wasn't later.' But she added, 'He asked me to sing. That was a good sign.' "[15]

The image of Gillespie carefully fostered in every press piece for over thirty years was not one that would easily admit the possibility that Dizzy had fathered a child outside his exemplary marriage, even less so a child with a white mother. Many jazz writers sprang to the defense of his reputation, angrily putting down Bryson's claims, and suggesting (unfairly, as she had landed her major recording contract before the main wave of publicity began) that she was cashing in on Dizzy's reputation. Her record company, Telarc, issued a statement from spokesman Donald Elfman that denied this: "That's not why we signed her. The fact that she's Dizzy's daughter didn't come up. She's just a good singer." As Jeanie herself was quick to point out, "Musicians know about me, but the public doesn't." This is borne out by her tutor at Rutgers and her father's one-time pianist Kenny Barron: "I met her when she was four. I was working with Dizzy when her mother brought her by. He didn't really talk about her, at least publicly, but I'm sure he was proud."[16]

Although one faction crowded to dispute the idea that Bryson could possibly be Dizzy's daughter, others, including the co-author of his autobiography, Al Fraser, were convinced. " 'Dizzy did recognize her as his daughter, but not publicly,' he says. 'He didn't want anything that would reflect negatively on his relationship with Lorraine. . . . After all he'd been married for years when Jeanie was born. She's Dizzy's child, and in many ways you can see that, especially musically. If anybody doubts it, watch the way she shakes her tambourine. I told Gillespie if he wanted to deny it, he would have to get a nose job.' "[17]

So how did it come about that Jeanie Bryson was born on March 10, 1958? "I first met him in 1953 at Birdland," says Connie Bryson. "I was a sophomore at high school, and I went in with a boy—not a boyfriend, just a boy I knew. From that time on, I'd come and see Dizzy at the club every time he was there. He was charming, wonderfully funny, and in lots of ways a real contrast to his 'canned' humor on stage, because that wasn't nearly as vital and spontaneous as he was in the flesh. I was around sixteen when I first met him, and while our relationship clicked very early on, he didn't lay a finger on me until I was over eighteen, although he did make it quite clear what his intentions were.

"My family lived out on Long Island, where my father was a microbiologist at Cold Spring Harbor, a place chock-full of Nobel prize-winners. Later he moved to the Institute of Microbiology at Rutgers University, but before the family went there, I attended a boarding school in Locust Valley. I guess I was a pretty eccentric kid, never a follow-the-crowd person, and very much a loner, although I was also class president. I suppose if I'd been a typical teenager, I doubt this would have happened. At home, there was music all around, my father listening to Duke Ellington, Jimmie Lunceford, and my mother listening to the classics, Bach, Beethoven, Chopin. I was in love with music, and I think it was the music that drew me to Dizzy. You can imagine having a terrible crush on someone, well, he was thirty-five and wonderful.

"I knew he was married, of course, but my feelings for him were very strong. He lived in fear of his wife finding out about me. Years later, I discovered his many aberrations, with what, I suppose, might have been hundreds of women. Dizzy had lots of things he didn't necessarily want people to know. He was very intent on his image, and that involved him being very upright and a respectable public figure. He was capable of always being 'on'—in other words, he could always display the side of himself that was appropriate in the circumstances, keeping other sides of his personality suppressed. In some ways that's pretty close to being self-ish—it's a very singleminded focus.

"It was a real surprise when I found I was pregnant, since he was sure he couldn't have children. I wanted to go through with it because this was 'his' baby, the child of a man I was insanely in love with. He wanted her, but he didn't want to go through with all that it meant. It was more complex than him just not wanting the responsibility. Our relationship continued, but when it came to being a mother I was on my own.

"I had Jeanie at a clinic in New York, and quickly moved back to my small apartment near Riverside Drive. I was all on my own and terrified. There was no heat in the apartment and roaches, and I had to leave the baby while I ran out to get food. Once I virtually started hemorrhaging on the way to buy things, because really I was up and about too soon. My parents found out what was going on, and the two of us moved in with them. We lived there while I finished my degree and started teaching, until Jeanie was about three and a half.

"Later, we moved to Highland Park, and then to an East Side studio while I worked in a public library. I continued to have as close a relationship with Dizzy as it's possible to have with someone who's on the road. This continued up until the time my daughter's support became an issue, especially once lawyers got involved in the proceedings, because he was adamant no mail went to the house in case his wife found out.

"There was a blood test done, and on the instructions of a lawyer, all three of us went down to the medical office. In the end there was an agreement, and a monthly check came from the Associated Booking Corporation. When Jeanie was eighteen, Dizzy agreed to continue her support until she was twenty-one."[18]

An unmarried mother in the late 1950s faced a very different set of social attitudes from today's. "There were a whole bunch of problems," said Jeanie. "And these included racial problems for her, and indeed for my grandfather in his work at Rutgers, when her little brown child appeared, as we were living with my grandparents. He got some thinly veiled threats about his job security. He told them if they didn't like it they knew what they could do with his job, and in the end everything was fine. He didn't like being pushed around."[19] Not sure whether she wanted to bring Jeanie up as a black child, but aware that she needed to give her some ethnicity, Connie invented an absentee father for her daughter with the Hispanic name of Carlos Tomas. This was also to protect Dizzy, since if Connie was to benefit from any kind of welfare, the authorities would immediately want to know who the father was. For a while, the child was known as Jeanie Tomas, but in due course, she and her mother went back to the name Bryson. "There never was a Carlos," says Connie. "He was a figment of my imagination."

It was under the name Jean Tomas that the New York Family Court, in a judgment of May 26, 1965, awarded maintenance to Jeanie Bryson. The document ends all speculation as to her parentage, since annexed to it is a paternity agreement signed by Dizzy on March 29. In it, Dizzy acknowledges "paternity of the said child and his legal liability for the support thereof." He could perfectly well have made equivalent provision for her without electing for this form of agreement. In doing so, he both provided for her education and upbringing and acknowledged that she was indeed his daughter.[20]

None of Jeanie's school friends had any idea about the real identity of her father, and, although there was some speculation, the truth did not emerge during her childhood. "I always knew who my father was," said Jeanie. "He saw me from the time I was a baby. My first real memory of him is when I was about two and a half or three, going to Seattle, my Mom and I, to see him. We traveled there by bus from New Jersey, and it was an epic journey. I remember looking out of the bus window and seeing purple mountains, like in the lyrics of the 'Star-Spangled Banner.'

"I saw him as a child quite often until I was about seven or eight. Then there was kind of a gap. I remember when I was given my first flute (the instrument I played right through high school), and I taught myself to play 'The Age of Aquarius' from *Hair*, and I played it for him, and he was pretty impressed, as I'd only had the instrument a week or two. At that time I'd have been ten, going into sixth grade, and then I didn't see him for a few years. I remember going in to see him as a young woman for the first time, when I guess I was about fourteen. I remember the shock that registered on his face, because the difference between ten and fourteen for a girl is considerable, and I was an early bloomer, tall for my age. Then for five or six years I saw him quite a bit, until I was nineteen or twenty or so. It was more contact than I'd ever had with him. Every couple of months I'd hear from him, and go along by myself to see him (rather than when I was younger, when, even after their relationship ended, my mother took me along). I'd hang around with him at the gigs, and that's how I met people like Mickey Roker, Earl May, Rodney Jones, Jon Faddis—all the people who were around him at the time."

It would be hard to assess the degree to which seeing Dizzy so often influenced Jeanie's own career as a musician, but her stage presence bears obvious similarities to his. Some of the nuances of expression, the way she counts off a tune or moves to the music, are uncannily similar. For his part, once she did start singing, he took notice. "My father told me

Jeanie Bryson and Dizzy, 1972. (Courtesy Jeanie Bryson)

that he had a tape of me that he was playing one time during a European tour, and Carmen McRae, who was on the same tour, heard it, and asked who I was. He told her, 'It's my daughter,' and she borrowed the tape. She wouldn't let him have it back for a couple of days."

Seeing Dizzy sporadically, without the opportunity to develop the normal closeness of father and daughter, Jeanie learned early what it meant to share a famous father with the world. "I grew up seeing from backstage what it is to be surrounded by people that adore you," she says. "People would appear that hadn't seen him for years and they'd go off into paroxysms of laughter about somebody spilling some soup over somebody else in 1949, and I'd think, 'Why's he talking to them when he could be talking to me?' But I also saw that he could make people feel so special. He could be so sweet and charming that a person would go away with a broad smile on their face. It wasn't, as you might think from some of what's been written, a black or white issue—if he liked you, he was the same whether you were a dishwasher or a king. He was always laughing, full of life, and, I think, truly larger than life."[21]

Outwardly, Jeanie's existence had little effect on the pattern of Dizzy's life. When it came to choices, there was little doubt—even before she was born—that he would choose the stability of his marriage and his life with Lorraine and that Connie would choose to have the baby knowing it would eventually mean she would forfeit her liaison with Dizzy to bear his child. But Jeanie's arrival coincided with the start of a growing humanity in him, a growing concern for social issues, and in due course a growing spirituality. In the decade that followed, Dizzy became a Baha'i, and even though his mean streak would still surface from time to time, those who knew him through the latter part of his life noticed changes. Author Nat Hentoff, for example, wrote: "I knew Dizzy for some forty years, and he did evolve into a spiritual person. That's a phrase I almost never use, because many of the people who call themselves spiritual would kill for their faith. But Dizzy reached an inner strength and discipline that total pacifists call 'soul force.' He always had a vivid presence. Like they used to say of Fats Waller, whenever Dizzy came into a room he filled it. He made people feel good, and he was the sound of surprise, even when his horn was in its case."[22]

As his career moved into the 1960s and beyond, this spiritual element of Dizzy's character took a more prominent part. He also traded his sharp suits and beret for African robes and hats, consciously playing up his African patrimony. Yet although he decked himself out in what some saw as the trappings of black consciousness and began to speak out more openly against prejudice wherever he found it as well as act to deter divisive practices from segregated hotel swimming pools to broader social issues, Dizzy's main theme increasingly became one of unification: unification between races, unification between peoples.

"It was a time of pan-Africanism," remembered his early 1960s bassist, Bob Cunningham. "In that climate of black awareness, for sure Dizzy identified with Martin Luther King, Malcolm X, and so on. Diz felt part of that, and he wore African hats and robes, but actually, as I traveled with him, I noticed that in fact he wore all sorts of things— within the overall African impression he had various types of wear from all over the world."[23] Dizzy's ideological position was always closer to Amiri Baraka and the Congress of African Peoples or equivalent cultural nationalist movements than (as Cunningham's remarks might suggest) the revolutionary nationalist movement. After all, Dizzy was a perfect exemplar of what black cultural independence could aspire to, yet in addition to Jeanie's arrival, there were personal reasons why his own thinking grew broader and more to do with overall unification of the world's peoples and races.

In 1959, not long after his mother's death, and on one of the first of a number of visits back to Cheraw at which the town honored him (yet where he still found it impossible to be served in a white barber's shop, despite his fame), Dizzy discovered two interesting facts that shaped his attitudes. His great-great-grandfather had been a chief in

West Africa. "He lived in Northern Nigeria, [and] his given name was Iwo," said Dizzy (who subsequently named his music publishing business Iwo).[24] He learned this from a man he had met through his mother's family, James A. Powe.

It was commonplace in Cheraw for former slaves to take the surname of their ex-owners' families. Dizzy's mother's family, the Powes, had taken the name of the family who had bought Iwo's daughter, Nora, at a slave auction in Charleston. James A. Powe was white and still lived in the large house where his own grandfather, Dr. Powe, had been renowned for owning the largest number of slaves in the area. As a child, John Birks would not have been able to turn up at the front door; indeed, his earlier visits to the house had been strictly confined to the servants' quarters, but now, as an internationally famous musician and the representative of the United States on State Department tours, he was welcomed (after a slightly stiff reception) by the older man.

During their conversation he learned not only about his Nigerian background, but that the father of Nora's children had almost certainly been James Powe's own father. As Dizzy told a newspaper reporter a year or two later: "I told him, 'Just call me your majesty.' My great-grandfather was a white man, and this white man there now calls me 'cousin.' 'That's all over the South, you know,' he concluded."[25]

The demise of his big band, which, following the lean times of the early 1950s had brought a couple of years of direction, certainty, and development to Dizzy's musical career, led to a period in which he tried various different approaches to small-group playing. In January and February 1958, he built on his studio associations of the end of the previous year and so teamed up with Sonny Stitt in his front line.[26] Later that year, and running on into 1959, he moved as close as he ever got to the cooler approach of Miles Davis, fronting a rhythm section of Junior Mance on piano, Lex Humphries on drums, and initially Sam Jones and then Art Davis on bass. His front-line partner was Les Spann, who doubled on guitar and flute, using the latter on Latin numbers where a percussionist was often also added to the mix. Granz's album titles like *Have Trumpet, Will Excite,* or *The Ebullient Mr. Gillespie* suggested a hotter, more assertive Dizzy than the majority of the tracks they cut, in which his muted horn blows uncharacteristically coolly over a minimalist backing.

There are moments of assertive, dominant trumpet of the kind his big band audiences would have recognized—for example, in "Swing Low Sweet Cadillac," a remake of the 1950 Dee Gee track, in which after what seems an eternity of pseudo-African chanting, the group suddenly bursts into a straightahead four-four backing for Dizzy's open horn.

More typical of the small band's output are tracks like "Lorraine" or "There Is No Greater Love," when in the latter piece, Dizzy's close-miked muted horn works slowly through the ballad sequence before a rhythmic interlude on guitar and a return to the ballad style. There is more light and shade in Dizzy's playing than there might have been in a Miles Davis reading of the piece, and his inveterate harmonic ingenuity explores twists and turns in the chord sequence that few others would even have noticed, let alone investigated. Overall, however, the effect is lackluster compared to the brash authority of his big band or his majestic ability to superimpose an intimate ballad over the power of a large jazz orchestra.

The self-conscious Africanisms of "Ungawa" are no more successful, and the effect is of a group still in search of its own distinctive style. In part this is because Dizzy had taken on Sam Jones and Junior Mance from a very different band that had already achieved its own quite in-dividual sound. Both had played with Cannonball Adderley's pioneering soul jazz unit, which broke up in early 1958 for lack of work.

"I saw Dizzy on the street one day in New York," remembered Mance. "Knowing that Cannonball had broken up, he said, 'What are you doing now?'

"I said, 'Nothing. I just did some things with Carmen [McRae].'

"He said, 'The rehearsal's at my house,' and gave me the address. ... It was such a relaxed rehearsal! Les Spann was in the group play-ing guitar and flute. [Quite recently] Les died. ... he ended up on skid row, at rock bottom. Somebody rescued him and checked him into the hospital to dry him out. Cats were taking him music paper, because he loved to write. They gave him every encouragement. One day, he checked himself out of the hospital and back to skid row. He died in the Bowery."[27]

Spann rehearsed with Dizzy, but did not actually join the touring band until May 1958, when its short-term members saxophonist Junior Cook and drummer Jimmy Cobb left. Mance stayed for over two years because he felt he had much to learn from Dizzy. Furthermore, the two men were near neighbors on Long Island. Dizzy's home was in Corona, and Mance's a short walk away in East Elmhurst. They played knocka-bout games of tennis and plenty of more serious games of chess, devel-oping a close friendship that underpinned their working lives together. They were locked in a game of chess when bassist Art Davis turned up at Dizzy's home for his audition to replace Sam Jones (who had gone back to the re-formed Adderley band).

"I'd first met Dizzy a year or two before in a club in Philly," recalled Davis. "I went up and introduced myself, but I committed a cardinal error, since I called him 'Dizzy.' 'My name is John Birks,' he told me. He'd take 'Dizzy' from the audience but not from musicians. So I was quite apprehensive when we were due to meet again at the time I joined the band. I'd recently left Max Roach, and Milt Hinton had recommended me to Dizzy. So I turned up at his house out in Queens. Diz was there with Junior Mance, playing chess. They carried on, and I looked nervously round for a drummer or guitarist, but nobody showed up. Half an hour later, the chess game was over, and I auditioned by myself. He put some sheet music in front of me and I sight read the intro and that complex bass figure from 'Night in Tunisia.' Dizzy turned to me and said, 'D'you want the job?' That was all I played, and although I never brought up the subject that he'd met me earlier, he said, 'I know who you are, I've heard you before.' "[28]

Characteristically, Dizzy was not quite so casual about Davis's recruitment as he made it seem. He phoned Milt Hinton later to congratulate him on the "phenomenal" bassist he'd found and he admitted to Davis in due course that it was his exceptional sight-reading that had gotten him the job because "he always had trouble with bassists . . . that came in the group."[29] The incident concerning Dizzy's name is also illuminating. Friends and intimates generally called him "John Birks," and had done so since his childhood. The public, bandleaders like Kenton or Calloway who employed him, and journalists regularly knew him as "Dizzy." Art Davis's experience draws attention to the point in Dizzy's life when he began to care what his closest associates called him. Just as Duke Ellington is alleged to have told Dizzy that his music deserved a better name than "bebop," at this point in his life, when his image began to matter more, Dizzy himself seems to have preferred his real name to the nickname that went with the image he had created for himself.

With two rhythm partners who were sympathetic and ready to learn, plus the wayward but original Les Spann, Dizzy's group gradually began to acquire a distinctive sound of its own. It avoided the almost emotionless cool of Miles Davis and his preoccupation with modes, and it also steered clear of the passionate intensity that John Coltrane brought to the work he did independently from Miles. Dizzy arrived at a middle ground that gave his bebop legacy room to breathe, but bound it into a neat mixture of his comic and entertaining songs, his established repertoire, and the soul-tinged playing of Mance. His African-influenced pieces were less successful, but their rhythmic variety paved the way for his subsequent association with Lalo Schifrin.

Although the group with Spann, Mance, and Davis recorded a fair amount for Norman Granz, it was for the most part a working band, grinding around the country on the club and concert circuit during those months when Dizzy was not engaged for world tours of Jazz at the Philharmonic. In due course, Granz booked Dizzy's entire band on his packages, and it became part of the fabric of his touring entourage in the early 1960s as, say, Gene Krupa's quartet had been in the early 1950s. Aside from that, they played some fairly undistinguished venues. One such was the Midway Lounge in Pittsburgh, described as "a singles low-life bar inhabited by young people who were mostly under the age for drinking. It was a long thin room with the bar itself extended along one whole side of the lounge. The musicians played on an elevated stage behind the bar. The stage only held four people comfortably, but most of the time it was crowded with more."[30]

In his long years in the music business, Dizzy had developed a strategy for putting himself over to such audiences. "He played a lot of rooms that were not jazz rooms," recalled Mance. "He didn't care. He still knew how to get an audience. Like, say, we'd start off with one of his compositions, some bebop tune and get polite applause, audience indifference. Then he'd go right into a tune (and he knew we didn't like this tune) 'School Days.' After that everybody is clapping, with it. And then he'd go right back into some of his other stuff and the attitudes had changed.

"I said, 'You have a reason for playing 'School Days'?'

"He said, 'Yeah. If I don't get 'em, 'School Days' will. And after 'School Days' they're into this other rhythm. And from that, everything is going to sound good to them.' And he was right."[31] Mance realized Dizzy's ability to shape a program to win over an audience was masterly, as was his talent for starting a set at the same heat and intensity as most bands would reach over the course of an evening.

During August 1959, as the Gillespie Quintet wound its way around the clubs and theatres of the United States, altoist Leo Wright took over from Les Spann. Wright had been playing in Charles Mingus's band at the Five Spot in New York when a telegram arrived from Dizzy asking him to join the group in one week's time at the Regal in Chicago.[32] Mingus let Wright go without holding him to his notice, and Wright arrived at the South Side's main theatre to find he was expected to play in the pit orchestra supporting the other headline act, singer Dinah Washington, and then join the Gillespie band on stage.

"My first appearance with Dizzy was competely unrehearsed, and it was pretty scary," recalled Wright, who had had no time even to scan the music and whose attempts to second-guess the arrangement of "Blues After Dark" led to puzzled looks from the band as he fluffed his way through the sequence of breaks and tags. In the course of the week, he studied the band book and learned what was expected of him, but in his memoirs he also offers a helpful insight into Dizzy's working method with his small band.

"I put in a lot of time trying to get the arrangements down to perfection," he wrote. "The only trouble was, Dizzy didn't want them that way. This sort of synchronization was acceptable from the rhythm section, but he wanted the front line to be a bit looser, more flexible. Interestingly, this concept is precisely the opposite from the South American music that he plays so well. But this meant that I had to be extra sharp on stage, or it would look like I didn't know the tunes. So I got into the habit of watching his breathing and fingers at the same time. That way I could spot which micro-second Birks would be using to lead into the next riff. Through that we got to be a helluva front-line team."[33]

Wright's gutsy, bluesy Texan alto, with its simultaneous debts to Charlie Parker and the broad ballad playing of Johnny Hodges, made him a far more robust counterfoil to Dizzy than Spann had been. The nod in the direction of Miles and cool jazz was over for good, and even Wright's flute playing managed to convey heat rather than an impression of cool. With Wright and Davis in place, and Mance beginning to show signs that he had ambitions to be a leader in his own right, the scene

Dizzy's quintet in Europe, 1959, with Leo Wright, alto. (Photo: David Redfern)

was set for the arrival of Lalo Schifrin on piano to act as the catalyst in another creative phase of Dizzy's musical development.

Before that, however, two events occurred that showed to what degree the jazz revolutionary of the 1940s had become a pillar of the jazz establishment by the late 1950s. The first was in January 1959, when Dizzy's band was a guest act on the Timex TV show. In the middle of their regular "Umbrella Man" routine (yet another of the lightweight songs Dizzy had included in his club act to win over general audiences) they were joined by Louis Armstrong. Twenty years earlier, the most startling thing about seeing and hearing these two trumpeters together might have been their radically different styles, but in their cameo television appearance, what stands out is the basic similarity in their approach. Dizzy mugs his way through the opening vocal, rolling his eyes knowingly before starting his trumpet solo. The two horns then trade eight-bar phrases in a manner well honed on Dizzy's part by years of Jazz at the Philharmonic practice, and on Armstrong's by the instrumental routines of his All Stars. Each manages to create a series of fleeting miniatures of his characteristic style, Armstrong with searing high notes, plenty of use of space between them, and a natural balance in each phrase; Dizzy bubbling all over the horn in just as finely controlled a display. As Dizzy sings the final "looks like rain" vocal, Armstrong cowers from his saliva and jokes about being showered with Dizzy's "mouth juice"—the kind of spontaneous mugging both men experienced in their respective apprenticeships on the variety circuit. They were both to be roundly criticized in print by Miles Davis for their stage demeanor, but what is obvious here is both men's almost instinctive ability to play an audience for laughs while creating more than incidental music.

The second event, just over a month later, took place when Dizzy dropped in on a Duke Ellington recording session for Columbia. The days of Dizzy's frosty reception in Duke's 1940s horn section were long forgotten, and Dizzy knew many Ellington sidemen from festival appearances and Jazz at the Philharmonic tours. He ended up cutting a trumpet feature with the band on "U.M.M.G." (a piece Ellington had dedicated to his personal physician Dr. Arthur Logan and the "Upper Manhattan Medical Group"). "It was an accident," Dizzy recalled. "I didn't have no record date that day. I just went down to say hello to the guys. I was playing five minutes later. You can't say no to the Master. You say, 'Yes, Master, and what would you like?' "[34]

Irving Townsend, who produced the disc, had set the event up as a welcome home session for Ellington after a tour of Florida. Other guests, including pianist Jimmy Jones and vocalist Jimmy Rushing, appeared elsewhere on the album, along with a vast percussion section. He recalls that Duke responded to the suggestion of recording something with Dizzy by searching through the band library to find all the parts for "U.M.M.G." "Dr. Arthur Logan was there to hear it recorded," he remembers. "Dizzy learned the piece in no time and led off with an exciting muted solo."[35]

This solo benefits from the sparse accompaniment of just Jimmy Woode on bass and Sam Woodyard on drums, with Duke himself staying well out of the way after setting up the atmosphere and tempo with a characteristic piano introduction. This rhythm section had proved, since its remarkable 1956 Newport Festival performance of "Diminuendo and Crescendo in Blue," to be consummate masters of the slow build, and Woode was harmonically well up to the task of catching the passing chords in Dizzy's solo, having spent part of his formative period as a player accompanying Charlie Parker at Boston's Storyville Club. Dizzy states the theme, emphasizing the pedal notes and moving into a remarkably fluent solo of his own on the second chorus, which paves the way for the whole orchestra to sweep in quietly behind him and for his old Frankie Fairfax colleague Jimmy Hamilton to take a ravishing clarinet solo. The trumpet reenters as an open horn over orchestral chording, with Woodyard stepping up the strength of the rhythmic backing before the whole band sets up an exchange between Dizzy and baritone player Harry Carney. After some characteristic Ducal band chords, Dizzy sees out the piece on muted horn, occasionally "popping" the microphone by his very proximity to it. The whole piece is a perfect example of Ellington's ability to fashion a setting to show off a soloist to great advantage and of Dizzy's ability to adapt his playing to almost any environment without compromising his highly personal style.

The following year, Dizzy worked with arranger Clare Fischer on a studio big band album of Ellington's music. It is one of the least successful of Dizzy's big band ventures, lacking the authentic stamp of Ellington's own personality that so enlivened the "U.M.M.G." session. It took the arrival in New York, later in 1960, of Lalo Schifrin, complete with his new green card and some unusual ideas for arrangements, to give Dizzy a setting that offered the same kind of new impetus that the Buster Harding, Quincy Jones, and Ernie Wilkins charts had provided for the State Department band. Dizzy's own playing, as suggested earlier, did not progress greatly after the late 1940s, apart from his ever-deepening ability to adapt to different surroundings, but what makes some parts of his later work far more interesting than others is the level of new ideas that fed the bands and small groups he led.

Schifrin's role as pianist in Dizzy's small group and his contribution to the breadth and depth of the music that band played has consistently been underestimated by critics. *Jazz Journal's* Barry McRae, for example, usually so accommodating to different approaches, is typical, criticizing Schifrin's playing for its "studied air [that] suggested a book-taught jazz-man."[36] He overlooks the way in which Schifrin took Dizzy's workaday quintet of 1959 and helped create music for it that steered it gently away from "School Days" and "Umbrella Man" into a more appropriate repertoire, as well as igniting widespread interest in bossa nova through broadening Dizzy's appreciation of Latin American music. Furthermore, Schifrin's playing on a feature like his May 1962 "Taboo," despite a fiendishly out-of-tune piano, is far from the stilted work of a "book-taught" player.

Even before Schifrin joined, the quintet had begun to tour internationally, with a late 1959 trip to Europe. With Mance still in the piano chair, they began in England, traveled to Scandinavia, and then to Germany, for much of the time back-to-back on programs with Dave Brubeck and Buck Clayton's All Stars (a band that included Dizzy's old Teddy Hill adversary, trombonist Dickie Wells). In Germany, where Leo Wright had made many friends during his army service, audiences went wild for the saxophonist. "They kept on clapping during Dizzy's solo," he recalled. "Birks . . . merely smiled and grabbed the microphone, 'Leo's back home!' he said."[37] Wright always wondered if even then Dizzy knew he would eventually move to Europe for good. The band made its way home via Algiers, where the civil disturbances against French rule were under way. Everyone was glad when the time came to return to the United States, and for once there was little fraternizing with native musicians.

When Junior Mance decided to leave the quintet in 1960, he did so as a firm friend of Dizzy's, with no acrimony. Indeed, just the opposite was true because Dizzy had given him solo space on one of the band's albums and helped to set up Mance's inaugural record date as a leader via Norman Granz—a trio with Ray Brown and Lex Humphries—some months before his eventual departure. Mance went on (after a period with Johnny Griffin) to lead several of his own trios during the early 1960s.

Mance was still ensconced in Dizzy's band when Schifrin appeared with the first arrangements Dizzy had suggested he produce for him. "Dizzy had asked me to write something," remembers Schifrin, "so I had prepared sketches for *Gillespiana*, and I mean just that—not orchestrated, not developed—which he asked me to take over to his house and play for him.

" 'How would you like to orchestrate it?' he asked.

"I told him I could hear a brass band in my head, playing the full band sections with his jazz quintet out in front. I told him I thought I could achieve the sound I wanted by replacing the five saxophones of a regular big band with four French horns and a tuba, along with the usual four trumpets and four trombones. Immediately he picked up the telephone and called Norman Granz at Verve. While he was being put through he turned to me and asked, 'How long d'you think it will take to orchestrate?'

"I told him about three weeks, and there and then he agreed with Granz to record it in two sessions just over a month away. It seemed to me to be quite fantastic—but we did it.

"When I got to the studio, besides Dizzy there were people like Clark Terry, Ernie Royal, Julius Watkins, Gunther Schuller, Urbie Green. I looked around and realized this was an amazing band, the best band you could put together in New York, composed of New York's elite. I thought back to my childhood, to that conversion when I heard the discs by Charlie Parker and Dizzy, and I felt like a Moslem must feel on arriving in Mecca. Just seeing them I was very nervous.

"Then, in a moment, I overcame the nerves. The music dictates how you feel, and I began to conduct and play. It was very rewarding then, and I find it is still very rewarding now, in the late 1990s, that something I wrote all those years ago is still alive and has become a classic in a real sense with regular performances recently by Jon Faddis or James Morrison with orchestras and bands all over the world."[38]

The five movements of *Gillespiana* were conceived as a form of *concerto grosso*, the baroque form in which a small group of musicians takes the role of a concerto soloist, playing above and between sections by the full orchestra. In Lalo's vision, the regular Gillespie quintet (with himself on piano) would become the group of soloists and the full band would take the role of the orchestra. As his sketches became a finished piece, each movement took on a distinctive character, as Gunther Schuller (who played French horn in the band) relates: "Schifrin wished to pay homage to the many facets of Dizzy's enormous musical talent. Lalo felt that it was not possible to do this in some kind of 'synthesis.' He therefore resolved to write a work in which each movement would reflect a different aspect of Dizzy's personality ranging from the melancholy 'Blues' to the vigorous 'Toccata,' from allusions to Dizzy's African forebears to his interest in Latin American music." Lest this seems too much like Schuller with his academic hat on, he also shared in the extraordinary atmosphere of the date already described by Schifrin: "I think I am speaking for all my colleagues on the date when I say that we were all visibly excited by the work and Dizzy's sovereignty on his horn, undimmed in my opinion by the passing of the years."[39]

Gillespiana opens with a grand orchestral statement from full orchestra, with brass chords piled up one on top of another and Art Davis's bowed bass buzzing away alongside Don Butterfield's tuba at the very bottom of the range. The quintet, spurred by some dramatic drumming from Chuck Lampkin, takes over and then continues alongside the full band, until Dizzy enters for an extended solo. What distinguishes Schifrin's writing from that of Dizzy's other arrangers is the melodic strength of the countermelodies that surge up through the arrayed brass from time to time. These are no mere accompaniment, but additional developments, with the same kind of headlong drama that Schifrin was already used to creating for the cinema screen. He extends the idea behind Leo Wright's subsequent alto solo, with sinister low notes from trombones and tuba adding darkness and strength to the atmosphere, while the brass almost engulfs his own piano solo.

The second movement, "Blues," begins as a feature for Art Davis on bass—an effect, daring for its time, of projecting a solo pizzicato bass over a full orchestra playing dark chords. The next part of this section makes a fascinating contrast with the mid-1950s writing of Quincy Jones, as Leo Wright's flute and Dizzy's muted trumpet exchange phrases with the muted brass. Schifrin's harmonies are denser and more complex than Jones's and his use of what outwardly seem to be similar tonal effects is put to a more dramatic purpose.

Schifrin had hit on a new and different direction for big band arrangement that neither followed the full orchestral route of Gunther Schuller's or William Russo's third stream music, nor simply continued the Jones/Wilkins thinking of the 1950s. It also contained a vitality and excitement missing from most of Kenton's excesses. A clue to this originality lies in the brass riffs that back up Dizzy's solo on "Blues" (with the same idea extended into the backing for Wright's flute). While Dizzy explores the conventional flattened thirds, fifths, and sevenths of blues harmonies (demonstrating in the process how far he had come in being capable of and interested in playing convincing blues compared with his apparent rejection of the form in the 1940s), Schifrin has the riffs in the final chorus of the solo centered on a major fifth of the underlying chord. This runs counter to accepted arranging practice because most jazz arrangers would emphasize rather than deliberately sidestep the "blue" notes of the scale, and it creates a strangely modernistic effect (especially since it means there is often a semitone between band and soloist). Yet through the integrity of the soloing, the blues feeling remains strong. Just these two opening movements demonstrate the spark of originality Dizzy must have heard in Schifrin's writing for his own Argentinean band when he invited him to New York.

The paramount reason for inviting Schifrin to join him, however, emerges in the next movement, "Panamericana." During the previous two and a half years, Miles Davis and Gil Evans had been exploring the idea of setting trumpet solos in an orchestral context using French horns and woodwinds. In particular, *Sketches of Spain*, made in late 1959 and early 1960, explored Hispanic sounds, but with little of the visceral energy Dizzy had found in his 1940s experiments in Afro-Cuban music. Dizzy (at a time when he was consistently head-to-head with Davis in jazz polls) was conscious that he should not be left behind in the race to produce work for the concert hall with an orchestral setting. So he followed his instincts to reinvestigate Latin American jazz; Schifrin's easy assimilation of Argentinean and African rhythms and themes gave him the ideal opportunity. "Panamericana" shows Dizzy and Schifrin's partnership at its creative best, uniting the rhythms of North and South America in one joyous mixture. Equally, the more somber "Africana" that follows takes many of the rhythmic and harmonic ideas from Chico O'Farrill's 1954 *Afro* and works them through in a more mature context. The final "Toccata" is built on a repetitive ostinato figure that picks up another of Dizzy's earlier ideas (from "Pickin' the Cabbage" through to "Night in Tunisia") and shows each section of the band moving in apposition, with sometimes three separate rhythmic layers coexisting. Wright's solo is a perfect example, with his almost straightahead bebop timing floating over Latin rhythms, slower riffs, and (in the center) a half-speed swing rhythm.

The suite was an unqualified success with the public and continues to be performed, as Lalo pointed out, forty years later. It was also a success with some critics. *Down Beat*'s John Tyson voted it five stars, and *Gramophone*'s Alun Morgan suggested (perhaps somewhat erroneously in the context of the instrumental forces used) that it was an "immensely rewarding" counterattack against the "third-stream menace." Other writers were not so sure, including Nat Hentoff, who felt it was "weak" and "rather conventional."[40]

The logical development from recording *Gillespiana* in a studio was to play the music in concert. This was not long in coming, with a midnight recital at Carnegie Hall extending into the early hours of March 4, 1961. In addition to *Gillespiana*, there was to be a set of Dizzy's older pieces, reworked by Schifrin for the new instrumentation and crowned by "Tunisian Fantasy," an extended rewrite of "Night in Tunisia." The whole thing was billed as the "*African Suite*, dedicated to the new nations that have thrown off their colonial shackles."[41]

This was difficult music to present in concert, not least because of the "studio dynamics" Schifrin had created. In the recording studio it is easy to balance a solo double bass against a thirteen-man brass section, and Schifrin's experience of writing for film studios in Paris and Buenos Aires had given him a compositional background in which such techniques were common. It is far harder to achieve such a balance in a natural concert hall acoustic.

When the author asked Schifrin how he had managed to achieve such a satisfying end result, he said: "By the time we got to Carnegie Hall I was becoming not exactly blasé, but certainly more confident. This was because we had done a tour of New England first to try out the music. It was a bit like taking a musical on an off-Broadway try-out. By playing Hartford, Connecticut, and other such towns, we had a good idea of how to achieve what we wanted in the one hall that really mattered. My only sadness is that when the original album was released of what had actually been a three hour concert, they chopped off the last movement of 'Tunisian Fantasy.' In fact I'd written it in three parts, but there are only two on the disc, and it wasn't until one of my 1990s *Jazz Meets the Symphony* discs that the entire work finally got recorded."[42]

There was almost another crisis over the Carnegie Hall concert because the lynchpin of several arrangements, Art Davis, had decided to leave Dizzy's band. Despite his prominent role in Schifrin's charts, he felt he was not being adequately featured, but agreed to play a European tour in the fall of 1960 and return for the Carnegie Hall engagement. "I agreed to stay on until he found a regular bassist," he recalled.[43] "I went back into the band for the Carnegie Hall concert, for which I did one rehearsal and the live recording of the actual concert. I enjoyed it because in the intervening months I'd done much more symphony work and studio work, which is what I went on to do afterward, as well as working with John Coltrane the following year."[44]

The "rehearsal" was almost certainly a warm-up concert on the afternoon of March 3 at Middletown, Connecticut, at Wesleyan University. Even though he almost certainly missed out on the other New England concerts, Davis was a vital ingredient at Carnegie Hall—his bass patterns setting up even the most familiar pieces, such as "Manteca," in what Dizzy called "our 1961 version." Schifrin had opened out the arrangement in a most convincing way, brightening up the riffs and adding some of his characteristic new countermelodies, as well as reharmonizing the brass flares. Dizzy solos sublimely, feeding off the excitement of the New York crowd. Dizzy's own "Kush" and the new "Tunisian Fantasy" also depend heavily on Davis, who supplies the regularly repeated ostinato patterns for both pieces and a spectacular higher register solo on the latter.

"Tunisian Fantasy" is perhaps the most significant piece to come from this Gillespie/Schifrin partnership during 1961 because it is a thorough recomposition of Dizzy's original with new variations by Schifrin. From the abstract opening on piano, to the ethereal quality of the French horns taking the melody of the channel, this reveals itself as characteristic of Schifrin's diligent approach to the task of arranging. He manages to make the whole piece sound entirely fresh, but not unfamiliar, and above all to provide a truly inspirational framework for Dizzy as a soloist. Dizzy's first solo allows him to extend himself over several choruses, his speed, range, and mobility as remarkable as in any solo he ever recorded, but combined here with an unusual quality of relaxation. There is aggression, passion, and power in his playing, but his timing and his ability to unfold his ideas make it sound as if he is so completely at home in the surroundings Schifrin provides that he is not, for once, trying to supply all the drama on stage himself, but able to focus on playing his own role to perfection. Mort Fega, who acted as announcer and master of ceremonies at the concert, commented on Dizzy's "indefatigable vitality" at the event, and on how Schifrin had given him a setting in which he could display several moods on trumpet: "wailing, plaintive and lyrical."[45]

In September 1961, at the Monterey Festival, *Gillespiana* and "Tunisian Fantasy" were performed again in a "jazz workshop" setting, coordinated by Gunther Schuller. The concert saw the premiere of a related commission for Dizzy from J. J. Johnson, who wrote what Dizzy described as a "difficult" piece of music called "Perceptions" for trumpet, brass, and percussion, recorded earlier in the year at a studio session led by Schuller.[46]

In the few months since his rather lackluster discs with Les Spann, Junior Mance, and Sam Jones, Dizzy seemed to have regained all his old energy and enthusiasm, winning the trumpet section of the 1961 *Down Beat* Readers' Poll. The period of 1960–61 was a high point in his career as significant as the 1948 band with Chano Pozo, Massey Hall in 1953, or the 1956 State Department band, but during this time his best work was not restricted to a handful of big band dates, high-profile concerts, and recording sessions. Anyone who heard Dizzy's small group then could testify that Dizzy had hit a peak of form that was on show night after night.

The November 1960 tour of Europe was a good example. British critic Brian Priestley heard the band play all the movements of *Gillespiana* in a quintet arrangement at their London concert and wrote how he felt "privileged to hear [Dizzy] extend himself." It was, he felt, an amazing contrast to the band Dizzy brought back to England in 1965 with James Moody and Kenny Barron, where "roughly speaking, one knew what to expect from Dizzy's group through records," and he described his trip to hear this later group in Bristol as "a wasted journey."[47]

The explanation for Dizzy's renewed vigor stems entirely from Schifrin's arrival in the band. Bassist Bob Cunningham, who took over from Davis, believes this was because, in Schifrin, Dizzy had found a man who matched his own musical curiosity. "Lalo was like a sponge, he was so eager to learn. We'd be playing something, and he'd hear a thing he hadn't heard before, a new voicing, and Lalo would be right there asking Dizzy 'How do you do this?' And that was the way he was, his enthusiasm was infectious, he loved the music so much."[48]

This exceptional small band made a handful of representative discs, but the best of them is unquestionably the "Electrifying Evening" concert cut at the Museum of Modern Art in New York on February 9, 1961. It was Bob Cunningham's debut with the band, but it was also very nearly a disaster. Leo Wright recalls that the other musicians were totally exhausted from touring and had only flown into New York that morning. "We decided the only way we could get through the evening was to get juiced up out of our heads . . . we made every mistake a musician could make in a lifetime during the first song. And the second song was worse. But we just laughed drunkenly and kept on going." Leo was never averse to the odd drink, and during the interval he was opening his second bottle of Johnny Walker when an irate Dizzy, who was the only one in the band not drinking, put his head round the door and tartly informed the band that their efforts were being recorded. "We started rushing around looking for black coffee and spent the intermission drinking gallons of it. And then we went out and played some music."[49]

Whether the effects of the alcohol or the surge of adrenaline that followed the discovery that the session was being taped prompted the band into its best efforts we will never know, but the four tracks from the next set that made up the album are everything small-group jazz should be: intimate, relaxed, dramatic, and with a tremendous sense of everyone listening and feeding off one another's ideas. "Kush," with its repetitive bassline, was a physical challenge for Cunningham (who had taken a few lessons from Davis and was recommended to Dizzy by the ever-vigilant Milt Hinton), but over his foundations Wright produces a *tour-de-force* solo. The whole ensemble is at its best on Ellington's "The Mooche." This is partly due to the rapport between drummer Chuck Lampkin and bassist Bob Cunningham. They had both grown up in Cleveland, Ohio, where they attended the same school, Audubon Junior High, and as teenagers had played together in a band led by Lampkin. Although Cunningham had not played publicly with Dizzy's band until the museum concert, before the band's tour he had been out to Dizzy's house on Long Island to practice the long runs for bass and piano that introduce each section of "The Mooche" and create the framework for the drama provided by each successive soloist.

The small group made one other highly significant contribution to the course of 1960s jazz, besides as its exceptional concert discs. It was the band that, even before Stan Getz, brought bossa nova to the American jazz public. Cunningham vividly remembers the band's 1961 tour to South America, on which it added these tunes to the repertoire, because the flight to Argentina was his first time ever in an airplane. "It was quite an experience for me, sixteen hours in the air, on the way to Buenos Aires," he recalls. "It was that particular group that was responsible for bringing back from that trip the now-popular bossa nova. We came back with these songs 'Desafinado,' 'Chega De Saudade,' and quite a number of others, and I was fortunate while being in Rio and also São Paulo to be able to meet some of the local musicians, one of which happens to live here now, in New York, Dom Salvador, who plays frequently at the River Café in Brooklyn. These fellows showed me the local and natural feeling of the bossa nova and samba, so I got the authentic feeling, and not so much of a jazz rhythm."[50]

At Monterey, on September 23, 1961, the band played a number of these South American tunes in its set; among those recorded was "Desafinado," cut some six months before Stan Getz made his famous recording of the piece with Charlie Byrd. It would be too much to claim that Dizzy made a comparable impact with his bossa-nova discs to that of Getz, whose recording both in single and LP form went on to the pop charts (an unlikely feat for a jazz disc at the time, let alone by a player consistently bested by John Coltrane in jazz polls). But what Dizzy did, almost a year ahead of Getz, was to bring authentic bossa nova and samba music to the international jazz audience and to feature the music of Antonio Carlos Jobim in all his programs.

Although Dizzy made a number of changes of bassist and drummer during 1962, the key relationship of himself, Schifrin, and Wright remained constant until late in the year, when James Moody, Dizzy's old colleague from the 1940s big band, took Wright's place. To some extent this had to do with the band's still playing clubs and theatres that expected entertainment as well as good music. Wright was never much of a comic foil for Dizzy, leaving most of the comedy routines to Dizzy and singer Joe Carroll and only playing straight man on the band's regularly requested performances of "Salt Peanuts." Moody's witty stage presence and his formidable musicianship, let alone the length of his friendship with Dizzy, made him a natural front line partner for Gillespie.

Also, Dizzy was not overly keen on sharing the limelight with another soloist in his own quintet, and Wright made up for any lack of stage presence with ever more blistering and crowd-pleasing solos. Dizzy seemed better able to accept Moody (who had made a name for himself as a bandleader since leaving Dizzy) on the same kind of equal terms as Charlie Parker, but he was less well disposed to a young upstart (as Wright once described himself) stealing the limelight. He also felt nervous that Wright showed signs of wanting to leave, was making albums under his own name, and had strong ties to Europe, but these alone would not have been enough to ensure his departure. The main reason Wright believed he was given notice is that he had incurred the displeasure of Lorraine Gillespie, who was still Dizzy's manager.

With Moody back in the fold, Dizzy and Schifrin made their final large-scale collaboration from this period in September 1962. *The New Continent* was more of a through-composed suite than *Gillespiana*, demonstrating Schifrin's instinctive ability (as he put it) to "improvise with a pencil." It is also, as recorded by an impressive collection of Hollywood freelance musicians conducted by Benny Carter, very much a "studio" record rather than a recording that eavesdrops on the atmosphere of a live concert. This is not to suggest that the piece did not work in a live setting. Indeed, it was premiered at Monterey at the time of its recording, with a formal East Coast premiere at Philharmonic Hall in New York's Lincoln Center in November 1962, conducted by Schifrin and featuring Dizzy in white tie and tails—a sharp contrast to the light blue Italian suit he had worn for his warm-up set of bossa novas, in what turned out to be the inaugural jazz concert in the venue. However, as preserved on disc it has a somewhat more remote quality than the 1960–61 pieces. Schifrin intended from the outset to produce "a complex work, but one that would still be essentially geared for Dizzy by taking advantage of his love for a variety of forms, modes and rhythms."[51]

This is the closest Dizzy ever got to the kind of collaboration that Gil Evans and Miles Davis achieved with *Porgy and Bess* or *Sketches of Spain*. It is less approachable music than either of those pieces, but has a technical excellence and musical homogeneity that make it an intriguing pointer to what might have been if Schifrin had remained in Dizzy's quintet and created further works for him. It is full of memorable moments, from the opening "Legend of Atlantis," with the vibraphone featured over the "bubbling" effects of muted brass and massed reeds, to the dramatic baroque-inspired piano solo that Schifrin produces after the bass and flutes in the next movement, "The Empire." A writer of such masterful effects, with such an original orchestral palette and melodic imagination, was not likely to make the best of his talents, commercially speaking, by being the piano player in a touring jazz band, however distinguished. Within the next few months, Hollywood beckoned and Schifrin left Dizzy to become one of the most prolific composers for the silver screen.

There were occasional reunions between Schifrin and Dizzy, but albums like their attempt at soul jazz from 1977, *Free Ride* (which featured an all-star cast including Ray Parker Jr., Lee Ritenour, Oscar Brashear, and Jerome Richardson), get nowhere near providing Dizzy with so challenging an environment as their 1960s work.

Dizzy's clear-toned clarion calls at the end of the "Chorale" section of *New Continent* are, effectively, the valedictory moments of a remarkable partnership and a period during which the high standard of Dizzy's own playing never faltered. There were to be few such musically fulfilling moments again in Dizzy's career until the late 1980s.

18
Dizzy for President

Exactly when the slide began is hard to tell, but, as the 1960s went along, Dizzy's music lost its direction again. This time the doldrums were not so acute as a decade before, and he never stopped working at the highest international level, but from the magnificent peak of his playing on *Gillespiana*, or at the Museum of Modern Art, there was a gradual decline. Perhaps it coincided with acquiring the nickname "Sky King," which according to Gene Lees was conferred on him by fellow musicians when he began to spend most of his life on airplanes, traveling from one job to the next.[1] Perhaps it coincided with the departure from the quintet of Lalo Schifrin, whose ready thirst for knowledge, quickness to turn sketches into arrangements, and grand orchestral vision had given Dizzy so much direction from 1960 to 1962. Perhaps it was to do with the fact that Norman Granz sold Verve records to MGM, leaving Dizzy to move first to Philips and then to Limelight for record contracts that lacked Granz's mixture of trust in Dizzy's instincts and vision for what would sell. Or perhaps it was simply because, as he occasionally admitted to colleagues, he was no longer interested in innovation, just earning money.

As ever, there were peaks at which his playing regained its former inspiration, but the occasions on which he hit the top of his form tended to become surprise exceptions rather than the general rule. Stylistically, he remained very much himself, a masterly instrumentalist firmly rooted in bebop, but he was clearly searching for the right kind of setting for his playing during the late 1960s. This was at a time when Miles Davis confidently moved first into free jazz and then into jazz rock. What Miles was doing mattered a lot to Dizzy, not least because, although he beat Davis in the 1963 *Down Beat* critics' poll, the readers' poll was a different story, with Davis way ahead, setting a pattern for the years that followed. Yet however he tampered with the ingredients of his backing band, Dizzy was never likely to reinvent himself in the way Davis did, especially since he had already begun to view himself as the fount of much that Davis's generation played. Dizzy's inclusion of an electric bass in his regular band and his subsequent decision to replace Moody with a guitarist, leaving himself as the only front-line horn, are signs of a search for a suitably hip setting for his own unreconstructed playing. His attempts to make a soul jazz album in 1970 show that he could get this disastrously wrong, and it took the all-star Giants of Jazz group, formed for an international series of concerts in 1971, to put him back in a suitable forum for his playing to blossom. British critic Mark Gardner, writing at the time of that tour, pointed out, "It seems an awfully long time—five or six years at least—since Dizzy Gillespie made a really good record."[2] This sentiment was echoed by his fans.

Another quite plausible explanation for Dizzy's musical decline in the 1960s is that there were plenty of other things going on in his life alongside music as a result of his high public profile and willingness to speak out on social and other issues. He had actively backed Norman Granz's 1961 action to introduce musicians' contracts in the United States that would only allow them to appear if the audience was unsegregated. He was also a vocal participant in the debate within the American Federation of Musicians to integrate the separate black and white regional associations or "locals" that existed in many U.S. towns and cities.

Such activities took place against a background of change in the United States, heralded by the election of John F. Kennedy as president in 1960 and his inauguration in January 1961. In the 1950s, Dizzy had often acted in a small-scale way against prejudice; his famous attempts to desegregate hotel swimming pools (and there are numerous apocryphal stories about the varied and humorous ways he went about this) are just one example.[3] The 1960s put the racial divide in the United States at the top of the social agenda and Dizzy found himself there alongside it. Like many Southerners, the racial issue was so much a part of his life that he had developed mature and comparatively tolerant views on the subject. He always fought in the corner of black people who were put upon or discriminated against, but he also reacted angrily to the implications of reverse racism when Tulane University asked him to replace the white Lalo Schifrin with a black pianist for a concert there on the grounds that it was his business who played in his band.

Even at the height of the development of bebop, Dizzy had never been a musician who allowed racial issues to cloud his musical judgment. He always respected those who knew what they were about musically, recalling that when Monk was at Minton's: "There wasn't something that he wrote to try to scare off the other musicians, it was just hard, so not even many black guys played it. But that didn't stop Johnny Carisi [a white trumpeter] playing it, he did all of Monk's tunes and all of mine, and he never did get off the bandstand, he just stayed there."[4] In his own band, he had frequently employed white musicians from Al Haig and Stan Levey onward. He also showed no special favors to anyone if they failed to meet his own high standards. There is a famous story of bassist Chris White, who had to play a pedal note on one beat in every bar during one of the regular comic routines that Moody and Dizzy introduced to the act in 1962. As Lalo Schifrin and drummer Rudy Collins played a free Latin rhythm, White joined in the comedy and, in doing so, lost the beat he had been on. Dizzy turned to him and the audience caught on to his error. Finally, after trying several changes of rhythm, he landed back where he was supposed to be. As Dizzy began his solo, he whispered, "I give you *one note* to play, and you *fuck it up!*"[5]

The 1960s mark a point when Dizzy began to reflect more seriously on ideas that affected his own views about music. There had been a time when in music and in words he mocked the blues. In the 1940s, he had not compromised his bop playing one iota when he backed blues singers like Rubberlegs Williams or Albinia Jones, but in 1962, on a visit to Britain, some of those who had paid six shillings each to hear his quintet heard Dizzy as he "spoke out seriously about blues-hating Negro musicians, explaining that 'they see an association between blues music and their unhappy past, and they're ashamed of it.'"[6]

In the months leading up to President Kennedy's assassination in November 1963, there were signs that the more tolerant climate that Kennedy had started to usher in, backed by the controversial policy of affirmative action, might be under threat. The year had started with Martin Luther King's speech at the Lincoln Memorial, setting out his dream for racial unity. But the events of the months that followed made this look less, rather than more, likely, especially after the National Guard were called in to protect black students trying to enroll at the University of Alabama in June, and with the firebombing of a church in the same state on September 15, killing four black schoolchildren and injuring dozens more—one of the most extreme acts of urban terrorism in modern American history.

Threats to the democratic ideal of a more tolerant society were symbolized by Senator Barry Goldwater, front-runner for the Republicans in the 1964 election against Kennedy (and, after the assassination, against his successor, Lyndon Johnson). Goldwater, from Arizona, had resisted the recent civil rights legislation and was seen by some as a beacon of the old right, prepared to stand against the current of the time and defend the "freedom not to associate."

As the electoral bandwagon of nominations and primaries gathered momentum, from the unlikely setting for any political action of the Monterey Jazz Festival an even unlikelier candidate was put forward for the White House—Dizzy Gillespie himself. The whole thing began some years before as a joke, when Associated Booking Corporation produced lapel buttons that proclaimed "Dizzy for President." This stuck in the memory of critic Ralph J. Gleason, who, with Jimmy Lyons, had founded the Monterey Festival in 1958.

Jazz festivals were still a relatively new phenomenon in the early 1960s. Following the example of Nice, France, which began in 1948, various events were established throughout the two decades that followed, in due course leading to the present-day festival circuit, and the position of festivals as the most important events in the jazz calendars of many areas of the world. The Newport Festival was seen, despite its occasional rioting or crowd problems, as the model event, and imitations were beginning to spring up, at Randall's Island in New York and in various parts of Europe, notably Paris and Warsaw. With John Lewis of the Modern Jazz Quartet as artistic director, and the enthusiasm of Lyons and Gleason, Monterey, California (situated on a peninsula south of San Francisco), was set to join the list of main U.S. festivals.

Dizzy had appeared at the very first Monterey event and from 1961 was a regular return attraction, forming close personal and professional links with both Lyons and Gleason in the process. He improved from a chaotic to a masterly compere, and, as Jimmy Lyons put it, "It's very difficult to do a Festival without Dizzy—he's a very festive kind of guy!"[7] Over the years, Monterey helped mount performances of some of Dizzy's major works, but in 1963 he appeared with just his regular quintet. This time, prompted by Ralph Gleason, he had political ideas on his mind.

Some months earlier, in time for Newport and a number of civil rights rallies that took place in the summer of 1963, Gleason and his wife Jean had initiated a campaign of support to try and win Dizzy a nomination in the state of California. They felt the chill possibilities embodied in the Goldwater candidacy and reasoned that America needed a figure above party politics who could bring some common sense (as well as good humor) to the whole proceedings. They did not so much target the local California population as the national jazz community who would be sympathetic to the idea of Dizzy as a prospective occupant of the White House (a name he vowed to change), and articles and interviews about it appeared mainly in the music press.

"Ralph Gleason and his wife organized this big rally in a park in Chicago that's famous for political meetings," recalled Dizzy, in 1989. "And there was my name all over everything—automobile fenders, buttons, tires, balloons, everywhere . . . DIZZY FOR PRESIDENT! It was amazing. Everybody was very amused."[8]

The whole thing came to a head at Monterey, the weekend of September 20, just a matter of five days after the Alabama firebomb incident and with feelings running high. Dizzy arrived in time to spend the afternoon before his concert helping to man a booth raising funds for the NAACP and, as author Ross Firestone recalls, "John Lewis's announcement that he was dedicating the MJQ's performance of *The Sheriff* to Martin Luther King was greeted with a burst of applause. When Jon Hendricks asked for a moment to honor the dead children of Birmingham, the crowd fell into a reverential silence. . . . The spirit-rousing sounds and unrelentingly good feeling that flowed from both sides of the bandstand over the course of that long weekend did, in their own way, echo the vision of community that Dr. King's impassioned oration had called for."[9]

In the recording that survives of Dizzy's set, there are even political overtones in the banter between him and Moody. Introducing the "Morning of the Carnival" from the film *Black Orpheus*, after Dizzy announces the title, he says, "Excuse the expression."

Moody comes in with, "It's all right to say *Black* Orpheus."

"Yeah?"

"Yeah, *black*! Malcolm told me!" [A reference to Malcolm X.]

"Well, if Malcolm say so, it's bound to be cool."

After more to-ing and fro-ing about the title, Moody then says, to laughter from the crowd, "And if they don't like it we can lie down and demonstrate right here, now!"[10] All this, however, is preparation for Jon Hendricks's appearance singing what he calls the "campaign song": a thinly veiled rewrite of "Salt Peanuts" called "Vote Dizzy!"

Hendricks's song and Dizzy's "campaign addresses" became features of the group's appearances on the West Coast that fall, and the "campaign" was all good, lighthearted fun, helping the band to do brisk business everywhere it appeared prior to the events in Dallas in November. After Kennedy's death, with Vice President Lyndon Johnson sworn in to replace him and suddenly heading an election campaign of his own, the Goldwater threat seemed to have grown. Almost in spite of himself, Dizzy spent a lot of time on his campaign in early 1964, during his usual January and February residency at Birdland in New York.

In the event, he was not nominated for any primaries, and the write-in vote was insufficient to carry him through to the California contest. Johnson won the eventual election with a majority massively increased over Kennedy's slender margin of victory. Yet Dizzy did not treat his brush with politics lightly. "I liked the idea of running for President," he wrote, "and it would've been fun to be elected. I'd have fought for a disarmament program and the establishment of a world government."[11] In 1972 he was tempted to stand again, and for a few weeks the whole campaign paraphernalia started once more. He even met President Nixon in the White House to discuss the election. Later he commented, "In the period when I stood, the voters really didn't have a lot of choice, when it came down to Goldwater or Nixon! But I made my candidature absolutely a-political. I principally advocated a message of peace."[12]

This time, however, it was Dizzy himself who withdrew. He had by 1972 become a Baha'i and learned that presidential elections were not in keeping with the principles of his faith. "I discovered the fact that I couldn't run for president. I couldn't be associated with any political party. So I had to turn it loose. I made this big speech at the Monterey Jazz Festival that, 'Upon reflection, I hereby withdraw!' When I said 'withdraw,' all the people said 'Ah! No, no, no!' . . . I had a nice little speech made up but I couldn't hardly say it because the people were hollering so loud out there in Monterey."[13]

Candidly, he would admit, "I was known as the modern-day equivalent of Norman Thomas, the socialist who must have run for election at least ten times. I didn't think that I would get it any time, but I was trying to point out some of the things that were necessary for the formation of a government that was really seeking peace and harmony—being a musician—between nations and between peoples."[14] Even after the election of 1972 was long forgotten, he would continue to work for peace and human understanding, as that very quality of spirituality mentioned in the last chapter by Nat Hentoff continued to develop in him.

His adoption of the principles of Baha'i did not begin until the late 1960s after the death of Martin Luther King. In the years leading up to that, the slow deterioration of his playing continued, but this was frequently alleviated during his annual appearances at Monterey, where that crowd, at least, still voted for him with their enthusiastic presence.

In 1964, the festival grew bigger than ever before, with such attractions as Duke Ellington's Orchestra, Charles Mingus, Horace Silver, Woody Herman's 1964 Herd, the Modern Jazz Quartet, Pee Wee Russell's All Stars, and Gerry Mulligan, alongside Dizzy's Quintet, spread over five main concerts. The relaxed atmosphere was in contrast to Newport, where advance publicity reassured would-be attendees of the presence of "100 policemen in riot helmets."[15]

That same year, Dizzy was involved in a number of film projects, including cutting the soundtrack music of Mal Waldron's score for a *cinema-verité* look at Harlem called *The Cool World*. Gloria Foster starred in the movie of what James Baldwin termed "one of the finest novels about Harlem to come my way." Although its advertisements screamed: "Hooker! Junk! Rumble!," critics at the time were less impressed, suggesting that the music (in which Dizzy was joined by Yusef Lateef, Aaron Bell, and Art Taylor, alongside Waldron himself) was "the brightest note in this dismal picture of a sordid kind of life in Harlem."[16] Dizzy made his own album of the music from the film with his regular quintet, and this was a markedly more musical piece of work than his next disc, his first effort for Limelight, *Jambo Caribe*, which featured Dizzy, Moody, and Chris White doing comic routines in West Indian accents that have not stood the test of time.

The year 1965 saw a new event, the *Down Beat* Jazz Festival in Chicago, added to the Festival calendar. There, Dizzy was just one of a number of headline acts that appeared, as he was at the second Jazzfest Berlin, started the previous year by critic Joachim-Ernst Berendt. Even so, the festival bandwagon was gathering international momentum and was soon to start taking up as much of his time as Dizzy's regular club residencies or concert appearances. Before the festival season got under way in the early summer, Dizzy spent April and May at the Village Gate on Bleecker Street in New York, where his band worked six nights a week, joined on weekends by Gerry Mulligan.

He then moved, rather surprisingly, to the Metropole, where he substituted during June for veteran trumpeter Henry Red Allen.[17] This club was a New York institution, in which the musicians were ranged on a long stage that closely resembled a shelf behind the bar. It took some getting used to playing there, as its one-time resident pianist Sammy Price told the author, because with the band in a long row and a minimal PA system, it was simply impossible to hear what was happening at the other end of the stage. Allen had attuned himself to the vagaries of the building and had held down a residency there for many years, but in the mid-1960s he discovered a new lease on life. His international touring career had revived following a European trip with fellow New Orleans pioneer Kid Ory in 1959, and he now took frequent tours, often to Britain, as a soloist. His playing was still unique, idiosyncratic, and, in its way, influential, and it did not seem to have dated at all. Because he had been a one-off, even in the Swing Era, Allen was able to continue to mature on his own terms, and in his declining years was hailed by some critics (as was his erstwhile partner, clarinetist Pee Wee Russell) as a modernist icon. His blurry phrases, unexpected dashes to the extremes of his range, and sporadic bursts of energy were seen as a kind of abstraction every bit as fascinating as that of Ornette Coleman or Cecil Taylor, who were emerging as champions of free jazz.

In a tit-for-tat arrangement, Allen was one of the guest trumpeters who joined Dizzy's quintet at Monterey for a "Trumpet Kings" set that was reminiscent of Norman Granz's 1950s barnstorming Jazz at the Philharmonic sessions, and part of a "Tribute to the Trumpet" loosely linked to Louis Armstrong's sixty-fifth birthday celebrations. Dizzy was joined by Allen, Clark Terry, and "Rex Stewart, with a borrowed trumpet,

[who] bounced on stage late in the set." In front of 30,000 people, according to *Down Beat*'s Don De Michael, the trumpeters "did a set that, while not outstanding, offered a good opportunity to compare three approaches to jazz. . . . Allen played and sang beautifully on a slow blues, his rough voice matching his raw-edged hot trumpeting."[18] Recalling the apparent influence of Allen on Dizzy's 1937 recording of "Blue Rhythm Fantasy" with Teddy Hill, this offered a rare opportunity to compare both men's playing, but, although the event was broadcast by Voice of America, the music has never been issued on a commercial disc, denying us the chance to compare Dizzy and Allen in the same way as Granz's many discs allow comparison between Dizzy and Roy Eldridge.

History was heavy in the air at the 1965 Monterey Festival, and Gil Fuller was called in by Jimmy Lyons to assemble a big band to recreate some of the spirit, if not the sounds, of Dizzy's 1940s orchestras. The open-air concert was not a particularly happy affair, and the issued recording bears out De Michael's description that "much of the writing sounded dated and hackneyed (the kind of music played for those big-city-rainswept-streets-scenes on television and in movies). The band played soggily and more often than not, the music came out heavy. Gillespie, who seemed distracted by some of the playing behind him, performed competently, but without the inspiration he brings to his music when he is at his best."[19] Fortunately, having assembled such a band, it was arranged to go into a commercial studio and record rather more material than was played at the concert for Dick Bock's Pacific Jazz label. The resulting disc is one of the minor triumphs of this otherwise undistinguished period for Dizzy.

Dizzy produces a remarkable solo on just his mouthpiece, duetting with altoist Buddy Collette on Fuller's "Angel City" before coming in on open horn over the full band. There is also a Monterey-related piece— Johnny Mandel's "Love Theme from *The Sandpiper*," a ballad for Dizzy, is taken from a film shot in and around Monterey and Big Sur (where Jimmy Lyons kept the local store). Then, as Dizzy recalled, "They naturally wanted to get as many notes out of me as possible, as I was the soloist, and they forgot all about Harry Edison sitting there [in the band]. During one of the numbers while the band was playing, I said to Harry: 'Come out here.' We played together, and when the record came out, several people said, 'Man that was a *bad* solo you played on the tune "It Be's That Way".' I said, 'That was two of us; he played his part, I played mine, and it just went together like that.' "[20]

The separation of the two parts over the rock-inflected New Orleans drumming of Earl Palmer is clearer than Dizzy supposed, and, since Edison is slightly underrecorded, it is easy to tell them apart, but the track does offer the chance to hear Dizzy and the man he was to have replaced in Lucky Millinder's band all those years before. It is an irony of Monterey in 1965 that in defying us the chance to hear Dizzy along-side one of his 1930s influences, he should have ended up cutting a disc that briefly features him with another former rival from the same period. Not every aspect of Dizzy's playing is as crystal clear as his work with his own 1960–61 big band, and some of the trumpet runs on his own "Things Are Here" are fumbled, but this is still a sign that Dizzy could produce work well above the level of his touring quintet. It was the same fall, in 1965, that they toured Europe as openers for Jimmy Smith and drew uniformly poor notices from critics, who despite the odd moment of inspiration from pianist Kenny Barron found the routines dull and the music uninspired.

In his way, Dizzy had gotten trapped inside his own repertoire just the way Louis Armstrong was cocooned inside a predictable All-Stars routine that invariably began with "Indiana" and "Sleepy Time Down South." If Dizzy's act was starting to seem stale by 1965, it was positively desiccated ten years later when Barry McRae heard the band on a routine visit to Ronnie Scott's in London: "It would be churlish to expect one of the great pioneers of modern jazz to remain an inspirational source nearly thirty years after his greatest years. He has been playing the clubs and concert halls since that time, and invariably lost his zest for involve-ment at a mind-stretching level. . . . It is only when he takes off on an odd half-chorus of sheer inspirational genius that we wish he had more to motivate him. But then playing 'Manteca,' 'Tunisia' and 'Summertime' as often as he has could kill the enthusiasm for anyone."[21]

In his most damning observation, McRae suggests that, because of the leader's coasting and fooling on piano and bongos, the band is ef-fectively a "four-piece quintet." Things had not slid that far in the mid-1960s, but the signs were there, assisted by a worrying tendency for Dizzy to seek solace in the bottle. He had never been much of a drinker, en-joying a taste after playing or smoking a small amount of marijuana, but, as he said himself in the late 1960s, "If something hurt or impressed me badly—or just out of plain boredom—I'd lapse into getting drunk and act extremely uncivil, until it occurred to me I was going round the world making myself look foolish before people who respected me and the music we played."[22]

Pianist Mike Longo, who took over from Kenny Barron, recalls that overindulgence slackened the muscles that held Dizzy's distended cheeks in place and that he would begin to look "like a beagle." The signs were therefore always obvious to his close associates. Nevertheless, Dizzy and

Moody (who, as he told the author, had had "a serious brush with alcohol" at the time he became famous in the late 1940s with "Moody's Mood for Love") believed for the most part that they could keep their occasional bouts of drinking secret from one another. Furthermore, if Dizzy was coasting on stage, so was Moody, who had developed little as a player after his brilliant debut in the 1940s. Whereas Leo Wright had brought an element of competitiveness to the band and helped push Dizzy to musical heights, Moody seldom challenged Dizzy musically. He was a brilliant stage partner, joining in the comic routines and inventing their famous duel for the microphone where each tried to solo at the same time, their jostle for position leading to both apparently squaring up for a fight, before joining together in a comic dance. Yet, on one occasion in Japan, both had overindulged, and the on-stage scuffles between them became real. If Dizzy's fans looked to him to continue the kind of high-flying musical creativity he had presented as recently as 1961, they were not going to find it in his regular quintet, except when it traveled to new countries, like Mexico. Instead, his finest work would emerge from the small number of stimulating one-off concerts he played each year.

In 1966, one such example came from the unlikely pairing of Dizzy with the American Wind Symphony Orchestra at an open-air festival at Point Park, Pittsburgh, in July. On an impromptu stage created on a moored barge on a bend of the Allegheny River, Dizzy played to an outdoor audience of 7,000, in the premiere of a newly written work for trumpet and wind orchestra by composer and arranger Oliver Nelson.[23] Within a few days of that event, Dizzy had also charmed a festival crowd almost ten times bigger with an appearance at George Wein's Newport "Trumpet Workshop." Over 54,000 people attended the 1966 Newport Festival, and they were held spellbound by what Dan Morgenstern described in *Down Beat* as "one of those things that only happen at festivals."[24]

Temperatures soared into the hundreds as Kenny Dorham, Thad Jones, and Howard McGhee began the event. They were replaced by Clark Terry, Ruby Braff, and Henry Allen before Dizzy emerged with a man who had made his name as a Dixielander, Bobby Hackett. "Despite the marked dissimilarity in rhythmic accents and phrasing," wrote Morgenstern, "the two trumpeters complemented each other perfectly, perhaps because both are masters of using chord changes as a basis for improvisation. Playing together on ''S Wonderful,' the two made delightful relaxed music and obviously appreciated each other's work. . . . Gillespie returned accompanied only by guitarist Kenny Burrell. With harmon mute he essayed a remarkably relaxed and delicate 'Siboney.' Though there was no tempo as such, the trumpeter's every note was loaded with swing."

Clearly, out of the fetters of his own group, Dizzy could stretch out, and if these two examples showed glimpses what he was capable of, his competitive instincts prompted him to Eldridge-like feats in the finale— a massed trumpet choir playing "Disorder at the Border." "Gillespie," Morgenstern recalled, "egged on by spontaneous riffs, constructed a se- ries of phenomenal choruses, swinging, leaping and getting off some runs that seemed to defy the laws of gravity and human breath control. It was a performance that brought a standing ovation and afterward backstage, hugs, kisses and compliments from all the other players."[25]

So successful was the partnership between Dizzy and Hackett that a few years later in January 1971 the two of them cut a disc together at New York's Overseas Press Club. Chuck Folds, who was a regular mem- ber of both Henry Allen's and Roy Eldridge's bands and later for many years with Doc Cheatham, had been Hackett's pianist throughout the previous summer and was in the audience. He vividly recalls the concert at which the disc was cut: "I was sitting next to Eubie Blake, and spoke to him during the break. Mary Lou Williams was on piano, George Duvivier on bass and Grady Tate on drums. It was a special event for Bobby, with whom I'd done the 1970 summer season up in New Hamp- shire, because the gig was on his fifty-sixth birthday, January 31. I was particularly interested in how Bobby and Dizzy would sound together, because to me they were musical opposites. In fact they sounded won- derful together and they liked each other very much. The styles somehow gelled, and they were both such very musical people that everything worked. It was a terrific group, and for a while there was talk of it be- coming a band that would appear from time to time."[26]

Despite individual events like this, the number of times that Dizzy was prompted to exceptional displays of his abilities was still limited to a handful each year in the late 1960s. In 1967, his regular group stirred itself beyond the regular routine to make a visit to Mexico, for a one-off Mexico City Jazz Festival sponsored by American Airlines to mark twenty-five years of scheduled flights to the city. Behind Dizzy and Moody, fender-bassist Russell George joined the lineup, a small conces- sion to 1960s fashion at a time when the band was largely playing its usual standards, "Manteca" and "Con Alma."[27] On this tour, however, Dizzy rediscovered his natural talent for international diplomacy, and, fascinated as ever by a new country and its sounds, he got out and about to hear the local music. He was tempted into an impromptu open-air concert in the streets near the festival with a brightly clad band of local mariachi musicians, as usual winning over their hearts with his informality and sheer musicality.[28]

Another overseas tour, late the following year, featured Dizzy in front of a big band that played several dates in Europe after an inaugural date at Newport. The idea was to celebrate the twentieth anniversary of the band he brought to Europe in 1948, and, although there were personnel changes and a tightly packed itinerary, the group briefly rekindled the spark of Dizzy's earlier big bands.

As the 1960s drew to a close, Moody left Dizzy's band to be replaced by a guitarist. At that time, in 1969, Dizzy himself may still have been adrift musically, but he was making significant strides in terms of his own life. He had reached his lowest point at the time of Martin Luther King's assassination in 1968, which happened on a day when, as luck would have it, Dizzy was back in South Carolina, revisiting Cheraw and Laurinburg, with all their associative memories of segregation and the old South. His reaction to the news was to get spectacularly inebriated, and Mike Longo, his pianist, tells the part-tragic, part-comic story of trying to extricate Dizzy from the area, with Dizzy drunk and bleeding from where a woman had bitten him in a fight. Longo was petrified about what the state police might think if they were to stop the car on a night when racial unrest was expected to find a severely beaten up Dizzy semiconscious on the back seat of their borrowed car.[29]

Within a year or so of this saga, Dizzy forsook drink for good. It was just one of his undertakings when he decided to become a Baha'i. Clues as to why he took this step are apparent in his earlier comments about drinking when things got him down, or just from sheer boredom. As his life involved yet more and more traveling from place to place or weeks at indifferent clubs in anonymous American cities, the boredom quotient grew higher and higher. For a figure of such seminal importance in jazz, Dizzy had somehow failed to capitalize on his position. While Miles Davis aspired to and acquired expensive Italian sports cars and a flamboyant lifestyle, promoting himself as a pop icon, and soul stars like James Brown sold their records in the millions, Dizzy was consigned, between festivals and the occasional overseas tour, to the old rounds of clubs. The Plugged Nickel and the Village Gate might have replaced Birdland or Snookie's in his itinerary, but the life was the same. Some musicians were angered by this, including trumpeter Donald Byrd, who followed Miles into the fringes of 1960s rock music. He told Leonard Feather: "Do you think it doesn't break my heart to see Dizzy working in some small club? We're talking about respect and dignity." Although

Byrd himself was by this time surrounding himself with backing vocalists and a funk beat, he knew exactly how important Dizzy's contribution to the development of jazz had been.[30]

Ironically, it was on his endless rounds of the club circuit that Dizzy encountered the woman who helped him change his life: Beth McKintey, who contacted him in Milwaukee—initially to talk about Charlie Parker. Their conversations turned from music to religion and it turned out that while Dizzy toured the nation playing in clubs, she traveled from place to place promoting the word of the Baha'i faith.

Contrary to some perceptions, Baha'i is not in itself an ancient religion, but is based on the nineteenth-century fulfillment of an Islamic prophecy that in "the year sixty" a Messiah or Qá'im would arise to establish the final victory of Islam on Earth. A mystical prophet known as the Báb ("the Gate") made a proclamation at Shiraz in what was then Persia in May 1844 that led him to be seen by many in the Islamic world as this expected Messiah, who would establish and purify Islam. As the Báb's earthly mission continued, it soon became apparent that he was proposing to replace rather than reform some of the laws of Islam, and, after a turbulent few years defying the Islamic orthodoxy, he was shot by a firing squad in 1850.

Persia put down the Babis—the followers of the Báb—with vicious force, and over 20,000 people are reputed to have been killed in the aftermath. However, as is so often the case, a new leader emerged in 1863, known as Bahá'u'lláh, who was accepted by the surviving Babis as a new prophet whose coming had been foreseen by the Báb, a kind of Jesus Christ to the Báb's John the Baptist. Bahá'u'lláh was forty-six in 1863, and from that time on spent much of the remainder of his life in prison: in Tehran, Baghdad, and eventually 'Akká, in what was then Palestine, where he died in 1892.

Despite his exile and imprisonment, Bahá'u'lláh managed to exert considerable influence and his teachings gained wide support in the Middle East and beyond. His son Abdu'l-Bahá was able to travel freely about the world before the 1914–18 war, and established groups of followers of Baha'i (as Bahá'u'lláh's teachings were known) in Egypt, Europe, and, principally, the United States. Beth McKintey worked for the U.S. branch of the faith, which he had established around 1912. Briefly, the teachings of Baha'i involved a continual process of divine revelation, of one being revealing one evolving truth, and of the unification of humanity into one faith and one order. Under such tenets, religion becomes the very bedrock of society, the supreme law for civilization.

It might be trite to suggest that Baha'i filled the vacuum created in

Dizzy's life by endless touring, but there is more than a little truth in it. There was a limit to the number of photographs Dizzy could take in a new place with his latest camera or the number of games of chess he could play, despite always carrying a portable board. People were not always available or willing to join him in other social pursuits. After meeting Beth McKintey and her husband, he filled the empty hours of his touring life by reading endlessly on the subject of Baha'i. This squares with the time in the late 1940s when John Coltrane was in Dizzy's big band searching for some kind of religious enlightenment. Then, although interested, Dizzy had left the long discussions into the night to Yusef Lateef and Coltrane, perhaps preferring to follow Jesse Powell's example and go for a drink. Now, in sharp contrast to his recent behavior, he eschewed alcohol and devoured books and pamphlets, in particular a work called *Thief in the Night* by Bill Sears.

By 1970, Dizzy had become a member of the Baha'i faith and managed to use its principles to rationalize some of what he must have felt about his musical career, about why it was that he still worked in those dingy clubs Donald Byrd got so irate about, while others who had based their work on his had gone on to greater things. "Every age in music is important," he said. "Equally as important as the previous one, and is as important as the one that's coming after that. The same thing with religion you know, like when religion reveals itself. God has got it set up now. His education of mankind is through these prophets, and each one's supposed to come for a specific age, so they just keep coming, and after his is over another one takes their place. That's what the Baha'is teach you. They got a really intelligent way, looking at God's work on the planet. So I believe that music is the same, too. Messengers come to the music and after their influence starts waning, another one comes with a new idea, and he has a lot of followers."[31]

In numerous interviews as well as in his autobiography, Dizzy expanded on this theme, the upshot of which was that he had defined his place in the succession of trumpeters and musical innovators within jazz. He could now look back at the lineage that led from King Oliver to Armstrong, to Roy Eldridge, to himself and onward to Miles Davis in terms of the principles of the faith he espoused. Other musicians who were devout Baha'is sometimes questioned the strictness of Dizzy's devotion to its rules, including Quentin Jackson, who spoke contemptuously to John Chilton of Dizzy's "carrying on" about the religion.[32] But this was to miss the point of its importance to Dizzy. Belief in the succession of "messengers" and application of the idea to music allowed him to regain belief in himself and reinvent himself as a teacher and prophet for the generation of younger musicians he encouraged over the years to come. As we will see, the kind of encouragement he offered Jon Faddis and Arturo Sandoval was very much more substantial than his 1950s championing of Lee Morgan and Joe Gordon. Acceptance of the principle of unification gave his growing spirituality the nourishment it needed; in due course, this, too, would find expression in his music.

19

Giant of Jazz

The 1970s saw the renewal of Dizzy's close working relationship with Norman Granz, after Granz founded his new record company Pablo in 1973, intending to carry on more or less where he had left off when he sold Verve to MGM a decade before. In keeping with his long-established principles, Granz frequently assembled all-star groups for his label, putting Dizzy, in particular, into a series of settings that removed him from his regular quintet and stimulating some high-quality playing alongside old colleagues like Ray Brown and Oscar Peterson as well as newer ones like Joe Pass and Freddie Hubbard.

It did not always work, and some Pablo lineups are either too much of a good thing, in which none of the distinguished cast gets a distinctive word in edgeways, or a repeat of the worst excesses of Jazz at the Philharmonic, where dueling leads to cliché rather than creativity. However, a couple of years before the new label got off the ground, Dizzy was part of a very different all-star lineup, which, at least to start with, suffered from neither problem and was the brainchild of an entrepreneur who had emerged during the 1950s as a serious rival to Granz: George Wein.

Wein had made his name as the founder of the Newport Festival in 1954, although before that he had established himself in the Boston area both as the owner of the Storyville Club and a pianist in various traditional and mainstream bands. He had a similar keen business brain to that of Granz and was the first entrepreneur to spot the gap in the market for a production company to manage the artist and repertoire side of the burgeoning jazz festival industry. His company, Festival Productions Inc., was set up to maximize the benefits of what was, in effect, a common artistic policy for a large number of European and American festivals. By supplying the musicians for as many events as possible throughout a summer season, he could hire the best players for several weeks and guarantee them work. The geographical separation of his venues meant that few ordinary festivalgoers would be worried that the Nice Grande Parade du Jazz was carrying a virtually identical program to the North Sea Festival in the Hague or Montreux in Switzerland, or that all the same artists had earlier appeared at Newport or one of its New York–based successors, and a number of other U.S. events.

As the 1970s went on, Dizzy (plus his own band) became one of a number of high-profile artists who played regularly for Wein. What seemed at the time to be an exhilarating possibility for audiences all over Europe and the United States to hear the very best musicians looks in retrospect like a treadmill every bit as stifling as Jazz at the Philharmonic eventually became. Dizzy's itineraries were almost identical from one year to another, and, just as he had been a regular favorite at Monterey, he was adopted by the public as an icon in many of the newer festivals promoted by Wein, even though his quintet often sounded no more inspired than it had in the late 1960s.

All this appears to detract from what was a shrewdly managed and well-chosen series of festival packages, which is, perhaps, unfair. Wein's concept was as new and fresh as Granz's had been in the 1940s, and in the early 1970s each festival created a buzz of excitement. For a relatively modest price it was possible for ordinary members of the public to hear a remarkable range of players, and, since Wein himself was a musician, within the limitations of a festival environment, he was generally sympathetic to the kind of setting in which most players would perform best. Not only Dizzy but musicians like Charles Mingus and Elvin Jones benefited from Wein's booking policy.

In 1971, Wein came up with a rather different idea. This was to put together a group of the best surviving members of the bebop generation and book the band on a two-month international tour, from mid-September to mid-November. They started in New Zealand and Australia, went on to Japan, then flew to Israel, and criss-crossed virtually all of Europe. Wein's choice of what he called "leaders of their own fine groups" could hardly have been bettered; alongside Dizzy (the automatic selection on trumpet) he brought in Sonny Stitt on alto and tenor, Kai Winding on trombone, Thelonious Monk on piano, Al McKibbon on bass, and Art Blakey on drums.

There were risks in assembling such a band, both from the possible collision of egos and from the fact that Monk had been suffering a period of ill health that led his own quartet to play only intermittently. "The rumor has been gaining ground in these past few years that Thelonious Monk is not the man he was. Or even that he never was what he was cracked up to be in the first place," wrote Brian Priestley at the time. Admitting the errors of this perception, he goes on: "True, he has been seriously ill in the last year, but this seemed to have been successfully surmounted by the time George Wein booked him for a world tour with the all-star Giants of Jazz in the autumn of 1971. Monk's solo work and his concentrated comping behind Dizzy Gillespie, Sonny Stitt and Kai Winding was enough to reassure anyone that he was not only back, but ready to play."[1] For the forty-two concerts they played, there were no obvious conflicts between the musicians either. George Wein recalled: "Personality clashes? Forget it. The respect and love each had for the other was evident from the start. The first rehearsals were a story in themselves. Dizzy learning Monk's music. Monk listening to the Parker and Gillespie tunes that the group played. Listening, listening. Then he decided what he wanted to play, coming up with some of his most creative ideas in years. Dizzy [was] the spokesman, but they all decided no leader. They would walk out on stage together. They asked not to be introduced individually so there would be no order of appearance."[2]

The tour finished in London on November 14, from where the best results from two successive houses at the the New Victoria Theatre were issued on disc. This is more than simply a memento of the evening, and the recordings represent the distillation of bebop into the *lingua franca* of jazz, played from the heart by many of the key figures in the development of the music. As Barry McRae (who was in the audience) recalled, the group "teamed Gillespie with five men who ate, slept and breathed the same music . . . and not without justification they called

The Giants of Jazz, New Victoria Theatre, London, 1971. Sonny Stitt, Dizzy, Kai Winding, Al McKibbon, Art Blakey. (Photo: David Redfern)

themselves the Giants of Jazz. Their first British concert . . . proved to be a triumph for all concerned. From the moment that the sounds of 'Blue 'n' Boogie' echoed through the old art-deco cinema, raw bebop was on show."[3]

McRae was not alone among critics who heard this band on tour in noting that there was no question of this being a stilted recreation of the music of twenty-five years before—it sounded completely fresh, as if, as he put it, it was "being performed for the first time." Virtually every track on the resulting album demonstrates the vigor and strength the group discovered within itself, but the best moments come in a haunting rendition of Monk's " 'Round Midnight." Dizzy plays his familiar introduction over long notes from the other horns before they fall back, allowing him a solo break where he half-valves and squeezes out his notes to introduce Monk's oblique statement of the theme, with some further judicious long notes from the horns. Stitt takes a strong solo on the channel, with some outrageous high note punctuations from the others, before Winding reenters with the theme. The equality and balance between the players are noticeable, and there is a sense in which each allows the others space to play in their own characteristic manner.

Perhaps the best thing that could have happened was for the band to complete the tour and call it a day. For all the obvious reasons, Wein was keen to rebook such a remarkable package the following year, but in January 1972 it almost looked as if this would not be possible at all. Dizzy had collapsed and ended up in intensive care after suffering heart failure during a two-week stint at the Village Vanguard. It appears that he was slipped either a cocktail of drugs or a spiked drink. This was an unlikely occurrence since he had forsworn drink when he became a Baha'i, but he put it down to a one-off attack of "dizziness." His protégé Jon Faddis was in the audience and remembers that "he went into hospital and almost died. I remember that night and have it on tape. He was playing and he fell over and his horn got smashed. . . . It was a very sad occasion because we didn't know what to do."[4]

After two weeks off, Dizzy went back to work with his own band, and then in May, as the festival season began, the Giants of Jazz reconvened. Unfortunately, tensions between the members of the band that had been suppressed in the sheer enjoyment of the initial tour began to surface. Some of these had been apparent to Art Blakey as early as November 15, 1971, the day after the first tour ended, when he, Al McKibbon, and Thelonious Monk went into the recording studios to make a trio album for Alan Bates of Black Lion Records. "Monk wanted to make the records there," Blakey recalled, "but he wasn't in shape because he was tired. He didn't feel like playing and he went within himself, he didn't feel like it. I knew what he was talking about, but then people said, 'He sure is weird!' He wasn't weird, it was just that the man went within himself. He got tired of that mess out there, you know, he was real funny."[5] There was a small audience crammed into the Chappell Studios in London where the recording took place, and, whereas Blakey was his usual gregarious self, Monk was increasingly withdrawn, from time to time simply launching into the next tune without waiting for a cue or for quiet in the studio.

Even so, in late 1971, despite his world weariness, Monk still had something of the sense of humor his closest associates always averred was buried somewhere under his taciturn exterior. Just before the trio cut one of its numbers, as Blakey recalled, "McKibbon said, 'Hey, Monk, let's rehearse those changes again—it's been about thirty years since we played these things together.'

"He said, 'But we've been playing the tune every night!'

"McKibbon said, 'Well, you played the wrong changes on the stage!'

"He said, 'If I played the wrong changes on the stage, then I'll play the wrong changes on the record, too!' "[6]

Such moments of levity were rare, for as it turned out this was the beginning of the final phase in Monk's career, and shortly after the final 1972 tour by the Giants of Jazz he slipped into almost complete reclusiveness, only appearing again for a handful of dates at Carnegie Hall in the mid-1970s. On the 1972 tours, his behavior was markedly different from first time around, and this was a contributing factor to the rapid decline in the band's musical standards. His withdrawal prompted ever more extroverted displays from the others, and any disagreements over chords were no longer resolved with a smile. Author and biographer Tom Bethell caught them at the Municipal Auditorium in New Orleans, battling an inadequate sound system in front of a crowd of 9,000 people. "Art Blakey, I noted, seemed to be having a ball thrashing about on the drums, while Thelonious Monk, who stared directly ahead with a haunted expression throughout the performance, seemed alone to be attempting to convey a feeling of lyricism," he wrote.[7] More worryingly, what had been a strongly unified band first time out was now resembling the kind of battlefield familiar from Granz's concerts. In Bethell's view, each player "was dedicated to a cult of individualism which supposedly demonstrates itself in the attainment of great technical proficiency on one's instrument. I was particularly interested in watching Dizzy Gillespie. I could observe his fingering clearly from my seat, and there's no denying the exceptional technical command he demonstrates in the stratospheric passages, executed with great rapidity." Bethell goes on to suggest that, by this time, such proficiency rather than "the normal musical virtues of tonal beauty, melodic beauty and articulacy of phrasing" had become the band's goal and, despite "manic badinage and jaunty back-slapping," the cooperative creativity of the previous year had been subsumed into mere display, with little content.

By the time the band—whose 1972 dates were stretched over several months of sporadic activity in the United States, Mexico, and Europe—reached London for the second year running in November, the cracks were even more obvious. "Those of us who were lucky enough to catch the Giants last year must have left their recent performance . . . feeling a trifle disappointed," wrote Pete Gamble. "It was patently obvious that the important spark was missing, and that the rapport between musicians and audience engendered last year had waned . . . one expected something special from the second set, but this was not to be, for it was appallingly short and consisted of only three numbers."[8] From Dizzy, there were the first signs of a trait that was to recur more and more often as he grew older and less able to sustain the pyrotechnics of his heyday: " 'Night in Tunisia' . . . turned out to be the closer. Dizzy really cooked on this one, producing some sparkling high note work which a man of his age has no right to. His solo completed, he strolled off stage, followed by Messrs Winding, Stitt and McKibbon, leaving Monk with a few bars and a final magnificent burst from Blakey to bring things to a close." Such behavior conveyed the fatal signs of indifference to the audience, and however rational the explanation that no one could expect Dizzy to keep up the same standard as he had once managed for evenings on end night after night, shuffling off stage in this way destroyed the easy rapport with the crowd that the band's initial enthusiasm conveyed. In time, Dizzy became masterly at concealing his limitations and managed to balance his sets with aplomb, always finishing on an energetic burst of playing such as Gamble had witnessed, but leaving his crowd wanting more, rather than just leaving them in the lurch.

In the more prosaic surroundings of his own quintet, Dizzy was under less competitive pressure than in the Giants of Jazz and could dictate the pace of each show. In 1973, his lineup had settled to include Al Gafa on guitar, Earl May on electric bass, Mike Longo on piano, and Mickey Roker on drums. Perhaps spurred in the aftermath of his own brush with health trouble, and in the wake of the Giants tours, he was in top form when he appeared at Ronnie Scott's for three weeks in 1973, momentarily allaying fears that the decline of the late 1960s was terminal.

Although he was to be withering in his criticism of the same group a year or so later, Barry McRae was impressed: "His three week spell at Ronnie Scott's was an unqualified success musically and an object lesson in professional presentation. Gillespie is so hip that his banter never dates and he must be the only guest at the club who has carved the proprietor in this respect. [An allusion to Scott's running jokes with his audiences.]

"He never settles for the safe phrase and he reworks the numbers associated with him in a highly inventive manner. The rambling codas still present the most sustained creative readings of the theme, but his brilliant instrumental control and artfully employed use of dynamics add a further dimension to solos that are familiar, if not known in detail. Gillespie's sheer perfection is a barrier to some listeners, although it is difficult to see how he can be criticized for playing not only with tremendous technical facility, but also with faultless intonation."[9]

In a supreme irony, the man who was consistently beating Dizzy in jazz polls as top trumpeter, Miles Davis, appeared at London's Rainbow, a short-lived jazz venue converted from a cinema into a large auditorium, at the same time, and it seems his playing was not quite so polished. His lineup was relatively similar to a Gillespie small group, but there the similarities ended: "Miles has grasped with his usual unerring judgement, how to succeed with the wider audience he now aims at," wrote Ron Brown. "The emphasis is on visuals, and Miles himself, wearing beautiful clothes and looking wonderful for a man of forty-seven, is visuals epitomized. He's managed to whip his line-up of saxophonist, guitarist, bassist (and an electric sitar player inaudible on the night) drummer and conga player into an exciting swirling rhythmic unit, as recognizable as a Miles Davis 'sound' as were the quintets with Coltrane and [Wayne] Shorter. . . . Dave Liebman got off some reasonable solos on tenor and soprano. The amazing and almost heart-breaking crunch lies in the fact that Miles himself hardly plays at all; he just spits a strangled beep into the action every couple of minutes and we're left with an efficient backdrop with nothing to back up. The stretches of compelling trumpet over a similar accompaniment on the *Live/Evil* album showed what he can do in this situation, but he just doesn't do it any more."[10]

Many, many reviews of Davis were to reinforce this view during his various appearances (either side of a long gap) over the next decade or so, and at least Dizzy's comparative musical conservatism, remaining true to the music he had developed, stood him in good stead when it came to his best moments from the same period. Perhaps stung by suggestions that he was coasting, he replaced May and Gafa in 1976 with guitarist Rodney Jones and bassist Benjamin Franklin Brown. In interviews he was quite candid about this: "I thought it was time for a change in my group. Sometimes it is necessary to have your appendix removed. It is probably a painful thing, but the overall picture of your health improves. So I figured it was time. I wouldn't call those other two musicians, Al Gafa and Earl May, my appendix, because they meant much more to me than that, than my appendix does, but it was time for a change. I have some ideas that haven't been formulated yet, and maybe they wouldn't fit into the picture, but these two young guys, Rodney Jones and Ben Brown, they're ready for anything. Anything you want, up to their capabilities."[11]

To many festival audiences, however, his own band was no longer the setting in which Dizzy appeared. With the reappearance of Norman Granz on the recording scene, some of the artistic packages that traveled the international circuit of events were to provide his new label, Pablo, with a staple diet of live concert recordings. Dizzy was often paired up with such famous colleagues as Milt Jackson, Ray Brown, and Johnny Griffin, in a latter-day reincarnation of the Jazz at the Philharmonic atmosphere. More important, Granz's studio dates brought Dizzy (and more often than not his own drummer Mickey Roker) into more controlled all-star settings. As suggested earlier, these were somewhat uneven in quality, but Dizzy's reemergence on what quickly became a major label was significant, and the high points show that he was capable of reversing the slow decline engendered by constant touring with his own band and its limited repertoire.

The first of Dizzy's Pablo discs is also one of the best: his *Big 4*, cut in September 1974, which put him together with guitarist Joe Pass, along with Ray Brown and Mickey Roker. His high-speed open horn playing is not as edgy or incisive as it had been thirty years before, but "Bebop," that old staple of his and Pettiford's Onyx Club repertoire, still shows that Dizzy could negotiate high-speed twists and turns with remarkable aplomb. Joe Pass takes a virtuoso first solo at incredible speed, shadowed every step of the way by Mickey Roker, before Dizzy enters. His first chorus is blurry, his softer embouchure suggesting that he might not attack his notes with his former precision, but after a couple of fluffed high notes he then zooms into his highest register and proceeds to show that he can still dominate the trumpet across its whole range. English saxophonist and critic Benny Green recalled that, when he first saw the sheet music for this tune, he could not understand what all the fuss was about, until he realized that he had been playing it at a quarter of its proper speed. Commenting on this session he noted: "It is surely a tribute to Dizzy's magnificent technical awareness and agility when he first arrived that so long afterward an outcome of his youthful exuberance like 'Bebop' is still stretching the best contemporary players to their very limits."[12]

Elsewhere the disc is full of surprises, not least Irving Berlin's "Russian Lullaby" transformed into a quickish bop number, no longer in three-four time but a headlong four-four. Fats Waller's "Jitterbug Waltz" keeps its original meter, but is stretched into more of a six-eight feeling, which allows a subtle Latin lilt to creep into Dizzy's wily muted solo, showing that his rhythmic ingenuity is still as crafty as ever.

Chamber jazz of this kind might not seem Dizzy's natural forté after his pioneering bebop quintets and brash big bands, but he adapted painlessly to the genre, not least in his duo set with Oscar Peterson from late 1974, or a series of recorded meetings with Yale music professor Willie Ruff (on French horn or double bass) and pianist Dwike Mitchell. Yet his various Pablo recording projects also allowed him from time to time to open up his full firepower in a larger band setting. Even the best of these sessions sometimes suffered from Dizzy's hectic touring schedule. He undertook an incredible amount of traveling for a star of his level and age, betraying the fact that he was still for the most part managed from home, without much of the sophisticated office backup and scheduling that many other artists of his stature enjoyed.

A case in point is his *Trumpet Summit* from March 1980, cut in Los Angeles, between a concert in South Carolina the night before and a date next evening in New York. For the most part the music is mildly combative rather than competitive. Freddie Hubbard is restricted from playing in his natural style by the square-cut rhythm of Peterson's quartet; Clark Terry relies on self-parody; and only Dizzy shows any originality or ingenuity across all his solos. The best moments come in the slowish "Chicken Wings," which has each trumpeter working with different rhythm permutations; after Dizzy's exceptional muted solo, Hubbard growls his way through some heartfelt blues choruses. Overall, there is a perfunctory quality about the whole affair, and the recording balance (in which Hubbard is frequently off-mike) sounds amateurish for what must have been the considerable expense involved. Norman Granz, in his most proprietorial mood, wrote: "I asked him [Dizzy] if he'd like to fly to Los Angeles to record. 'Not really,' he said, 'Why fly out to record there? Why not later in New York?' I told him who was on the date and Dizzy immediately replied, 'I'll be there.' He flew in on the afternoon of the session, went directly to the studio, did the date (we recorded from nine o'clock at night until three o'clock in the morning), and returned to the airport immediately after the session to go to New York. That's his love for jazz."[13]

Such incidents became more and more common, and Gene Lees's famous portrait of Gillespie, *Waiting for Dizzy*, is built around just such a flying visit to Rudy Van Gelder's New Jersey studios, which, despite being a few minutes' walk from the Englewood Cliffs house to which Dizzy had recently moved from Long Island, left him no time to go there. Dizzy did not travel light; his traveling wardrobe, oddly sized trumpet case, and inevitable camera or two were joined by a sleeping board for his back, a festoon of small items of hand baggage, and a stick covered in Coca-Cola bottletops that he took everywhere and incorporated into his act as a home-made percussion instrument. (This last item acquired a folklore of its own. Mundell Lowe tells of a frustrated Jimmy Lyons, working on schedules for Monterey rehearsals, being so incensed by the incessant jingling of Dizzy's rhythm stick that he hurled it into the far corner of his office. Gene Lees remembers producer Creed Taylor having a new one made for Dizzy after the original vanished in transit somewhere, and bassist Bill Crow recalls Dizzy lying on the baggage claim conveyor at La Guardia, the stick placed on his chest, shouting, "Somebody claim me!"[14])

Although his traveling schedule barely lessened until a couple of years before his death, Dizzy did acquire some unofficial help in moving his cache of chattels around the world. While he was playing the Carl Sandys Club in the Boston area in 1975, he met a man who was doing various promotional jobs for local radio stations in the area. His name was Charles Lake, and he remembers a call from France being put through to Dizzy's hotel room the next day, extremely early in the morning in U.S. time, and Dizzy's falling asleep for two hours while the exasperated caller hung on to the other end. With this and a handful of other incidents that took place, including narrow misses for the constant mixture of planes and cars that were required to ferry the trumpeter around, Lake offered himself as road manager to Dizzy. It was a good arrangement, not least because Lorraine tended to stay at home rather than keep up with Dizzy's incessant traveling, and Dizzy often needed help wherever he found himself.

Lake spent the best part of fifteen years on the road with Dizzy, whenever he could. The two men shared a love of cameras, and Lake, known to all and sundry as "The Whale," kept a constant record of their life on tour by snapping everyone and everything they encountered. Dizzy took him on with not much more formal agreement than a nod and a handshake, but if ever there was any coolness between them, Lake would remind Dizzy: "You can't fire me, because you didn't hire me!"[15]

Amid the traveling, the festivals, and the Pablo recording sessions, the 1970s also saw Dizzy work with Al Fraser to produce his autobiography, which was eventually published in 1979. Perhaps prompted by the intimations of mortality that committing one's life to paper often engenders, Dizzy also stepped up his efforts to ensure his trumpet lineage would continue by fostering the careers of his two main protégés, Jon Faddis and Arturo Sandoval. One was a California-born trumpeter who first met Dizzy in the late 1960s when he handed him a pile of records to autograph at Monterey; the other was a Cuban prodigy who encountered Dizzy on his first visit to Cuba in 1977 and rekindled much of the warmth and creativity Dizzy had experienced with Chano Pozo in the 1940s.

Faddis had first come across Dizzy's music in 1964, when he was eleven, and started with a new trumpet teacher in his native Oakland, Bill Catalano. Together they worked through transcriptions of Dizzy's solos and Faddis began to acquire some facility in playing in his idol's style. In due course, the young trumpeter joined the high school band at Pleasant Hill near Concord, having also worked in other local rehearsal bands around Oakland, where older players like Lew Soloff recognized his talent and offered him help and assistance.

Around the time Faddis was due to leave high school, he applied to the New England Conservatory, but was only awarded half fees; his family could not afford the balance, so he did not take up the place. Instead he ended up—age eighteen—in Lionel Hampton's band, with whom he came to New York. By then, he had already played at least once alongside Dizzy, who had noticed the young man's enthusiasm and brought him up on stage during a gig at the Jazz Workshop in San Francisco. "No minors were allowed," he remembered, "but I took my horn anyway. He was playing 'Night in Tunisia,' and I said, 'Dizzy, you gonna play the ending?' and he said, 'You do it!' I was fifteen years old with a big afro hairstyle wearing a sweatshirt which read 'Dizzy for President!' He got me up on stage and we played Jimmy Owens's tune 'Get That Moody Blues' and 'Satin Doll.' I almost fainted I was so nervous. I started shaking and the room started spinning, but I was playing with Dizzy."[16]

Having witnessed Dizzy's collapse in January 1972, Faddis was concerned for his idol, but Dizzy showed up in the audience at the Avery Fisher Hall on February 4, when Faddis took the solo role with Charles Mingus's big band in a piece written for Roy Eldridge called "The Little Royal Suite." Mingus joked that Faddis was "a newcomer to improvisation. At least he said he was before he came in—he sounds like he's been doing it before."[17] The eighteen-year-old trumpeter played completely convincingly, in the style of Dizzy's mentor, and when Dizzy caught up with Faddis backstage he said, "I came out of the death bed to see you, boy!"[18]

By this time, Faddis had left Hampton and played a few more jobs for Mingus before joining the Thad Jones–Mel Lewis Orchestra. From time to time, he caught up with Dizzy, and the two of them would play together. One of Dizzy's most joyous recordings from his Pablo period was made at the 1977 Montreux Festival in Switzerland, where master and pupil played together in an informal jam-session setting with Milt Jackson, Ray Brown, and Jamaican pianist Monty Alexander (all of them hastily recruited when Dizzy's own rhythm section lost their instruments and baggage in transit). In the old jam-session warhorse "Get Happy" their muted chase shows an intuitive understanding of Dizzy's style on Faddis's part, and an old master still able to pull out some convincing new ideas of his own, all the while prompted by the relentless jabbing chords of Alexander and Brown's metronomic beat. In the decade that followed, Faddis was to be a regular member of the trumpet section in Dizzy's various projects for which he reassembled a big band, and increasingly he relieved Dizzy of a substantial proportion of the solo burden. So, too, did Arturo Sandoval, four years older than Jon Faddis and a leading light of the Cuban band Irakere.

Formed out of a pioneering band called the Orquestra Cubana de Música Moderna, Irakere was Cuba's leading modern jazz group in the late 1970s, but when Dizzy first came to the country in 1977, they had not been able to travel outside Cuba and their work was only available on one local recording. For Dizzy, the experience of discovering musicians like Sandoval, the group's saxophonist Paquito D'Rivera, and percussionist Oscar Valdés was almost as overwhelming as the emotional impact that Cuba itself made on him.

During a television documentary on his Cuban travels, Dizzy told interviewer Allen Honigberg that on the journey there, as part of a Caribbean jazz cruise, the 320 American passengers on the boat, who were the first official U.S. visitors since the 1961 missile crisis, were exceedingly nervous, especially since the dictator Fidel Castro's sister had organized a dockside protest in New Orleans at which a jeering horde chanted derogatory slogans about the Cuban leadership.[19] "I feel like Christopher Columbus," Dizzy told Leonard Feather, who was accompanying the trip as a journalist, "Damned if I know what we're going to discover." To counteract their nerves, Dizzy and Stan Getz decided to arrive playing their horns and walked down the gangplank to a storm of applause.

"Gillespie, one of the first to emerge, was the most widely acclaimed," wrote Feather. "Within moments he was caught up in an orgy of cheering, greeting, handshaking and T-shirt autographing. 'Dee Zee!' called a group of subteeners. 'Mucho gusto!' replied Gillespie. A half hour elapsed before he could extricate himself and whisk off in the company of a local trumpeter."[20]

The trumpeter was Arturo Sandoval, but at first he did not let on to Dizzy that he was a musician. "I met him at the harbor in Havana," he told the author, "and then I drove him all over the island, showing him everything and introducing him to the musicians. I didn't tell him I was a trumpeter myself. I never told him that. But this made it especially nice for me because we connected so well from the very first minute. And at that time I couldn't speak any English at all—I mean *nothing*! But somehow we communicated. I guess it had been the same with Chano Pozo, because he had never learned to speak English properly before he was killed. In Cuba, every single day, Dizzy talked about Chano Pozo and what a big impression he had left.

"Of course, Dizzy made the same kind of impact on me. Every little thing I know about jazz I feel I learned from Dizzy. I first heard him on record when I was just sixteen years old. I remember the impact of hearing him and Charlie Parker and saying to myself, 'Goodness! What kind of music is this?' And it's still my goal to try to learn to play bebop as well as that."[21]

Once Dizzy discovered Sandoval's interest in playing trumpet, the bond between the two men deepened immeasurably. This was also because there was a considerable similarity in their backgrounds. Sandoval had grown up in a poor rural community, and none of the rest of his family was remotely interested in music. He was entirely self-taught as

Arturo Sandoval and Dizzy, Cuba, 1990. (Photo: David Redfern)

a trumpeter and also as a pianist (a pursuit his father strongly discouraged because he felt the piano was "just for girls"). "Until I was in my late 'teens, I only played classical music or traditional Cuban music," recalled Sandoval, "and I discovered my first jazz on those bebop records." His natural ability as a pianist, combined with a formidable technique on the trumpet, had given him a set of autodidactic ideas about harmony and melody that coincidentally mirrored many of Dizzy's own.

He was twenty-eight when Dizzy and Leonard Feather first heard him playing with Irakere. According to Feather, he was the band's pride and joy, "a trumpeter who welded 40s Harry James, 50s Maynard Ferguson and a hint of Rafael Mendez into his own persona. When he ended spectacularly with a skyscraping quote from Gillespie's 'Groovin' High,' Dizzy ripped off a tablecloth in a 'tossing-in-the-towel' gesture."

Dizzy himself said, "I've been involved with Afro-Cuban music for more than thirty years, but when I hear the real masters, I feel I'm just a country boy from South Carolina."[22]

There was more to this observation than meets the eye. Dizzy felt that his home in South Carolina much more closely resembled the rural communities he visited in Cuba than it did his adopted homes of Philadelphia and New York. He talked openly during his later visits to Cuba in 1985, 1986, and 1990 about the oppression of poor black families during his upbringing in the South and how he felt this helped him to identify with poor Cubans. This was aided on his very first visit by his conversations with Fidel Castro himself, who invited Dizzy to meet him in his private office following a riotously successful concert by the Jazz Cruise stars and local Cuban musicians at the Mella Theatre in Havana. Castro probed into Dizzy's background and upbringing, his sporting days at Laurinburg, his education, and his music itself. Dizzy quickly realized that Castro was well aware of what he had done to popularize Afro-Cuban music in the United States and that he was being treated as a specially honored guest.

This experience prompted a number of ideas that Dizzy had been mulling over for years to coalesce into a loosely knit theory. He could explain his fascination with Caribbean, Brazilian, and particularly Cuban rhythms by recognizing that in these areas African slaves had been allowed to keep their music, their drums, and their religion—as well as, in Cuba, their languages. He began to look back at his own background in Cheraw, at a social structure that was riven through with memories of the era of slavery, with the imposition of Christianity and the rule of the slave masters, and to see connections in music, in social life, in the faces of his family, and even in the superstitions and black magic that involved hexes or love potions, both with his African heritage on the one hand and with those other slaves and their children who had settled all over the Caribbean. Cuba awakened memories of his African tours where, in particular, he remembered seeing (just as Louis Armstrong had done before him) the face of a woman in a Nigerian crowd who closely resembled members of his immediate family.

In some respects, Dizzy's ideas that arose from his trip to Cuba were not entirely new. Many had been expressed or half expressed over the years, especially in response to the 1948 big band with Pozo. But that first Cuban tour in 1977 acted as a catalyst to consolidate Dizzy's thinking. His Baha'i faith talked of unity, of breaking down barriers and the cyclical arrival on Earth of messengers who would carry ideas of unification forward. Slowly but surely, in the remaining years of his life, his musical projects came closer and closer to achieving this kind of unity in his music. Central to his thinking was the incorporation into his groups of Cuban players like Arturo Sandoval and Paquito D'Rivera; of Latin American players like Flora Purim, Airto Moreira, and Claudio Roditi (another of Dizzy's trumpet disciples); as well as Americans from younger and older generations of jazz musicians, like Jon Faddis and his old colleague James Moody. His supreme achievement of the late 1980s was to be his United Nation Orchestra, a musical melting pot that combined the rhythmical and emotional charge he felt for the music of Brazil and Cuba with the harmonic and melodic ideas he had himself introduced to jazz.

As these ideas gradually took hold, their application was not always successful. When the inaugural North Sea Festival was held at The Hague, Dizzy took part in a televised jazz cruise on the *S.S. Rotterdam* in which his playing was dismissed as vacillating "between ersatz African cabaret pieces and his current fad of Latin American muzak."[23] His African garb, the by now well-worn chanting routine on "Swing Low Sweet Cadillac," plus the ubiquitous "Manteca," were not in themselves enough to indicate the level that would be reached by Dizzy's 1980s achievements. Nor, too, although it was a nod in his future direction, was a 1979 Carnegie Hall event called "Unity with Diversity" that pitted Dizzy's solo horn against nine percussionists.

The hints about his future achievements came on overseas tours where his own sense of excitement and discovery of new sounds was matched by the enthusiasm with which he himself was discovered by a new public. At the first São Paulo festival in Brazil, for example, "Benny Carter, along with Dizzy Gillespie and others, kicked off this world series by giving a free concert at a . . . subway station entrance for a very youthful audience, an event that found them on the next evening's television news."[24] That took place in September 1978, shortly after Dizzy had already undertaken another jazz cruise to the Caribbean, visiting several West Indies islands along with George Shearing and the Thad Jones–Mel Lewis orchestra. Such events kept Dizzy in touch with ordinary people and their musical tastes and enthusiasms in a way that was not strictly necessary for such a high-profile star. Meanwhile, proof of the level of his recognition as a father figure in jazz came with the famous June 1978 White House party at which he cajoled President Jimmy Carter into singing "Salt Peanuts" along with himself and Max Roach.

In contrast to performing for the great and the good at the White House, films of Dizzy's visits to Cuba show him dancing, joining in with folk ensembles, and jamming with local musicians, which, even though partly staged for the cameras, reveal a completely genuine involvement in the music of the country. His enthusiasm for doing this, even when endless touring made him tired or grumpy, was to be the main element that went into making his United Nation Orchestra a success.

20
Old Man Time

Once upon a time there were two trumpeters who both played with the most famous saxophonist of his day. One of them went cool, then hot, rock, electric and funk, and sold albums by the million. The other continued to play what he had always played and gradually sunk from view. 'Enough is enough,' he said, as he finally disappeared from sight. 'I'm tired of being ignored. I'm as hip as the next trumpeter and far hipper than any new upstart.' So out he went and nicked the upstart's brother, signed up half his rival's band and grabbed a megastar from the big bad world of pop, and recorded the most embarrassing record of almost all time."[1]

This withering review by Simon Adams of Dizzy's 1984 Atlantic album, *Closer to the Source*, aptly sums up the lowest point in Dizzy's 1980s career. Despite the presence of Branford Marsalis (the "upstart's brother") and Stevie Wonder (the pop "megastar"), it is a poor production, with Dizzy playing well below his best, and the kind of aberration that most musicians make once or twice in their working lives. In Dizzy's case, it was no juvenile mistake, since it was released in 1986, his sixty-ninth year. It looked very much as if, in reaction to all the touring, the Norman Granz–inspired festival jams of the 1970s, and the often uninspiring surroundings of his own band, Dizzy had opted for a disastrous career move. Furthermore, it was not an accident, although it did involve a slightly world-weary cynicism, since Dizzy had said in an interview shortly before it was recorded: "My plan for the future is to make me a disco album. I figure the money is there, it's nothing that I haven't heard before. I can do it, so why not do it and get the money?"[2]

Fortunately, it was a one-off disaster, and Dizzy's life for the early 1980s was spent much as he had passed the last decade—fronting his own small band, in better shape musically than he had been in the low points of the 1960s, but now needing to pace himself carefully to produce (at least once in every set) the kind of trumpet pyrotechnics his audiences had come to expect. All the while his ideas about unification rumbled along quietly in the background.

Despite the extraordinary commercial success of Miles Davis, Dizzy had not sunk nearly as far from sight as Adams suggests, and throughout the 1980s, generally fronting his own quintet, he was a popular and welcome fixture on the world's festival circuit, ever more established as the avuncular father figure of jazz. He was a frequent guest at Monterey, Montreux, Montreal, the North Sea, London's Capital Festivals, and a host of others. His frame was more portly, his movements more deliberate, but otherwise his exuberant stage presence was undimmed since the 1940s, and, perhaps to accommodate his need to pace himself as a trumpeter, Dizzy had developed his talents as a comedian.

Cedar Walton, who undertook one mid-1980s world tour with Dizzy's small group—which also included Bobby Hutcherson, Steve Turré, Phil Woods, Mickey Roker, and Rufus Reid—recalls titters from the audience at one of the festivals they played, during a particularly quiet and sensitive introduction to "Con Alma," which featured just him and Dizzy. He looked up during his own solo to see Dizzy mouthing soundlessly to the crowd in mock annoyance "You motherfucker, you don't have to play that!" This put Walton off his stride momentarily, but he was to see the trick repeated many times, to best effect at the Grande Parade du Jazz in Nice, when their guest soloist, Stan Getz, was ten minutes late on stage. Dizzy said not a word, but had the audience in fits of laughter from the soundless expletives he mouthed during Getz's opening solo.

Cedar's main memory of life on the road with Dizzy was that it was always fun, especially if you were a pianist. "He loved to play piano, and if you were the piano player in the band he would kidnap you to talk about ideas. Art Tatum used to do this, too, and the two of them were similar in that they always had music on their minds. At the same time, Dizzy was completely adjusted to touring. He made sure he was always on time, his suits were never wrinkled, and he was always immaculate. I do remember, though, that he only traveled with two pairs of shoes, one brown and one black. They were kind of cowboy boots, very elaborate. He was standing in the wings at the North Sea Festival during Miles Davis's set, and, when Miles came over to talk to him, he looked him up and down, and the first thing he said was, 'How can you play in those shoes?' "[3]

The humor and Dizzy's serious side as a musician seemed, to the public and some of his close colleagues at least, completely intertwined. Not everyone who knew him was so sure. Trombonist Milt Bernhart, for example, often worked with Dizzy during his long career as a studio musician and recalled: "Dizzy either played or was funny, but not at the same time. Once on a TV special I worked on, Diz was a guest and pre-recorded his solo. But his horn was full of spit and it had no spit valve

... they kept stopping the take and asking him to do something about the bubble in his sound. Diz was not in a mind to co-operate. He just shook his head and said let's try another one. He was not jovial about it. ... On stage with lights and a big audience, Diz played his image as a lovable character to the hilt. But when he was still able to play and decided to play (mainly on record dates) he played and it was no jokes allowed. As for the missing spit valve, I remember saying something to him about that TV special, and getting a look that would have frozen a taco."[4]

Two illuminating stories from Gene Lees illustrate the two sides of Dizzy's character: the super-attuned musical personality and the stage clown. As Bernhart suggests, these came together most often on stage in front of an audience. Lees recounted these in his book *Waiting for Dizzy*, but in a letter to the author he paraphrased them as follows.

"Some years ago, when I was living in Los Angeles, I was invited to an opening at a hotel in downtown L.A. that had decided to 'try' a jazz policy. The bill was Dizzy's group and Carmen McRae. Carmen opened. The piano was dreadful, horrible tone and all that. About half-way through a ballad, the entire harp fell off, so that her pianist couldn't handle sustained chords in ballads. Dizzy saw this from backstage and came out to play behind her, to help. That is one little example of his generosity. He helped her through her set.

"Then there was a break. After that, someone set up his micro-phone—the mike very high on the stand, where he liked it. He was introduced and came onstage alone, oddly enough. The cord was spi-ralled around the mike stand. Dizzy looked at it as if in total bafflement. And then he did something of Jack Benny, who could get an audience laughing before saying a word. He stood his horn on its bell, and of course the rest of the horn was at a 45 degree angle on the stage. That's funny already.

"He affected to be completely alone in the world, as if there were no audience there. He walked around that mike stand, stood to one side studying it, as if trying to solve some profound problem. And then he picked it up, base high in the air, and spun it, so that the cord uncurled from it. The audience roared with laughter, and he looked startled as if he had not been aware there was anyone in the room until now. Then the laughter really got heavy. I have always said that he could have made his living as a standup comic. (And of course his solution to the problem was ingenious; I would probably have taken the mike off the stand and laboriously unwound the cord.) Anyway, after doing his nonsense about noticing he had an audience, he took the mike off the stand, looked to one side and then the other, as was his wont, and said, 'It's quite a few years since Charlie Parker and I played Los Angeles.' A well timed pause. 'It still ain't shit.'

"The audience (and most Los Angeles people don't really like the place) went up in smoke."[5]

The Dizzy described by Lees is the one that the world will remember. For the most part, by the 1980s, established in the Baha'i faith and moving toward his principles of unification and global peace, Dizzy's presence was benign, wise, and funny, combined with profound musicianship. Only occasionally were there glimpses of the firebrand youth from Cheraw—such as the occasion at the Fifth Jazz Latino Plaza International in Cuba in 1985, when he was rehearsing three bands together in a complex version of "Manteca." His avuncular personality encouraged each section of the large group to play their riffs in turn, until suddenly he drew a vicious looking knife and said, "You're gonna get it right or I'm gonna cut you!"

Such incidents were isolated, and Dizzy's natural humor bubbled out even in times of sadness, as increasing numbers of the bebop pioneers predeceased him. When Howard McGhee died in 1987, Grady Tate was sitting behind Dizzy in the congregation at St. Peter's Church on Lexington Avenue. Dizzy was to read the lesson, but when the moment came he was slow to get out of his seat, obviously worried about the safety of his elaborate camera gear that was slung over his shoulder. "Don't worry, I'll keep an eye on it!" said the stranger in the next pew. Everyone waited expectantly as Dizzy began to remove the straps—then he thought better of it, and slung the camera back over his shoulder. "Who's gonna keep an eye on *you*?" he asked in a stage whisper that had the congregation in peals of laughter before he got to the lectern.[6]

For his media appearances, Dizzy also adopted the kind of paternal "personality" role that Louis Armstrong had in the 1960s, assuming a gravelly tone of reminiscence in dozens of radio interviews, and making cameo appearances in many kinds of film and television productions. Some of these were serious, like Carlos Ortiz's 1988 film about Machito, *A Latin Jazz Legacy*. Others were frivolous, like his famous appearance on the *Muppet Show*, which meant children everywhere in the world recognized Dizzy's inflatable cheek pouches and crazily upturned trumpet. In 1991, he even followed Dexter Gordon's example and tried his hand in the kind of acting and playing role that Dexter had made famous in Bertrand Tavernier's film *Round Midnight*. In Dizzy's case, *Winter in Lisbon* featured the trumpeter as Bill Swann, a once-famous musician who moved to Europe to avoid the U.S. political and social situation, but is coaxed back to music by a young pianist played by Christian

Vadim. Leonard Feather noted, "The movie is worth seeing, if only for Gillespie's contribution," and also draws attention to the score by Slide Hampton.[7] Grady Tate, who played drums on the soundtrack, remembered: "Diz was a delight to be with, because his childlike enthusiasm propelled us to another plane. He was a wonderful guy, and I directed the band in the studio for that last film. He played on the sound track, too, of course, and so there really wasn't that much directing for me to do. To get the timing right we synchronized to a click track, and I'd give the cues and conduct the band."[8]

Tate told the author that to his regret he had only ever worked with Dizzy on one-off sessions and as part of recording groups, but that on almost every occasion Dizzy had been keen to pass on his accumulated knowledge. Perhaps also prompted by the visions of mortality engendered by his autobiography, the 1980s were a time when Dizzy seemed more eager than ever to teach others what he had painfully learned for himself. "When I asked Dizzy who helped him and shared things when he was coming up," recalled Jon Faddis, "his response was 'Nobody showed me shit!' That makes his contributions to jazz education the more remarkable. No one showed him anything, but he shared his music with everyone. His legacy continues with us, sharing Dizzy's music with the younger musicians of today."[9]

Of course, Dizzy did not suddenly become a responsible educator overnight. He had taken part in the "License Series" of jazz workshops and seminars at Tennessee State University in Jackson back in 1956 with his State Department band. Alto saxophonist Hank Crawford was a student there and remembers that Dizzy followed an earlier workshop by Duke Ellington, but that Dizzy's concert stuck in his mind because the band stayed on campus to play the Thanksgiving ball. Crawford remembers the difference between Dizzy's informative and humorous workshop, already structured to pass on information to younger players, in contrast with a far less formal visit to the same campus by Charlie Parker, before his death in 1955. "He came through on a concert package. I was playing in the band at an after-hours club called the Morocco, and he came by after his gig. It was the place to go late at night. He was very intelligent, funny, likable, I just sat and talked with him for three hours, over some Scotch, and I remember looking at what small hands he had for producing such great sounds."[10]

Many other musicians recall Dizzy's inspirational role at college workshops, especially during the 1980s, when he attacked the task with renewed vigor. Scott Stroman, now professor of jazz studies at London's Guildhall School of Music, remembers clearly the effect that Dizzy had in playing and rehearsing with the student band at the University of

Miami in 1981–82, where Stroman was taking his master's degree, and that he carried much of this knowledge forward into his own work in directing student bands.

There was never a danger that Dizzy would retreat full time into academia, as he told Charles Fox: "I expect to do some teaching through TV cassettes, half hour programs. And I'll do master classes at universities, and things like that. But not on a permanent basis. If I were to get hung up at a college, say Dartmouth, for five days every week, I'd go crazy up there, probably."[11]

Teaching (informally or by working alongside his fellow musicians on the road), incessantly touring, appearing at high-profile concerts, and representing jazz on television and film, Dizzy's life in the mid-1980s seemed to involve all the right things, yet somehow in practice the sum of all them failed to bring him the level of international recognition he deserved.

The tide began to turn in 1987, when he reached seventy and went on the road to celebrate with an outstanding big band. No commercial recordings appear to have been issued by this nineteen-piece orchestra, but its London concert on July 2 was broadcast by the BBC and displays a remarkably energetic band, featuring a cross section of old Gillespie favorites like "Things to Come," plus reworkings of Schifrin's *Gillespiana*. Dizzy's tone is blurrier than of old, and the highest register trumpet work is entrusted to Jon Faddis, but, spurred on by some pugnacious tenor solos from Sam Rivers and the young Ralph Moore, Dizzy rises to the challenge with some playing that belies his advancing years. With Steve Turré and Britt Woodman among the trombones, and his old sidekick Howard Johnson anchoring the reed section on baritone, this was a big band to rival any that Dizzy had led since the State Department tours.

There was no sense in this band, despite his age, that Dizzy was shirking the duties of a trumpeting leader. He split the soloing with Faddis on " 'Round Midnight" and "Emanon," took all the solos on *Gillespiana*, and led the entire trumpet section through the old routines on "Things to Come." Mildly upstaged by Steve Turré's conch shell playing on "Manteca," Dizzy then took the lead on the piece written by Jimmy Heath to encapsulate his alleged remark to Louis Armstrong: "Without You—No Me."

Everywhere the band played, it drew the kind of reviews that Dizzy had not enjoyed in years, and when Arturo Sandoval joined them for a guest appearance at the North Sea Festival in The Hague, the ideas were sown for a band that would take shape in 1989 and be Dizzy's crowning achievement as a leader.

This was the United Nation Orchestra, and it continued much that the seventieth anniversary big band had achieved. Its rhythm section, for example, was built around guitarist Ed Cherry, bassist John Lee, and Cuban drummer Ignacio Berroa, who had anchored the 1987 band. Steve Turré was once more on hand on trombone, but the rest of the lineup assembled by Dizzy and the band's *éminence grise*, Charles Fishman, was exactly the kind of geographical and stylistic mix that Dizzy's Baha'i principles espoused. Mario Rivera from the Dominican Republic played saxophones, along with Cuban Paquito D'Rivera and American James Moody. Arturo Sandoval sat alongside Brazilian Claudio Roditi in the trumpets, while big band veteran Slide Hampton joined Turré on trombone (and also provided many arrangements for the group). The rhythm section was filled out by the Panamanian pianist Danilo Perez, Giovanni Hildago on congas (from Puerto Rico), and Airto Moreira (from Brazil) on percussion, alongside his wife, the singer Flora Purim.

On stage, the band's layout was less formal than the serried rows of a conventional big band, and its repertoire was an intriguing blend from all stages of Dizzy's career, infused with a level of rhythmic complexity that gave it a startling contemporary feel, even on his old standards. In this context, the bass patterns of Lee and the guitar riffs of Cherry sound as natural and unforced as the disastrous 1984 *Closer to the Source* album had sounded contrived. Dizzy again drew strength from his orchestra to achieve a remarkable level of consistency in his own playing—still hitting the high notes on "Manteca" and never shirking solo duties, despite a continued blurriness in his tone, a fondness for muted solos, and a radio microphone clamped to the upturned bell of his horn.

Its live recording from the Royal Festival Hall in London captures much of the extraordinary atmosphere generated by this band, as does its Bristol concert from the same tour, recorded by the BBC a week earlier. The baby of the band, pianist Danilo Perez, recalled these were his first concerts with Dizzy. "They were recorded and all, but I was scared. But from then on, playing around the world with Dizzy gave me all the attention I needed and more. I joined through Paquito D'Rivera, who recommended me, as did Claudio Roditi, who I'd met earlier in Boston, while I was at Berklee Music School. That's also where I met Slide Hampton.

"Dizzy trusts Paquito's judgment, so when he said, 'I got this piano player,' I got the job. In fact up until the time of the European tour, Monty Alexander had been playing in the band. And I just got up on the bandstand on the first English concert, and that was my first gig. I was scared to death. After I got over that, it took me a while to realize that I really was there. It was like a dream. I'd never dreamed of being

Dizzy Gillespie and the United Nation Orchestra, London 1989. Back: Ed Cherry (guitar), Ignacio Berroa (drums), John Lee (bass); middle: Steve Turre, Slide Hampton (trombones); Arturo Sandoval, Claudio Roditi (trumpets); front: Mario Rivera (tenor), Paquito D'Rivera (alto), James Moody (tenor), Giovanni Hidalgo (congas), Dizzy. (Photo: David Redfern)

in a situation where I would be playing with people of that caliber. Every night I would have to wake up and rub my eyes, look around me and say 'It's true!'

"It was a big lesson, playing with Dizzy every day. On a daily basis he was amazing. After that you're cool for the rest of your life! I was just twenty-two when I started with the band."[12]

Dizzy undertook a touring schedule with his new orchestra that would have taken its toll on a much younger man. Yet, Flora Purim and Airto Moreira were amazed at Dizzy's stamina, as Airto recalled: "One day we were at Milan Airport, after four concerts in Italy. We had been five weeks on the road, and the band was very tired because of all the pressure and the lack of organization typical of that country. Flora and I approached Dizzy who was looking round the stores, whistling happily and looking as if he'd just enjoyed a good night's rest. We asked him: 'How do you manage to do this when all of us are feeling so miserable and exhausted?' He replied: 'You have to take it easy and don't worry about the past or the future. Life will take its natural course, and you just go with it. Nobody is going anywhere anyway, we are all here to-gether and we are all going to the same place."[13]

Charles Lake described Dizzy's stamina on tour as a godly gift, but by the age of seventy-two he was so accustomed to life on the road, that he did not know what to do with himself when he was at home for any length of time. He called Lorraine every day from wherever he was, but, as photographer Dany Gignoux remembers, "He didn't last longer than three days at home."[14]

In every interview, and in all the publicity for the band, Dizzy pre-sented his theories of unification and his desire for peace and harmony among people. One particularly poignant moment came when the band played in Nuremburg at the first post-unification Jazz Ost–West Festival in 1990, and, while reviewers regretted the fact that Dizzy seemed re-luctant to use the full resources of the band flat out for any great period, preferring to break it down into a series of complementary small groups, its message to the world was clear: "[It is] the hippest band led by a septuagenarian today. The drum section's a pan-African delight: Airto on percussion, Ignacio Berrio on traps, the incredible Giovanni Hildago on congas. With these men smouldering away beneath 'Manteca' and 'Tin Tin Deo' the old Chano Pozo charts breathe anew. . . . Arturo's all but taken over the eternal 'Night in Tunisia,' with the result that Tunis begins to sound like a mythological jungle town in a Latin American novel . . . a riot of vibrating humming birds and not a camel in sight."[15]

If the United Nation Orchestra had been Dizzy's only achievement in 1989, for a man of his age it would have been remarkable enough. As it turned out, he appeared on three other outstanding record dates that year, which showed the diversity of his Indian summer as a player, look-ing forward in one case and back at past triumphs in the others.

The first, and most forward-looking, session was a two-hour duo concert in Paris with Max Roach. At a time when his own big band was more heavily dependent than ever on a massive rhythm section and large numbers of brass and reeds to carry the harmonies, this would pit Dizzy against a master percussionist with no supporting harmony instruments and just his wits to rely on. Furthermore, apart from a hurried warm-up at their hotel, there had been no time to work anything out in advance. Max Roach recalled: "Dizzy got in town just prior to us going to the concerts, and they were making a film as well. All the events that were happening related to Bastille Day, and since we were all part of this whole year celebration the cameras were rolling and people were constantly asking us questions. So we barely had a moment alone together to talk about this except on the day of the concert when the car picked us up.

We got in together and looked at each other and Diz said, 'There's no piano and no bass.' He said 'What about the changes?' I explained to him how things worked with [Anthony] Braxton and this is what happened with Archie Shepp. Not that he didn't conceive of it or know of it—Dizzy is so wonderful, he really is like a fox. He said, 'Oh! You mean I'm free?' "[16] Max recalled also that there were many trumpet players in the audience to see if Dizzy was up to this challenge and whether he could sustain a lengthy session of free improvisation. In part, he sidestepped the problem by squeezing many of his old familiar bop themes into the program, which he and Roach picked up, ran with for a while, and discarded, before almost seamlessly moving to a new idea. Yet, taken as a whole, the concert is remarkable for a musician written off by many critics as a conservative, beached in his old and familiar repertoire and unwilling to embrace the changes of a new era in jazz. Some sections of the concert are poignant and melancholy, others joyous and celebratory, but none of it suggests a trumpeter unable to cope with the challenge, and the two old bop masters show that they can more than hold their own as free jazz players.

In quite a different reunion at the end of the year, the second of his unusual sessions, Dizzy found time to squeeze in a brief trip to Rudy Van Gelder's New Jersey studio to join in the making of Milt Hinton's eightieth birthday tribute album. Drummer Jackie Williams, who played on the date, recalled it was a bitterly cold December day, with snow on the ground, and that they met first at Dizzy's nearby house before setting off in the cold for the studio. Dizzy presented Milt with a jigsaw puzzle of a double bass that he had picked up in Europe—a continuation of the two men's regular exchanges of gifts that had begun so many years before in the Calloway band. They talked and joked in the studio, some of it on the resulting album, and played two tracks that included the tune from the fateful spitball incident "Girl of My Dreams." The results are touching and affectionate, and proof that in all the hurly-burly of his international career Dizzy had still got a soft spot for his fellow junior colleague in Cab's orchestra.

The third date is proof, if proof were needed, that Dizzy still had exceptional powers as a soloist in 1989, when he cut a set of arrangements of his old standards with the Rochester Philharmonic Orchestra. One of these was a touching slowish version of "Con Alma," arranged by Robert Farnon. Unlikely as it might seem, Farnon and Dizzy had also been firm friends from Calloway days, when Danny Barker, Milt Hinton, Dizzy, and Cozy Cole had gone for an after-hours jam session at Farnon's house in Toronto in 1939. In those days, Farnon was a cornet player, but he was just as involved in the study of arranging and harmony as Dizzy.

Later, Farnon went on to become one of the most successful of all commercial arrangers and composers, with dozens of albums and film scores to his credit. He would often call on Dizzy when Gillespie was in visiting distance of Farnon's home on the Channel Island of Guernsey. On at least one visit to Dizzy's London hotel Farnon had himself announced as "Beethoven," a nickname that stuck between the two men.

The 1989 session, even though only one Farnon chart was used, saw the ultimate completion of a long-held ambition. The two men had tried to work together in the 1950s, first in London and then in Berlin, but had been blocked by the protectionist attitudes of the AFM, who threatened Dizzy with expulsion from the union if he recorded for Farnon with the Berlin Philharmonic.

The Rochester Philharmonic sessions were an attempt by the Pro Arte label (a classical imprint) to diversify into jazz, but in a manner that might not frighten off its regular customers (a similar strategy to Telarc, which released Dizzy's last sad sessions from the Blue Note in New York in 1992). Producer Steve Vining had discovered that the company had a contract with the orchestra that allowed it to make a certain number of discs a year at a fixed cost, so he set up a series that also featured New Orleans trumpeter Al Hirt and ex-Ellingtonian Barry Lee Hall. The musical director was John Dankworth, the English saxophonist whose association with Dizzy went back many years. Dizzy had even sat in with the Dankworth band one year at the Barrylands Ballroom in Glasgow.

"I was there in my capacity as someone who could control a symphony orchestra in a jazz context," Dankworth told the author. "I didn't play myself on that occasion, but I conducted the arrangements by Mike Crotty, J. J. Johnson and Robert Farnon. I think the main problem with it from my point of view is that the engineers in the control room didn't put enough emphasis on the rhythm section, making some of the results rather echoey and ill-defined. As the session went on, Dizzy got rather absent minded, and there were a couple of places he forgot to come in, but his tenor player, Ron Holloway, was quite used to leaping in and playing solos, and he helped to avert a disaster on all fronts!"[17]

The best of the tracks, the ubiquitous "Manteca," shows no sign of Dizzy nodding off, and his soloing has an unusually incisive edge to it for this late period in his career. All the aspects that characterized his playing over the years were on show—brisk runs, the oblique attack of high notes that sounded irresistibly hip, corkscrewing figures that spiraled downward at speed. On this disc, Dizzy no longer has the same vigor as in his 1940s and 1950s heyday, but it offers a chance to hear him on sole display in a role he was often content to leave to Roditi or Sandoval in his United Nation Orchestra.

Throughout 1990 the United Nation Orchestra continued to travel the world for the festival season, and the beginning of 1991 saw him in Paris, where he returned in April, also touring in Germany later in the summer. In the middle of 1991 Dizzy was treated in Switzerland for deterioration in his hearing, and, as the year went on, photographs show him looking less vibrant than before. His face, up until mid-1991 youthful and full of fun despite greying hair and the sagginess of his cheek pouches, started to show his age.

At the start of 1992, Dizzy went back to old habits and played a month-long residency at a New York club, the Blue Note. The results were recorded and eventually issued by Telarc, but, compared with the vibrancy of his 1989 Indian summer, Dizzy's own playing sounds uncharacteristically tentative and it did him no service to issue this material where he is so far below his best form. Several guest trumpeters were booked to appear with him at the start of what promised to be a frenetic year to celebrate his seventy-fifth birthday in October. One of them was eighty-seven-year-old Doc Cheatham, who told the author he took one look at Dizzy and knew he was ill: "He was in poor shape, and I felt it was serious."

With a media army descending on the Blue Note, and publicist Virginia Wicks flown in from Los Angeles to try and impose some order on the chaos, it seemed that Dizzy's efforts of the last few years had paid off. His United Nation Orchestra, his grand vision of world music, peace, and unity, had touched the hearts of many all over the world, and the venerable trumpeter's seventy-fifth year was to be big news.

In February, Dizzy took off for California and the opening of a photographic exhibition that was intended to follow at least some of his frenetic world travels that were planned to take in Argentina, England, Paris, South Africa, Germany, the United States, Germany again, Sweden, and Japan. Clowning and inflating his cheeks for the cameras with photographer Herman Leonard at the exhibition preview in Emeryville, Dizzy's eyes have a rheumy sadness not visible in earlier pictures. Within a few weeks, he had cancelled his travels, and although the exact nature of his illness was not revealed at the time, the cancer that killed him had begun its work.

Against doctor's orders, he made a few low-profile non-playing appearances in 1992, not announcing until very shortly before it set off that he would be absent from the Jazz Cruise planned to celebrate his birthday, sailing on October 17 from Fort Lauderdale on the *M.V. Zenith*. To keep his illness quiet, his visits to the hospital in Englewood Cliffs were shrouded in secrecy, and the world knew little of how serious his illness was until not long before he died. With James Moody, Jon Faddis, and a small number of other friends at his bedside, he died on January 6, 1993.

With his death, the world lost a man who had revolutionized jazz, given it a set of principles on which it could develop musically, and shown by example how to create within those principles at the highest level. His legacy of recordings is unparalleled in jazz history, and, in his most fertile period, from 1944 until 1961, nobody else in jazz matched his combination of range, vision, and instrumental prowess in settings from small groups to large orchestras. His determination to foster the talents of younger trumpeters from the mid-1950s onwards also ensures that his musical legacy will not just live on through recordings but through the playing of a generation of skilled younger musicians who learned from him firsthand. But by far Dizzy's greatest achievement in his final years was to bury forever the image of the hothead, quick to draw his knife and stand his corner, and to suppress his childhood mean streak once and for all. From the ideal platform of his United Nation Orchestra, with its pathbreaking fusion of musical styles from North, Central, and South America and the Caribbean, he had demonstrated his commitment to the principles of unity, peace, and brotherhood of which he spoke so often. He ended his autobiography with the wish that he would be remembered as a humanitarian.

It is the greatest tribute to him to say that his wish came true.

Notes

Chapter 1

1. Taylor, p. 193.
2. Dizzy Gillespie interviewed by Charles Fox for BBC Radio, February 28, 1980.
3. Dizzy Gillespie interviewed for *Norman's Conquest* (a history of Jazz at the Philharmonic transmitted on BBC Radio, April–June 1994).
4. Dance, *Basie*, p. 149.
5. Letter to the author from Dave Brubeck, July 9, 1994.
6. Letter to the author from John Chilton, March 8, 1994.
7. Dizzy Gillespie interviewed by Zane Knauss for *Cheraw for Dizzy* documentary for South Carolina Educational TV, January 1975.
8. Ibid.
9. Stanley Dance, "Dizzy Gillespie—Past, Present and Future," *Jazz*, vol. 2, no. 6 (July–August 1963), p. 8.
10. Fox interview, February 28, 1980.
11. Tape of Carnegie Hall concert by Dizzy's band and New York City All High School Chorus with guests, 1972, celebrating award of the Handel Medal to Dizzy.
12. Knauss interview, January 1975.
13. Ibid.
14. Dance, "Dizzy Gillespie—Past, Present and Future," p. 9.
15. Ibid.
16. Fox interview, February 28, 1980.
17. *Desert Island Discs*: Dizzy Gillespie interviewed by Roy Plomley, broadcast January 19, 1980.
18. Wilson, p. 2.
19. Mrs. McDuffy interviewed by Zane Knauss, January 1975.
20. Dizzy Gillespie interviewed by Charles Fox for BBC Radio, August 31, 1976.
21. Ibid.
22. Gillespie/Fraser, p. 45.
23. Author's interview with Norman Powe, January 13, 1998.
24. Clarke/Verdun, p. 37 (translated by the author).
25. Powe interview, January 13, 1998.
26. Wright, p. 156 ff.

27. Ibid. Oliver toured the Carolinas in late 1932–early 1933, June 19–July 5, 1934, October 15–28, 1934, and April 29–May 29, 1935. During the October 1934 visit the band made several broadcasts over WFBC from Greenville. This may have been too far away to reach Laurinburg. They also broadcast in May 1935 from Charleston and Greenville.

28. Powe interview, January 13, 1998.

29. David Griffiths, "Leslie Johnakins—Always a Big Band Musician," *Storyville*, no. 70 (April–May 1977), p. 137; other material on Taylor and Gunn from McCarthy, p. 91, and Schuller, p. 776.

30. Powe interview, January 13, 1998.

31. Much speculation, initially fueled by Albert McCarthy, Brian Rust, and Laurie Wright and later accepted by Gunther Schuller, concerns Gunn's trombonist, whose lively playing is the main feature of "Star Dust," "I've Found a New Baby," and "Slats' Shuffle." The player in question is not the eponymous "Slats" but John "Bones" Orange.

32. Chilton, *Jazz Nursery*, p. 40 ff. Author's interview with Chilton, January 8, 1998, confirms that Dizzy heard this band from a conversation that took place when Chilton presented Gillespie with a copy of the *Jazz Nursery* book at Ronnie Scott's in London after its publication in 1980. "He talked in great detail about the various players who came from that source, saying, with what seemed to be genuine emotion (and pride) how pleased he was that someone had written about the South Carolina musicians" (letter to the author from John Chilton, March 8, 1994).

33. Powe interview, January 13, 1998.

34. Gillespie/Fraser, p. 41.

35. Mrs. McDuffy interviewed by Zane Knauss, January 1975.

36. Clarke/Verdun, p. 79.

37. Dance, "Dizzy Gillespie—Past, Present and Future," p. 9.

38. Knauss interview, January 1975. It is actually unlikely that Dizzy did go to Laurinburg during the 1946 tour with Ella, but most probable that this took place the previous year, with the Hep-sations tour when the singer was June Eckstine. See Chapter 12, note 38.

Chapter 2

1. Gillespie/Fraser, pp. 46, 60.

2. Ibid., p. 59.

3. Hultin, p. 44, is a typical reference to Gillespie's womanizing. See Chapter 17 regarding his liaison with Connie Bryson.

4. Irv Kline, "The Philadelphia Story," *Jazz FM*, issue 9 (Autumn 1991), p. 20.

5. Frankie Fairfax was born around the turn of the century. He died in 1972. The exact date is not recorded, but his obituary appeared in a local AFM

publication in April 1972. I am grateful to John Chilton for supplying this information from his work in Philadelphia libraries. Although Fairfax was concentrating on trombone by the time Dizzy joined him, Charlie Shavers (*Metronome*, February 1950, p. 28) recalls that "Fax" still played trumpet.

6. Author's interview with Doggett, April 30, 1996.

7. Bernhardt/Harris, p. 60.

8. Hoffman, *Jazz Advertised*

9. Panassié, "Chappie Willett." In a conversation with various musicians Dizzy once said: "You remember Chappie Willett? He used to write a lot of way out things for the Millinder band in crazy times—3/8; 5/8; 12/8; 16/95— you name it. Well Lucky would just sit there and watch while Chappie rehearsed the band a couple of times. Then Chappie would say 'You got it, Lucky?' " (Interview kindly supplied by Steve Voce. A paraphrase appears in McRae, pp. 25–26.)

10. Author's interview with Chilton, April 23, 1996.

11. Gillespie/Fraser, p. 51.

12. Doggett interview, April 30, 1996.

13. Author's interview with Jimmy McGriff, January 22, 1994.

14. Author's interview with Bill Dillard, March 24, 1993.

15. Details from Howard Rye as part of his research into *International Musician* AFM listings.

16. Smith, *Sideman*, p. 47 ff.

17. Gillespie/Fraser, p. 53.

18. Sinclair Traill, "Charlie Shavers," *Jazz Journal*, vol. 23, no. 5 (May 1970), p. 8.

19. Smith, *Sideman*, p. 40.

20. Barker/Shipton, *A Life in Jazz*, p. 153.

21. Gillespie/Fraser, p. 33.

22. For example, Enstice/Rubin, p. 174.

23. Shipton, pp. 30–31. A comparison of the recording dates of Waller's 1928–29 sessions with the times the discs were first advertised as new releases.

24. *New York Age*, August 10, 1935.

25. *New York Amsterdam News*, July 13, 1935.

26. Gillespie/Fraser, p. 54.

27. Author's interview with Brown, April 11, 1996.

28. Barker/Shipton, *A Life in Jazz*, p. 57.

29. Gillespie/Fraser, p. 66.

30. Doggett interview, April 30, 1996.

31. Blakey interviewed by Charles Fox, BBC Radio 3, broadcast March 3, 1982.

32. Doggett interview, April 30, 1996.

33. Author's interview with Sweets Edison, November 2, 1992.

34. *Baltimore Afro-American*, October 30, 1937.

Chapter 3

1. Dance, *Earl Hines*, p. 257.
2. Dizzy Gillespie interviewed by Charles Fox for BBC Radio 3, broadcast January 3, 1977.
3. Clayton, pp. 107, 110.
4. Fox interview, January 3, 1977.
5. Author's interview with Bill Dillard, March 24, 1993.
6. Eric Townley, "From Down in Atlanta, Ga. An Interview with John Smith,"*Storyville*, no. 99 (February–March 1982), p. 92.
7. *New York Amsterdam News*, July 13, 1935; *New York Age*, August 10, 1935.
8. Schuller, p. 422.
9. Townley, *Storyville*, no. 99, p 92.
10. Dance, *Swing*, p. 246 (Howard Johnson interview).
11. Dillard interview, March 24, 1993.
12. Letter from John Chilton, March 8, 1994.
13. Howard Rye "Visiting Firemen, 6: Teddy Hill and The Cotton Club Revue,"*Storyville*, no. 100 (April–May 1982), p. 145 ff.
14. Virtually all accounts give the venue correctly as the Moulin Rouge, as evidenced by the review by Hugues Panassié in *Jazz Hot*, no. 18 (June/July 1937) that also includes an advertisement for the Moulin Rouge placed by the band's sponsors, Conn instruments. The exception is *Metronome* (July 1937), which says that Hill opened for six weeks on June 11 at the Café des Ambassadeurs.
15. Clarke/Verdun, p. 25.
16. Hugues Panassié, "Teddy Hill's Orchestra," *Jazz Hot*, no. 18 (June–July 1937), p. 3; Panassié/Gautier, p.112.
17. Coleman, p. 108.
18. Panassié wrote (*Jazz Hot*, no. 18) "John Gillespie has a tremendous swing: his style, very much like Roy Eldridge's, is not my ideal, but he is so sincere that I like him a lot." Undoubtedly, in addition to the reasons given in the text, Panassié's stylistic objections to Dizzy would have eliminated him from the recording sessions. Dizzy's views are quoted in Clarke/Verdun, p. 23.
19. "The only guy who was sort of sotto voce, a real quiet guy, was Smitty—John Smith Jr.—and he had the job of trying to convert a 19-year-old unmarried (w-o-w) trumpet player. And he was with me all the time." Dizzy interviewed by Charles Fox, February 25, 1980.
20. Author's interview with Benny Green, January 1994. This incident is quite possibly apocryphal. There is a very similar anecdote in Joe Darensbourg's *Telling It Like It Is* (Peter Vacher (ed.), London and Basingstoke: Macmillan, 1987), a book full of musicians' anecdotes that Darensbourg applies to himself. There is a strong chance that Dizzy, who also adapted the truth to suit his audience, applied the story to himself for dramatic effect.
21. Clarke/Verdun, p. 27 ff. The authors transcribe Smith's name as "Ro-

land," but *Melody Maker* includes him in the personnel of the revue as "Rollin'" Smith, a spelling confirmed by Madelaine Gautier in *Jazz Hot*, no. 18.

22. Clarke/Verdun, p. 26.

23. Dillard interview, March 24, 1993.

24. Chilton letter, March 8, 1994: "The following was imparted to me during a casual conversation at the Manchester Sports Guild c. 1967. I didn't know the man who told me the story. 'During the Teddy Hill band's visit to Manchester, Dizzy sat in with local musicians at the [Ritz?] ballroom. One of the locals was a trumpeter who had faulty vision which necessitated him having his trumpet bell bent upwards.'" The leader of the band at the Ritz, Rowland Hyatt, stated in *Musical News* (October 1937) that both musicians and dancers from the show made afternoon appearances at the dance hall. See p. 259.

25. Gillespie/Fraser, p. 80.

26. David Griffiths, "Still Very Much on the Scene: The Musical Life Story of Harvey Davis," *Storyville*, no. 115 (October–November 1984), p. 16. Davis lived a few doors away from the Gillespies and recalls the neighborhood. He was for a time a member of the trumpet section of Edgar Hayes's Orchestra, and was later to replace Dizzy in Benny Carter's Band.

27. Various dates are given for this tour, especially in Hennessey. The confirmed dates are that Hayes and the band sailed on the S. S. *Drottingholm* on February 19 (*New York Age*, February 12, 1938, p. 7) and returned on or around May 5 (*Pittsburgh Courier*, May 7, 1938).

28. Bernhardt, pp. 138–93.

29. Clarke/Verdun, p. 29.

30. Gillespie/Fraser, p. 92.

31. Herb Friedwald, "The Latin Tinge: The Alberto Socarras Story," *Storyville*, no. 90 (August–September 1980), p. 224. There is also a useful interview with Socarras in Fraser/Gillespie.

32. Dance, *Swing*, pp. 193 and 221.

33. Fox interview, January 3, 1977.

34. *Storyville*, no. 115, p. 16 ff.

35. A typical piece appears in the *Baltimore Afro-American* of March 11, 1939, reviewing Edgar Hayes's appearance at the Howard Theatre in Washington: "Theatrical rumors have it that the aggregation will be given a spot at the New York World's Fair soon."

36. *New York Age*, August 10, 1935.

Chapter 4

1. Dizzy Gillespie interviewed by Charles Fox for BBC Radio, August 31, 1976.

2. Gillespie/Fraser, p. 93.

3. Ibid., p. 72.

4. Letter to the author from John Chilton, March 8, 1994.

5. Schuller, p. 627.

6. This disc was never released on 78 and found its way onto the market as an LP, Polygram 423248, dated by Brian Rust as February 1936.

7. Schuller, p. 626, notates this: ex. 14. Gillespie himself acknowledges the Allen influence in his comments inserted in Martin Williams's liner notes on Smithsonian R 004: *The Development of an American Artist*: "You might hear traces of 'Hot Lips' Page or 'Red' Allen—but mostly Roy Eldridge."

8. Gillespie/Fraser, p. 72.

Chapter 5

1. *Desert Island Discs*: Dizzy Gillespie interviewed by Roy Plomley, broadcast January 19, 1980. Dizzy actually says "twenty-seven years old" but he was twenty-two at the time he joined Cab and he is meticulous about his age elsewhere in the interview, so this is obviously just a slip.

2. *Baltimore Afro-American*, March 4, 1939, p. 10.

3. Author's interview with Alan Cohen, May 19, 1995.

4. Author's interview with Danny Barker for *A Life in Jazz*, October 1984.

5. Author's interview with Milt Hinton, March 23, 1993.

6. Tanner, p. 11.

7. Author's interview with Jonah Jones, May 25, 1995. A similar account is in *Storyville*, no. 85 (October–November 1979), p. 7.

8. Gillespie/Fraser p. 111. "Dizzy was in Teddy Hill's band when I first heard him. I think he was recommended to me through, if I'm not mistaken, Jonah Jones."

9. Author's interview with Doc Cheatham, September 1991.

10. Hinton, March 23, 1993.

11. Ibid.

12. Gillespie/Fraser, p. 104.

13. Russell, p. 114.

14. Hinton, March 23, 1993.

15. Barker/Shipton, *A Life in Jazz*, p. 164.

16. Gillespie/Fraser, p. 111.

17. Calloway, p. 160.

18. Cheatham/Shipton, p. 35.

19. *Pittsburgh Courier*, March 25, 1939, carries a typical entry on Smith's record-breaking run in Chicago's Blue Fountain Room at the LaSalle Hotel. That would have been instrumental, along with Smith's reputation from his earlier residency at the Onyx Club, in Cab's original request to Jonah to join the band. Further pieces about Smith appeared over the following years, confirming Cab's view that Jones was a hot property.

20. Jones interview, May 25, 1995.

21. Popa, pp. 18–21.

22. Charts of "Pickin' the Cabbage" do not survive in the Calloway Archive at Boston University. However, second and third trumpet parts do survive

for "Paradiddle," in Dizzy's hand (no. 102 in the Calloway pad) and show some interesting harmonic ideas, especially where these two trumpet parts descend with the interval of a flattened fifth between them in the first and second bars after the introduction.

23. Hinton interview, March 23, 1993.
24. Barker/Shipton, *A Life in Jazz*, p. 146.
25. Dates culled from the black press, Franz Hoffman's scrapbooks, and the Cab Calloway Archive at Boston University. Hinton almost certainly telescoped time in his recollections, confusing the year they were at the Cotton Club and jammed at the Uptown House (1939) with the year that Minton's opened (1940) when the band was not at the Cotton Club during the summer.

In 1939, the band was in New York from the July 17 record session with Bauza, through to the recording with Dizzy in New York on August 30. Their last appearance of the year at the Cotton Club was the week beginning on September 15; they then left by September 22 for Hartford, Connecticut. They were back playing in Brooklyn and the Bronx for the first week of October, and were at the Audobon Theatre, 165th and Broadway, during mid-October. They then went to Jamaica, Long Island, for a week, and reached the Palace Theatre, Akron, Ohio, by October 31.

During the equivalent period in 1940, they were in New York for parts of August, cutting two sessions on August 5 and 28 and appearing at the Paramount in Times Square, but union depositions show transfers from Memphis, Nashville, Knoxville, the Meadowbrook Inn (Cedar Grove, New Jersey), Indianapolis, Louisville, and Minneapolis, so they were around far less than the previous year, although it would have been easy for Hinton and Dizzy to get to Minton's after work during the latter part of August and early September, when after leaving the Paramount, they were again at the Flatbush in Brooklyn and the Windsor in the Bronx.

26. Jones interview, May 25, 1995.
27. Barker/Shipton, *A Life in Jazz*, p. 164.
28. Gillespie/Fraser, p. 117.
29. Pearson, p. 208.
30. Ibid.
31. Taylor, p. 121.
32. Jay McShann interviewed by Charles Fox for BBC Radio 3, February 8, 1980.
33. Gillespie/Fraser, p. 118.
34. Pearson, p. 207.
35. Enstice/Rubin, p. 177.
36. Ibid.
37. Jones interview, May 25, 1995.
38. *Lima (Ohio) News*, October 5, 1941. This cutting in one of Calloway's scrapbooks reviews a date not long before Dizzy's final appearance with the band, which had already happened by the time the review was printed.
39. Hinton/Berger, p. 94.

40. Hinton interview, March 23, 1993.
41. *Down Beat*, October 15, 1941.
42. Gillespie/Fraser, p. 111.

Chapter 6

1. Dizzy Gillespie interviewed by Charles Fox, August 31, 1976.
2. Dance, *Jazz Era*, p. 38.
3. "I'll Pray for You," from the Meadowbrook Inn session of July 27, 1940, is a good example.
4. Hinton interview, March 23, 1993.
5. Hinton/Berger, p. 83.
6. Collier, p. 183, gives a succinct account of how Hampton came to join Benny Goodman.
7. For a comprehensive survey of Hampton's recording activities, the author's liner notes to *Lionel Hampton 1929 to 1940* on Robert Parker's Jazz Classics in Digital Stereo series (BBC RPCD 852) released in 1991 summarize the period and comment on tracks from most of the main sessions.
8. Fox interview, August 31, 1976.
9. Hinton interview, March 23, 1993.
10. Lionel Hampton interviewed by Charles Fox for BBC Radio. Transcript of interview dated May 30, 1974.
11. Hampton, p. 70.
12. Hinton interview, March 23, 1993.
13. Fox interview, August 31, 1976.
14. Schuller, p. 346.
15. A not dissimilar idea is used in Gillespie's bebop composition "Salt Peanuts," where the interrupted main theme with its "Salt Peanuts" shout-back is alternated with a straightforward four-four channel.
16. Hennessey, p. 66. "Diz was an instructor as well as a creator in those early days." Other comments from Clarke elsewhere recall Gillespie's pedagogic skill in rhythmic matters, for example, Gitler, *Swing to Bop*, p. 55: "Diz, who plays the drums well, taught all the other drummers my way of playing."
17. Lees, *Waiting For Dizzy*, p. 244.
18. Owens, p. 260.
19. Schuller, p. 346.
20. Schuller, pp. 346–47, describes and notates this piece in detail.
21. Owens, pp. 102–3.

Chapter 7

1. Interview with Charles Fox, August 31, 1976.
2. Barker/Shipton, *A Life in Jazz*, p. 172.
3. 1940 is conventionally accepted as the date of Teddy Hill's arrival as manager, but it was not announced in *Jazz Information* until February 21, 1941, suggesting that his arrival was toward the end of 1940.

4. Gitler, *Swing to Bop*, pp. 60, 82. From this we learn that the apartment block was a musicians' building; Billy Eckstine and Shadow Wilson also lived there. Lorraine used to cook for the musicians who came by, according to Trummy Young. The piano was inherited from Chu Berry after his death in late October 1941.

5. Interview with Charles Fox, February 25, 1980: "Monk and I had been delving into harmony and I'd been looking into Afro-Cuban rhythms . . . I was getting the guys to do like . . . the bass player wasn't doing dung-dung-dung-dung; the bass player was doing figures like a 'Night in Tunisia.' " It would be inaccurate to assume that ostinato bass patterns had not already been used in jazz by this time, however, and Dizzy's ideas are prefigured by Israel Crosby on Teddy Wilson's "Blues in C Sharp Minor" (with Roy Eldridge) recorded on May 14, 1936, Brunswick 7684.

6. Jonathan Finkelman, "Charlie Christian, Bebop, and the Recordings at Minton's," in Berger, Cayer, Morgenstern, Porter, *Annual Review of Jazz Studies*, vol. 6 (Metuchen, N.J.: Scarecrow Press, 1993), p. 196. Further analysis can be found in De Veaux, p. 185. I have followed the late Martin Williams's view that Dizzy's four tracks were recorded at the Uptown House, as confirmed in his liner notes to the issued versions of the tracks on Smithsonian R 004: *The Development of an American Artist*.

7. Enstice/Rubin, p. 177.

8. Finkelman, "Charlie Christian, Bebop, and the Recordings at Mintons," p. 199. This also draws on Denny Brown's analysis of jazz drumming, originally published as a dissertation and later crystallized into his article on "Drum set" for the *New Grove Dictionary of Jazz*.

9. Feather, *Inside Bebop*, p. 8; Hennessey, p. 28. Hennessey himself dismisses this theory as "banal," preferring to see Clarke's innovations as consciously planned and his description of what happened as self-deprecating.

10. Fox interview, August 31, 1976.

11. Fox interview, February 25, 1980.

12. Hennessey includes Clarke's recollection that the residency was at the Cocoanut Grove. Other sources, including both Haskins and Nicholson's biographies of Fitzgerald, suggest Levaggi's, which is what Dizzy told Stanley Dance in the *World of Earl Hines*.

13. By a curious coincidence, McRae went from Ella's band into the Calloway Orchestra, where he replaced Chu Berry, who had been fatally injured in a car crash on the evening of October 27. (An Associated Press wire in Cab's scrapbooks says: "CONNEAUT, Ohio, October 27 AP: Leon Barry [*sic*] and Andrew Brown of New York, saxophonists with Cab Calloway's Orchestra, were injured when their automobile struck a concrete bridge abutment south of here today. Barry, the driver, was taken to hospital with a possible skull fracture, cuts and bruises. Brown was treated for bruises.")

14. Gillespie/Fraser, p. 133.

15. Hennessey, p. 35, gives a clear account of the complex history of the development of this theme.

16. "Sullivan–Carter Combo Clicking," *Baltimore Afro-American*, August 9, 1941; Kelly's Stable residency advertised in *New York Times*, October 29, 1941. Details of acts and dates from the *New Yorker* September 1941–March 1942, passim.

17. Barker/Shipton, *A Life in Jazz*, p. 152.

18. Hawk returned to New York when he again came into Kelly's Stable on Christmas Eve 1942. By then Dizzy was fronting his own band in Philadelphia prior to joining Earl Hines, so it is unlikely that Dizzy worked with Hawk for a few days then, or during Hawk's subsequent residency, which ran until Henry "Red" Allen took over the gig (with Hawk as a sideman) on February 11, 1943 (*New Yorker*, February 13, 1943); but *Metronome* noted that Dizzy worked there with Hawkins in the October 1943 issue: "Dizzy Gillespie, former Earl Hines trumpet is now with Coleman Hawkins" (p. 16), so we can be reasonably sure that this is when the incident related in Dizzy's autobiography took place.

19. The program is listed in *New York Times*, November 2, 1941.

20. Berger, pp. 194–95.

21. Berger, p. 259, quoting interview with Nesuhi Ertegun.

22. Berger, p. 196.

23. Gitler, *Swing to Bop*, p. 60.

24. Clancy, p. 55.

25. Lees, *Leader of the Band*, pp. 109–110.

26. *Metronome*, January 1942, pp. 11 and 47.

27. Gitler, *Swing to Bop*, p. 59.

28. Gillespie/Fraser, p. 154.

29. *Down Beat*, vol. 8, no. 24 (December 15, 1941), p. 4, and David Griffiths, "Still Very Much on the Scene: The Musical Life Story of Harvey Davis,"*Storyville*, no. 115 (October–November 1984), p. 18.

30. Gillespie/Fraser, p. 158.

31. A piece on Hill's London appearances by Steve Race from *Jazz Illustrated* in June 1950 (vol. 1, no. 7) does not make it clear that Race himself actually saw the band, and his description of Gillespie, "the most unpopular man in the band," is clearly based on Feather's book.

32. The *New York Amsterdam News* carries a typical piece by Feather: "London Swing Critic Lines Up Mixed British Swing Ork Here" on December 2, 1939. The "Pooh Bah" jibe came in one of his regular columns for that paper.

33. Feather, *Inside Bebop*, p. 24.

34. The film is listed in Meeker, *Jazz in the Movies* (London: Talisman, 1977). Dizzy's point about "Night in Tunisia" is in Gillespie/Fraser, pp. 171–72.

35. Gillespie/Fraser, p. 106.

36. Ibid., p. 207.

37. *New Yorker* listings, January–March 1942, passim.

38. *New York Amsterdam News*, February 21, 1942, p. 17.

39. Clancy, p. 45.

40. *New York Amsterdam News*, April 11, 1942, p. 17.

41. Ibid., May 23, 1942, p. 17. This details the transfer from Elite to Hit and gives a figure of prerelease orders

42. Data from Howard Rye and Josephine Beaton's search of *International Musician*. Later itinerary from *Pittsburgh Courier*, May 23, 1942, p. 21.

43. J. Patrick, "Al Tinney, Monroe's Uptown House and the Emergence of Modern Jazz in Harlem," *Annual Review of Jazz Studies*, vol. 2 (Metuchen, N.J: Scarecrow Press, 1983).

44. *Metronome* (November 1942), p. 27: "Gillespie, former Calloway and Millinder trumpeter is leading a small all-colored combination at the Downbeat Club, Philadelphia, Pa."

45. Irv Kline, "The Philadelphia Story Part 2," *Jazz FM*, issue 10 (1992), p. 37.

46. *Jazz Information*, September 27, 1942.

47. Gitler, *Jazz Masters of the 40s* p. 72.

48. Smith, *Sideman*, pp. 124–27.

49. Ibid.

50. Ibid. Levey himself, interviewed by Alun Morgan, *Jazz Monthly* (September 1961), recalled: "When I started working with Dizzy, I'd not heard Kenny Clarke or Max Roach. So Dizzy told me how to play and he used to talk about this drummer I'd never heard of before, Shadow Wilson. You can say Dizzy was my first teacher." De Veaux, pp. 17–29, tackles the subject of "Bebop and Race" in a measured review of the arguments surrounding the role of white musicians at this formative stage.

51. *Chicago Defender*, March 6, 1943, p. 13, has the photo of the band from February 27, with Dizzy clearly visible. His recordings from Bob Redcross's room in a Chicago hotel date from February 15. Both men had clearly joined Hines before the April 23, 1943, residency at the Apollo given by Feather in *Inside Bebop*, p. 26. Ira Gitler (*Jazz Masters of the Forties*) dates both men in Hines's band as "early 1943," and although Ross Russell in *Bird Lives* correctly dates the opening of Hines's tour to January 15, 1943, at the Apollo, he does not state categorically that both Bird and Diz were with the band at that pont.

Chapter 8

1. *Desert Island Discs*: Earl Hines interviewed by Roy Plomley, BBC Radio, recorded May 30, 1980.

2. Wilson, pp. 104–5.

3. Hines may have influenced bebop, but not the other way round. "The excellent recordings by his 1945–6 band proved, to me, that bebop hadn't made a great impression on him, although Duke Ellington later told me that the seeds of bebop were in Earl's piano style." Stanley Dance, letter to the author, November 7, 1996.

4. *Chicago Defender*, November 28, 1942.

5. Dizzy Gillespie interviewed by Charles Fox for BBC Radio, August 31, 1976.

6. Details supplied by Howard Rye and Josephine Beaton from their

research into band personnel listed in *International Musician*. A useful list of the band a few weeks later, showing some changes, is in Gourse, p. 21.

7. *Metronome* (March 1942).

8. Gillespie/Fraser, p. 176: "I couldn't swear he was even using or addicted to dope. I couldn't swear on it because I never saw it, and I became as close to him as anybody."

9. Reisner, p. 85.

10. Ibid., p. 108.

11. Ibid., p. 110; Russell, p. 147; Gillespie/Fraser, p. 178.

12. Hines/Plomley interview, May 30, 1980.

13. Gillespie/Fraser, p. 178.

14. Dance, *Earl Hines*, p. 266. Many sources suggest Sarah's date of arrival as April 4, but she was billed with the band as "America's New First Lady of Song" for a military ball that the band played in Boston on March 19 (*Baltimore Afro-American*, March 20, 1943). In a *Down Beat* article from April 15, Hines said that she had joined "about three months" before, suggesting that she joined the band soon after its Apollo residency ending on January 21. This contradicts Gourse, p. 22.

15. Weinstein, passim.

16. A broadcast transcription by Boyd Raeburn survives from late March or early April 1944 with Roy Eldridge playing the trumpet solo—it is discussed in Chapter 11.

17. Dance, *Earl Hines*, p. 260

18. Notes to *Dizzy Gillespie, Vol. 5*, Média 7, by Phillippe Baudoin and Alain Tercinet, summarize the complex history of this tune and its vexing copyright records at the Library of Congress.

19. Gitler, *Jazz Masters*, pp. 72–74.

20. Gitler, *Swing to Bop*, p. 130.

21. Information supplied by Howard Rye and Josephine Beaton.

22. Dizzy Gillespie interviewed by Charles Fox for BBC Radio 3, February 1980.

23. Ibid.

24. Gitler, *Swing to Bop*, p. 95.

25. Gillespie/Fraser, p. 179.

26. Jones, p. 238.

27. Chronology from Dance, *Earl Hines*.

28. Gillespie/Fraser, pp. 152–53; *Metronome* (October 1943), p. 16.

29. Stratemann, pp. 253–54.

30. Stewart, p. 214.

31. Gillespie/Fraser, p. 184. It seems odd, as John Chilton points out in a letter to the author, that Dizzy recalled Cootie Williams as one of the trumpets who gave him the cold shoulder, since Cootie was no longer in Duke's band by this time, but leading his own and soon afterward employing Bud Powell as his pianist.

32. Reisner, p. 181.

33. Author's interview with Billy Taylor, October 31, 1996.

34. *New York Amsterdam News*, December 11, 1943. De Veaux, p. 291, is incorrect in suggesting that Gillespie's name "did not appear on the bill"—it was Pettiford who suffered this fate.

35. Jimmy Butts, "Harlem Speaks," *The Jazz Record*, No. 15 (December 1943), p. 7, lists "Monk, piano, Petiford [*sic*], bass and Lester Young, tenor." Band billed on p. 2 of the same issue as "Dizzy Gillespie Band." In addition to the author's interview with Taylor, see Gitler, *Swing to Bop*, pp. 123-24. Büchmann-Møller, in *You Just Fight for Your Life*, p. 110, notes "the drummer was Harold 'Doc' West, later replaced by Max Roach" but other sources including Roach himself give the impression that Roach was there virtually from the outset.

36. Taylor interview, October 31, 1996.

37. Groves/Shipton, pp. 31–34, covers this segment of Powell's life.

38. Author's interview with Al Casey, October 31, 1996.

39. Taylor interview October 31, 1996.

40. Ibid.

41. Jon Faddis quoted in insert notes to *Dizzy's Diamonds: The Best of the Verve Years* (Verve 314 513 875-2).

42. Quotes from Gillespie/Fraser, and additional material from Mark Gardner: "George Wallington—Obituary," *Jazz Journal International*, vol. 46, no. 5 (May 1993).

43. Ibid.

44. Author's interview with Ray Brown, April 11, 1996.

45. Haydon/Marks, p. 87.

46. Chilton, *Song of the Hawk*, p. 208.

47. Taylor interview, October 31, 1996.

48. Roach interviewed by Charles Fox for BBC Radio 3 and broadcast in *Drum Beats*, December 1989–January 1990.

Chapter 9

1. *Desert Island Discs*: Hines interviewed by Roy Plomley, BBC Radio, recorded May 30, 1980.

2. Taylor, p. 118.

3. Ulanov, p. 270.

4. Ibid.

5. Gillespie/Fraser, pp. 202–3.

6. Ibid.; Gitler, *Swing to Bop*, p. 124.

7. *The Jazz Record*, no. 18 (March 1944), p. 2.

8. *New York Age*, March 18, 1944, p. 10; March 25, 1955, p. 10; Gillespie did appear at the Downbeat in May 1944 as a Monday night guest with Coleman Hawkins's band, reported in the *New York Age*, May 27, 1944.

9. Eckstine movements and Pettiford dates from *New York Age*, April 15, 1944; May 6, 1944; May 27, 1944. The last notice of Dizzy and Budd

Johnson's "swingsational band" at the Yacht Club is *New York Age*, April 29, 1944, noting Coleman Hawkins as the other band. Gitler, *Jazz Masters*, p. 76, suggests that Dizzy was replaced on Kirby's broadcasts, but the Média 7 Gillespie edition includes the airshots of May 19–24.

10. Art Hodes, ed. by Chadwick Hansen, *Hot Man* (Oxford, Miss.: Bayou Press, 1992), pp. 61–62.

11. Ibid. p. 60.

12. Gitler, *Swing to Bop*, p. 127.

13. Gillespie/Fraser, p. 204.

14. "Eckstein" is the spelling in almost all billings for the Hines Orchestra in 1943, and in the *New York Age*, April 15, 1944; September 23, 1944; *Chicago Defender*, August 19, 1944; "Eckstine" is the spelling in *New York Age*, May 27, 1944; September 2, 1944; *Chicago Defender*, November 18, 1944.

15. See Feather, *Inside Bebop*, and also quotes from Feather in Jim Burns "The Billy Eckstine Band," *Jazz Monthly*, vol. 13, no. 11 (January 1968), p. 6.

16. G. Hoefer, "The First Bop Big Band," *Down Beat* (July 29, 1965).

17. Ted Yates, "Billy Eckstine, Singer and Orchestra Leader Being Mentioned for Hollywood," *New York Age*, September 2, 1944, p. 10.

18. Ibid. The reason Deluxe was only "able" to supply a specified number of discs was because, in common with all other record companies, it was allocated a shellac ration; the raw materials for record manufacture were largely imported to the United States and subject to wartime restrictions. It is often argued that these shortages contributed to the length of the AFM ban on recording—see Chapter 10. De Veaux, p. 342, contains interesting commentary and transcriptions from "Good Jelly Blues," including pointing out the link between the opening theme and Rachmaninoff's Prelude in C Sharp Minor.

19. Jones, p. 239.

20. Gitler, *Swing to Bop*, p. 125; J. Burns, "The Billy Eckstine Band," *Jazz Monthly*, vol. 13, no. 11 (January 1968), p. 6.

21. J. Burns, op. cit.

22. Jones, p. 240.

23. *Chicago Defender*, August 19, 1944, p. 9.

24. Feather, *Inside Bebop*, p. 30.

25. Art Blakey interviewed by Charles Fox for BBC Radio, recorded February 18, 1982, and broadcast on March 3, 1982.

26. Ibid. In various other sources, Eckstine himself suggests that the band used to shoot at cows (not crows) through the bus windows, a suggestion that drew some incredulity from readers when I incorporated it in his obituary for *The Guardian*.

27. Gitler, *Swing to Bop*, p. 128.

28. Details of Dizzy's draft record from Selective Service System, Arlington, Virginia.

29. Letter to the author with drafts of an autobiography, October 11, 1988.

Chapter 10

1. Russell, pp. 156, 191, et seq.
2. Continental was founded in early 1944 by an ex-Victor artists and repertoire man, Sascha Gabor. Manor was a successor to Regis Records who recorded "the elite in sepian blues-spirituals-jazz," and a part of the Clark Record Company of Newark, managed by Irving Berman, who later went on to record more modern jazz on his Arco label in the 1950s. Guild went out of business in late 1945; its masters passed to Musicraft and were later issued on other labels. There are brief histories of all three labels in the *New Grove Dictionary of Jazz*, but Mark Gardner's statement in his entry for Guild that it "was the first company to record Charlie Parker and Dizzy Gillespie together" is incorrect because their first discs were for Continental on January 4, 1945, under Clyde Hart's name.
3. Airshots of Dizzy with Raeburn are included on the Média 7 edition of Gillespie, Volume 5, and producer Alain Tercinet believes "he was often a member of the orchestra at this time, even undertaking a brief tour in its ranks." Dizzy was reported in *Down Beat* (February 15, 1945) with Raeburn at the Apollo, and earlier he had broadcast on January 17 and 24, as well as appearing on two studio dates on January 26 and 27.
4. J. Burns; "Early Birks," *Jazz Journal*, vol. 23, no. 3 (March 1971), p. 19.
5. Jordan, from the unedited manuscript.
6. There were various different names used; one of the most eccentric turned up the following year with clarinetist Tony Scott, for whom Dizzy adopted the pseudonym "B. Bopstein."
7. "Omission of Basie and Sgt. Clayton From 'All American Jazz Concert' A Mystery" *New York Age*, February 10, 1945, p. 10.
8. Balliett, p. 21.
9. Vail, p. 12 (uncredited press cutting).
10. Russell, p. 181.
11. Dizzy Gillespie interviewed by Charles Fox for BBC Radio, broadcast January 3, 1977.
12. Personnel (captioning a photograph) from Feather, *Inside Bebop*, p. 34. Another, similar caption is in Vail, p. 13.
13. Changes are noted in the interviews in Gillespie/Fraser, pp. 222–30.
14. Fox interview, January 3, 1977.
15. Haydon/Marks, p. 90.
16. *Pittsburgh Courier*, June 30, 1945, p. 13. This gives the band itinerary in the form of a panel advertisement. They played a mixture of armories and auditoriums in the Carolinas, Tennessee, Florida, Georgia, Alabama, Louisiana, Texas, Oklahoma, Kansas, Missouri, and Ohio.
17. Gillespie/Fraser, p. 223.
18. Feather, *Inside Bebop*, p. 34.
19. *Pittsburgh Courier*, October 13, 1945, p. 10; November 10, 1945, p. 16 (both from the "Rowe" gossip column)

20. Author's interview with Bill Doggett, April 30, 1996.

21. Author's interview with Ray Brown, April 11, 1996.

22. The only element of doubt in Brown's account is that almost immediately after he remembers leaving Snookum Russell in Florida, the band made a tour to the north and passed right by New York as they traveled between Syracuse, New York, on November 22 and Richmond, Virginia, on November 23, 1945. But it is sensible to assume that Brown did not wait for Russell to pay for the trip north and left a few weeks earlier than this at his own expense.

23. The reminiscences by Brown are all from my April 11, 1996 interview. Powell's medical history is discussed in Groves/Shipton, which also contains a full discography of Powell's work.

24. Lees, *Peterson*, p. 138.

25. Milt Jackson interviewed by Charles Fox for BBC Radio 3, May 6, 1976, broadcast May 31, 1976.

26. Feather, *From Satchmo to Miles*, p. 161.

27. Chilton, *Song of the Hawk*, p. 224 et seq.

28. Porter, pp. 53–56.

29. Ibid.

30. George Orendorff interviewed by Peter Vacher (who kindly supplied the transcript). Orendorff's views about the new jazz are consistent with those of most of his generation, such as Kid Ory, who allegedly lamented the fact that Coleman Hawkins "no longer played the way he used to" during Hawk's stay on the Coast.

31. Gordon, p. 6.

32. Bob Porter and Mark Gardner, "The California Cats" [interview with Sonny Criss], *Jazz Monthly* (April 1968).

33. Gioia, p. 20.

34. Author's interview with Ray Brown, April 11, 1996.

35. Gillespie/Fraser, pp. 248–49.

Chapter 11

1. Author's interview with Ray Brown, April 11, 1996.

2. Gitler, *Swing to Bop*, pp. 149–50.

3. Dizzy Gillespie interviewed by Charles Fox for BBC Radio, recorded February 25, 1980.

4. Wilber, p. 49.

5. Alain Tercinet, notes to Média 7, *Dizzy Gillespie, Volume 5, 1945*, p. 13.

6. McRae, p. 38.

7. Unbroadcast sections of a BBC Radio interview between Dizzy Gillespie and Charles Fox, transcribed by Radio Recording Services, August 31, 1976.

8. Ibid.

9. Gillespie/Fraser, p. 217.

10. Fox interview, August 31, 1976.

11. Gillespie/Fraser, p. 254.

12. Joe Marsala interviewed by Leonard Feather, *Down Beat 14th Yearbook* (1969).

13. Owens, p. 14.

14. James Lincoln Collier, *The Reception of Jazz in America: A New View* (Brooklyn: I.S.A.M. monographs, no. 27, 1988), p. 2.

15. André Hodier, "Vers un renouveau de la musique de jazz?" *Jazz Hot*, no. 7 (May–June 1946).

16. *Down Beat* (June 15, 1945), reprinted in Vail. "Don" was staff writer Don C. Haynes.

17. *Down Beat* (December 10, 1945).

18. *Down Beat* (August 1, 1945).

19. Hodier, op cit. (translated by the author).

20. Dance, *World of Swing*, p. 327 (interview with Ram Ramirez).

21. Ulanov, p. 271.

22. Ibid., pp. 274–75.

23. "Broadway Chatters," *New York Age*, June 2, 1945, p. 10. The piece suggested that Dizzy was to star in a "negro movie musical" for Bud Pollard called *Y' Hear Gabriel!* This does not appear to have happened.

24. Tony Williams, notes to *Red Norvo's Fabulous Jam Session*, Spotlite SPJ 127.

25. John Mehegan, notes to *The Charlie Parker Story*, Savoy MG 12079.

26. Russell, p. 195.

27. By October, Parker's quartet no longer regularly included Roach or Russell. Photographs and ads show Stan Levey on drums and Leonard Gaskin on bass, with Sir Charles Thompson on piano.

28. Owens, p. 18.

29. Besides Owens's analysis mentioned above, there is more on this session in Groves/Shipton, pp. 34–35.

30. Priestley, *Charlie Parker*, pp 29–30.

31. Lees, *Waiting for Dizzy*, p. 239.

32. This session is preserved in its entirety on Spotlite SPJ132. I have not devoted space to a review because the session was not of the same historical importance as those discussed in detail. Max Harrison's excellent notes to the Spotlite issue provide a concise and informed commentary, pointing out that "Dynamo A" and "B" are both versions of "Dizzy Atmosphere," and noting about Dizzy: "His ideas are finely honed but, as the alternative takes prove, wholly spontaneous, and his use of phrases at double tempo, interplaying with the basic pulse is masterly."

33. Ulanov, pp. 272–73.

34. Stan Levey interviewed by Alun Morgan, *Jazz Monthly* (September 1961).

Chapter 12

1. Milt Jackson interviewed by Charles Fox for BBC Radio, May 6, 1976.

2. Ray Brown interview, April 11, 1996.

3. The majority of sources, backed up by reviews, confirm Parker's presence, even though he is listed in several discographies as still recording with Billy Eckstine's band in March 1946. Dizzy's autobiography names Sonny Stitt as the additional member of the group, but it would appear that he joined later in the year, in time for the May 15 Musicraft session, and thereafter stayed only intermittently.

4. *Chicago Defender*, March 9, 1946, "Band Routes," p. 25.

5. Feather, *From Satchmo to Miles*, p. 162.

6. *New York Times*, January 5, 1947.

7. Stanley Dance, "J. C. Heard," *Jazz Journal International*, xxxix/11 (November 1986), p. 10.

8. Dance, *Earl Hines*, p. 259.

9. Taylor, p. 179.

10. Dance, *World of Swing*, p. 247.

11. Taylor, p. 232.

12. John Shaw, "Kenny Clarke," *Jazz Journal*, vol. 22, no. 10 (October 1969), p. 4.

13. Author's interview with Ray Brown, November 19, 1995.

14. Ibid.

15. John Shaw, "Kenny Clarke," *Jazz Journal*, vol. 22, no. 10 (October 1969), p. 4.

16. Jack Cooke, "Sixteen Men Stone Dead," *Jazz Monthly*, no. 175 (September 1969), p. 2 ff.

17. Dance, *World of Swing*, p. 247.

18. Ibid.

19. Ibid., p. 222.

20. Milt Jackson interviewed by Charles Fox for BBC Radio, May 6, 1976.

21. *Metronome* (January 1946). A discussion of Monk's playing in Hawk's band is in Chilton, *Song of the Hawk*, p. 233.

22. Author's interview with Ray Brown, April 11, 1996.

23. "MJQ Views—on Bebop's Beginning," *Crescendo International*, vol. 24, no. 9 (September 1987), p. 28.

24 Author's interviews with Ray Brown, November 19, 1995 and April 11, 1996.

25. Milt Jackson interviewed by Charles Fox for BBC Radio, May 6, 1976.

26. *New York Amsterdam News*, April 19, 1947, p. 21.

27. Author's interview with James Moody, May 19, 1995.

28. Author's interview with James Moody, July 6, 1995.

29. Gitler quoted in *Jazz Times* (October 1992), p. 27; Parker in a conversation with the author February 18, 1997; Gleason in notes to *Dizzy Gillespie: In the Beginning*, Prestige PR 24030 (issued 1973).

30. Author's interviews with Ray Brown, November 19, 1995, and April 11, 1996.

31. Ibid.

32. Dance, *Count Basie*, p. 193.

33. Author's interview with Benny Golson, April 2, 1996.

34. Letter from Grover Sales, October 22, 1996.

35. Clayton, p. 130.

36. Apollo billing from *New York Age*, June 29, 1946; Chicago billing from *Chicago Defender*, July 20, 1946.

37. *Chicago Defender*, October 5, 1946.

38. This almost certainly means that those of Dizzy's friends and family who recall in his autobiography seeing him on tour with a big band caught him in the previous year's Hep-sations tour, which included seven dates in the Carolinas.

39. *New York Age*, November 9, 1946.

40. "Billie Holiday Sounds Off Against Segregation in Gotham Niteries," *Baltimore Afro-American*, December 21, 1946; "June Eckstine on $2000 Bail on 'Dope' Moral Charges," *Baltimore Afro-American*, January 18, 1947—an article that summarizes charges against Mrs. Eckstine of drug abuse and committing acts of sodomy.

41. Haskins, *Ella Fitzgerald*, pp. 86–88.

42. Nicholson, p. 94.

43. Author's interviews with Ray Brown, November 19, 1995, and April 11, 1996.

44. Milt Jackson interviewed by Charles Fox for BBC Radio, May 6, 1976.

45. Gitler, *Jazz Masters*, p. 60, quoting a *Down Beat* interview with Dizzy.

46. *Time*, October 11, 1948.

47. Ulanov, p. 280.

48. Barnet, p. 143.

49. Dance, *Count Basie*, p. 340.

50. Dizzy Gillespie interviewed by Charles Fox for BBC Radio, August 31, 1976.

51. Ibid.

52. George Russell interviewed by Ian Carr for BBC Radio, June 29, 1992.

53. Author's interviews with Ray Brown, November 19, 1995, and April 11, 1996.

54. Author's interview with Benny Bailey, April 27, 1993.

55. Ibid.

56. *Chicago Defender*, December 18, 1948.

57. Clarke/Verdun, p. 26.

58. Author's interview with Benny Bailey, April 27, 1993.

59. *New York Amsterdam News*, February 21, 1948, p. 25.

60. Article from *Jazz Hot* reprinted in notes by Claude Carrière and Don Waterhouse to *Pleyel 48*, Vogue 74321134152.

61. Vian, p. 30.

62. Ibid., p. 31.

63. Hennessey, p. 71.

64. Vian, p. 31.

65. Ibid., p. 33.

66. Author's interview with Benny Bailey, April 27, 1993.

67. *New York Times*, December 5, 1948.

68. Michael Levin and John S. Wilson, "No Bop Roots in Jazz: Parker," *Down Beat* (September 9, 1949).

69. John S. Wilson, "Bird Wrong; Bop Must Get A Beat: Diz," *Down Beat* (October 7, 1949).

70. Dizzy Gillespie interviewed by Charles Fox for BBC Radio, August 31, 1976.

Chapter 13

1. James Moody interviewed by Steve Voce at the Nice Jazz Festival 1983. (An article based on this interview appeared in *Jazz Journal* in June 1983, but I have referred to the original tape of the discussion, kindly made available by Steve Voce.)

2. Gillespie/Fraser, pp. 267–68.

3. Voce/Moody interview.

4. Priestley, *Charlie Parker*, p. 34.

5. Author's interview with Ray Brown, April 11, 1996.

6. Author's interview with Joe Wilder, March 24, 1997.

7. Author's interview with Benny Bailey, April 27, 1993.

8. Author's interview with Joe Wilder, March 24, 1997.

9. J. Simmen, "George 'Big Nick' Nicholas," *Jazz Journal*, vol. 25, no. 9, (September 1972), p. 6.

10. McRae, pp. 44–45.

11. Dance, *Duke Ellington*, p. 175.

12. Priestley, *Charlie Parker*, pp. 37–39.

13. Cole, p. 43.

14. Thomas, p. 45.

15. Ibid.

16. Simkins, p. 41.

17. Pepper, p. 112

18. Dance, *Duke Ellington*, p. 166.

19. Steve Race, "Dizzy Gillespie," *Jazz Illustrated*, vol. 1, no. 7 (June 1950), p. 12.

Chapter 14

1. Dizzy, billed as "the man with the trumpet, the big glasses and . . . the infectious personality" was alongside the "Real Gone Gal" Nellie Lutcher, singing her hit songs "Fine Brown Frame," "Cool Wafer," and her theme, "Real Gone." Ballad singer Johnny Hartman, who had recently left the band to go

solo, was reunited with Dizzy for the week, alongside Joe Carroll. The comedians Spider Bruce "and his gang of laugh getters" were accompanied by the novelty skaters Virgie and Elree. *New York Amsterdam News*, March 25, 1950.

2. Crow, *Jazz Anecdotes*, p. 309.

3. Tormé, p. 92.

4. *New York Age*, September 2, 1950.

5. Crow, *Jazz Anecdotes*, p. 309.

6. Chambers, p. 99.

7. Davis, p. 153.

8. Ibid., p. 73.

9. Gillespie/Fraser, p. 359.

10. Clarke/Verdun, p. 58.

11. Leonard Feather, *Dee Gee Days*, notes to Savoy CD ZD 70517.

12. Clarke/Verdun, p. 58.

13. Büchmann-Møller, p. 115.

14. Cole, p. 27.

15. Initially Bird and his string section opened opposite Slim Gaillard and Erroll Garner, but for the week from March 29, the All Star Quintet became the main attraction.

16. Paudras, pp. 19–21.

17. Alun Morgan, *Professor Bop*, notes to Charly Le Jazz CD 25.

18. Gitler, *Jazz Masters*, p. 61.

19. Feather, *Dee Gee Days*, notes to Savoy CD ZD 70517.

20. Ruppli, *Savoy*, pp. 240–242, is a listing of all Dee Gee sessions acquired by Savoy.

21. Milt Jackson interviewed by Charles Fox for BBC Radio, May 6, 1976.

22. Smith, *Pure at Heart*, p. 26 ff.

23. The sibilant "Nobody Knows" and jumping "Bluest Blues" are Louis Jordan-like vehicles for singer Joe Carroll, with Dizzy playing relaxed, behind-the-beat trumpet, stretching briefly into the upper register in "Bluest Blues," but betraying nothing of the innovative soloist who had easily kept pace with Charlie Parker at Birdland only a few months before. The rest of the session is made up of standards, including a delicate and sensitive reading of "Star Dust" by Dizzy and the novelty of Milt Jackson singing "Time on My Hands" over a backdrop of his own organ-playing and Stuff Smith's violin obbligato. "Nobody Knows" is not, as Dizzy suggests in his autobiography, anything to do with the spiritual "Nobody Knows the Trouble I've Seen."

24. Harrison, p. 94.

25. Büchmann-Møller, p. 156, quoting *Metronome* (October 1951).

26. Letter to the author, July 6, 1994.

27. *New York Amsterdam News*, April 18, 1952, and April 25, 1952, p. 8, advertisement for Snookie's Nite Spot.

28. *New York Age*, April 12, 1952, p. 16.

29. Alain Tercinet, *Dizzy in Paris 1952–3*, liner notes to Blue Star 80713.

30. Don Waterhouse, *Dizzy Songs*, liner notes to Vogue CD 7432115464-2.

31. "Blue Moon" has a most unusual effect when Dizzy reenters after the piano solo, as he rapidly repeats one note but alters his fingering for each repetition, minutely changing the timbre. Fingering and valve control were an interest of Dizzy's bordering on an obsession, as John Chilton discovered during a conversation with Benny Carter: "I recall discussing a method of playing the scale of C using a hundred different fingering combinations. Benny said instantly, 'Oh yes, Dizzy knows all about that—he's got all that inside his head.' One technical quirk of Dizzy's was that he used paraffin [kerosene] to lubricate his valves, and my own observation was that his fingering technique was awesome." Letter from Chilton to the author, March 8, 1994.

32. This is partly due to the head arrangements for "Dizzy Song" and "Wrap Your Troubles in Dreams," which have some cleverly understated voicings for two saxophones and trombone below Dizzy's lead and partly due to Pierre Lemarchand's subtle brushwork.

33. McRae, p. 62; Gillespie/Fraser, p. 360.

34. *Chicago Defender*, June 14, 1952, p. 16.

35. *Jazz Monthly* (April 1965).

36. *New York Amsterdam News*, November 1, 1952.

37. Author's interview with Ahmad Jamal, January 10, 1994.

38. McRae, p. 61.

39. *Jazz Monthly* (April 1965).

40. *Jazz Monthly* (May 1968) summarizes the problem.

41. Owen Peterson, "The Massey Hall Concert," *Jazz Journal*, vol. 23, no. 3 (March 1970), p. 8.

42. Groves/Shipton, pp. 53–56.

43. Max Roach interviewed by Charles Fox for BBC Radio, December 1989.

44. Owen Peterson (op. cit.) has an excellent analysis of most of Dizzy and Bird's solos, including attribution of a large number of the quotes that they employ. The comments from Dizzy are from the interview by Charles Fox for BBC Radio, February 25, 1980.

45. Reisner, p. 195.

46. Dizzy Gillespie interviewed by Charles Fox for BBC Radio, August 31, 1976.

47. Max Roach interviewed by Charles Fox for BBC Radio, December 1989.

48. Ibid.

Chapter 15

1. Gillespie/Fraser, p. 367.

2. Ralph J. Gleason, "The Rhythm Section," *This World*, February 12, 1954.

3. Ibid., p. 337.

4. Stan Kenton interviewed by Brian Priestley for BBC Radio, March 1975.

5. Ibid. Dizzy's repertoire included "Festival in Cuba" and "Cubana Be–Cubana Bop" from September 1947; Kenton first recorded "Cuban Carnival" (with Machito on maracas) on December 6 that year.

6. Maggin, p. 128.

7. Gillespie/Fraser, p. 364.

8. Steve Voce, "Buddy Childers—Part 2," *Jazz Journal International*, vol. 50, no. 11 (November 1997), p. 12.

9. Gillespie/Fraser, p. 366.

10. Russell, p. 323.

11. Nat Hentoff, "Dizzy Designs New Trumpet, Claims Improvement in Tone," *Down Beat* (July 11, 1954), p. 29.

12. *Desert Island Discs*: Dizzy Gillespie interviewed by Roy Plomley, broadcast January 19, 1980.

13. Letter to the author, March 8, 1994.

14. Pat Brand, "On the Beat," *Melody Maker*, November 24, 1956, p. 9; December 1, 1956, p. 9.

15. Jon Faddis interviewed by Kenny Washington, liner notes to *Dizzy's Diamonds* (Verve 314 513 875-2).

16. Author's interview with Ray Brown, April 1996.

17. Dizzy interviewed for *Norman's Conquest*, a history of Jazz at the Philharmonic transmitted on BBC Radio April–June 1994.

18. Ibid.

19. Feather, *From Satchmo to Miles*, p. 173 ff.

20. Author's interview with Illinois Jacquet, July 11, 1992.

21. Ibid.

22. Dizzy Gillespie interviewed by Charles Fox for BBC Radio, August 31, 1976.

23. McRae, p. 77.

24. Feather, *From Satchmo to Miles*, p. 180.

25. *Boston Sunday Herald*, October 9, 1955

26. Conversation with Voce, January 12, 1998.

27. Lees, *Peterson*, pp. 65–67, et seq.

28. David Aaberg, "Dizzy Gillespie's and Roy Eldridge's Trumpet Battle on 'Blue Moon,'" *Down Beat* (September 1996), p. 64.

29. Alun Morgan, liner notes to *Trumpet Kings* (Verve 2683 022).

30. Lees, *Peterson*, p. 115.

31. Author's interview with Ray Bryant, October 16, 1993.

32. Author's interview with Benny Golson, April 2, 1996.

33. Norman Granz, liner notes to *Afro* (Columbia CX 10002).

Chapter 16

1. John S. Wilson, "Bird Wrong; Bop Must Get A Beat: Diz," op. cit.

2. Jones began arranging while playing alongside Clifford Brown in the

Hampton trumpet section. "I loved the way Brownie played," he recalled. "I said, to play like you I would have to play all the time. He loved the way I wrote, and he said to write like that I would have to write all the time. I had always loved the idea of arranging, right since I was a small kid, but that was when I decided to concentrate on it." K. Mathieson, "Quincy Jones: The Dude Is Back," *Wire*, vol. 82, no. 3 (New Year 1991), p. 50.

3. Alfred Appel Jr., "Trois mois du jazz au Birdland," *Jazz Hot*, no. 127 (December 1957), pp. 12–13.

4. Sheridan, pp. 359–60.

5. Brian Priestley, "Big Band Sound of Dizzy Gillespie" (liner notes to Verve 2317 080).

6. Basin Street residency noted in *New York Amsterdam News*, November 12, 1955; the same source lists the Birdland gig (opposite the Commanders) in the issue of January 7, 1956.

7. Gillespie/Fraser, p. 414; Alun Morgan, "The Best of the Dizzy Gillespie Big Bands" (liner notes to Verve VLP 9076).

8. Gillespie/Fraser, p. 416.

9. Ibid., p. 417.

10. *Pittsburgh Courier*, June 2, 1956.

11. Ibid.

12. Ibid.

13. *New York Amsterdam News*, April 21 and May 19, 1956.

14. *Pittsburgh Courier*, June 9, 1956.

15. *New York Amsterdam News*, April 21 and May 19, 1956.

16. McRae, p. 70.

17. *Pittsburgh Courier*, June 9, 1956.

18. Ibid.

19. Alun Morgan, "The Best of the Dizzy Gillespie Big Bands" (liner notes to Verve VLP 9076). Interestingly, despite a protracted correspondence with Jones, Horricks does not quote this letter in his book on Dizzy. He does report Quincy as saying: "Diz was always with cobras or camels or something for publicity purposes, but really I think he enjoyed every minute of it" (p. 45).

20. Dizzy Gillespie interviewed by Charles Fox for BBC Radio, August 31, 1976.

21. Basie's version was cut in Chicago on January 23–24, 1959, and issued on Roulette R52024. Jones offered one interviewer an illuminating view as to why the two treatments sound so different, despite being fundamentally the same chart: "I usually write for specific players. There are some pieces which are pretty standard, and might fit any band, but for the most part I like to take the Duke Ellington approach and write exactly for the people you have." K. Mathieson, op. cit., p. 50.

22. Author's interview with Benny Golson, April 2, 1996.

23. Author's interview with Lalo Schifrin, January 9, 1998.

24. Dance, *Count Basie*, p. 206.

25. Horricks, p. 48.

Chapter 17

1. *Chicago Defender*, January 5, 1957.
2. *Esquire* article quoted in *Pittsburgh Courier*, May 18, 1957, p. 23.
3. Dizzy's appointment here dated from August 11, 1957, not in 1955 as Dizzy suggests in Gillespie/Fraser, p. 403. Correct dating is in "Leading Jazz Men on School Faculty," *New York Amsterdam News*, April 20, 1957.
4. *Village Voice*, April 2, 1958.
5. *Chicago Defender*, August 18, 1959.
6. Gillespie/Fraser, p. 379.
7. Barker/Shipton, *Bolden*, p. 127.
8. Gillespie/Fraser, p. 414.
9. *Chicago Defender*, September 14, 1963, pp. 1–2.
10. Hultin, p. 44.
11. Philippe Adler, "Dizzypoppin,'" *Jazz Hot*, no. 180 (October 1962), p. 17 ff.
12. George Kanzler, "Sound Waves in Jazz: Jeanie Bryson Enters the Limelight with a Voice and Style That Bring the Lyrics to Life," *The Star Ledger* (New Jersey), September 6, 1990.
13. James T. Jones IV, "Jazz Singer Claims Dizzy's Musical Legacy," *USA Today*, February 11, 1993.
14. Ibid.
15. Richard D. Smith, "Dizzy's Daughter Has Her Own Career in Jazz," *New York Times*, March 28, 1993.
16. "Going Public as Her Father's Child," *USA Today*, February 11, 1993.
17. Ibid.
18. Author's interview with Connie Bryson, January 26, 1998.
19. Author's interview with Jeanie Bryson, January 22, 1994.
20. Notice of Agreement, Family Court of New York, May 26, 1965, Docket No. 1218/1964.
21. Author's interview with Jeanie Bryson, January 22, 1994.
22. Hentoff, p. 82.
23. Author's interview with Bob Cunningham, March 23, 1993.
24. *Chicago Defender*, September 14, 1963, pp. 1–2.
25. Ibid.
26. *New York Amsterdam News*, January 25, 1958.
27. Junior Mance interviewed by Gene Lees, letter to the author, March 1997.
28. Author's interview with Art Davis, June 1, 1994.
29. Val Wilmer, "Art Davis: A Struggle for Recognition," *Jazz Monthly*, vol. 7, no. 12 (February 1962).
30. Cole, p. 3.
31. Junior Mance interviewed by Gene Lees; letter to the author, March 1997.
32. The band opened at the Regal on Friday, August 14, for one week.

Chicago Defender, August 15, 1959, p. 14. Also on the bill: Dorothy Donegan and Timmy Rogers; the movie was *Warlock*, starring Richard Widmark, Henry Fonda, Dorothy Malone, and Anthony Quinn. This shows that even as late as 1959 Dizzy was appearing as part of variety programs at major U.S. theatres, as he had done thirty years earlier with Calloway.

33. Leo Wright, with Kevin Lambert, *God Is My Booking Agent* (forthcoming from Cassell, London and Washington).

34. Dizzy Gillespie interviewed by Charles Fox for BBC Radio, August 31, 1976.

35. Irving Townsend, "Ellington Jazz Party" (liner notes to Columbia CK 40712).

36. McRae, p. 81.

37. Leo Wright, with Kevin Lambert, op. cit.

38. Author's interview with Lalo Schifrin, January 9, 1998.

39. Gunther Schuller, "Gillespiana" (liner notes to Verve 314 519 809-2).

40. All quoted in John McDonough, "Gillespiana" (liner notes to Verve 314 519 809-2).

41. *Baltimore Afro-American*, February 18, 1961.

42. Author's interview with Lalo Schifrin, January 9, 1998.

43. Val Wilmer, "Art Davis: A Struggle for Recognition," op. cit.

44. Author's interview with Art Davis, June 1, 1994.

45. Mort Fega, "The Dizzy Gillespie Big Band," reprinted in "Gillespiana" (liner notes to Verve 314 519 809-2).

46. *Baltimore Afro-American*, September 2, 1961, p. 15.

47. Brian Priestley, review of Dizzy's band's November 28, 1965, concert in *Jazz Monthly*, vol. 11, no. 12 (February 1966).

48. Author's interview with Bob Cunningham, March 23, 1993.

49. Leo Wright, with Kevin Lambert, op. cit.

50. Author's interview with Bob Cunningham, March 23, 1993.

51. Quoted in Dan Morgenstern, "Dizzy Gillespie and the Big Band" (liner notes to *The New Continent*, Trip TLP 5584).

Chapter 18

1. Lees, *Waiting for Dizzy*, p. 245.

2. Mark Gardner, "The Ebullient Mr Gillespie" (review), *Jazz Journal*, vol. 24, no. 11 (November 1971).

3. Crow, *Jazz Anecdotes*, p. 142; Hentoff, *Listen to the Stories*, p. 86; Leo Wright, with Kevin Lambert, op. cit.

4. Dizzy Gillespie interviewed by Charles Fox for BBC Radio, August 31, 1976.

5. Crow, *Jazz Anecdotes*, pp. 311–12.

6. *Wire*, no. 9 (November 1984), p. 33.

7. Lyons quoted in Ross Firestone, "Dizzy for President" (liner notes to Douglas ADC1).

8. Clarke/Verdun, p. 65.

9. Ross Firestone, "Dizzy for President" (liner notes to Douglas ADC1).

10. "Dizzy for President" (Douglas ADC1) band 2.

11. Gillespie/Fraser, p. 460.

12. Clarke/Verdun, p. 65.

13. Dizzy Gillespie interviewed by Charles Fox for BBC Radio, February 28, 1980.

14. Ibid.

15. *Chicago Defender,* June 20, 1964; Monterey billing from Baltimore *Afro-American,* July 18, 1964.

16. Advertisement and review from *Chicago Defender,* June 19, 1965.

17. Village Gate dates from *New York Amsterdam News,* April 10, 1965, and *Village Voice* April 15, 24, and May 1; Metropole details (Dizzy appeared alongside the Watusi Girls) from *New York Amsterdam News,* June 19, 1965. Dizzy's quintet had also topped the bill at an All Star Carnegie Hall concert on March 27 to remember Charlie Parker, ten years after his death.

18. Don DeMichael, "Monterey 1965," *Down Beat* (November 4, 1965). Armstrong was, in fact, only sixty-four in 1965, as recent research on his birth-date has proved.

19. Ibid.

20. Taylor, p. 129.

21. Barry McRae, "Dizzy Gillespie at Ronnie Scott's: Jazz in Britain," *Jazz Journal,* vol. 28, no. 1 (January 1975), p. 19.

22. Gillespie/Fraser, p. 472.

23. *Pittsburgh Courier,* July 16, 1966, p. 13.

24. Ibid., and Dan Morgenstern, "Newport Trumpet Workshop," *Down Beat* (August 11, 1966).

25. Ibid.

26. Author's interview with Chuck Folds, June 1, 1994.

27. McRae, p. 92.

28. *Pittsburgh Courier,* June 3, 1967, p. 13, and June 17, 1967, p. 13.

29. Gillespie/Fraser, pp. 467–70.

30. Feather, *Passion for Jazz,* p. 100.

31. Dizzy Gillespie interviewed by Charles Fox for BBC Radio, August 31, 1976.

32. Letter to the author from John Chilton, March 8, 1994.

Chapter 19

1. Brian Priestley, "Thelonious Monk: Something in Blue" (liner notes to Black Lion/Polydor 2460 152).

2. George Wein, "Giants of Jazz" (liner notes to Atlantic K 60028).

3. McRae, p. 98.

4. "Jon Faddis Talks to Martin Richards,"*Jazz Journal International*, vol. 39, no. 3 (March 1986), p. 11.

5. Art Blakey interviewed by Charles Fox, BBC Radio, broadcast March 3, 1982.

6. Ibid.

7. Tom Bethell, "Jazzfest Number Five," *Jazz Journal*, vol. 25, no. 6 (June 1972), p. 6.

8. Pete Gamble, "The Giants of Jazz," *Jazz Journal*, vol. 25, no. 12 (December 1972), p. 26.

9. Barry McRae, "Dizzy at Ronnies," *Jazz Journal*, vol. 26, no. 9 (September 1973), p. 19.

10. Ron Brown, "Miles at The Rainbow," *Jazz Journal*, vol. 26, no. 9 (September 1973), p. 19.

11. Dizzy Gillespie interviewed by Charles Fox, BBC Radio, August 31, 1976.

12. Benny Green, "Dizzy Gillespie's Big 4" (liner notes to Pablo 2310 719).

13. Norman Granz, "The Trumpet Summit Meets the Oscar Peterson Big Four" (liner note to Pablo Today 2312 114).

14. Author's interview with Mundell Lowe April 5, 1995, Lees, *Waiting for Dizzy*, p. 246; Crow, *Birdland to Broadway*, p. 246.

15. Author's interview with Charles Lake, June 12, 1994.

16. "Jon Faddis Talks to Martin Richards," op. cit., p. 11.

17. Priestley, *Mingus*, pp. 188–89.

18. "Jon Faddis Talks to Martin Richards,"op. cit., p. 11.

19. "Dizzy in Cuba," TV documentary first broadcast in 1988.

20. Feather, *Passion for Jazz*, p. 37 ff.

21. Author's interview with Arturo Sandoval, August 7, 1997.

22. Feather, *Passion for Jazz*, p. 37 ff.

23. Liam Keating, "Jazz Ship," *Jazz Journal*, vol. 29, no. 7 (July 1976), p. 16.

24. Feather, *Passion for Jazz*, p. 37 ff., and p. 84.

Chapter 20

1. Simon Adams, "Dizzy Gillespie: Closer to the Source," *Jazz Journal International*, vol. 39, no. 9 (September 1986), p. 32.

2. Dizzy Gillespie interviewed by Charles Fox for BBC Radio, February 28, 1980.

3. Author's interview with Cedar Walton, June 22, 1995.

4. Milt Bernhart, from an internet correspondence with Steve Voce.

5. Letter to the author from Gene Lees.

6. Author's interview with Grady Tate, June 1, 1994.

7. Leonard Feather, "American Notes," *Jazz Express* (April 1991), p. 10.

8. Author's interview with Grady Tate, June 1, 1994.

9. Program note from 23rd IAJE Conference, Atlanta 1996.

10. Author's interview with Hank Crawford, January 22, 1994.

11. Dizzy Gillespie interviewed by Charles Fox for BBC Radio, February 28, 1980.

12. Author's interview with Danilo Perez, November 12, 1997.

13. Gignoux, p. 40.

14. Ibid., p. 85.

15. "Jazz Ost West Festival 1, Nuremburg" *Wire* (New Year 1991 issue: December 1990/January 1991).

16. Max Roach interviewed by Charles Fox for BBC Radio, December 1989.

17. Author's interview with John Dankworth, May 1996.

Bibliography

Balliett, Whitney. *Dinosaurs in the Morning*. London: Phoenix House, 1962.

Barker, Danny. *Buddy Bolden and the Last Days of Storyville*. Ed. Alyn Shipton. London and Washington: Cassell, 1998.

———. *A Life in Jazz*. Ed. Alyn Shipton. London and Basingstoke: Macmillan, 1986.

Barnet, Charlie, with Stanley Dance. *Those Swinging Years: The Autobiography of Charlie Barnet*. Baton Rouge: Louisiana State University Press, 1984.

Berger, Morroe, Edward Berger, and James Patrick. *Benny Carter: A Life in American Music*. Metuchen, N.J.: Scarecrow Press, 1982.

Bernhardt, Clyde. *I Remember*. Ed. Sheldon Harris. Philadelphia: University of Pennsylvania Press, 1986.

Büchmann-Møller, Frank. *You Just Fight For Your Life—The Story of Lester Young*. New York: Praeger, 1990.

Calloway, Cab, with Bryant Rollins. *Of Minnie the Moocher and Me*. New York: Thomas Y. Crowell, 1976.

Chambers, Jack. *Milestones 1: The Music and Times of Miles Davis to 1960*. Toronto: University of Toronto Press, 1983.

Charters, Samuel B., and Leonard Kunstadt. *Jazz: A History of the New York Scene*. 2nd ed. New York: Da Capo, 1981.

Cheatham, Doc. *I Guess I'll Get the Papers and Go Home*. Ed. Alyn Shipton. London: Cassell, 1996.

Chilton, John. *A Jazz Nursery, the Story of the Jenkins' Orphanage Bands of Charleston, South Carolina*. London: Bloomsbury Book Shop, 1980.

———. *The Song of the Hawk*. London: Quartet, 1990.

Clancy, William D., with Audrey Coke Kenton. *Woody Herman: Chronicles of the Herds*. New York: Schirmer Books, 1995.

Clarke, Laurent, and Franck Verdun. *Dizzy Atmosphere: Conversations avec Dizzy Gillespie*. Arles: Actes Sud, 1990.

Clayton, Buck, with Nancy Miller Elliott. *Buck Clayton's Jazz World*. London and Basingstoke: Macmillan, 1986.

Cole, Bill. *John Coltrane*. New York: Schirmer, 1976.

Coleman, Bill. *Trumpet Story*. London and Basingstoke: Macmillan, 1990.

Collier, James Lincoln. *Benny Goodman and the Swing Era*. New York: Oxford University Press, 1989.

Crow, Bill. *From Birdland to Broadway: Scenes from a Jazz Life*. New York: Oxford University Press, 1992.

————. *Jazz Anecdotes*. New York: Oxford University Press, 1990.

Dance, Stanley, ed., *Jazz Era: The Forties*. London: Macgibbon and Kee, 1961.

————. *The World of Count Basie*. New York: Charles Scribner's Sons, 1980.

————. *The World of Duke Ellington*. New York: Charles Scribner's Sons, 1970.

————. *The World of Earl Hines*. New York: Charles Scribner's Sons, 1977.

————. *The World of Swing*. New York: Charles Scribner's Sons, 1974.

Davis, Miles, with Quincy Troupe. *Miles the Autobiography*. New York: Simon and Schuster, 1989.

De Veaux, Scott. *The Birth of Bebop: A Social and Musical History*. Berkeley: University of California Press, 1997.

Enstice, Wayne, and Paul Rubin. *Jazz Spoken Here*. Baton Rouge: Louisiana State University Press, 1992.

Evensmo, Jan. *The Trumpets of Dizzy Gillespie (1937/1943)—Irving Randolph—Joe Thomas*. Norway: Jazz Solography Series, no. 12, 1982.

Feather, Leonard. *From Satchmo to Miles*. London: Quartet, 1974.

————. *Inside Bebop*. New York: J. J. Robbins, 1949.

Gentry, Tony. *Dizzy Gillespie, Performer, Bandleader and Composer*. New York: Chelsea House, 1991.

Gignoux, Dany. *Dizzy Gillespie*. Kiel: Nieswand Verlag, 1993.

Gillespie, Dizzy, with Al Fraser. *Dizzy: To Be or Not To Bop*. London: W.H. Allen, 1980.

Gioia, Ted. *West Coast Jazz: Modern Jazz in California 1945–1960*. New York: Oxford University Press, 1992.

Gitler, Ira. *Jazz Masters of the Forties*. New York: Macmillan, 1966.

————. *Swing to Bop*. New York: Oxford University Press, 1985.

Gordon, Robert. *Jazz West Coast*. London: Quartet, 1986.

Gourse, Leslie. *Sassy: The Life of Sarah Vaughan*. New York: Charles Scribner's Sons, 1993.

Groves, Alan, and Alyn Shipton. *The Glass Enclosure: The Life of Bud Powell*. Oxford: Bayou Press, 1993.

Hampton, Lionel, with James Haskins. *Hamp: An Autobiography*. London: Robson Books, 1990.

Harrison, Max. *A Jazz Retrospect*. Newton Abbot: David and Charles, 1976.

Haskins, James. *Ella Fitzgerald: A Life Through Jazz*. London: New English Library, 1988.

Haskins, James, with Kathleen Benson. *Nat King Cole: The Man and His Music*. London: Robson Books, 1986.

Haydon, Geoffrey, and Dennis Marks. *Repercussions: A Celebration of African-American Music*. London: Channel Four Books/Century, 1985.

Hennessey, Mike. *Klook: The Story of Kenny Clarke*. London: Quartet, 1990.

Hentoff, Nat. *Listen to the Stories: Nat Hentoff on Jazz and Country Music*. New York: HarperCollins, 1995.

Hinton, Milt, and David G. Berger. *Bass Line—The Stories and Photos of Milt Hinton*. Philadelphia: Temple University Press, 1988.

Hoffman, Franz. *Jazz Advertised in the Negro Press*. 5 vols. Berlin: Franz Hoffman, 1980–96.

———. *Jazz Reviewed 1910–1967. Vol. 1, Out of the New England Press 1910–1950*. Berlin: Franz Hoffman, 1995.

Horricks, Raymond. *Dizzy Gillespie*. Tunbridge Wells: Spellmount, 1984.

Hultin, Randi. *I Jazzens Tegn*. Oslo: H. Aschehoug, 1991.

Jones, Max. *Talking Jazz*. London and Basingstoke: Macmillan, 1987.

Jordan, Steve. *Rhythm Man: 50 Years in Jazz*. Ann Arbor: University of Michigan Press, 1991.

Kreibel, Robert C. *Blue Flame: Woody Herman's Life in Music*. West Lafayette, Ind.: Purdue University Press, 1995.

Lees, Gene. *Leader of the Band: The Life of Woody Herman*. New York: Oxford University Press, 1995.

———. *Oscar Peterson: The Will to Swing*. London and Basingstoke: Macmillan, 1988.

———. *Waiting for Dizzy*. New York: Oxford University Press, 1991.

Lyons, Len. *The Great Jazz Pianists*. New York: Morrow 1983.

Maggin, Donald L. *Stan Getz—A Life in Jazz*. New York: William Morrow, 1996.

Martínez, José María García. *Del Fox-Trot Al Jazz Flamenco, El Jazz En España, 1919–1996*. Madrid: Alianza Editorial, 1996.

McCarthy, Albert. *Big Band Jazz*. London: Barrie and Jenkins, 1974.

McRae, Barry. *Dizzy Gillespie His Life and Times*. Tunbridge Wells: Spellmount, 1988.

Nicholson, Stuart. *Ella Fitzgerald*. London: Gollancz, 1993.

Owens, Thomas. *Bebop: The Music and Its Players*. New York: Oxford University Press, 1995.

Paudras, Francis. *La Danse Des Infidèles*. Paris: Editions de l'Instant, 1986.

Panassié, Hugues, and Madeleine Gautier. *Dictionary of Jazz*. Trans. Desmond Flower. London: Cassell, 1956.

Pearson, Nathan W. Jr. *Goin' to Kansas City*. London and Basingstoke: Macmillan, 1988.

Popa, J. *Cab Calloway and His Orchestra*. Discography. Zephyrhills, Fla., 1976.

Porter, Roy, and David Keller. *There and Back*. Oxford: Bayou Press, 1991.

Priestley, Brian. *Charlie Parker*. Tunbridge Wells: Spellmount, 1984.

———. *Mingus: A Critical Biography*. London: Quartet, 1982.

Reisner, Robert. *Bird: The Legend of Charlie Parker*. London: Quartet, 1962.

Ruppli, Michel, with Bob Porter. *The Savoy Label, A Discography*. Westport, Conn.: Greenwood Press, 1980.

Russell, Ross. *Bird Lives: The High Life and Hard Times of Charlie "Yardbird" Parker*. London: Quartet, 1973.

Rust, Brian. *Jazz Records 1897–1942*. 5th ed. Chigwell, Essex: Storyville, n.d.

Schuller, Gunther. *The Swing Era*. New York: Oxford University Press, 1989.

Sheridan, Chris. *Count Basie—A Bio-Discography*. Westport, Conn.: Greenwood Press, 1986.

Shipton, Alyn. *Fats Waller—His Life and Times*. Tunbridge Wells and New York: Spellmount/Universe, 1988.

Simkins, C. O. *Coltrane: A Biography*. New York: Herndon House, 1975.

Smith, Stuff. *Pure at Heart*. Ed. Anthony Barnett and Eva Løgager. Lewes: Allardyce, Barnett, 1991.

Smith, W. O. *Sideman*. Nashville, Tenn.: Rutledge Hill Press, 1991.

Stewart, Rex. *Boy Meets Horn*. Ed. Claire P. Gordon. Oxford, Miss.: Bayou Press, 1991.

Stratemann, Klaus. *Duke Ellington Day by Day and Film by Film*. Copenhagen: Jazz Media, 1992.

Tanner, Lee. *Dizzy—John Birks Gillespie in his 75th Year*. Rev. ed. San Francisco: Pomegranate Art Books, 1992.

Taylor, Art. *Notes and Tones*. New York: Da Capo, 1993.

Thomas, J. C. *Chasin' the Trane: The Music and Mystique of John Coltrane*. Garden City, N.Y.: Doubleday, 1975.

Tormé, Mel. *Traps, the Drum Wonder—The Life of Buddy Rich*. New York: Oxford University Press, 1991.

Ulanov, Barry. *A History of Jazz in America*. London; Hutchinson, 1959.

Vail, Ken. *Bird's Diary: The Life of Charlie Parker 1945–1955*. Chessington, Surrey: Castle Communications, 1996.

Vian, Boris. *Round About Close to Midnight: The Jazz Writings of Boris Vian*. Trans. Mike Zwerin. London: Quartet, 1988.

Weinstein, Norman C. *A Night In Tunisia—Imaginings of Africa In Jazz*. New York: Limelight Editions, 1993.

Wilber, Bob, assisted by Derek Webster. *Music Was Not Enough*. London and Basingstoke: Macmillan, 1987.

Wilson, Teddy, with Arie Lighart and Humphrey Van Loo. *Teddy Wilson Talks Jazz*. London and New York: Cassell, 1996.

Wölfer, Jürgen. *Dizzy Gillespie, Sein Leben, Sein Musik, Sein Schallplatten*. Waakirchen: Oreos Verlag, 1987.

Wright, Laurie. *Walter C. Allen and Brian Rust's "King" Oliver*. Chigwell: Storyville, 1987.

Index

Page numbers in **bold** indicate illustrations.